3D Printing with RepRap Cookbook

Over 80 fast-paced recipes to help you create and print 3D models

Richard Salinas

[PACKT] PUBLISHING

open source *
community experience distilled

BIRMINGHAM - MUMBAI

3D Printing with RepRap Cookbook

First published: June 2014

Production reference: 1170614

Published by Packt Publishing Ltd.
Livery Place
35 Livery Street
Birmingham B3 2PB, UK.

ISBN 978-1-78216-988-8

www.packtpub.com

Cover image by Gagandeep Sharma (er.gagansharma@gmail.com)

Credits

Author
Richard Salinas

Reviewers
Richard Horne (RichRap)
Miro Hrončok
Eugene Medvedev
Clarence 'Sparr' Risher

Commissioning Editor
Aarthi Kumaraswamy

Acquisition Editor
Vinay Argekar

Content Development Editor
Azharuddin Sheikh

Technical Editor
Shashank Desai

Copy Editors
Janbal Dharmaraj
Karuna Narayanan
Alfida Paiva

Project Coordinator
Wendell Palmer

Proofreaders
Simran Bhogal
Maria Gould
Paul Hindle

Indexers
Hemangini Bari
Mehreen Deshmukh

Graphics
Ronak Dhruv
Yuvraj Mannari

Production Coordinator
Sushma Redkar

Cover Work
Sushma Redkar

About the Author

Richard Salinas is a scenic artist in the film industry, where he has worked for over 20 years on numerous television and motion picture productions.

He was educated at the University of Missouri where he studied sculpture and three-dimensional design. He also has a formal education in the field of electronics. He developed an interest in computers in 1981 when he began programming on his university's mainframe and one of the first affordable personal computers: the Commodore VIC-20.

Since 2012, he's constructed five 3D printers of various designs and hacks. His aim is to explore the possibilities of creating fine art sculpture with DIY technology. You can follow his progress at `www.3dprintedsculpture.com`.

I'd like to thank Adrian Bowyer and the rest of the RepRap community for sharing their work. Their vision and hard work has made it possible for the rest of us to explore the potential of this technology.

I'd also like to thank the reviewers and editorial staff at Packt Publishing for their expertise and guidance in helping make this book possible.

Last but not least, I'd like to thank my family for the time afforded me. A lot of quality family time has been lost in favor of writing and playing with robots.

About the Reviewers

Richard Horne (RichRap) is well known in the 3D printing community as RichRap. He has over two decades of experience in the electronics industry, first as an electronics engineer and more recently, commercially, in both a Sales and Marketing capacity. His work spans over a wide range of technologies and industries for both consumer and industrial sectors. From arcade games to washing machines, he has designed and developed products used by millions of people around the world.

He is part of the board of advisors for the 3D Printing Association and a highly passionate advocate of 3D printing for the home, education, and industrial sectors. Since joining the open source maker movement and then the RepRap project in 2009, he has been blogging, developing, and sharing ideas for greater consumer interest in 3D printing. His work is helping make this high-tech industry a little easier for everyone to join in and collaborate, while also pushing the technical boundaries of design and personal manufacturing.

His blog can be found at `www.richrap.blogspot.com`, and further printing advice and open source 3D printing projects are available at `www.richrap.com`. The 3D Printing Association is available at `http://the3dprintingassociation.com/`.

Miro Hrončok is a Fedora Ambassador and Packager. He maintains the 3D printing stack in Fedora (see `http://fedoraproject.org/`), and he wants Fedora to be the best operating system for makers. Miro Hrončok works as a developer for Red Hat Czech. He studies at the Faculty of Information Technology at Czech Technical University in Prague, where he also helps run a 3D printing lab for students and teaches 3D printing. More information (in Czech) about the 3D printing lab can be found at `http://3dprint.fit.cvut.cz/`.

Eugene Medvedev is a Russian sociologist from Moscow, who started his career in home 3D printing by writing a paper about the social effects of the coming home manufacturing revolution. Once the paper was halfway complete, a realization that he didn't really know what he was talking about led to a successful attempt to recreate the entire technology from scratch, deliberately using nothing but what could be obtained in local hardware and electronics stores, which mostly amounted to fiber boards and bits of string. This eventually led to a rapid reinvention of the wheel, which became a much-cited source for the Russian 3D printing community, as the paper about social effects gave way to explanations of technical underpinnings of the craft. However, the actual business is still struggling to get off the ground. He can be contacted at `http://reprapology.info`.

Clarence 'Sparr' Risher is a technical geek with a passion for obscure and cutting-edge technologies. He finds himself involved in open source and collaborative projects, ranging from 3D printing to large scale art to robotics and software development. Starting with a RepRap Mendel at a local hackerspace, he soon upgraded to a modified MendelMax design and then started tinkering on low-cost printers such as the Printrbot and not-printer-specific three-axis Cartesian platforms such as the ShapeOko.

www.PacktPub.com

Support files, eBooks, discount offers, and more

You might want to visit www.PacktPub.com for support files and downloads related to your book.

Did you know that Packt offers eBook versions of every book published, with PDF and ePub files available? You can upgrade to the eBook version at www.PacktPub.com and as a print book customer, you are entitled to a discount on the eBook copy. Get in touch with us at service@packtpub.com for more details.

At www.PacktPub.com, you can also read a collection of free technical articles, sign up for a range of free newsletters and receive exclusive discounts and offers on Packt books and eBooks.

http://PacktLib.PacktPub.com

Do you need instant solutions to your IT questions? PacktLib is Packt's online digital book library. Here, you can access, read and search across Packt's entire library of books.

Why subscribe?

- Fully searchable across every book published by Packt
- Copy and paste, print and bookmark content
- On demand and accessible via web browser

Free access for Packt account holders

If you have an account with Packt at www.PacktPub.com, you can use this to access PacktLib today and view nine entirely free books. Simply use your login credentials for immediate access.

Table of Contents

Preface

There's a wealth of information available on the Internet about 3D printing. For a novice, just starting out with a RepRap 3D printer and with limited or no experience with 3D modeling, this can create a daunting task of online searching for what is relevant and helpful.

This book will help plot a course for you and bring to your attention what a designer, artist, or creative hobbyist will find most useful.

Each chapter of this book will introduce you to simple methods of creating original content and at the same time, expose you to the technical aspects of the 3D printing process. Each chapter will ease you into more complex techniques and at the same time expose you to new software tools, which will help expand your technical abilities.

For those who are more experienced, this book will provide a handy reference for comparing the two slicers, Skeinforge and Slic3r. It will also provide you with a quick reference of software functions for some of the more advanced programs such as MeshLab and TopMod.

Overall, this is my 3D printing bible. I'm an artist with serious intentions of making some really cool stuff. This book is the culmination of a year's worth of 3D modeling and printing. Over 600 individual prints were created to test the functions and possibilities of the technologies covered in this book.

If you follow the recipes in this book, you'll learn how to master what is sometimes a frustrating, annoyingly fickle, and time-consuming process, but a process that will open the doors to a wonderful world of new and exciting objects.

What this book covers

Chapter 1, Getting Started with 3D Printing, will get you moving quickly by 3D scanning some common everyday objects with an ordinary digital camera and Autodesk 123D Catch. We'll move into 3D printing our 3D scanned objects and take a basic look at the mechanics of the process.

Chapter 2, Optimizing the Printing Process, will introduce us to Meshmixer, a surface-modeling program that will help us clean up our 3D scanned objects and optimize them for better printing. We'll move into 3D printing by looking at how we can control the interior of our models. By experimenting with the infill of a 3D model, we'll see how different infill patterns are created and how important the surface perimeters are for the structure and surface details.

Chapter 3, Scanning and Printing with a Higher Resolution, will introduce us to 3D scanning with an ordinary, inexpensive red laser, a webcam, and a DAVID Laserscanner software. MeshLab, a very powerful mesh editing program, will be introduced. This will help us with our final 3D scanned results. We'll move into 3D printing by learning how to adjust our printing resolution for finer results.

Chapter 4, Modeling and Printing with Precision, will introduce us to SketchUp Make. It's a 3D modeling program that has an easy learning curve for making precision mechanical parts. We'll move into 3D printing by learning how we can control a slicer and mechanical functions for higher precision printing.

Chapter 5, Manipulating Meshes and Bridges, will introduce us to TopMod. It's a 3D modeling program that works by manipulating the mesh structure. MeshLab will also be examined more closely for its mesh manipulation tools. We'll move into 3D printing and learn how to achieve the difficult task of bridging, the task of printing filament over an empty space.

Chapter 6, Making the Impossible, will examine the tools of TopMod in more depth. We'll move into 3D printing by learning how to create a removable support material for complex models.

Chapter 7, Texture – the Good and the Bad, will examine an easy method to create textures and patterns on our models using Meshmixer and Paint.NET. We'll move into 3D printing by learning how we can control and eliminate some of the unwanted textures created by the 3D printing process.

Chapter 8, Troubleshooting Issues in 3D Modeling, will examine common issues such as inverted face normals and non-manifold geometry that arise in 3D modeling.

Chapter 9, Troubleshooting Issues in 3D Printing, will review the basic systems that make a 3D printer work and how we can troubleshoot some of the issues that occur.

Appendix A, Understanding and Editing Firmware, provides information on how to upload firmware and make some basic changes.

Appendix B, Taking a Closer Look at G-code, provides information on how to access G-code and make some basic changes.

Appendix C, Filament Options for RepRap Printers, is a list of filament materials and their characteristics.

Who this book is for

This book is for novice designers, artists, or makers who own home-based 3D printers and have fundamental knowledge of how it works but they desire to gain better mastery over the printing process. Its focus is on introducing easy approaches to create original objects that can be 3D printed and how to 3D print them with good results. Each chapter will focus on digital modeling and then conclude with a section devoted to 3D printing.

What you need for this book

All the software featured in this book is either open source or free for use and can be downloaded with an Internet connection. A PC running on Windows 7 was used for all the examples shown in the book, but most of the software can be downloaded for use on a Mac or Linux system.

A 3D printer is required. Considering the proliferation of designs, it's impractical to list them all. This book utilizes two different RepRap-based 3D printers to print its examples. Any RepRap-based 3D printer that utilizes fused deposition modeling (FDM) will suffice, whether purchased fully assembled or by kit.

You'll also need your choice of host software. This is the user interface that controls your 3D printer. This book utilizes two of the most popular host programs: Pronterface and Repetier-Host.

Pronterface

Pronterface is a G-code sender and the graphical user interface of the host. It has a simple set of movement and temperature controls, as shown in the following screenshot:

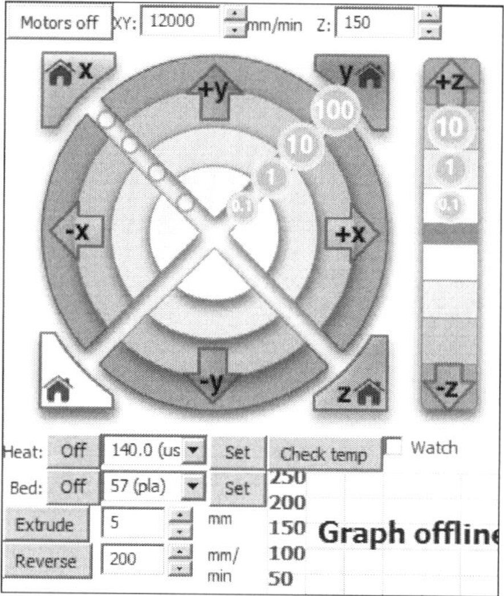

By clicking on the model in the plate window, a pop-up window will appear. By holding *Shift* on the keyboard, the print layers can be examined by scrolling the mouse wheel. Refer to the following screenshot:

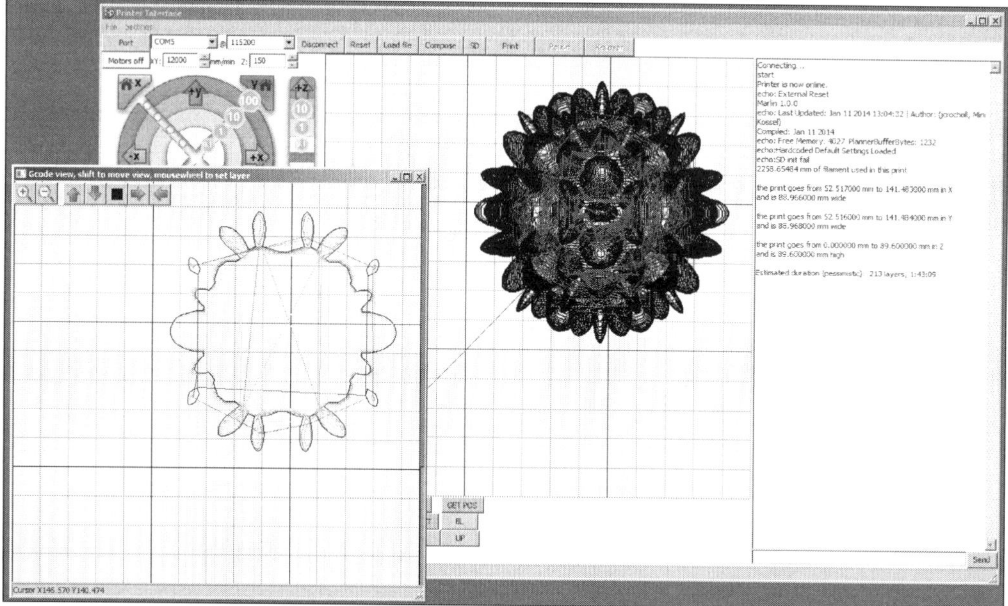

Printrun's easy interface and good operating features makes it a popular host for many RepRap machines. Its interface is not as sleek as some of the others, but it's a no-frills, dependable work horse.

A good tutorial on using Printrun can be found at `http://www.plasticscribbler.com/tutorial/getting-started/item/21-getting-started-with-pronterface#.UxzyAPldUps`.

A precompiled version can be downloaded from `http://koti.kapsi.fi/~kliment/printrun/`.

Repetier-Host

Repetier-Host has an easy GUI and includes a great G-code visualizer. It features a large collection of unique options, which we'll explore further in *Chapter 8, Troubleshooting Issues in 3D Modeling*. Its slicing options include configured versions of both Slic3r and Skeinforge, making it easy to switch from one slicer to the other when needed. Refer to the following screenshot:

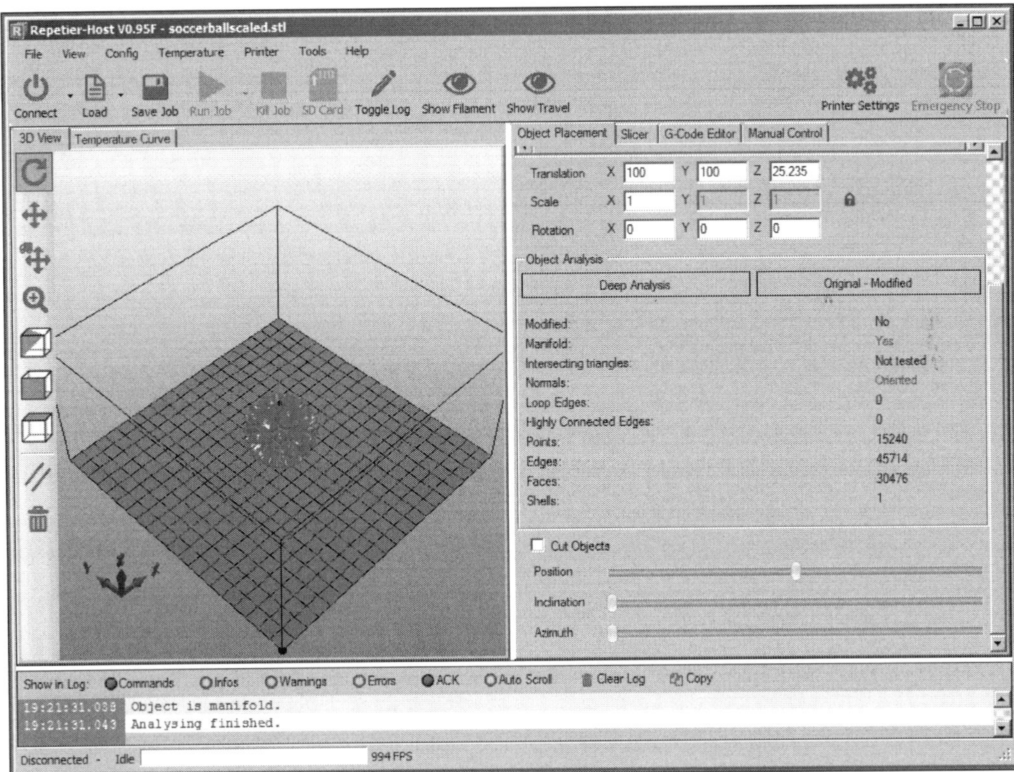

User information and download options are available at `http://www.repetier.com/`.

Conventions

In this book, you will find a number of styles of text that distinguish between different kinds of information. Here are some examples of these styles, and an explanation of their meaning.

Code words in text, database table names, folder names, filenames, file extensions, pathnames, dummy URLs, user input, and Twitter handles are shown as follows: "Scroll down the file list and open the `configuration.h` file by double-clicking on it."

New terms and **important words** are shown in bold. Words that you see on the screen, in menus or dialog boxes for example, appear in the text like this: "Fill this out and click on **Send**."

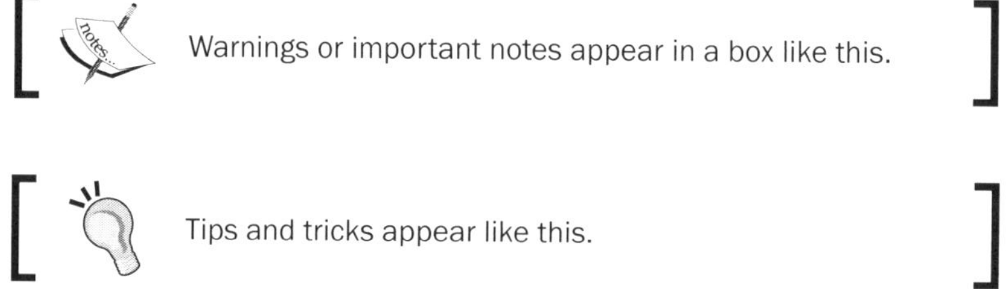

Warnings or important notes appear in a box like this.

Tips and tricks appear like this.

Reader feedback

Feedback from our readers is always welcome. Let us know what you think about this book—what you liked or may have disliked. Reader feedback is important for us to develop titles that you really get the most out of.

To send us general feedback, simply send an e-mail to `feedback@packtpub.com`, and mention the book title via the subject of your message.

If there is a topic that you have expertise in and you are interested in either writing or contributing to a book, see our author guide on `www.packtpub.com/authors`.

Customer support

Now that you are the proud owner of a Packt book, we have a number of things to help you to get the most from your purchase.

Downloading the color images of this book

We also provide you a PDF file that has color images of the screenshots/diagrams used in this book. The color images will help you better understand the changes in the output. You can download this file from: `https://www.packtpub.com/sites/default/files/downloads/9888OS_ColoredImages.pdf`

Errata

Although we have taken every care to ensure the accuracy of our content, mistakes do happen. If you find a mistake in one of our books—maybe a mistake in the text or the code—we would be grateful if you would report this to us. By doing so, you can save other readers from frustration and help us improve subsequent versions of this book. If you find any errata, please report them by visiting `http://www.packtpub.com/submit-errata`, selecting your book, clicking on the **errata submission** form link, and entering the details of your errata. Once your errata are verified, your submission will be accepted and the errata will be uploaded on our website, or added to any list of existing errata, under the Errata section of that title. Any existing errata can be viewed by selecting your title from `http://www.packtpub.com/support`.

Piracy

Piracy of copyright material on the Internet is an ongoing problem across all media. At Packt, we take the protection of our copyright and licenses very seriously. If you come across any illegal copies of our works, in any form, on the Internet, please provide us with the location address or website name immediately so that we can pursue a remedy.

Please contact us at `copyright@packtpub.com` with a link to the suspected pirated material.

We appreciate your help in protecting our authors, and our ability to bring you valuable content.

Questions

You can contact us at `questions@packtpub.com` if you are having a problem with any aspect of the book, and we will do our best to address it.

1
Getting Started with 3D Printing

In this chapter, we will cover the following recipes:

- 3D scanning with a digital camera
- Processing a 3D scan with 123D Catch
- Viewing your scene with 123D Catch
- Stitching photos with 123D Catch
- Changing mesh resolutions with 123D Catch
- Cleaning up the model with 123D Catch
- Using the Autodesk 3D Print Utility
- Slicing the models with Slic3r
- Slicing the models with Skeinforge

Introduction

3D printing is an amazing technology for creating physical objects from a digital design. However, for many of us the digital fabrication of our idea is the most difficult aspect of the process. 3D modeling programs generally have a steep learning curve and for the inexperienced, the journey required for building the necessary skills can become a time consuming endeavor. One simple solution is to 3D scan an existing object.

We'll learn how the 3D scanning process works by scanning some common objects. Almost any object can be chosen, irrespective of whether the object can be handheld or is the size of a house. We'll learn how to make a model from a 3D scan that's suitable for printing. It's the perfect solution for creating some models that we can use as learning examples in the course of this book.

We'll also be introduced to a variety of software options that will help us improve our 3D scans for printing. They will become important components in our toolbox for making repairs of surface imperfections and modifying the integrity of the model's mesh, for optimal printing.

At the close of the next few chapters, we'll continue using these models for testing purposes, when we focus more on the mechanics of 3D printing. Each of these models will introduce different challenges in the 3D printing process and in turn, give us an opportunity to explore solutions for solving difficult printing issues.

3D scanning with a digital camera

The 123D Catch scanning process requires the use of an ordinary digital camera to take a series of 40 or more photographs while moving around an object. Virtually, any stationary object can be chosen, provided that you have a complete 360-degree unobstructed view around the object, and it can be photographed with good lighting.

For the following recipes to be more useful as a learning exercise, it will be helpful if you find objects that are similar to the ones shown in the following image:

The following are the specifications of the objects shown in the preceding image:

- A coin measuring 30 mm across (any small object with very fine surface details)
- A toy block measuring 60 x 30 x 55 mm (any basic geometric form with solid walls and some curves)

- A statue measuring 68 cm high (any human form that is squatting or kneeling would be best)
- A monument measuring 4 m high (any simple object that tapers towards the top with minimal obtrusions)

It is important to choose objects that do not contain protrusions, which span far out from the object, such as the outspread arms of a standing figure. It's also best to avoid large recesses or holes. Simplicity of the object's form is best when making your choice.

Acquiring objects with a variety of sizes and complexities, similar to the preceding examples, will help us test the basic capabilities of 123D Catch. They will also help us test different problems in the 3D printing process.

Getting ready

For this recipe, you'll need a digital camera with a good focus and exposure control. You'll also need the four objects that you have selected for scanning. For smaller objects, a flat surface such as a tabletop is required.

How to do it...

Prepare your work surface for the smaller objects. Try to avoid a shiny surface where there can be a lot of reflection. If possible, mask out a work area with a sheet of newspaper. This will provide a dull surface. For all of the objects, make sure there is consistent illumination. Don't use flash! If you are photographing outside, an overcast day or shade is preferable rather than the harsh lighting of direct sunlight, which can create deep shadows.

We will proceed as follows:

1. With the smaller objects, place them at the center of your work surface.
2. Position the camera at about a 45-degree angle, looking down on the model.
3. When photographing the large objects, position the camera as high as possible and place the object at the center of the picture frame, keeping the background detail behind the object in focus.
4. Take a photograph and continue to move around the object, taking photographs every 18 degrees or so. You'll need to move completely around the object. By the time you circle the object and reach your starting point, you should have about 20 evenly spaced photos.

5. Position the camera lower this time, almost at eye level with the object. Repeat the process by taking another 20 shots at this angle.

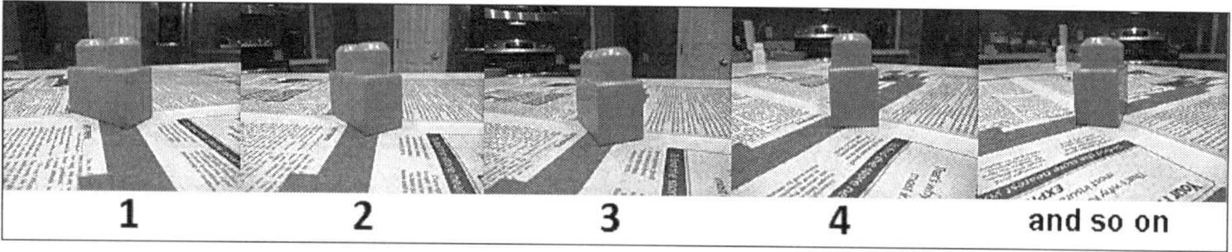

6. Save the series of photographs for each object in its own folder.

How it works...

When we photograph smaller objects, the camera's depth of field is short, and this will generally produce a blurred background. It's good to have an initial series of photographs that retains the sharp detail around the object. By placing a smaller object on a newspaper, the printed lines will act as registration points and help in sequencing all of the photos in proper order. With the larger objects, the camera's depth of field will generally be longer, and the background will be in focus, providing enough background information for registration. Moving around the object twice and photographing with high and low angles will help record more detail of the object's form.

There's more...

Sometimes, when photographing an object, there can be a glare on the surface from a light source that is improperly angled or is too close to the object. If possible, adjust the object or the light source to remove the glare. Sometimes, a shiny surface will have reflections, which can cause distortion. The following are several solutions that can be implemented:

- Use light that has been softened with photographic diffusion gels or umbrellas.
- Apply a dulling spray to the object. This can be purchased at many craft stores.
- Coat the model in a water-soluble tempera paint that can be washed off when you are finished. This will flatten out the object's sheen.

In this case, the toy block was reflecting too much of its surroundings. 123D Catch interpolated the reflections as holes. By painting the block grey, the block was properly modeled, shown as follows:

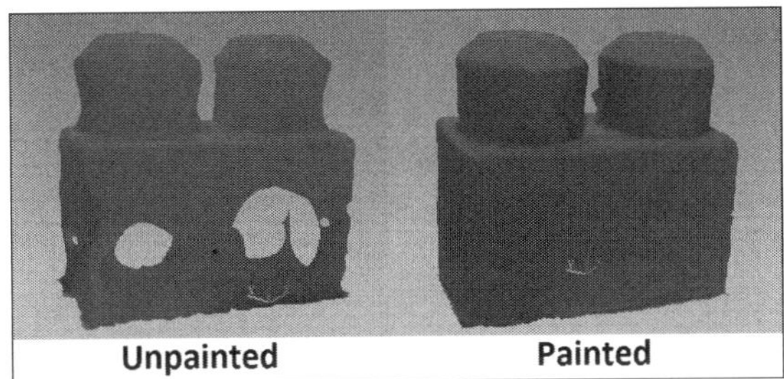

Processing a 3D scan with 123D Catch

With the series of photographs that we took of our objects, we'll use 123D Catch to merge them together to make a three-dimensional scene.

Getting ready

You'll need to visit the Autodesk website at `http://www.123dapp.com/catch`. Here, you will be able to download the application for use on a PC, or use the web app if you're using a Mac or Linux OS. A free account will need to be set up with Autodesk, or you can use your social networking account, such as Facebook, to log in.

This book uses 123D Catch v2.3.3. It's also available for use on iPads and iPhones. These applications will have a different approach than what is outlined in this recipe, but the concepts are the same.

You'll also need the folder containing the series of photographs of your objects.

How to do it...

Connect to the Internet, open 123D Catch, and sign in to the Autodesk server, if necessary. Proceed as follows:

1. Select the top-left button, **Create a New Capture**. The **Select Photos** window will open, allowing you to find the directory containing the folder with your photos. Select all the .jpg files that create your scan, and click on **Open**.

2. At the upper-left side, you should see a large, green, check-mark button. Under this, the total count of photos should be selected for upload. Click on **Create Project**.

3. Initially, you'll see a pop-up window asking for a quick registration and your e-mail. Fill this out and click on **Send**.

4. Next, you'll be given an option to tag, categorize, and provide a description of your object before uploading it to the Autodesk cloud for processing. These fields must be filled in, or the upload will not complete.

5. Now, the photos can be uploaded. You'll be given a choice to wait for your scene to be compiled, or you can have the results e-mailed. For this recipe, choose the e-mail option. Processing can take up to 45 minutes or more.

6. Repeat these steps for each of the four objects that you have photographed.

How it works...

A photograph is basically a flat two-dimensional record of a three-dimensional space. It contains most of the information of this three-dimensional space, except for the data needed to provide information about its depth. By taking more photographs, we supply more information. When we took a series of photographs around our object, we not only recorded the shapes, colors, and textures, but also mapped out a three-dimensional scene.

When the photo files are uploaded to the Autodesk servers, their system begins the tedious process of correlating all the images together. It first determines the camera position and aiming angles of each photograph and then uses a system of triangulation to map out the space. It then creates a 3D mesh of your scene from this information.

Viewing your scene with 123D Catch

In this recipe, we will cover some of the basic operations of 123D Catch. These include operations such as loading a scene and navigation.

Getting ready

You'll need a processed 3D scene of your object. Autodesk will e-mail you with a notification that your capture has been successful. A link will be provided to download the Photo Scene data file (`.3dp`). The filename will start with the word `Capture`, the date it was created, and a series of numbers. Create a new folder and download the file into it.

How to do it...

Open 123D Catch and proceed as follows:

1. Select the middle-left button, **Open an Existing Capture**. From the **Select the project to open** window, find the directory containing the folder with your Photo Scene data file. Select the file and click on **Open**. The workspace appears, and Autodesk loads the project files. This takes several minutes. When the scene appears, it should look similar to following screenshot:

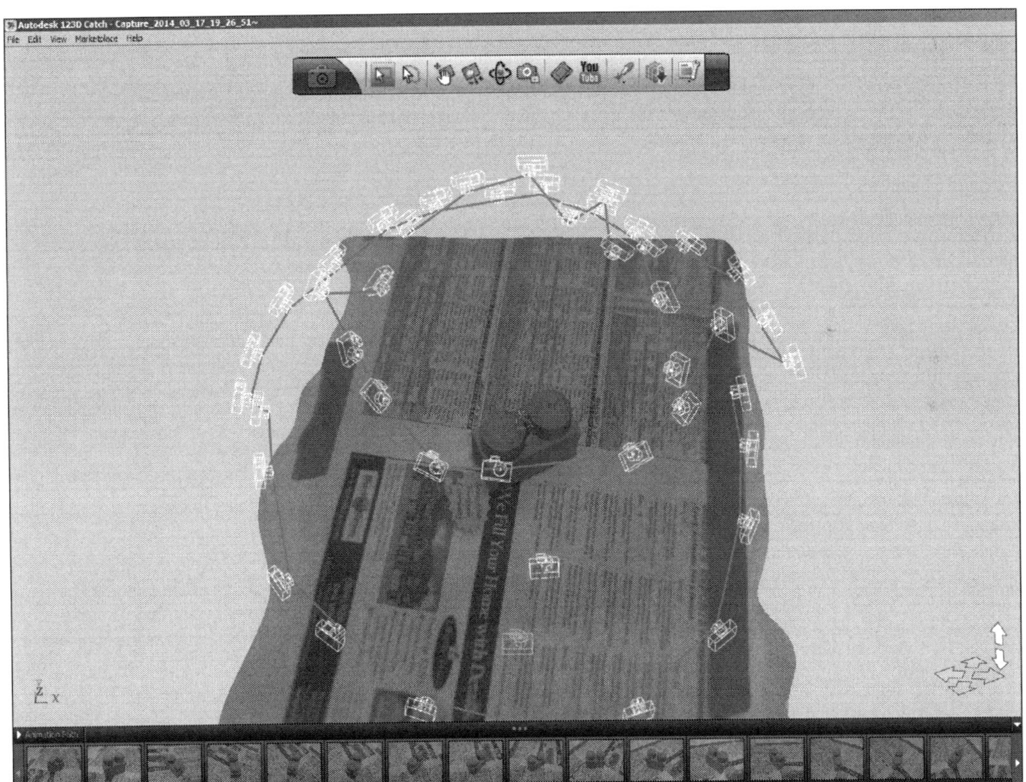

2. At the center of the workspace, we see the object that we scanned and the area that surrounds it. This is the content of the 3D scene. A series of cameras connected by a line surround the model. This shows the chronology of the photos taken. Below the workspace is a thumbnail strip containing the photos you took. Click on **Animation Path** at the top of the first thumbnail. From the drop-down menu, choose **Create default animation path**.

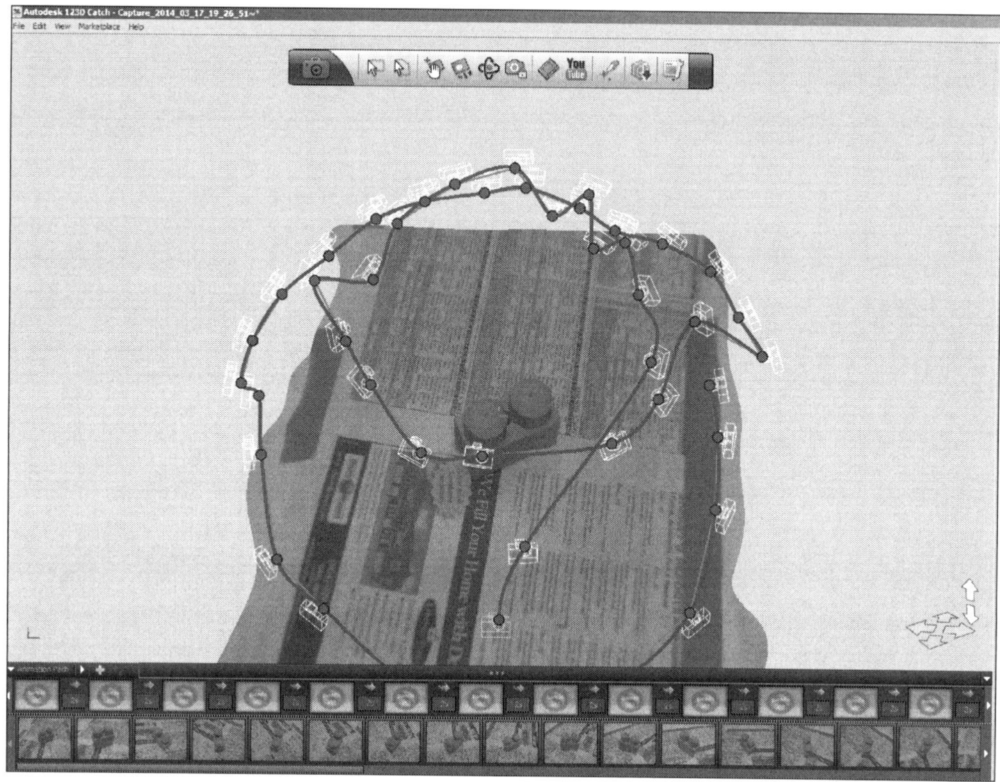

3. The camera track of the scene is now highlighted, as shown in the preceding screenshot. A new thumbnail series also appears. These are the keyframes of the animation. To play, click on the arrow pointing to the right, and to stop, click on the square icon.

If the animation is not playing in fullscreen, slightly move the corner of the program's window in or out.

4. Let's return to the global view. We'll do this by pressing Space bar twice.

5. We can view the individual thumbnails by scrolling along the bottom. Each thumbnail will be highlighted if we hover over it. Select a thumbnail by left- clicking on it. The photo will now be in view.

6. To return to the global view, press Space bar once. The view will show the particular camera within the chronology track (which took the selected thumbnail) highlighted in green.

How it works...

When you opened the Photo Scene data file, two things happened. First, there were additions made to the folder where the .3dp file is stored; photos that comprised your scene were added, and another folder was created with the same name as your .3dp file (this folder contains two Autodesk files that we should not touch). Secondly, the scene was loaded on your workspace.

This scene includes a visual track of the movements you made when photographing your object. This enables a convenient review of the photos for the purpose of editing or fixing stitching problems that may occur. Stitching is the term that 123D Catch uses for describing the correlation of photos in a sequence. We'll examine stitching in greater detail in the next recipe.

The animation that we played in this recipe can be saved to the desktop or uploaded on YouTube. While the animation is loading, right-click on the workspace for a pop-up window and choose **Export Video**.

Stitching photos with 123D Catch

Stitching is the correlation of the photos you took of your object. It aligns the photos to each other to make a proper sequence. Sometimes, the Autodesk server will have a difficult time choosing the proper photo for stitching; it will either discard the photo from the sequence or choose the wrong placement of a photo. These problems can be fixed by manually stitching the photos. In this recipe, we'll learn how to do this.

Getting ready

Hopefully, you don't have any stitching problems with the four objects you scanned, but we will need a photo sequence with stitching problems for this recipe. There's an easy way to illustrate the repair of unstitched photos, even with a good processed scan. Choose one of your Photo Scene data files for the following recipe, and make a copy of the folder and all of its contents. Use the copy for this recipe.

How to do it...

Open 123D Catch and sign in. Open an existing capture and proceed as follows:

1. Choose a photo from the thumbnail strip at the bottom. Right-click on it, and choose **Unstitch Photo** from the pop up. As shown in the following screenshot, the thumbnail darkens with an embedded yellow warning symbol:

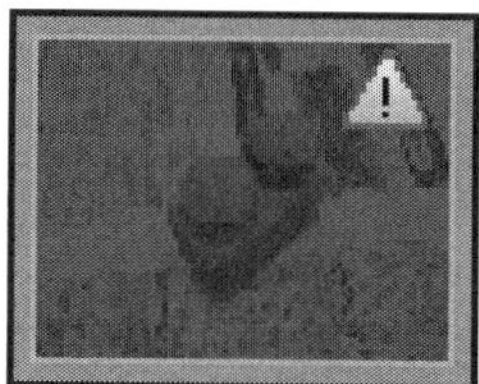

2. The photo sequence now has an unstitched photo. To repair it, double-click on the darkened photo. A new window opens, as shown in the following screenshot:

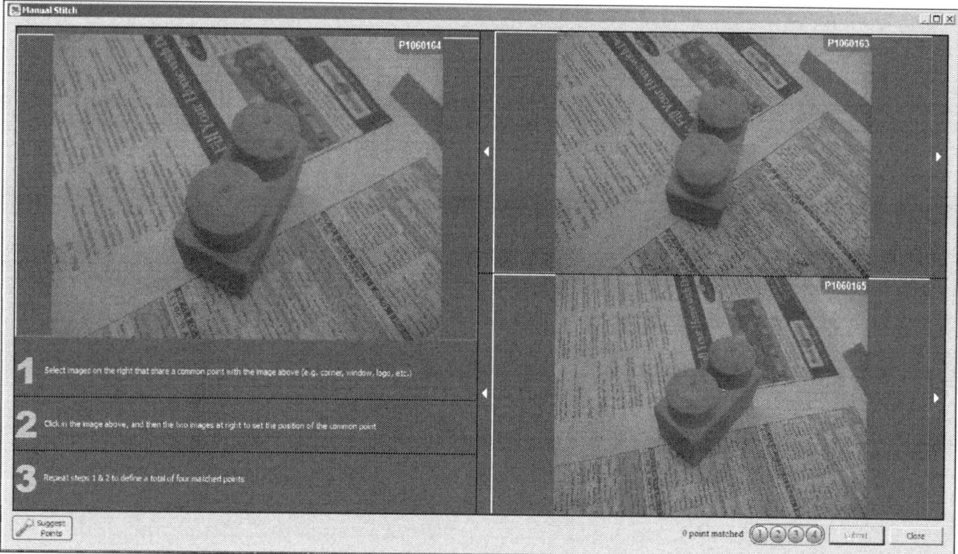

3. At the bottom-left side, the **Manual Stitch** window outlines the basic procedure in three steps. Review these steps before continuing.

4. The first step is to choose the best photos to align. 123D Catch chose two photos, and they are displayed on the right-hand side of the window. We can keep these or change them by scrolling through the thumbnails by clicking on the arrows.

5. For the second step, we need to choose a point on the unstitched photo that correlates with the same exact point on the other two photos. Left- click and hold on the point. A magnifier opens, giving us a better definition of the immediate area. This is illustrated in the following screenshot:

6. Release the mouse when you determine your point. A yellow marker appears. If you're not happy with your choice, right-click on the yellow marker and choose **Delete Point in Image** from the pop up.

7. On the photo in the top-right corner of the window, repeat the selection for the proper correlation point. When the point is accepted, a suggested point will be automatically made on the third photo in the bottom-right corner. Instead of a circle registration point, it will be a square. Left-click on it and hold to determine if it's correct. If it is, release the mouse. When all the points are accepted, they will turn green.

8. For the third step, repeat the first and second steps until all the four matched points are made. Your project should look similar to the following screenshot:

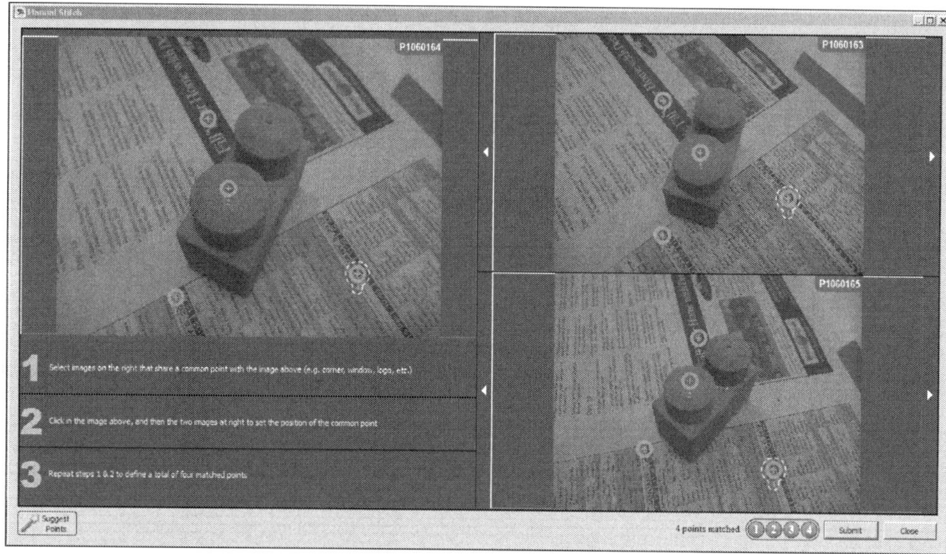

9. When all the four points are matched, a pop up will appear and prompt you to update your scene. Choose **Submit**. Another pop up will appear and prompt you with a **Continue** option. The processing must take place at the Autodesk server. This requires the upload of the changes and a wait time. When the processing of the scene is finished, a new file will be returned.

How it works...

For our recipe, we intentionally unstitched a photo from our sequence. This gave us a situation to repair it using manual stitching. Sometimes, we may find that it's important to unstitch a photo that has been incorrectly processed by the Autodesk server. This can occur when similar sides, such as the sides of a cube, are confused in the interpolation of the scene and an erratic camera track is produced. Sometimes, unstitching a photo out of sequence and restitching it where it belongs will solve the problem.

There are situations when the incorrect exposure or focus of an image is undesirable. This can be the case when the output is for export as an animation. By unstitching the problematic photo, the result will be better.

Changing mesh resolutions with 123D Catch

There are three different mesh resolutions available for our scene. The program's default setting produces a low-resolution draft. In this recipe, we will learn how to change the mesh resolutions of our scene for higher quality.

Getting ready

It is good practice to make a backup of your folder containing the Photo Scene data files and photos. Keep all the backups of the originals together in a folder. In the following recipe, multiple resolutions will be generated for each scene. Keeping all of your data files organized is very important!

How to do it...

Open 123D Catch and sign in. Open an existing capture and proceed as follows:

1. Click on the **Generate Mesh** icon [■] on the toolbar. A window opens, giving us three choices for the output quality of our mesh. Let's begin by choosing **Mobile**.

2. A new window will open, informing us that the scene will now close. Click on **OK**.

3. A **Create New Capture** window will open. Here, you can rename your model. It is a good idea to attach a tag to designate that it's a mobile mesh, as we'll be experimenting with all three mesh resolutions for all the four models. When you have renamed the model, choose the e-mail notification for processing it.

4. Repeat the preceding procedure, and save the model as a **Standard** and **Maximum** resolution file. Keep in mind that Autodesk will close your window each time after you request a resolution update. You will have to reload your initial scene for each save.

5. Repeat these steps for the remaining scenes.

How it works...

When Autodesk first processed your photos, it generated a very low-resolution draft of your scene. This draft is just a little lower in resolution than a **Mobile** resolution export. The following chart compares the resolution of a typical scene saved in all three resolutions:

Mobile	19,442 polygons	1.17 mb
Standard	63,701 polygons	4.02 mb
Maximum	306,015 polygons	20.2 mb

We would typically assume that picking the highest resolution would be the best for 3D printing. However, by experimenting with the various resolutions with each model, you may find that a lower resolution is either better or more interesting than a higher-resolution export.

Cleaning up the model with 123D Catch

A useful set of editing tools is available in 123D Catch. They provide us with the ability to remove all the unwanted 3D material that surrounds the model. In the following screenshot, we can see that a large portion of the 3D scene contains the newspaper surrounding the toy block:

In this recipe, we will learn how to use these tools to remove the unwanted 3D material from around our model.

Getting ready

Choose a scene with the mesh resolution you desire. Keep in mind that once you make changes to the scene, they will be permanent.

How to do it...

Open 123D Catch and sign in. Open an existing capture and proceed as follows:

1. First, we will clear the camera track from our view so that we can see our model better. We will do this by clicking on the **Display Settings** icon [🖼] on the toolbar and deselecting the **Cameras** button. This will give us a clear view of the model.

2. While in **Display Settings**, switch over to **Wireframe Only** by selecting the cube icon on the left-hand side [🧊⬤⬤].

3. We need to be able to move around the model. We'll do this by selecting the **Orbit** tool icon [⬡].

4. By left-clicking and holding on the model, we can move around it. By selecting the **Pan** tool icon [⬡], we can left-click and hold on the model and adjust its position on the workspace. Using the middle track on the mouse, we can zoom in and out of the model.

5. Select the **Rectangle Selection** tool icon [⬡] and drag it out on a large area of the background. When you release the mouse, the selected area will turn red. If you don't like the area or a part of the model has been accidentally selected, clicking on the red area will deselect it.

6. When you have finished selecting it, press *Delete* on the keyboard. The selected area is removed. Keep in mind that once an area is removed, it's permanent. There isn't an undo function.

7. Continue doing this, cleaning all the space around the model.

8. Select the **Lasso Selection** tool icon [⬡].

9. The tool works in a manner that is similar to the rectangle select tool. Use the lasso to clean up close to the model's base, as shown in the following screenshot:

10. Save the mesh. Go to the menu and select **File**. Scroll down and select **Export Capture As**. Choose `.obj` and click on **Save**.

How it works...

The editing tools in 123D Catch are similar in function to their counterpart tools in many 2D graphics programs, and therefore, they should be intuitive in their use. Care must be exercised, however, when selecting areas in the image. Unlike a 2D image, where the selection is clearly seen on a flat surface, a selection in a 3D scene is what you see and what you don't see on the back side of the model.

Cleaning up the model with these tools can be done offline, but the results can only be saved using the Autodesk `.3dp` file format. The ability to export as an `.obj` file can only be attained when you are online.

Using the Autodesk 3D Print Utility

From the 123D Catch menu, the **Autodesk 3D Print Utility** (**A3DP**) can be accessed. It's a standalone program that repairs and optimizes your model for 3D printing. Though many features of the A3DP are designed for specific commercial 3D printers, the results can be exported to a file for use on any 3D printer. In the following recipe, we'll use the basic functions to create a properly scaled and watertight model.

Getting ready

You'll need a 3D scene open in 123D Catch with a model that is cleaned and ready for export. Go to **File** in the menu and select **3D print.** Follow the download and install instructions for the utility. Once the initial installation has been completed, the program can be accessed from the menu.

This book uses 3D Print Utility v1.1.1. After downloading, it can be accessed as a standalone program from the `Autodesk` folder in your Windows OS `Program Files` folder.

How to do it...

We will proceed as follows:

1. With a scene ready for processing in 123D Catch, select **3D print** in the **File** menu. This will open the **Autodesk 3D Print Utility** window and immediately begin the automatic processing of your model. It makes repairs to the model's mesh and positions the model properly on the build platform.

2. Once the processing of the model is finished, it will appear in the build envelope. The pyramid object that's used as an example in this book can be seen in the following screenshot:

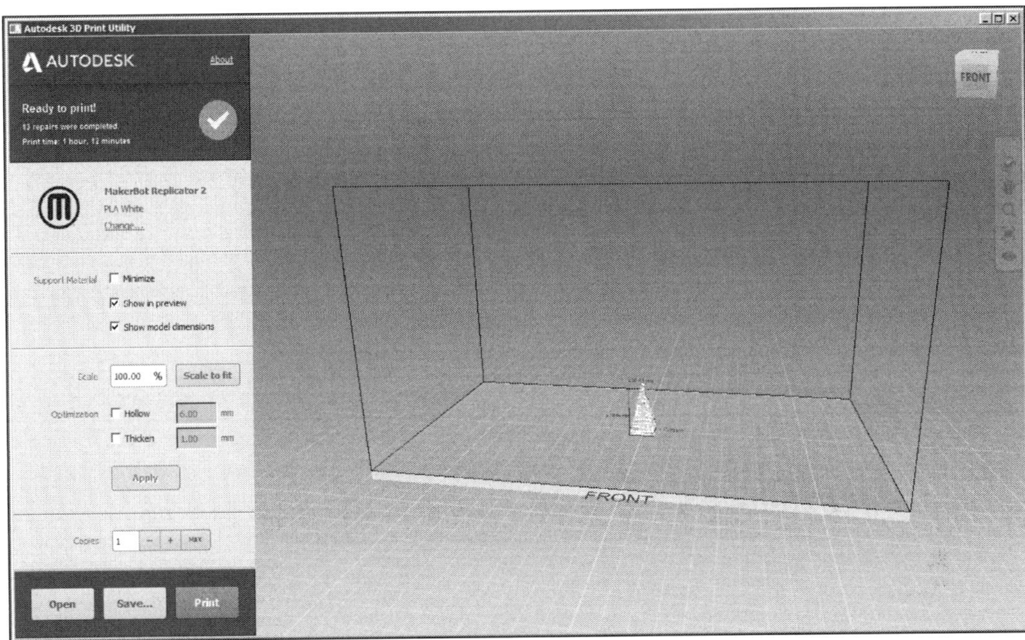

3. A series of navigation controls can be found in the top-right corner of the window. The basic controls allow for orbit, pan, zoom, center, and eye-level movements. They are accessed from the icon strip in which there's also a navigation cube icon [ ].

4. Left-click on the cube's front side. The view levels to a frontal view. Zoom in on the model using the magnifying glass icon, or use your scroll wheel on your mouse. The model should be clearly seen and should be similar to the pyramid model in the following screenshot:

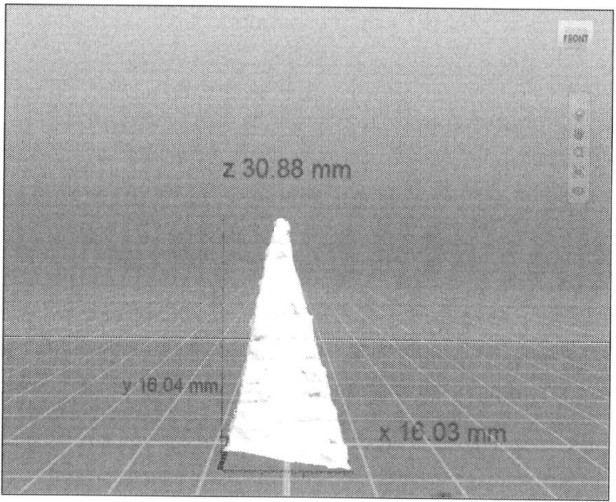

Be sure to deselect the **Show in preview** box under **Support Material**. This function is likely to distort your view of the model.

5. For each axis of the model, the A3DP Utility has given us a measurement in millimeters. This is the real-world measurement of our model if we were to print it. Our model was processed by 123D Catch without any information relating to its actual size in the physical world. Using the **Scale** function of A3DP, we can adjust the size of our model for final printing. To do this, take the recorded measurement of any one axis and determine its actual size. Enter the percentage of change for **Scale** and select **Apply**.

6. If you're not sure how much the percentage should be, but you know your target size, use the following method to calculate the percentage. In this case, I'm using the z axis, which shows a measurement of 30.88 mm. I would like this height to be changed to 53 mm. Divide 53 by 30.88 and then take the quotient, 1.72, and multiply it by 100. The product gives me a 172 percent change. Enter this percentage for **Scale** and select **Apply**.

7. Select **Save** to export the model as an STL file.

Stereolithography is a file format that describes only the surface geometry of a 3D object. It is the required file format for 3D printing.

How it works...

The A3DP Utility provides an easy solution for preparing a model, as follows:

- It automatically places the model properly on the build platform
- It repairs the holes and other mesh imperfections in the model
- It allows for manual scaling of the object

There are other options available in the utility, but they're not useful unless the model is exported for printing for one of the specified commercial machines, such as the MakerBot Replicator 2 (which is the default setting). These options are as follows:

- Support material
- Optimization
- Copies

Even with limited options, the A3DP Utility acts as an efficient tool in preparing models ready for slicing. A convenient feature of this utility is that it also works as a standalone program. Any `.obj` file, whether it is processed by 123D Catch or a 3D modeling program, can be loaded into the A3DP Utility, and it can be repaired and exported.

There's more...

When the A3DP Utility processes a model ready for printing, it also automatically decimates the model, that is, it reduces the polygon count of the mesh. This enables more efficient printing, but at the cost of losing detail. Let's compare the original model of the statue after 123D Catch processing and the same model after it was processed with the A3DP Utility.

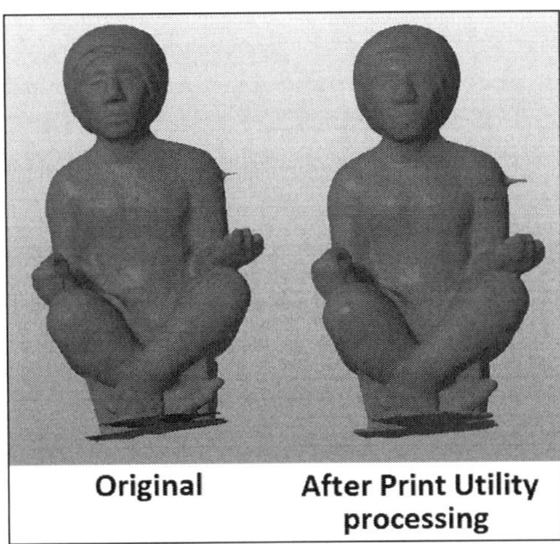

The original 123D Catch model has a polygon count of 151950, and the model processed with the A3DP Utility has a polygon count of 18670. This is a great difference, and it can be clearly seen in the preceding comparison. This is something to keep in mind when a higher-resolution print is required for finer details.

Let's print!

We began the chapter by choosing four objects from our physical world, and then we created a digital likeness of each of them. Using two programs, 123D Catch and the Autodesk 3D Print Utility, we were able to accomplish this with relative ease.

The resulting 3D models that were made of the example objects used in this book are shown in the following image:

Each of these models consists of a single watertight mesh. These models are saved as STL files, the proper file format for 3D printing. They are almost ready for printing, but one last step in the process is required.

We need to write a set of instructions for each model that tells our 3D printer how the model is to be printed. We do this using a slicer that generates G-code. G-code is a numerical control programming language that controls the automated functions of a 3D printer. The slicer generates G-code by taking the STL file of the model and slicing it up into many layers. For each of these layers, the variables set in the slicer profile are recorded. The finished G-code generated by the slicer will then instruct the extruder tool head how to move in an x, y, and z coordinate system. The 3D model will be built layer by layer.

In the next two recipes, we will become acquainted with two of the most popular slicers, **Slic3r** and **Skeinforge**. We will also run a basic print test of the models using both the slicers and then compare the results.

Slicing the models with Slic3r

It's fair to assume that if you are new to 3D printing and have limited experience, you've probably been using Slic3r. Slic3r has been in development since November 2011 and has become one of the most popular slicers in use. It has an easy user interface, good documentation, regular updates, and good user support on many forums.

Getting ready

You need a RepRap-based 3D printer and have the basic skills to operate it. If you are using Repetier-Host or another host that has Slic3r built in, use the standalone version. This can be found at `http://slic3r.org/download`.

This book uses Slic3r release v0.9.9. If you would like to use older versions, they can be downloaded at `http://dl.slic3r.org/win/old/`.

Download the application for your operating system (available for Windows, Mac, and Linux) and follow the installation instructions. This version will have a **Plater** window, as illustrated in the following screenshot:

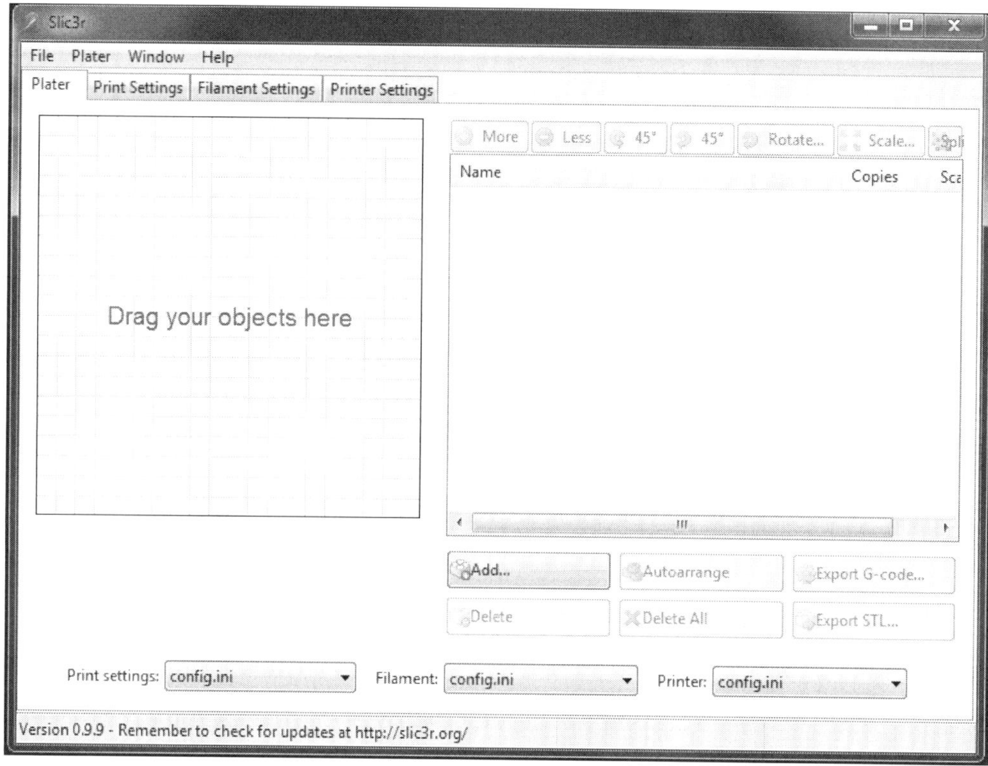

How to do it...

If you are presently a Slic3r user, you can ignore the configuration part of this recipe. Open Slic3r and proceed as follows:

1. When Slic3r is initially started, a configuration wizard will prompt you to supply some basic information about your printer. There are six settings in this configuration. They are as follows:

   - **Firmware Type**: This indicates the type of firmware to be used. Most RepRap kits will be using Marlin/Sprinter. This is the default setting in Slic3r. Check with the builder of your machine if you are not sure what firmware your printer is using.

   - **Bed Size**: This is the length of travel along the x and y axes. For most RepRap printers, this will be 200 mm by 200 mm. This is the default setting in Slic3r.

- ❑ **Nozzle Diameter**: This size should be specified by markings on the nozzle, by the extruder manufacturer or the builder of your printer. Common sizes are 0.35 mm and 0.5 mm. The default setting in Slic3r is 0.5 mm.

- ❑ **Filament Diameter**: This is the precise diameter size of the filament you are extruding. The two available sizes are 3 mm and 1.75 mm, but it can vary in size between manufacturers. Take multiple measurements and an average of the total. The default setting in Slic3r is 3 mm.

- ❑ **Extrusion Temperature**: Different filament materials require different extrusion temperatures. Enter the correct temperature for the material you are using. The default temperature in Slic3r is 200 degrees Celsius.

- ❑ **Bed Temperature**: Different filament materials require different bed temperatures. Enter the correct temperature for the material you are using. The default temperature in Slic3r is 0 degrees.

2. Choose one of your models to start. Take the STL file and drag-and-drop it on the **Plater**. The shape of the model's bottom can be seen when it is fully loaded. This is illustrated in the following screenshot:

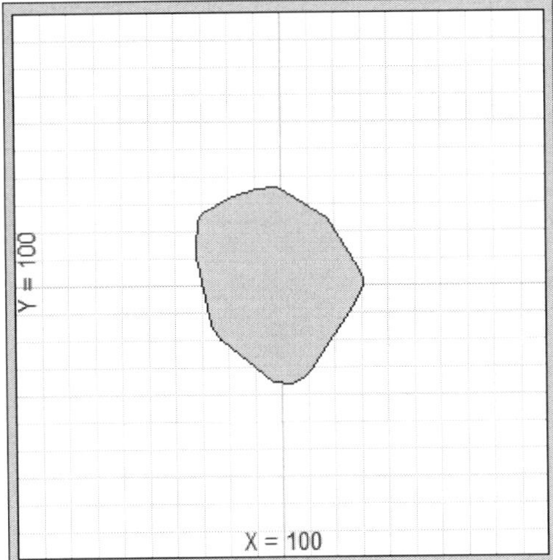

3. To generate the G-code, select **Export G-code**. A pop-up window appears, allowing you to name and save the G-code file. Choose a place to store the file. There's a progress bar in the lower-right corner of the **Plater**. When the G-code is complete, a message at the bottom of the window will show that the G-code has been exported.

4. Open your host and load the G-code. Your model is now ready to be printed.

How it works...

When you open Slic3r for the first time, a simplified interface version is presented. All of the configuration selections you made earlier are stored under the **Filament Settings** and **Printer Settings** tabs. Any changes you may need to make to your configuration can be done there.

The **Print Settings** tab has six sections where slicer settings can be made. We can see the options available in the following screenshot:

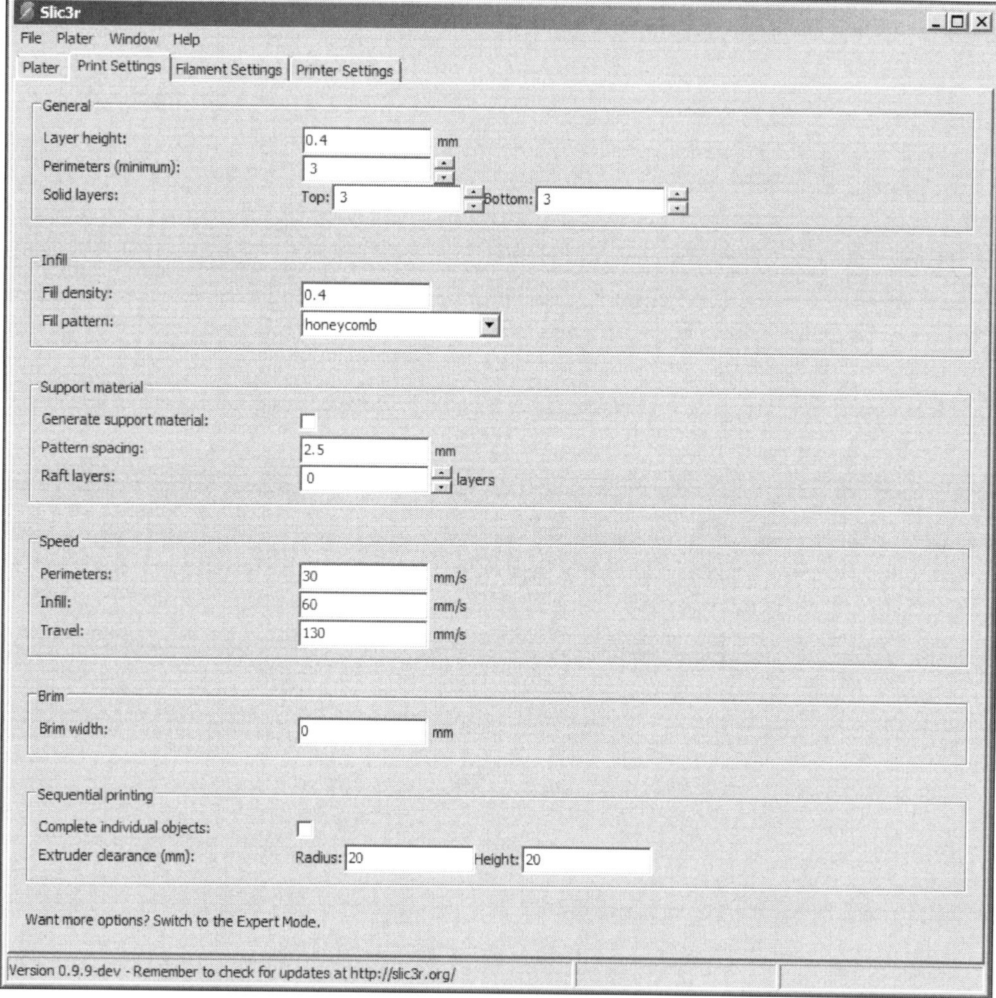

For this recipe, we used the default values as a starting point. This will become our reference point for all the future changes. Later, in the following chapters, we will open the expert mode and experiment with the various settings.

A manual created by Gary Hodgson can be found at `http://wiki.techstories.de/download/attachments/7143623/Slic3r-Manual2.pdf`.

Slicing the models with Skeinforge

Skeinforge is by far the most versatile slicer available, and it can be the most intimidating one because of its complexity. Taking the time to unravel its mysteries will pay off in the end. The amount of control one can exercise over the numerous setting options can sometimes overcome printing difficulties that other slicers cannot achieve.

Getting ready

You need a RepRap-based 3D printer and have the basic skills to operate it. If you are using Repetier-Host or another host that has Skeinforge built in, make sure you are using the latest version. Its latest update can be found at `http://fabmetheus.crsndoo.com/`. It has not been updated since March 15, 2012.

To use Skeinforge as a standalone program, you will need to install Python. Python can be found at `https://www.python.org/download/`. Install Python Version 2.7.6.

In order to create a default settings profile for Skeinforge, we will need to add a profile that is not included in the latest version. This profile will make a good starting point and also provide us with a reference point for future changes. It can be downloaded at `https://github.com/romscraj/skeinforge41/zipball/master`. Open the folder and navigate into the `.skeinforge` folder, then into the `profiles` folder, and finally into the `extrusion` folder. Copy the `Durbie-Normal` folder.

Locate the `.skeinforge` folder that is created by Skeinforge when it is initially opened. It should be in your computer's personal folder if you are using Windows or in your computer's home in Mac or Linux OS. Once it is located, add the `Durbie-Normal` folder into the `extrusion` folder nested in the `profiles` folder. Now, the added profile is available in the **Profile Selection** menu.

How to do it...

We will proceed as follows:

1. Open Skeinforge by double-clicking on the Skeinforge Python file in the `skeinforge_application` folder.

2. When the Skeinforge window opens, you will be confronted with a menu and an array of tabs for many different plugins. Initially, maneuvering through the selections can be overwhelming, but we are only going to concern ourselves with configuring the printer and filament settings. First, choose the **Profile** tab and select the **Durbie-Normal** option from **Profile Selection**. We can see how this looks in the following screenshot:

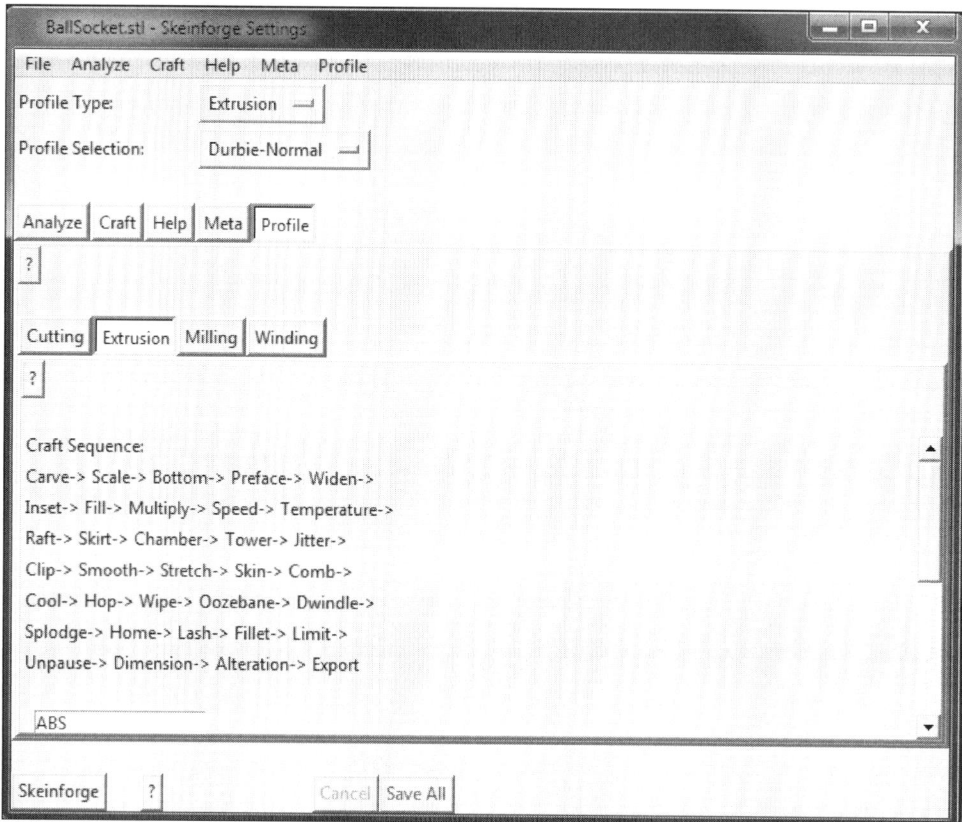

3. Now, we are ready to configure the slicer to your 3D printer. Select the **Craft** tab. There are 34 tabs that offer options to control your printer. These can be seen in the following screenshot:

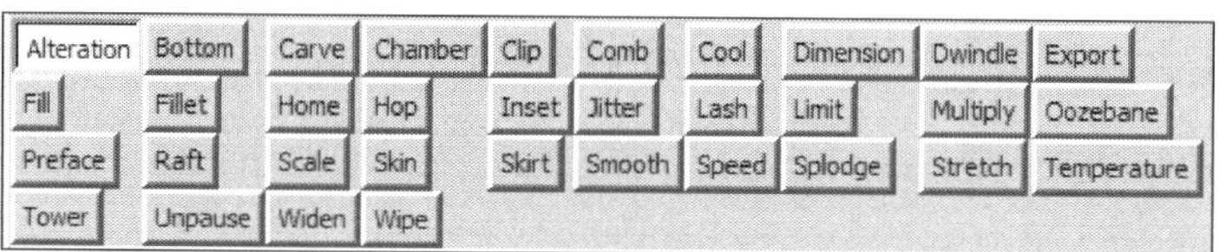

4. We'll make our configuration adjustments by selecting three of these tabs.

5. Select the **Carve** tab. This is seen in the following screenshot:

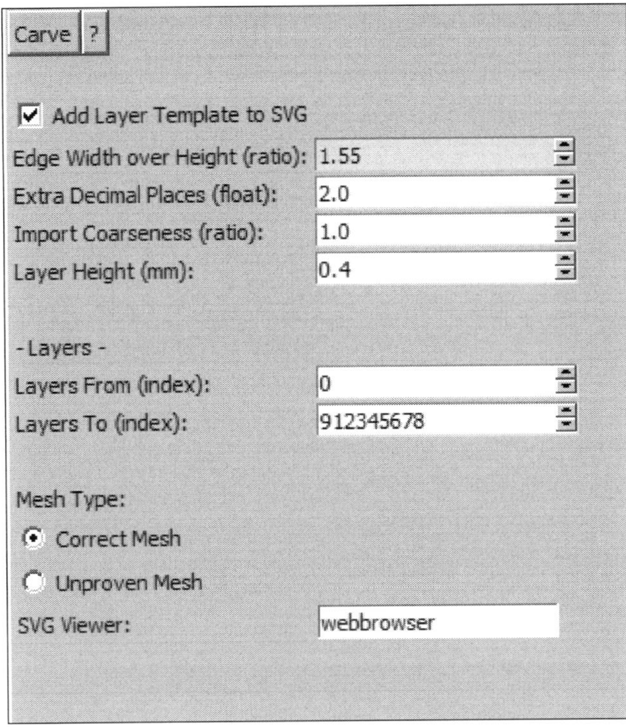

☐ Here is where we tell Skeinforge what size of nozzle we are using and how thick our printing layer will be. Unlike Slic3r, we don't simply enter a nozzle size. Skeinforge uses a ratio of edge width over height to determine the nozzle size. If you're using a 0.5 mm nozzle, this is the **Durbie-Normal** profile default. If you're using a 0.35 mm nozzle, change the 1.55 value in **Edge Width over Height (ratio)** to 1.4. Then, change the **Layer Height (mm)** from 0.4 to 0.3.

Refer to *Chapter 3*, *Scanning and Printing with a Higher Resolution*, to learn how these values are selected for different nozzle sizes and layer heights.

6. Select the **Dimension** tab. This is seen in the following screenshot:

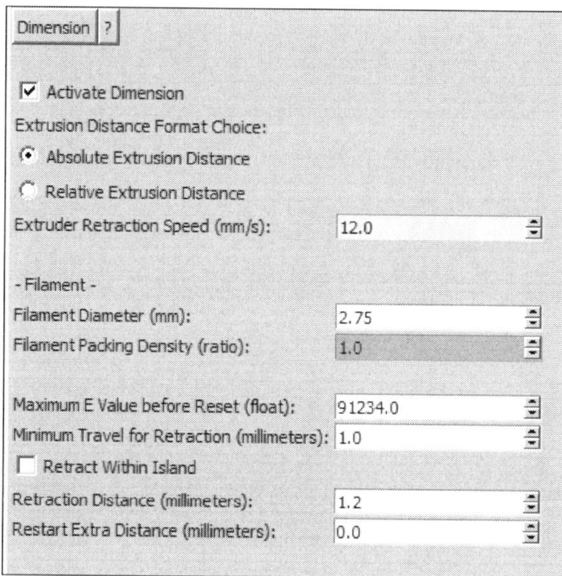

- ❏ Place your filament size in the **Filament Diameter (mm)** window. The **Durbie-Normal** default value is 2.75 mm.

7. Select the **Inset** tab. This is seen in the following screenshot:

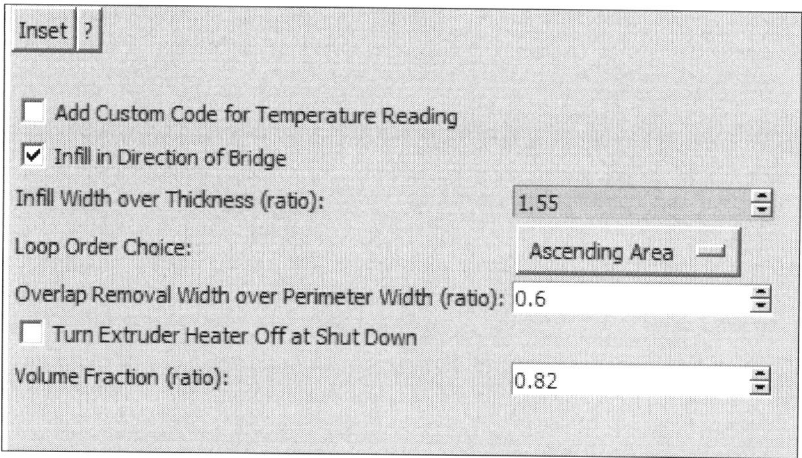

- ❏ The infill width over thickness ratio should be kept similar to the edge width over height ratio in the **Carve** plugin. The **Durbie-Normal** default value is 1.55.

8. Select **Save All** at the bottom of the window.

9. To generate the G-code, we need to left-click on the **Skeinforge** button at the bottom-left corner of the program window. From the pop up, choose **STL files** from the extension list.

10. Choose one of your models to begin with. Locate the STL file and click on **Open**. Skeinforge begins to compile the G-code.

11. When the G-code has been compiled, two windows containing analytical information will appear. Close these windows and locate the G-code file by checking the bottom lines in the **Python.exe** window. It will show you where the file was exported.

12. Open your host and load the G-code. You are now ready to print the model.

How it works...

For a new user, the adjustments in Skeinforge may seem arcane. For example, instead of simply entering the size of the print nozzle, Skeinforge requires a ratio of the width to height of the extruded filament. This becomes more complicated as variables change. This is just one aspect of Skeinforge's complexity in comparison to other slicers. Yet, with this additional complexity, far more control can be mastered. Throughout the course of this book, we'll be exploring many different features offered by the Skeinforge plugins.

There's more...

It won't be unusual for us to have many different profiles and a need to label and store them in **Profile Selection**. To make a profile, start by selecting one that's similar to your target profile. Make your alterations and select the **Profile** tab, as shown in the following screenshot:

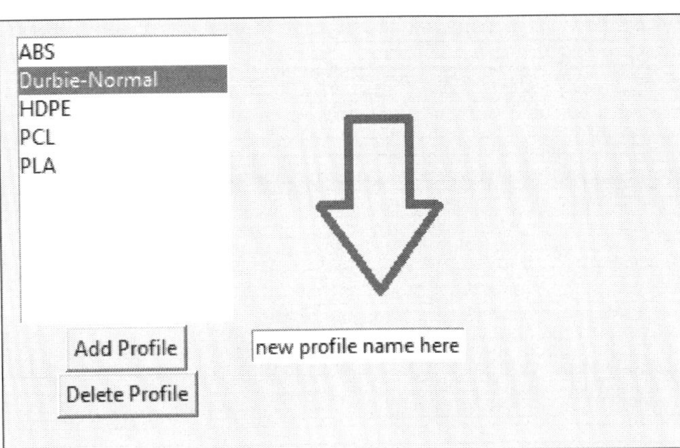

Enter the name of the new profile in the window and select **Add Profile**. This is shown in the preceding screenshot.

Reviewing the print results

Both the slicers, with their default settings, printed well with minor to average problems. The major difference between the two slicers was the amount of time it took to compile the results of the G-code. Slic3r is fast in comparison to Skeinforge.

In the following image, we can see that the coin suffers from a lack of detail. It's difficult for 123D Catch to capture fine surface detail.

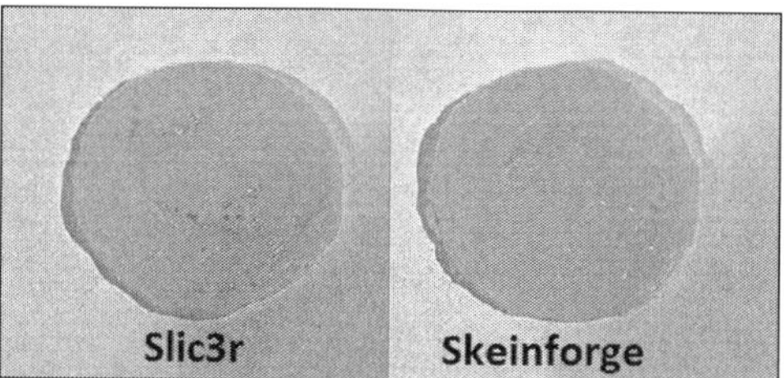

In the following image, we can see the results of the toy block. There's a lot of distortion caused by the 3D scanning process of the model. Both Slic3r and Skeinforge produced similar printing results.

The 3D scan of the following figure produced a successful result, but both suffer from a common problem encountered in 3D printing. When a complex model has angles of more than 45 degrees, the filament may lose support and sag.

Refer to *Chapter 6, Making the Impossible*, for a method of creating a removable support. This will eliminate the sagging filament.

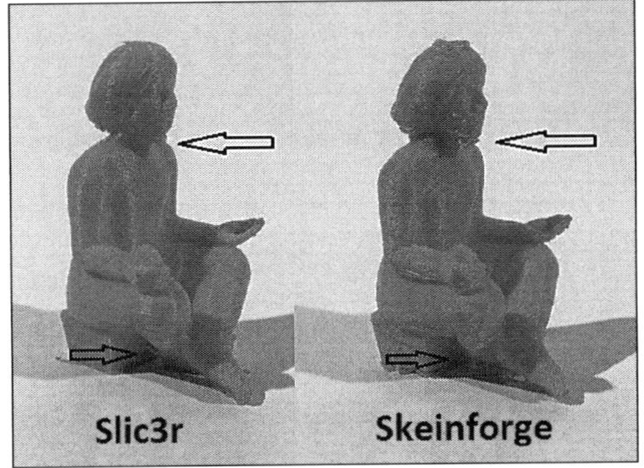

The 3D scan of the pyramid was successful, however, both slicers had difficulty with printing the uneven base of the pyramid, as seen in the following image:

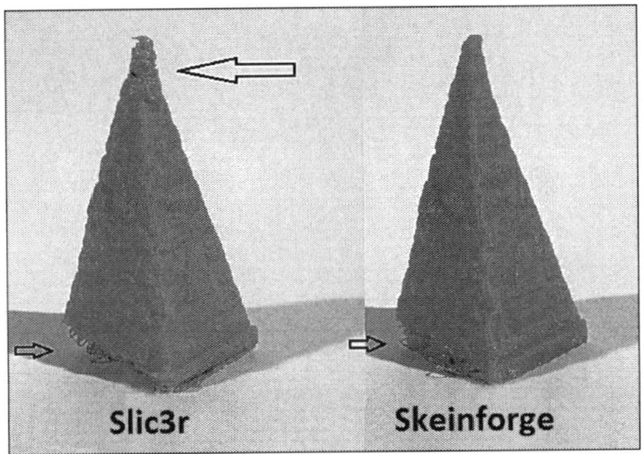

Slic3r has an additional issue at the tip of the pyramid. It's distorted is caused by inadequate cooling of filament layers. As each layer is extruded at more than 200 degrees Celsius, there must be an opportunity for each layer to cool for another hot layer to be deposited. The default cooling settings in Slic3r were not sufficient, but in later chapters we'll learn how to optimize Slic3r's cooling features in the following chapters.

2
Optimizing the Printing Process

In this chapter, we will cover the following recipes:

- Inspecting the model with Meshmixer
- Plane alignment with Meshmixer
- Scaling the model with Meshmixer
- Leveling the model with Meshmixer
- Removing scanning artifacts with Meshmixer
- Shaping the model with Meshmixer
- Optimizing infill with Slic3r
- Optimizing infill with Skeinforge
- Printing without fill with Skeinforge
- Tweaking shells and surface layers with Skeinforge

Introduction

In this chapter, we're going to take the models that we scanned with 123D Catch and make them better. We'll do this by using another free program offered by Autodesk called Meshmixer. It's a 3D modeling program that offers a variety of sculpting tools that manipulate the surface mesh of a 3D model. It also offers a series of tools that are geared to optimize a model for 3D printing.

We'll also take a look inside the model. There's a lot that can happen in the interior, which can affect both the structural integrity and surface quality. We'll see how infill options in both Slic3r and Skeinforge can be adjusted for different uses.

Inspecting the model with Meshmixer

In this recipe, we'll get familiar with Meshmixer by using the Inspector tool. This tool analyzes defects in the model's mesh and provides options for repairing it manually or automatically. We'll see how well it works by repairing the models that we made in 123D Catch.

Before we get started, let's get acquainted with the basic navigation controls. Meshmixer has an easy user interface called a Hotbox. It can be seen in the following image:

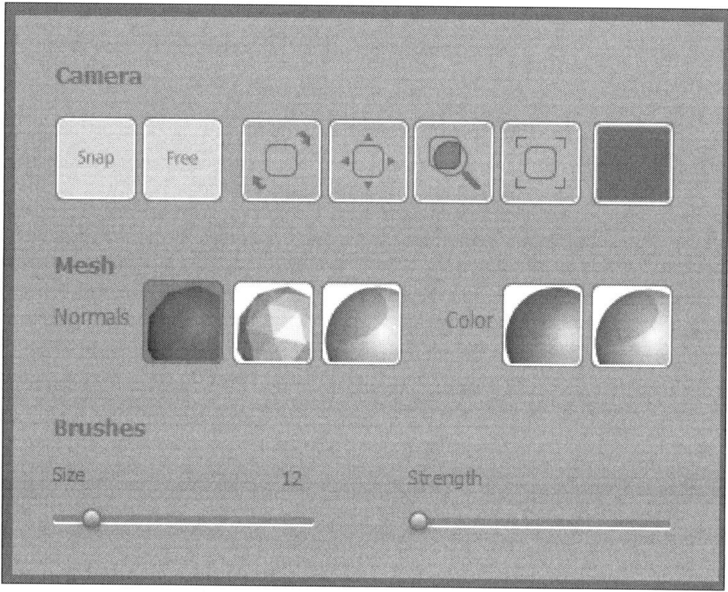

The navigation control buttons are in the **Camera** section. Experiment with them. While keeping the Space bar key pressed on the keyboard, click, hold, and move the mouse on each button. The first button will rotate the model along the axes. The second button will pan the model across the screen. The third button will zoom in and out on the object, and the fourth button will re-center the image.

There are two other buttons in the far left corner that will help in orienting your model precisely. The **Snap** button will keep your model snapped to the axes. The other button, **Free**, will allow full navigation around the model.

If you like the mouse navigation control that's similar to 123D Catch, this can be made possible by going to the menu and selecting **View** and then **Navigation Control**. From the cascaded window, choose **123D**.

Getting ready

You'll need to download Meshmixer from `http://www.meshmixer.com/download.html` and follow the instructions for installing it. You'll also need to choose a model that was scanned with 123D Catch. Don't choose a model that was repaired with the Autodesk 3D Print Utility. We need a model that has defects and is in need of repair.

 This book uses Meshmixer v10.2.32. It is available for Windows and Mac operating systems.

How to do it...

We will proceed as follows:

1. When you initially open Meshmixer, you'll see a big box that provides us with options to open a file. We'll need to use **Import+** to load our file.

2. The Meshmixer UI has a row of icons on the left that provides access to a variety of actions, from here choose **Analysis**. From the pop-up window, choose **Inspector**. What you should see is illustrated in the following image:

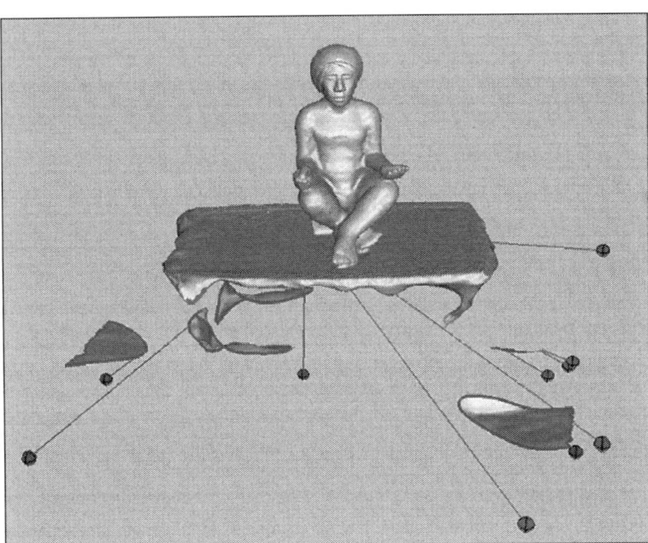

3. Lines will radiate from the mesh defects with an attached globe on each end.

4. There are three differently colored globes that represent three different problems. The first one that we'll look at is the magenta-colored globe. These markers indicate disconnected fragments that fill your scene, which should probably be deleted. To delete the fragments, left-click on the globe and it will disappear.

5. The second one is the blue-colored globe. This represents areas that have holes in the mesh. Left-click on one to repair the hole.

6. The third one is the red-colored globe. This indicates the non-manifold areas in the mesh. By left-clicking on the red globe, the non-manifold area will be repaired by discarding it.

7. Instead of selecting each globe one by one, all the repairs can be made by selecting from the pop-up toolbox or by right-clicking on any single globe.

8. If you don't like a repair, select **Actions** in the menu. Scroll down and select **Undo/Back**.

How it works...

When Meshmixer auto repairs the model, it's not unusual for the program to extrapolate a repair, which distorts a "repaired" area of the model. Sometimes, the automatic repair may remove portions of the model that we would like to keep. Using AutoRepair All is generally a fast and efficient way to clean up your model, but sometimes there are situations when a manual selection is preferable.

See also

▶ *Chapter 8, Troubleshooting Issues in 3D Modeling*, will provide more information on different kinds of mesh defects and how to repair them manually

Plane alignment with Meshmixer

In a 3D software program, we have to be able to orient ourselves in this virtual space to be able to work in it. This is typically achieved by modeling on a plane in the workspace. Meshmixer generates a grid plane and a model is then positioned somewhere on or within it. We can see this illustrated in the following image:

Meshmixer imports the rabbit sitting on the plane and imports the sphere with the plane bisecting it. Depending on how a model is positioned in the Cartesian space of another 3D program, the positioning, when importing into Meshmixer, can be anywhere in relation to this plane.

Meshmixer orients the *y* axis going up from the surface of the plane. You'll find that the other programs in this book will not have this configuration. The *z* axis will travel up from the plane. This isn't a problem when sculpting the model in Meshmixer, but it does make a difference when using a modification tool, which depends on the plane for orientation.

In this recipe, we'll learn how to make a manual change in this alignment.

Getting ready

You'll need one of the models from *Chapter 1, Getting Started with 3D Printing*. In this recipe, the pyramid model will serve as the example.

How to do it...

We will proceed as follows:

1. Select **Import+** to import the model into Meshmixer. In the following image, we can see how the pyramid is positioned in relation to Meshmixer's grid plane:

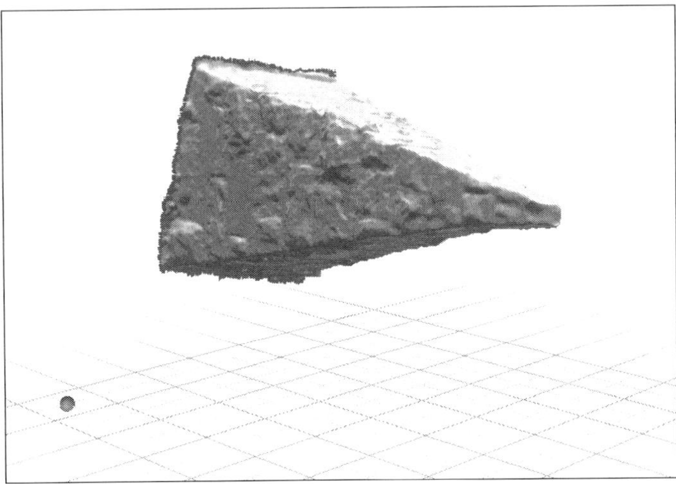

2. Go to **Edit**. From the pop-up window, choose **Align**. The workspace will now show another plane with the model. From here, manual movements can be made by clicking, holding, and dragging the blue arrow and arc controls. For now, let's use the alignment controls in the **Properties** window.

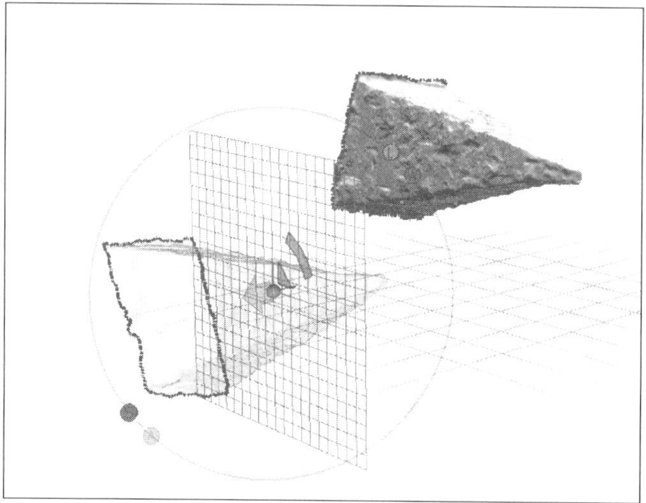

3. From the **Align** properties window, you'll have a choice in alignment by choosing an axis. Choose the axis that will orient your model on the plane. In this case, it's the *y* axis. We can see the alignment change in the following image:

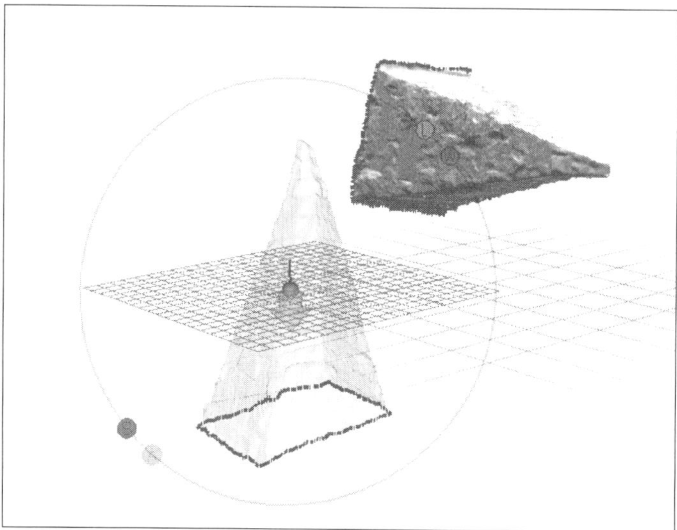

4. When you're happy with the orientation, click on **Accept** in the **Align** properties window.

How it works...

Aligning the model in relation to Meshmixer's plane is helpful when working in Meshmixer, but before the model is exported as an STL for slicing and printing, we'll have to realign the model back to its former position. If we don't, then the model will be positioned on its side for printing.

 Meshmixer allows for an automatic flip of the *z* and *y* axis during import and export. This is found in the menu under **View** and then **Config**.

There's more...

The red ball on the plane in Meshmixer is a marker that shows the origin of the coordinate system. This can be seen in the following image by comparing the top view of the pyramid in another 3D program:

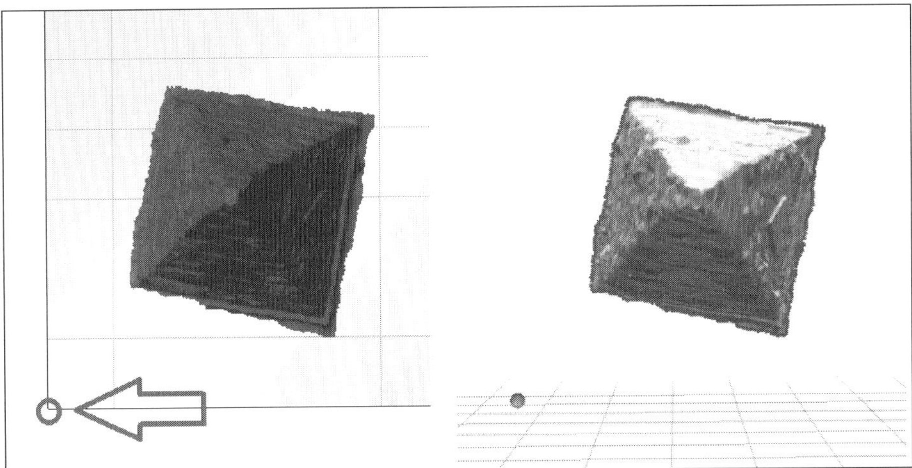

The image on the left shows a view that is seen by looking down the *z* axis onto the grid where the model is positioned. The origin is marked by the red circle on the grid that represents the *xy* plane. The image on the right shows the Meshmixer grid with its origin marked by a small red ball. Knowing where the origin is located in the virtual space is important. It always provides a point of reference no matter which 3D program your model is imported.

Scaling the model with Meshmixer

Measurement in the virtual space can be considered arbitrary; what matters is the relative scale. When a model is created by 123D Catch, the size of the object is measured in an arbitrary scale of units. These units can then be interpolated by other 3D modeling programs using metric or imperial units of measurement. We can see how Meshmixer interpolates the size of the pyramid in the following image:

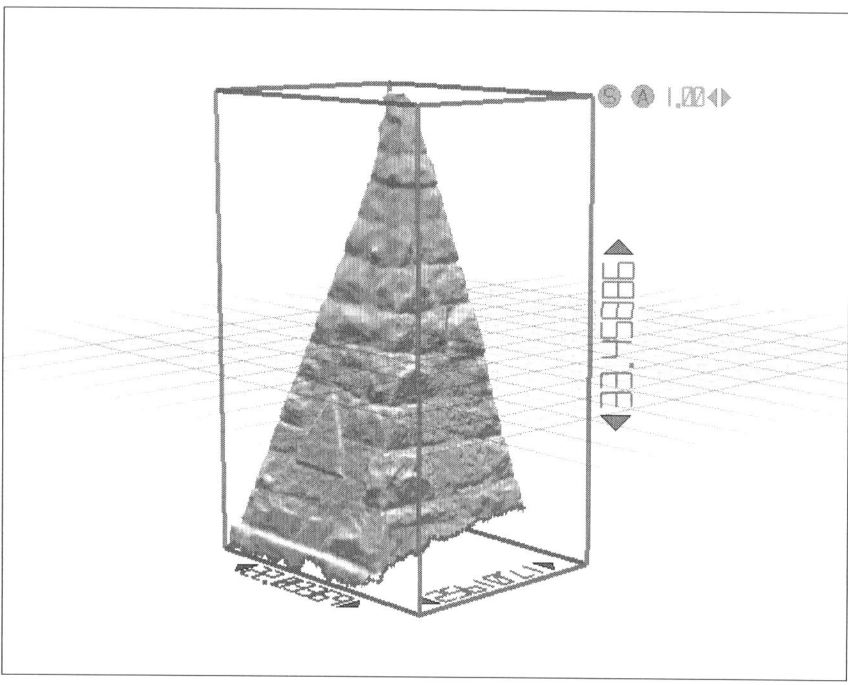

The pyramid measures roughly 23 x 17 x 33 millimeters. In reality, the pyramid is more than 4 meters high. What is important for us is a scale that will print on our 3D printer.

In this recipe, we'll learn how to scale our model for printing with Meshmixer.

Getting ready

You'll need the models that you created with 123D Catch.

How to do it...

We will proceed as follows:

1. Select **Import+** to import a model into Meshmixer.

2. Go to **Analysis**. From the pop-up window, choose **Units/Scale**.

3. In the **Units/Scale** properties window, enter the measurement that you want for your model. In this case, a measurement of 100 mm is entered for the *z* axis. The other axes are adjusted automatically for proper scaling of all the axes.

4. Save your model.

How it works...

When the model is scaled in Meshmixer, there's no visual indication of a change in size in the workspace. What changes are the measurement values and the **Grid Size** value in the **Properties** window.

Leveling the model with Meshmixer

Sometimes, we'll have a model that has an uneven bottom that needs to be leveled. The pyramid is a good example of this. When it was 3D scanned, its positioning on a slope concealed part of its base. This can be seen in the following image:

In this recipe, we'll learn how to fix this kind of problem by using a plane cut in Meshmixer.

Getting ready

You'll need to load one of your models in Meshmixer. Choose one that has an issue, which is similar to the example model.

How to do it...

We will proceed as follows:

1. Select **Import+** to import the model into Meshmixer.

2. Go to **Edit**. From the pop-up window, choose **Plane Cut**. The following image illustrates the cutting plane and colored axes controls:

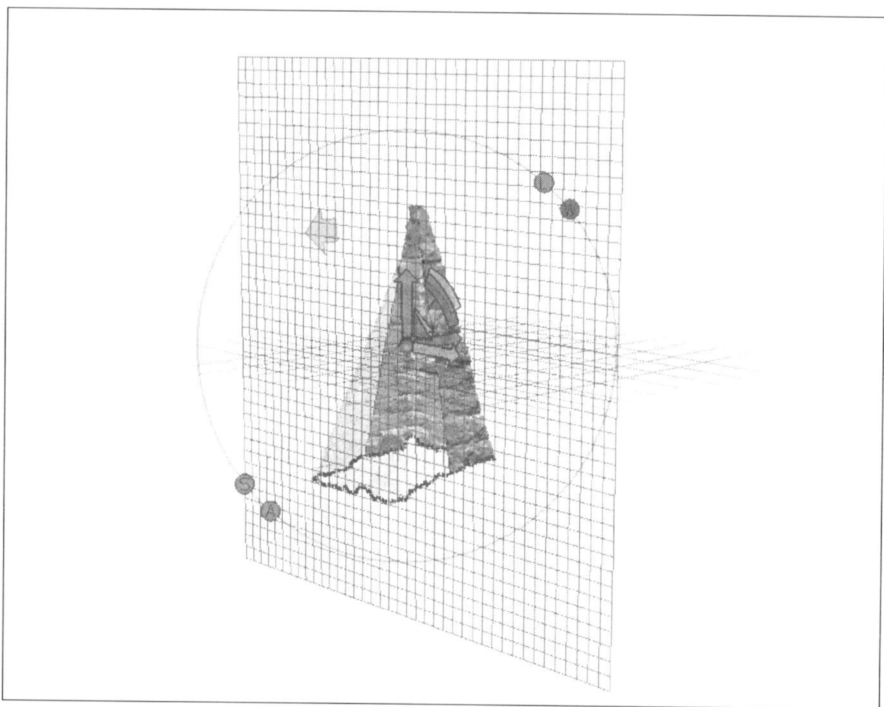

3. Click, hold, and drag and move the appropriate axis (it's the arc shape). In this case, it's the green axis that will lower the cut plane parallel with the base. It should look like the following image:

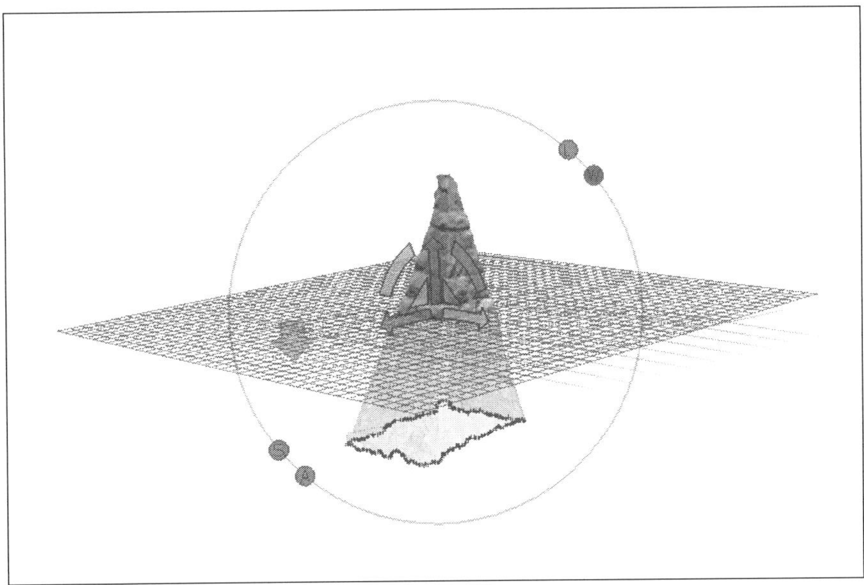

4. Now, click, hold, and drag the *z* axis arrow down, lowering the plane cut to the closest point where the base can be cut even. Go to the **Properties** window and click on **Accept**.

5. Save the model.

How it works...

The **Plane Cut** tool will also cut the model and fill with a flat surface. By choosing the **Delaunay** option in **Fill**, a solid base will be created that's water-tight.

Removing scanning artifacts with Meshmixer

Sometimes, we'll find odd distortions in our 3D scanned models. These are digital artifacts that are generated from glares, poorly focused photos, and other degraded information, which the scanning program processes. In this recipe, we'll learn how to remove these artifacts from the model.

Getting ready

You'll need to open a model in Meshmixer that has similar defects as shown in the following image:

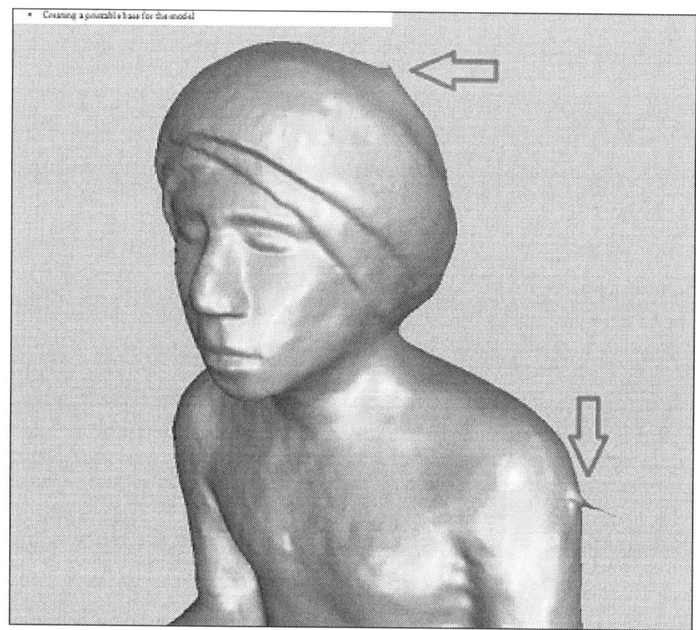

How to do it...

We will proceed as follows:

1. Zoom in on the artifact. Choose **Select**. From the pop-up toolbox, we'll use the default brush tool. Adjust its size by using the size slider and then select the end of the artifact. The pop-up toolbox will change and provide more options.

2. Go to the toolbox and select **Modify**. Scroll down the cascaded window and select **Expand Ring**. The selection will grow slightly larger.

3. We can also use the keyboard shortcut (*Shift* + >). This will also expand the ring. Continue using the keyboard shortcut until the area is selected up to the model. In the following image, we can see the selection illustrated:

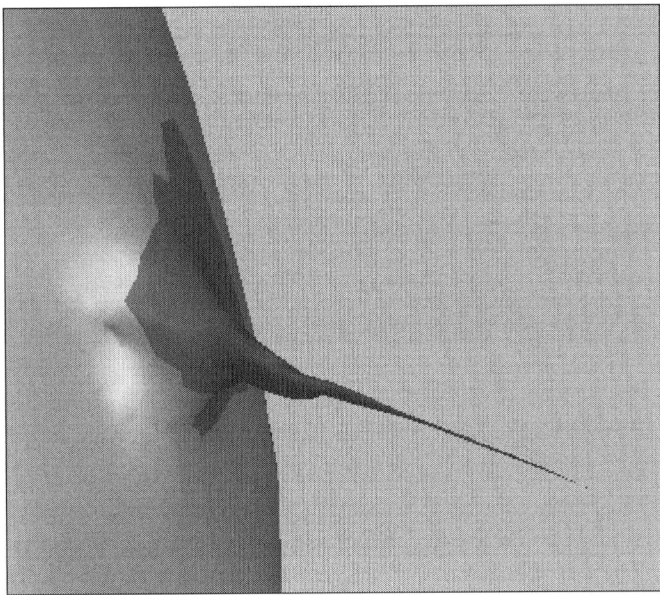

4. Now, let's get rid of it. Choose **Edit** from the toolbox. Scroll down the cascaded window and select **Discard**. You can also use the keyboard shortcut X.

5. We've created a hole in the model's mesh by removing the artifact. To repair it, choose **Inspector**. In the following left-hand side image, the hole becomes outlined in blue with its attached blue globe. Left-click on it to repair it. Now, we've removed the artifact, but as we can see in the image on the right, the area is still distorted. We can fix this with the smooth tool.

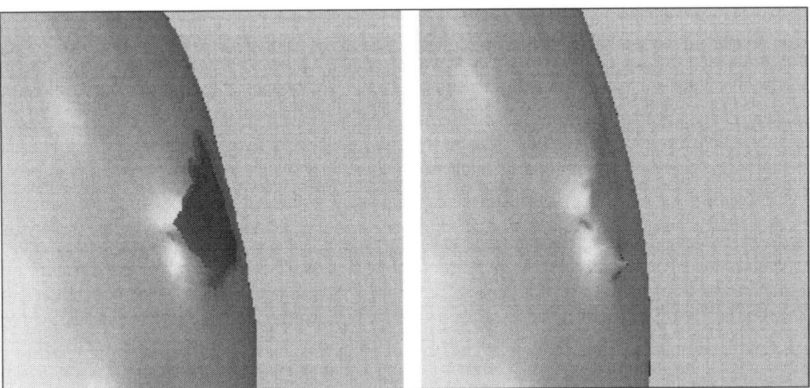

6. Choose **Sculpt** from the toolbar. From the pop-up toolbox, choose **Brushes**. You'll be confronted with a lot of choices. In this recipe, what we're interested in is the **ShrinkSmooth** brush. The brush can be adjusted for the size and strength in the **Properties** section.

7. Click, hold, and drag the brush across the distorted area as shown in the following left-hand side image:

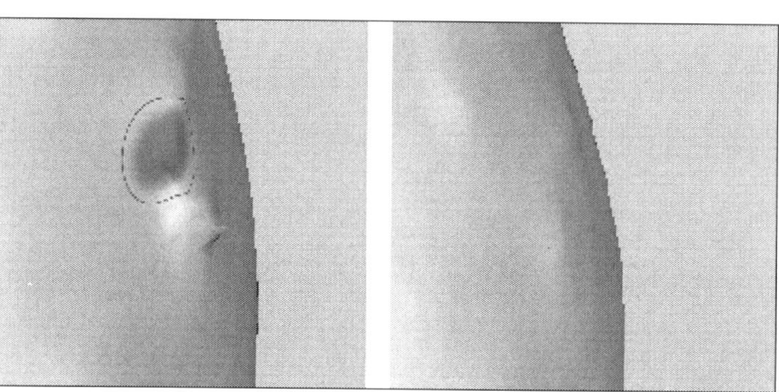

8. As you move over the area, it will become smoother. Experiment with different brush sizes and strengths for each of the artifacts that your model may have.

How it works...

Meshmixer has many different brushes that will perform very specific functions. Most of these functions are better understood by experimentation on a model. One of the best methods for doing this is by using a sphere. This can be found by going to **File** in the menu and selecting **Import Sphere**. Dragging each brush across its surface will give you a good idea of its capabilities.

These brushes are more useful when the functions of each brush are inverted. This is accomplished by holding *Shift* on the keyboard as you drag the brush.

Shaping the model with Meshmixer

In this recipe, we'll improve the surface of a model by working with its mesh. Meshmixer was designed to provide a modeling interface that frees the user from working directly with the geometry of the mesh. In most cases, the intent of the program succeeds, but in some cases, it's good to see how the underlying mesh works.

We'll use some brush tools to make one of our models better, thereby taking a look at how this affects the mesh structure.

Getting ready

We'll need the toy block that we scanned with 123D Catch.

How to do it...

We will proceed as follows:

1. Let's take a look at the model's mesh by positioning the model with a visible large surface. Go to the menu and select **View**. Scroll down and select **Toggle Wireframe** (*W*).

2. Choose **Sculpt**. From the pop-up toolbox, choose **Brushes**. Go to the menu and select **ShrinkSmooth**. Adjust your settings in the **Properties** section. Keep the size as 60 and its strength as 25. Use the smooth tool slowly across the model, watching the change it makes to the mesh. In the following example, the keyboard shortcut *W* is used to toggle between mesh views:

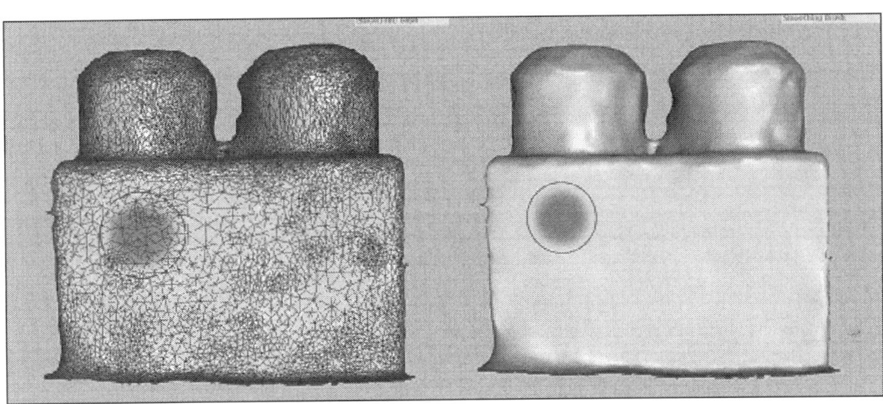

3. Repeat using the **RobustSmooth** and **Flatten** brushes. Use these combinations of brushes to flatten one side of the toy block.

4. Rotate your model to an area where there's heavy distortion. Make sure your view is in the wireframe mode. Go back to **Brushes** and select **Pinch**.

5. Adjust the **Strength** to 85, **Size** to 39, **Depth** to -17, and **Lazyness** to 95. Keep everything else at default values. If you are uncertain of the default values, left-click on the small cogwheel icon next to the **Properties** heading. Choose **Reset to Defaults**.

6. We're going to draw a line across a distorted area of the toy block to see how it **affects** the mesh. Using the pinch brush, draw a line across the model. Save your work and then select **Undo/back** from the **Actions** menu (*Ctrl + Z*).

7. Now, select your entire model. Go to the toolbox and select **Edit**. Scroll down and select **Remesh** (*R*). You'll see an even distribution of polygons in the mesh. Keep the defaults in the pop up and click on **Accept**.

8. Now, go back and choose **Clear Selection**. Select the pinch brush again and draw a line across the model as you did before. Compare it to the other model with the unrefined mesh.

9. Let's finish cleaning up the toy block. Click on **Undo/back** (*Ctrl + Z*) to the pinch brush line that you drew.

10. Now, use the pinch tool to refine the edges of the model. Work around it and sharpen all the edges.

11. Finish smoothing the planes on the block and click on **Save**.

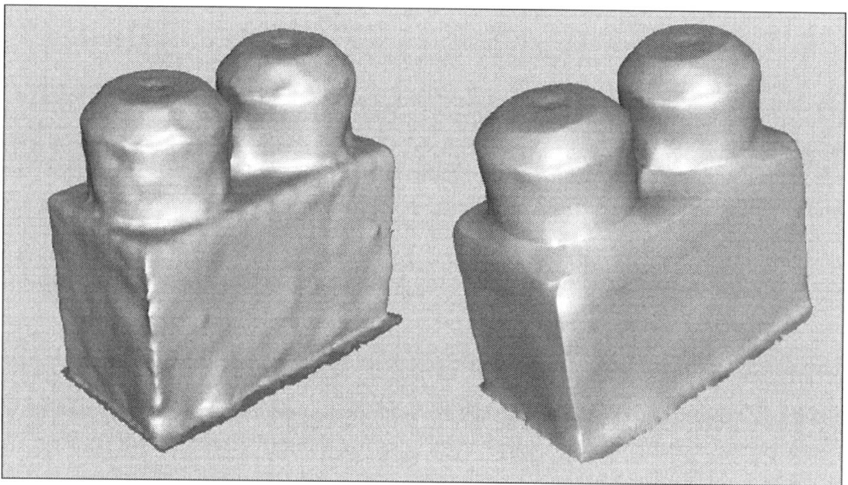

12. We can see the results clearly as we compare the original toy block model to our modified model in the preceding image.

How it works...

Meshmixer works by using a mesh with a high definition of polygons. When a sculpting brush such as pinch is used to manipulate the surface, it rapidly increases the polygon count in the surrounding area. When the pinch tool crosses an area that has fewer and larger polygons, the interpolation of the area becomes distorted. We can see this in the following example when we compare the original and remeshed model in the wireframe view:

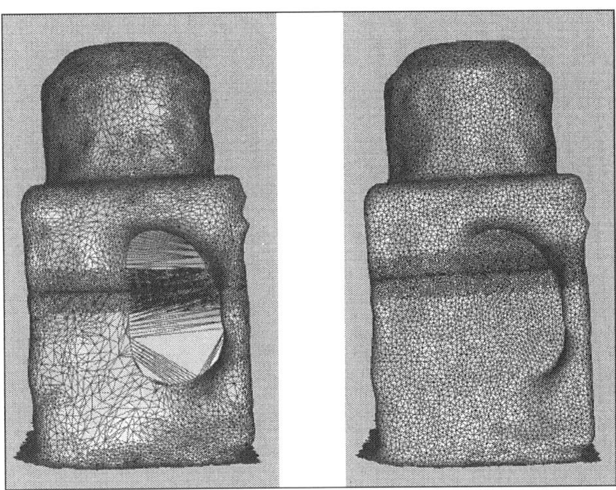

In the following image, when we hide the wireframe, we can see how the distortion in the mesh has given the model on the left some undesirable texture along the pinch line:

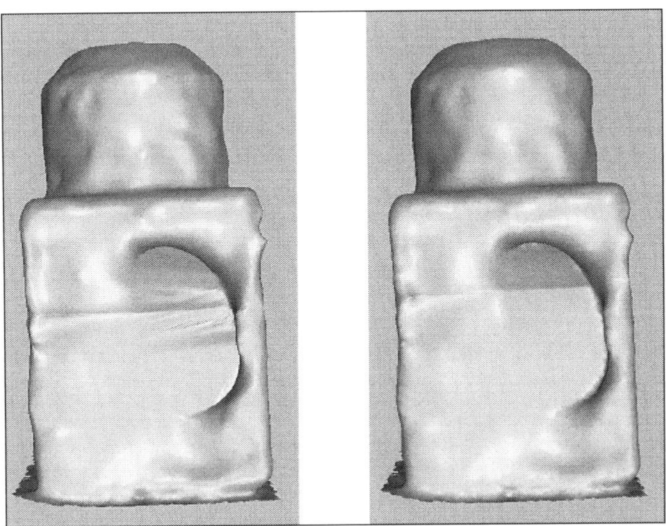

It may be a good idea to examine a model's mesh before sculpting it. Meshmixer works better with a dense polygon count that is consistent in size. By using the **Remesh** edit, a variety of mesh densities can be achieved by making changes in **Properties**.

Experiment with the various settings and the sculpting brushes while in the wireframing stage. This will help you gain a better understanding of how mesh surface modeling works.

See also

> ▸ *Chapter 5, Manipulating Meshes and Bridges*, has more in-depth information on meshes and how to manipulate them

Let's print!

We've spent the first section of this chapter learning how to optimize what we can see of the model. In the printing section of this chapter, we're going to learn how to optimize what we can't see of the model.

When we 3D print a model, we have the option of controlling how solid the interior will be and what kind of structure will fill it. How we choose between the options is easily determined by answering the following questions:

> ▸ Will it need to be structurally strong? If it's going to be used as a mechanical part or an item that will be heavily handled, then it does.

> ▸ Will it be a prototype? If it's a temporary object for examination purposes or strictly for display, then a fragile form may suffice.

Depending on the use of a model, you'll have to decide how the object falls within these two extremes. Most of the models that we'll print in the following recipes will be considered a prototype. We'll learn how to make them economical and sufficiently strong for our purposes. We'll also take a look at how to optimize a model for more stress-related use.

We'll accomplish this by controlling how we print inside the model using the slicer. With the following recipes in this chapter, we'll examine the infill and perimeter settings of both Slic3r and Skeinforge.

Optimizing infill with Slic3r

Slic3r has the capability of creating seven infill patterns. These patterns can be interesting and fun, but they also serve a practical function. Each pattern will offer different qualities in strength and have a different print time and material usage. In this recipe, we'll learn how to select the infill pattern and adjust its density.

Getting ready

You'll need the toy block that we optimized with Meshmixer.

How to do it...

Open Slic3r and follow the procedure:

1. Select the **Print Settings** tab and then choose **Infill**. The section where we'll be making our changes is illustrated in the following screenshot:

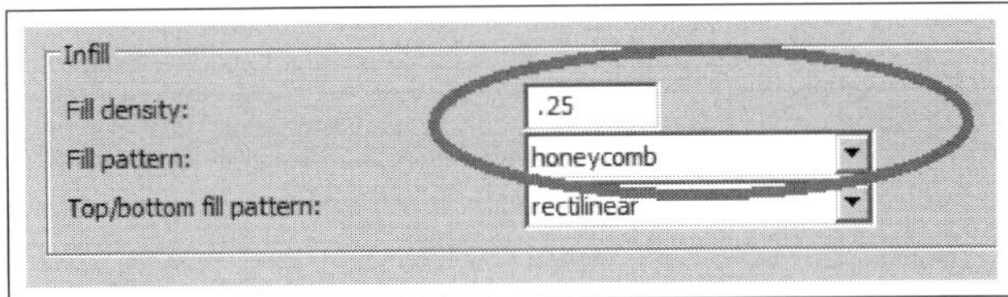

2. The default **Fill density** in Slic3r is `0.4`. For sampling the infill textures, we'll change this to `0.25`. This will create an infill that's less dense and easier for us to visually examine.

3. Now we'll choose the **Fill Pattern**. There are seven infill patterns as follows:

    - **rectilinear**
    - **line**
    - **concentric**
    - **honeycomb**
    - **hilbertcurve (slow)**
    - **archimedianchords (slow)**
    - **octagramspiral (slow)**

4. Choose each of these patterns and slice the model. Save each one, taking care to label them with the appropriate pattern name.

5. Now, we'll test the infill density by increasing and decreasing it by 50 percent from our starting infill of `0.25`. Choose an infill pattern and change the **Fill density** to `0.375` and then slice the model. Repeat using `0.125` for the infill.

How it works...

In the following image, we can see a composite of the first 10 print layers and the resulting pattern:

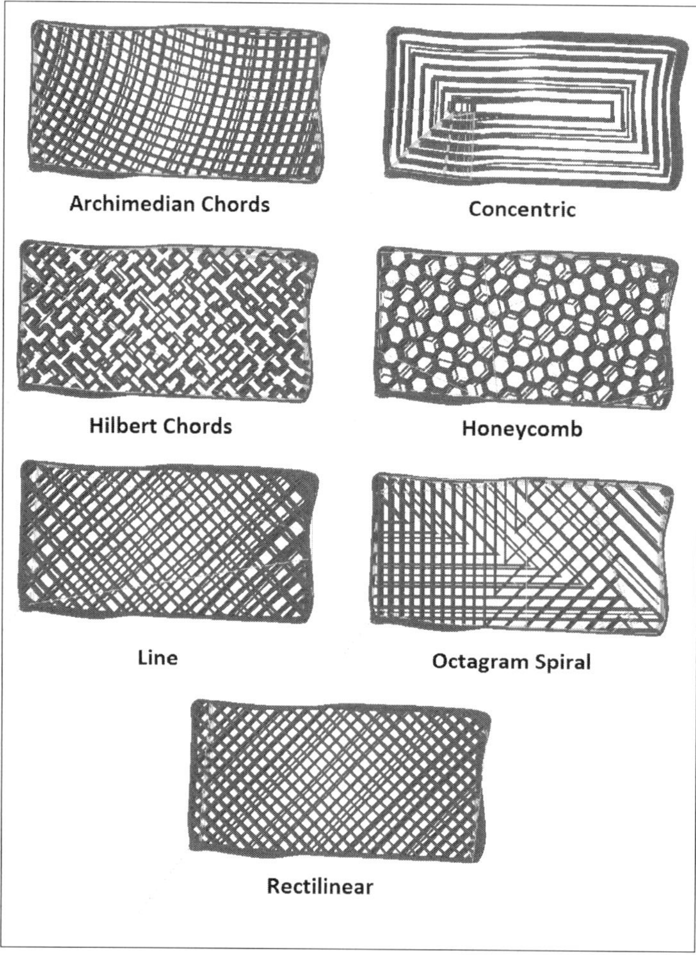

Each of these patterns is going to produce different results. Some of the differences may be as follows:

- **The strength of the pattern**: The honeycomb pattern is good for strength. It follows the hexagonal pattern vertically through the print. This makes it generally good for mechanical parts.

- **The print time of the pattern**: The line pattern is the fastest at printing infill. It's also a good infill for organic shaped forms.

- ❏ **The amount of filament to be printed**: The octagram spiral uses the least amount of infill than the others.

- ❏ **The amount of vibration of the print head**: When printing a pattern like the honeycomb, a lot of vibration can be caused by the rapid short moves of the print head. A pattern such as concentric produces less vibration in the print head.

In the following image, we can see the differences made in adjusting the infill density:

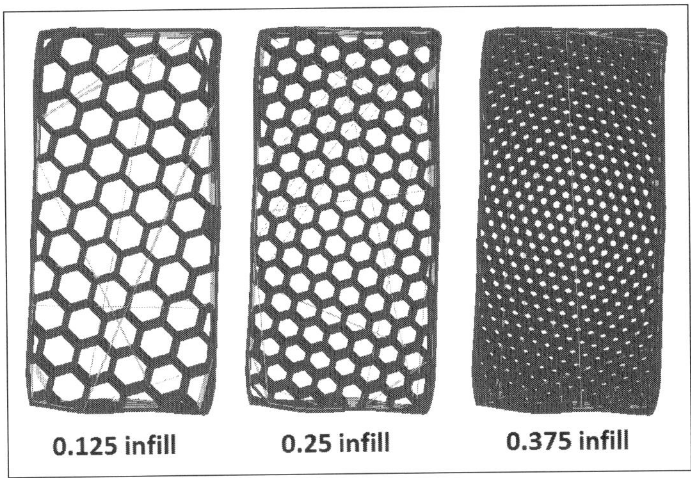

Most models will be strong enough with an infill of 10 to 25 percent. For gears and pulleys, a higher density of up to 50 percent or more may be best for durability. In principle, try to print with as little as possible. This will speed up the printing process and decrease the amount of filament you expend.

Experimenting with the infill as you progress with your future printing would be a good way to see how the infill patterns and infill solidity affect your model.

Optimizing infill with Skeinforge

Skeinforge has the capability of creating four infill patterns. In this recipe, we'll learn how to select the infill pattern and make the most common adjustments for better optimization.

Getting ready

We'll use the same toy block that we used in the previous recipe.

How to do it...

We will proceed as follows:

1. In Skeinforge, select **Craft** and then select **Fill**. This is where all of our changes will be made. We can see the section illustrated in the following screenshot:

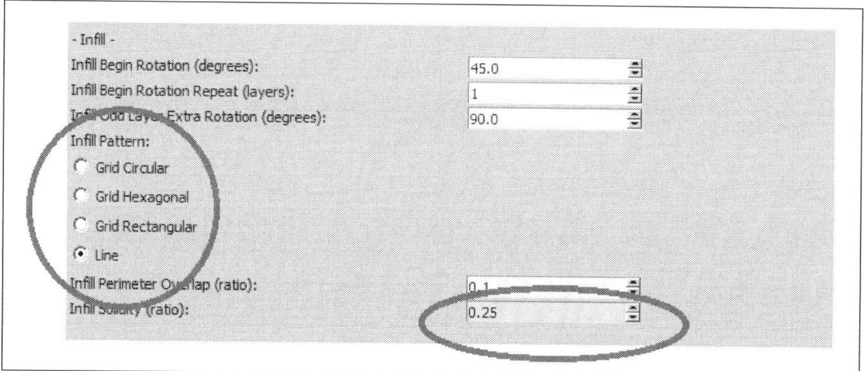

2. First, we'll set the infill density. For **Infill Solidity (ratio)**, make sure the default value is 0.25.

3. Next, locate the four infill patterns:

   - **Line**
   - **Grid Circular**
   - **Grid Hexagonal**
   - **Grid Rectangular**

4. Choose each of these patterns and slice the model. Save each one, taking care to label them with the appropriate pattern name.

5. Now, we'll test the infill density by increasing and decreasing it by 50 percent of our starting infill of 0.25. Choose an infill pattern and change the **Infill Solidity (ratio)** to 1.25 and then slice the model. Repeat using 0.375 for the infill.

How it works...

In the following image, we can see that the infill patterns that Skeinforge produces are very similar to Slic3r's infill patterns:

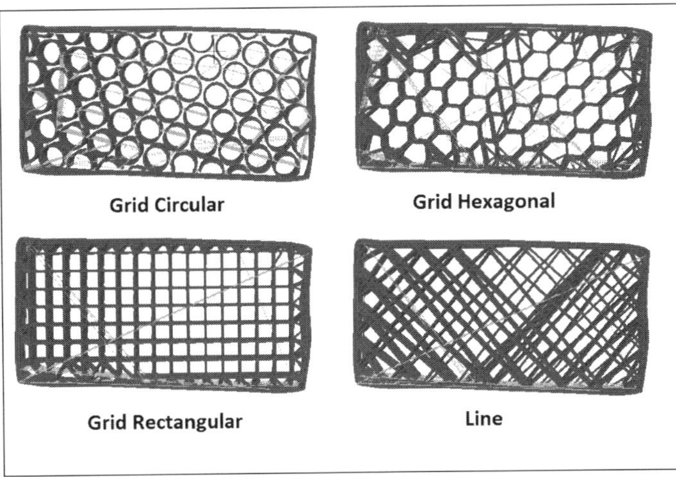

Similar attributes can be made with these patterns as were made with the Slic3r patterns. There are three main considerations to keep in mind with these patterns. They are as follows:

- When selecting the line pattern, it will be quicker to generate, and it doesn't add any extra movements to the print head. This will keep the vibration down.

- When selecting a grid pattern, there will be extra diagonal lines and more filament extrusion. Keeping the infill around 0.2 will give better results.

- The grid patterns are stronger except for the circular pattern. This pattern is weak but is good for minimizing warping of the print.

Printing without fill with Skeinforge

Both Skeinforge and Slic3r have a variety of choices that control infill and thickness. Both slicers have similar controls to make these adjustments, their major difference being nomenclature. Skeinforge will refer to the skin of a model as the shell, and Slic3r will refer to the vertical shells as the perimeter. Both slicers have options for specifying the number of base and top layers to be printed.

In this recipe, we'll see what happens when we print without infill and shells using Skeinforge. The same test could easily be made with Slic3r by reducing the perimeter and base layers to 0. Keep in mind that with both slicers, there is always one shell when printing a model.

Getting ready...

For this recipe, you'll need the models that you scanned with 123D Catch in *Chapter 1*, *Getting Started with 3D Printing*. In this case, I'm using the toy block, statue, and pyramid.

How to do it...

We will proceed as follows:

1. In Skeinforge, open the **Fill** plugin. We'll be making changes in the circled fields illustrated in the following screenshot:

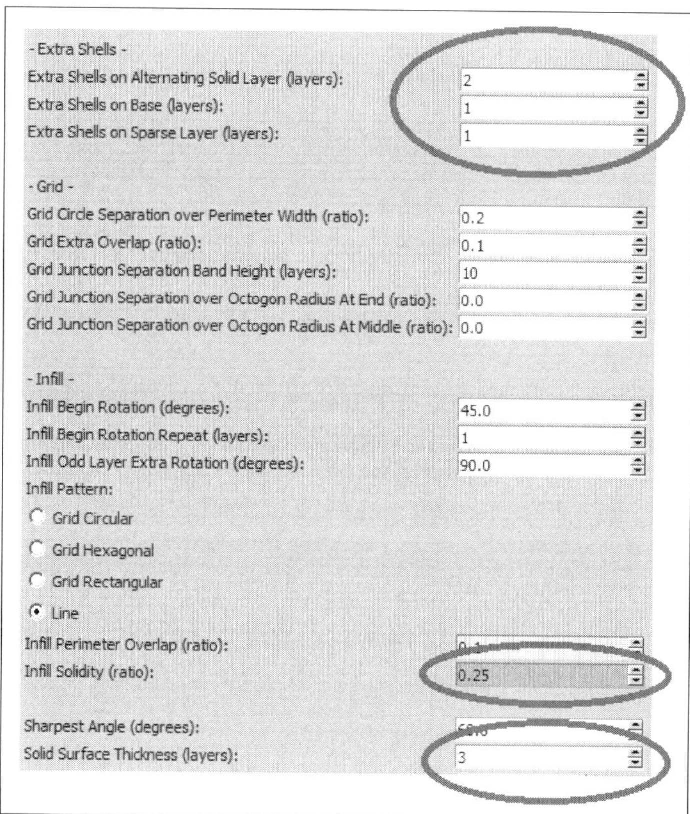

2. Enter 0 in **Extra Shells on Alternating Solid Layer (layers)**.
3. Enter 0 in **Extra Shells on Base (layers)**.
4. Enter 0 in **Extra Shells on Sparse Layer (layers)**.
5. Enter 0 in **Infill Solidity (ratio)**.

6. Enter 0 in **Solid Surface Thickness (layers)**.

7. Slice and print all three models with these settings.

How it works...

By changing the values of **Extra Shells** to 0, we've instructed Skeinforge to create a 1 shell thickness.

> The shell width is determined by the Edge Width over Height (ratio) in Skeinforge's Carve plugin. More information about this can be found in *Chapter 3, Scanning and Printing with a Higher Resolution*.

This is determined by the width size that our hot-end extrudes a line. By changing the **Infill Solidity (ratio)** to 0, we've instructed the slicer to keep the interior of our model empty. By changing the **Solid Surface Thickness (layers)** to 0, we've instructed the slicer to remove all solid layers (which is any area that would be printed across the entire model for that layer, such as the first flat layer that makes up the base of the model).

Let's look at the printing results of the three models in the following image:

We can see that distortion occurred in the toy block and statue; there are gaps in the horizontal surfaces. Without activating the solid layers, all of the flat surfaces could not print. The pyramid model printed well because its structure gradually builds on top of each layer in increments. This kept the filament fairly tight without sagging.

Tweaking shells and surface layers with Skeinforge

In this recipe, we'll run a series of tests to see what happens when we make changes in both the number of shells and the surface layers.

Getting ready

You'll need the toy block. It's a good model to create these tests because it has multiple solid layers.

How to do it....

We will proceed as follows:

1. In Skeinforge, open the **Fill** plugin. Enter 1 in **Extra Shells on Sparse Layer (layers)**.
2. Enter 1 in **Solid Surface Layer (layers)**.
3. Keep the value of **Infill Solidity (ratio)** as 0.
4. Slice the model and print.
5. Enter 1 in **Extra Shells on Sparse Layer (layers)**.
6. Enter 2 in **Solid Surface Layer (layers)**.
7. Slice the model and print.

How it works...

When we visually compare the results in the following image, we can see that by adding two surface layers with only one extra shell, it made a good print.

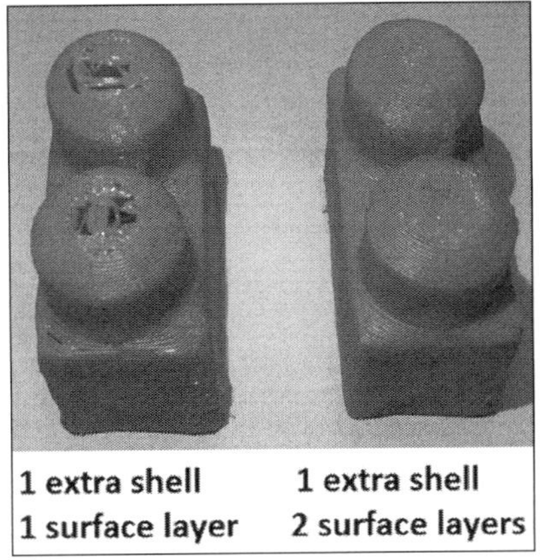

For this model, an equal number of shells and solid layers make a good economic model. Remember, we always start with one shell, so by adding one extra shell, we have a total of two.

Let's look deeper into the relationship between shells and layers. In the following image, we can see what happens when we print with extra shells:

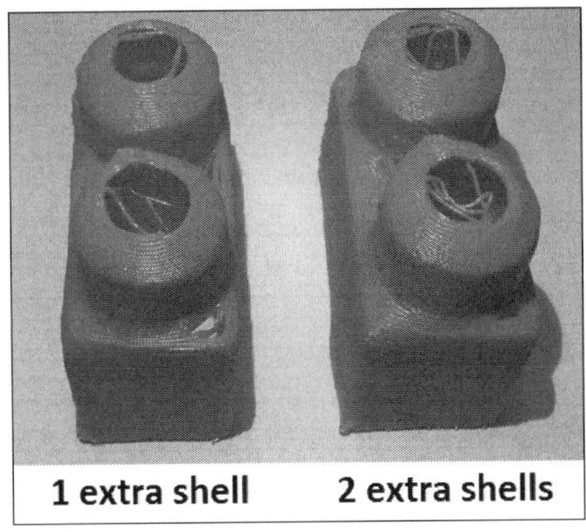

When we add shells, we are essentially adding extra thickness to the model's wall. In this model's case, the two additional shells did very little to change the overall appearance of the block.

What happens when we only adjust the surface layers? In the following image, we can see an improvement in the horizontal fill of the model. When more solid layers are added, the overall appearance of the block is better.

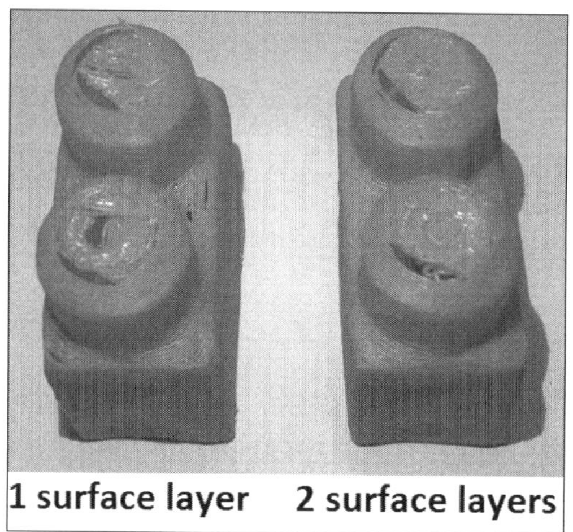

There are other factors to be considered as well, such as the width of the extrusion bead. A larger nozzle size would create thicker walls, and this would make a stronger print.

Layer height can also have an impact on the quality of the print. Printing at a lower height would create more layers to print. This will create a more gradual buildup and possibly enclose the gaps better.

Reviewing the print results

Let's take a look at the three different models after printing them with the most efficient settings for the number of shells and surface layers. We'll be able to see what settings work best with each type of model.

We can see the results of printing the statue in the following image. It required three layers and two shells for a successful print. This is the default setting for Skeinforge and proves to be a good starting point for any model.

Next, let's look at the pyramid shape in the following image. It required the least amount of layers and shells for a successful print. It required only one shell.

During the modeling process, any form that can be designed with a gradual build to a point or multiple points will print well. This is a good technique for building paper-thin and hollow models.

There's also another method of printing a hollow form. Slic3r has an option called **Spiral vase**. By activating it in **Layers and perimeters** under **Vertical shells**, this setting will raise the height continuously, thereby avoiding a layer-change point that would cause a visible seam. Just be sure to keep the infill set at 0.

Last, we'll look at the toy block. We can see that the block printed successfully with a reduced amount of both layers and shells; it took only two surface layers and shells to print without infill.

When we print without infill, the most problematic areas will be the horizontal surfaces. Without the support of adequate infill, there will be gaps in the horizontal layers that will have to be bridged. If the gaps are too large, the filament will sag. Bridging is the name of the technique that requires the printer to span a gap from two points. How the printer responds when bridging situations occur is determined by how adjustments are configured with the slicer.

See *Chapter 5, Manipulating Meshes and Bridges*, for more information on how bridging techniques work.

3

Scanning and Printing with a Higher Resolution

In this chapter, we will cover the following recipes:

- Setting up DAVID Laserscanner
- Calibrating DAVID Laserscanner
- Scanning with DAVID Laserscanner
- Viewing the model in MeshLab
- Cleaning the scans with MeshLab
- Aligning the scans with MeshLab
- Merging and remeshing the aligned scans in MeshLab
- Tuning up the printer
- Using Skeinforge with a 0.5 mm nozzle
- Using Skeinforge with a 0.35 mm nozzle
- Using Skeinforge with a 0.25 mm nozzle
- Using Slic3r to print different resolutions

Introduction

In this chapter, we'll look at how we can increase a model's resolution using a laser 3D scanning process.

We'll do this with a 3D scanning system called DAVID Laserscanner. DAVID is a program that utilizes an ordinary line laser and a web camera to scan an object and then takes this information and interpolates a 3D surface. It's a different process compared to what we used with 123D Catch. Instead of photographing an object from all sides, we'll rotate the object by 360 degrees and capture all the sides with a webcam video, as we move a laser line across its surface. Behind the object, a calibration screen that contains a grid of points is placed. The size of the calibration panel will depend on the size of object to be scanned—the larger the object, the larger the calibration panel. We'll find that this limitation can be overlooked when comparing the DAVID scanning results of smaller objects with 123D Catch. 123D Catch works well when scanning large to monumental sized objects, but it doesn't work well for scanning very small objects (as we found when scanning the coin in *Chapter 1, Getting Started with 3D Printing*). This is the advantage of using laser scanning. We'll explore this system by setting up an inexpensive scanning system and using the free version of DAVID Laserscanner.

We'll also learn how to make a printable model using our scans. We'll do this using an open source program called MeshLab. This program will be an invaluable tool for cleaning up and stitching our scans together.

We'll end the chapter by printing in low and high resolutions and compare the results and the differences in quality of the slicing made by Skeinforge and Slic3r.

Setting up DAVID Laserscanner

DAVID Laserscanner is a popular commercial software package. There's a free edition available that has limited save functions. We'll be using this one. Combined with some additional hardware, DAVID can 3D scan a variety of objects. The size and quality of these scans will be heavily determined by your choice in hardware. For this recipe, we'll use inexpensive components and set up a simple area for scanning.

Getting ready

You will need to download DAVID Laserscanner from `http://www.david-3d.com/?section=Downloads`.

This book uses DAVID_Setup_3.5.1. A newer version, DAVID_Setup_3.10, has been released and can be used as well. This version supports only XP, Vista, Windows 7, and Windows 8.

You will need the following hardware items for this recipe:

- A webcam (preferably an HD webcam) that supports WDM Video Capture Driver for Windows and a small tripod or other device to hold the camera. Some laptops have built-in webcams. These may also work.

- You'll also need an inexpensive 5 mW red-line laser (preferably, one that can be focused) and its power supply, as shown in the following image. This can be found on sites such as eBay.

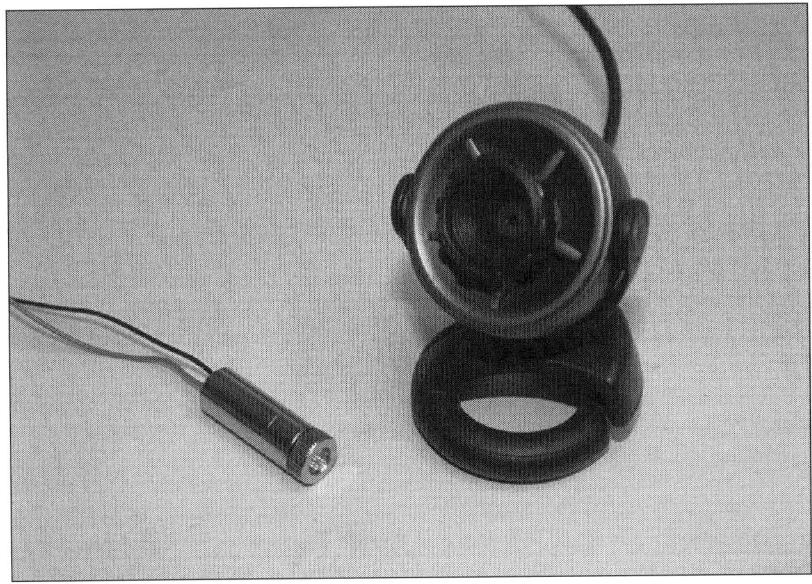

- A wall corner that has a 90-degree angle and a table surface that will fit snug into it.

- An inkjet printer and a few sheets of white bond paper.

- A metric ruler and an adhesive tape.

- Last, you will need some objects to scan. The examples used here are the coin and the toy block that were scanned with 123D Catch in *Chapter 1, Getting Started with 3D Printing*. You will also need a small box or any other item that can be used as a platform.

How to do it...

We will proceed as follows:

1. Launch the DAVID Laserscanner installer and follow the installation instructions. Once it is installed, open the `DAVID-LASERSCANNER3` folder in your `Program Files` directory. Locate the `Calibpoints_V3_A4` file in the `printout` folder and print the calibration points at full size and several scaled down by 25 percent. With smaller calibration panels, smaller objects can be scanned more efficiently.

2. Measure the small scale located on the side of the calibration points and take note of the length of the object in millimeters. Fold the sheet in half, precisely along the line running through the center.

3. Place a table or any other flat surface in a wall corner. Elevate the toy block on a box or on another item, as close as possible to the wall corner, but still far away enough so that it can be rotated by 360 degrees.

4. Carefully mount the calibration points on the wall behind the toy block, keeping the block centered in the calibration area. Try to keep the paper folded tight against the wall at exactly 90 degrees; otherwise, the calibration will not be successful.

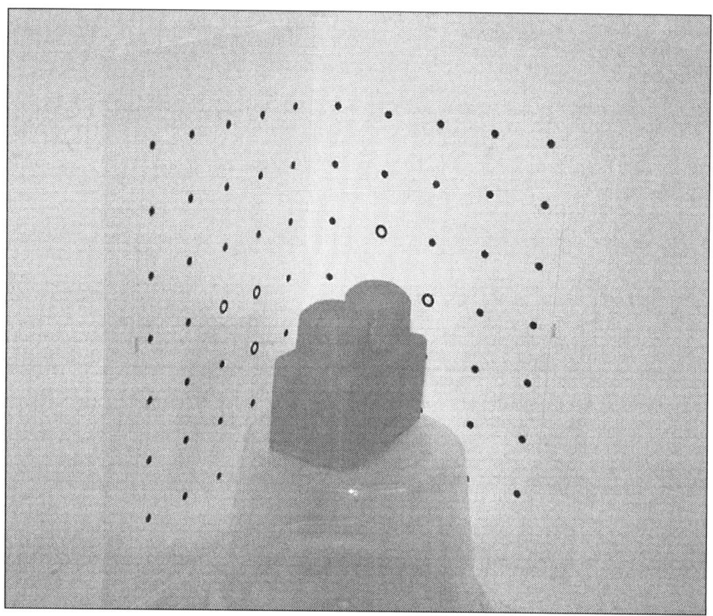

5. Mount the webcam on a small tripod or on another supporting device. A clear level view of the calibration points is necessary.

How it works...

The object that you scan should determine the size of the calibration corner. It's best to keep the object's width about one-third of the length across the calibration corner. The object's height should not extend past the top row of points. This will allow the camera to see enough of the laser line on each side of the object. With this setup, it's possible to scan very large or small objects if the calibration panels are the appropriate size. Keeping the points scaled correctly and the panels at a 90-degree angle is the key for a successful calibration.

See also

▶   You can find more information about setting up your scanning system at
    `http://wiki.david-3d.com/user_manual/getting_started`

Calibrating DAVID Laserscanner

In this recipe, we will set up our webcam to work with DAVID Laserscanner and learn how to calibrate it.

Getting ready

Connect your web camera to your computer and make sure that the camera drivers are installed.

How to do it...

We will proceed as follows:

1. Open DAVID Laserscanner. From the menu at the left-hand side of the window, choose **Hardware Setup**.

2. At the top of the window, under **Setup Type**, click on the rollout-box. Choose **Hand-Held Laser Setup**.

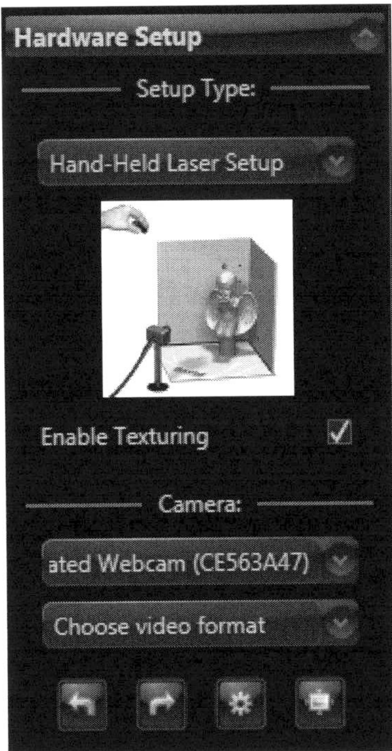

3. Under **Camera**, click on the rollout-box and choose your webcam. If you don't see it listed, try reconnecting it.

4. Click on the rollout-box option, **Choose video format**. There should be a listing of screen resolutions and frames per second (fps). Choose 640 x 480, 30 fps, or if you have a HD webcam, choose 800 x 600, 30 fps. If you do not see anything listed, select the **Camera Format** icon at the bottom-right side of the window. From the **Properties** window, you can make a selection.

5. From the side menu, choose **Camera Calibration**. At the top of the window, select **V3 pattern**, and enter the measurement you took of the scale on your calibration panel. In this case, its `120.0` mm, as shown in the following screenshot:

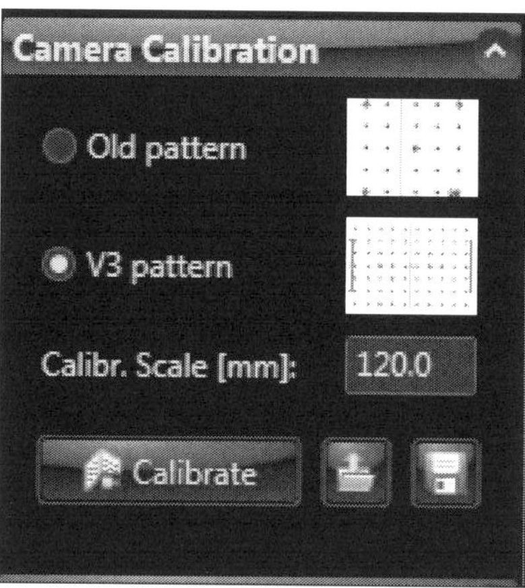

6. At the top of your workspace, there is another menu section. Under **Visibility**, make sure that the **Calibration panel visibility** and **Camera visibility** icons are selected. The icon's field will turn red.

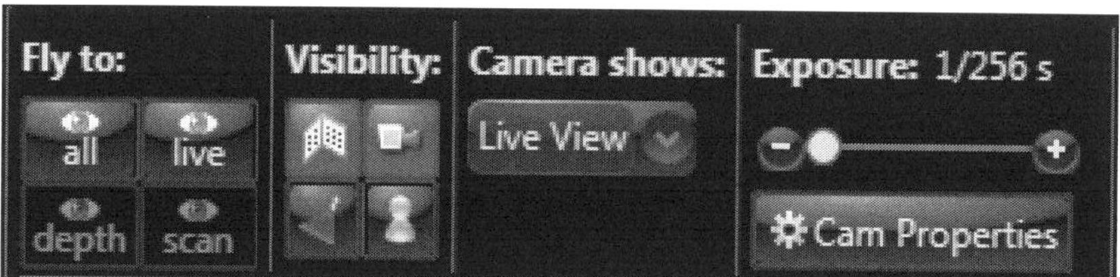

7. Under the **Camera shows** option, select **Live View** from the rollout-box.

8. Under the **Exposure** option, adjust the brightness so that you can see the calibration corner clearly. Now, take time to adjust the camera setup so that the calibration corner fills the screen and is centered.

9. Now, select **Cam Properties** under **Exposure**.

10. Depending on your particular webcam, you'll have a set of properties to choose in order to make your webcam view better. First, if your webcam can be focused, make sure that the camera is set to manual and focused on the calibration corner. Secondly, make sure that the **Gain** option is set as low as possible. Adjust the **Contrast** until the calibration corner has no mid tones and is sharp.

11. Now, select **Calibrate** from the side menu. If everything goes well, you should get a pop-up message confirming a successful calibration. Don't move anything!

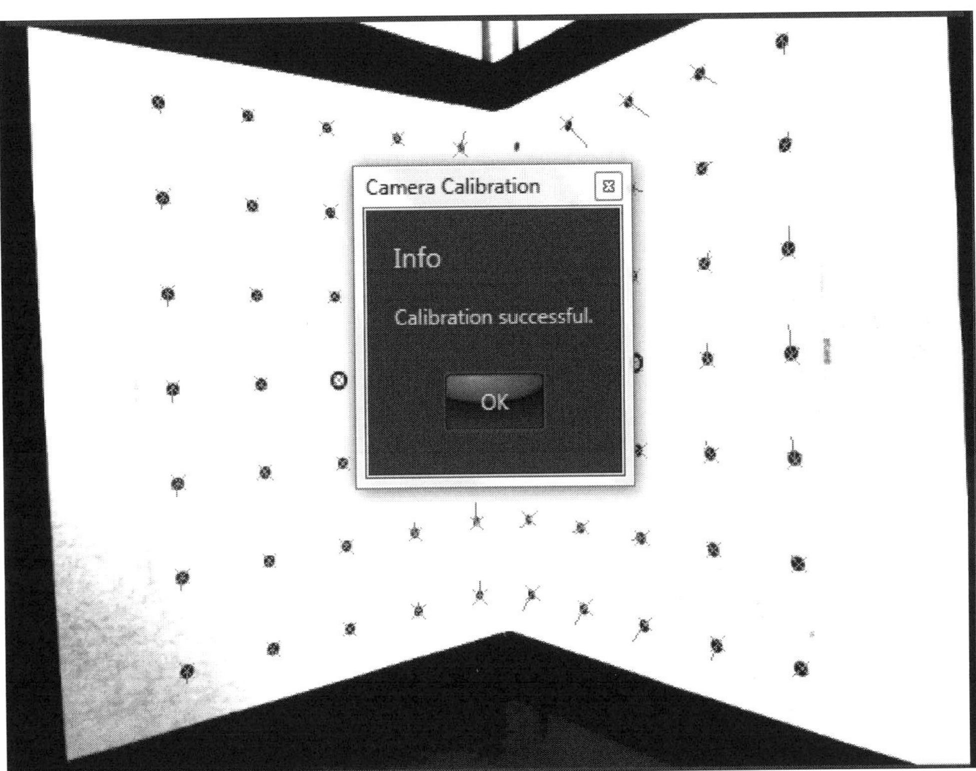

How it works...

It's very likely that you'll get a failed calibration the first time. Don't let this frustrate you if it takes several or more attempts. Sometimes, just tweaking the webcam's position slightly will be enough for a successful calibration. Also, adjusting the exposure, focus, and lighting conditions will help.

DAVID Laserscanner works by triangulating the laser line and projecting the rays back to the camera. For this to work properly, the camera's view must first be calibrated so that the laser's line can be accurately positioned and oriented in space. Pointing the camera's lens as close as possible along the bisecting plane of the 90-degree calibration corner will assure success.

See also

▶ More information about calibration can be found at `http://wiki.david-3d.com/user_manual/camera_calibration`

Scanning with DAVID Laserscanner

In this recipe, we'll learn how to scan an object from multiple views by carefully moving the object around a central point. Using the free edition of DAVID Laserscanner, we'll save the scans as low-resolution `.obj` files.

Getting ready

The camera should be set up and successfully calibrated. Before we make our first scan, we need to make a minor adjustment in our camera exposure. Position the toy block on its base, as close as possible to the calibration corner. Dim the lights and turn the red-line laser on. Focus the line on the block and adjust the camera exposure until only the line is visible and sharp. Try to keep the background as dark as possible.

How to do it...

We will proceed as follows:

1. From the side menu, select **3D Laser Scanning**. Under **Scanning**, choose **Red** in the rollout-box for **Laser Color**.

2. Under **Result Filtering**, keep the default values as shown in the following screenshot:

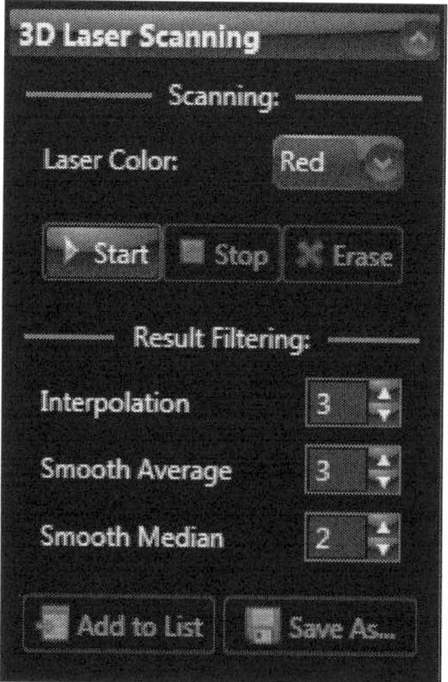

3. From the top menu under **Visibility**, select **Depth Map** from the rollout-box.

4. Hold the laser above the camera and position the laser line so that it falls across the top of the calibration corner. Try to keep the laser positioned from the same spot. From the menu, click on **Start**.

5. Very slowly, tilt the laser line down from the fixed position. The line needs to sweep down across the entire object, as shown in the following image:

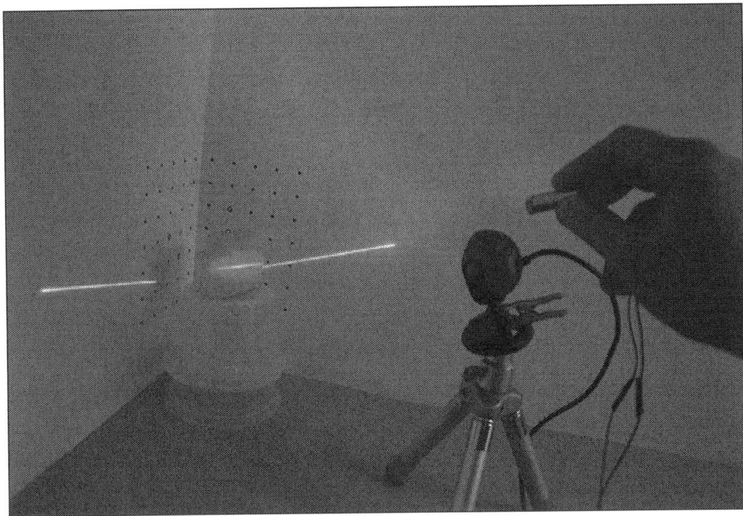

6. On the screen, you can see a live image of the color depth map of the scanned object. If the areas are not clear, a second pass could help.

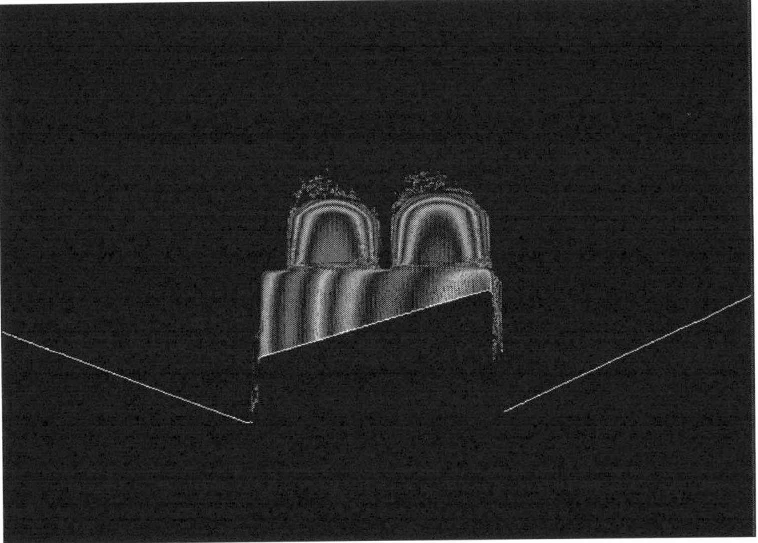

7. When the scan is complete, click on **Stop**. Save the scan as an `.obj` file. With the free edition of the program, a warning window will appear, alerting you that your scan will save at a reduced resolution.

8. Turn the block about 45 degrees clockwise. Be careful not to disturb your camera setup. Repeat the scanning process until you have a total of at least 6 scans representing a clear view around the block.

9. Repeat the process for the coin. Support the coin vertically on its edge, but only make one scan of the surface. We're only concerned about one side of the coin for this exercise.

How it works...

Before we save each scan, we can alter three variables in **Result Filtering**. The following comparisons will illustrate the changes made when adjusting **Interpolation**, **Smooth Average**, and **Median Average**.

By adjusting **Interpolation**, the program will fill holes in the scan. The following image shows the **Interpolation** values from **0** to **2**, without the smoothing filters:

By adjusting **Smooth Average**, the program will smooth the scan. The following image shows the **Smooth Average** values from **1** to **3**:

By adjusting the **Smooth Median**, the program will smooth the scan. The following image shows the **Smooth Median** values from **1** to **3**:

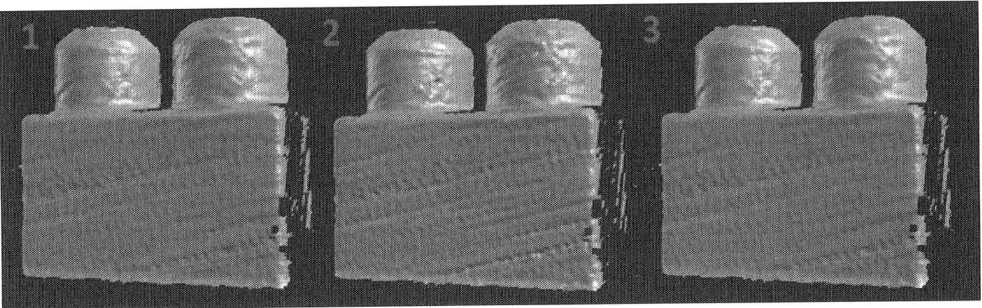

Once we make our final adjustments, we can save the scan as an `.obj` file. We'll now have a collection of scans that are essentially shells representing multiple views of our object. Using all the shells, we'll stitch them together to make a complete model. In DAVID Laserscanner, there's a feature called ShapeFusion that provides tools that will clean the scans and merge them together. The free edition will allow access to these tools, but all the work will not be saved. In the following recipes, we'll learn how to stitch the shells together with another program called MeshLab.

There's more...

Depending on the hardware you utilize, DAVID Laserscanner is a very versatile system that can be refined for extraordinary results. Changing from an inexpensive red-line laser to a more expensive green or blue laser will increase the scanning sensitivity. Controlling the laser movement precisely with a stepper motor equipped with a planetary gearbox will also give better results. For illustrative purposes, a comparison between the free version of DAVID that utilizes the inexpensive equipment, covered in the preceding recipes, and the Pro version of DAVID that utilizes a motorized green laser is shown in the following image:

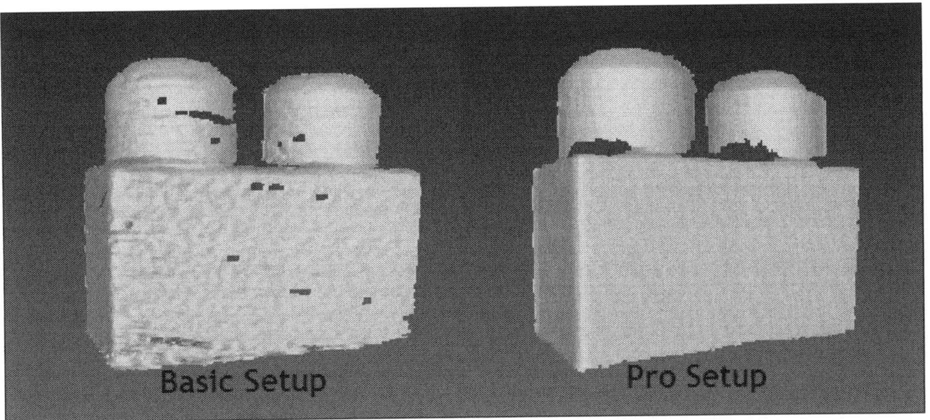

The fine detail of the coin (remember that it only measures 30 mm across!) is captured with a 1024 x 768 resolution, provided that it is only available in the commercial version. Purchasing the program and upgrading the equipment is worth the investment if your needs require finer detail scanning.

Viewing the model in MeshLab

In this recipe, we'll learn how to import/export a model into MeshLab and cover the basic navigation controls for the camera view. We'll also examine our model by changing the way we view its mesh.

Getting ready

You'll need to download MeshLab from `http://meshlab.sourceforge.net/`. This program is available for both PC and Mac platforms. Install the correct version for your computer. You'll also need your `.obj` files that you saved in DAVID Laserscanner.

How to do it...

We will proceed as follows:

1. When you open MeshLab, you will see a long bar displayed under **Menu**. It contains a row of icons that provides quick access to various program functions. Select the **Import Mesh** icon [▪] and locate the folder containing your `.obj` files.

2. In this recipe, the first scan of the toy block is opened. This can be seen in the following screenshot:

 You can also simply drag-and-drop the `.obj` file to the MeshLab's workspace.

3. To freely orbit around the model, simply left-click and drag.

4. To pan the model, hold down on the scroll wheel and drag. If you don't have a scroll wheel, hold *Ctrl* on the keyboard.

5. To zoom in on the model, rotate the scroll wheel. If you don't have a scroll wheel, hold *Alt* on the keyboard and drag.

6. Position and size your model until it fills your screen. At the icon bar, select each of the mesh views and observe the model, starting on the right-hand side with **Smooth**, **Flat**, **Flat Lines**, and **Hidden Lines**, and ending with **Wireframe**.

See also

- There are more precise options for maneuvering the object, which can be found on the MeshLab site: `http://sourceforge.net/apps/mediawiki/meshlab/index.php?title=Interacting_with_the_mesh`

- For a video tutorial, Mister P offers *MeshLab Basics: Navigation*, which can be accessed on YouTube at `http://www.youtube.com/watch?v=Sl0vJfmj5LQ`

Cleaning the scans with MeshLab

MeshLab has a variety of methods that can be used to remove the unwanted 3D artifacts that surround the model. We'll take a simple approach to clean our scans by learning how to use a cleaning filter and selection tool.

Getting ready

The first scan of your series should be positioned on your workspace, where the entire scene can be viewed.

How to do it....

We will proceed as follows:

1. Go to **Menu** and select **Filters**. Scroll down and select **Cleaning and Repairing**. In the next cascaded window, select **Remove isolated pieces (wrt face num)**.

2. In the pop-up window, keep the default values and select **Apply**. The small isolated pieces around your model should disappear, but it's very likely that there will be more of them. If this is the case, raise the minimum size value in the pop-up window. Try increasing it by 20 percent and select **Apply**.

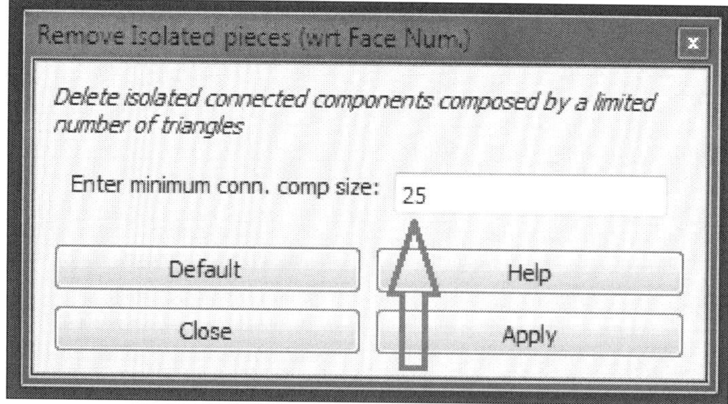

3. Continue cleaning until most or all of the isolated fragments are deleted. Take note of the last value chosen. You may find it useful as a starting point for the next scan. If you find that a section of your model has been mistakenly deleted, chose the **Reload** option icon [ ]. This will revert your model back to its original state.

4. Go to the icon bar and choose the **Selected Face Rendering** icon [ ].

5. While at the icon bar, choose the **Select Faces** icon [ ] in the rectangular region. An unusual effect of this procedure is that the entire model will initially be selected and turn red. This can be easily changed by selecting an area outside of the model's space. In fact, at any time when a selection is made, it can be deselected by choosing a selection elsewhere.

6. Left-click and drag out a rectangle on an area that contains unwanted scanned material. The selection will turn red. Go to the icon bar and click on the **Delete Selected Faces and Vertices** icon [ ]. Alternatively, press *Del* on the keyboard. To return to the orbit mode at any time, simply click on the **Select Faces** icon once again.

7. After all the unwanted pieces have been removed, export the model by going to the icon menu and choosing the **Export Mesh** icon [ ].

8. Continue cleaning all the scans in the series that you made of your model. Before you load each scan, clear the workspace by selecting **File** in **Menu** and **New Empty project** or *Ctrl + N*; otherwise, the scans will build up on top of each other.

Unfortunately, there isn't an undo function in MeshLab.

Aligning the scans with MeshLab

We have half a dozen or more shell segments that we made of our model with DAVID Laserscanner. How do we assemble all this into a completed model? One of the powerful features of MeshLab is the alignment tool, and in this recipe, we'll learn how to use it by stitching together all of our scans.

Getting ready

You'll need all the scans that you made of your model. They should be clean and free of all artifacts.

How to do it...

We will proceed as follows:

1. Open your folder containing the `.obj` files you made in DAVID Laserscanner. Select all of them and click on **Open**. All of the scan segments will merge together on your workspace, shown as follows:

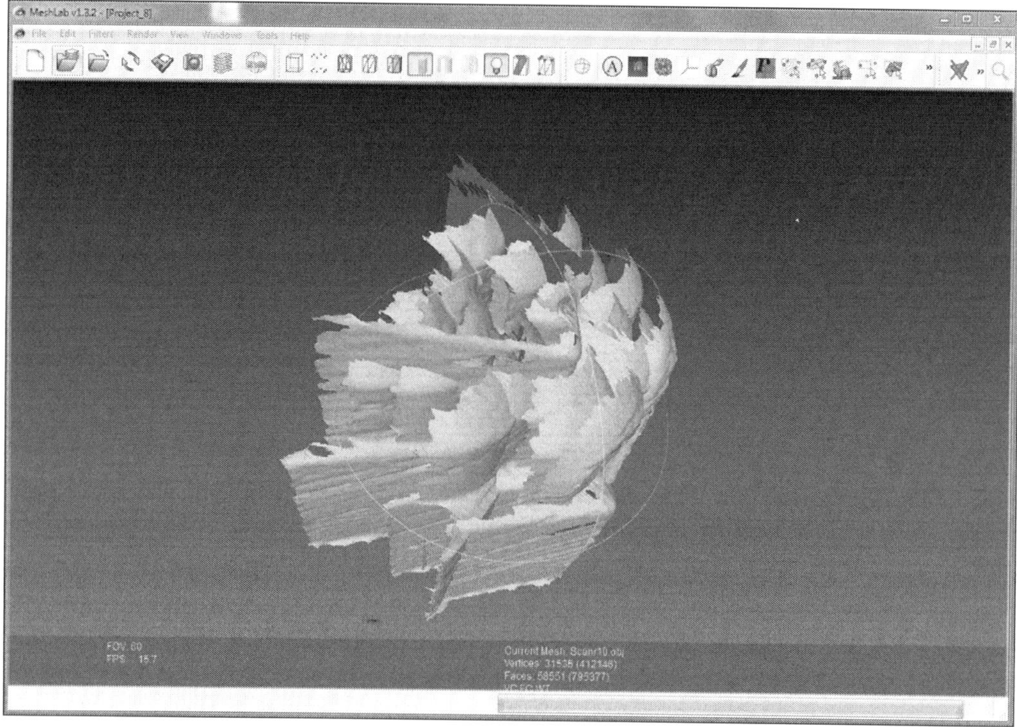

2. Go to the icon bar and select the **Show Layer Dialog** icon [▩]. This will open a box to the right of the workspace, displaying a list of the scan layers.

3. Go back to the icon bar and select the **Align** icon [ⓐ]. Two things will occur. First, a new window will pop open. This window contains a list of the open scan files (similar to the layer dialog box) with an addition of alignment options at the bottom. Secondly, the model segments have unique colors. This will help distinguish the segments from each other.

4. In the **Align Tool** window, click on each of the small green eyes that precede the scan file, leaving the first two scans open. Now, you should only see two scan segments open in your workspace.

5. To start the alignment process, we must first set a reference for the scans. To do this, select the first file in the list of scans. A gray bar will appear across the filename. Next, select **Glue Here Mesh**. An asterisk will appear before the filename.

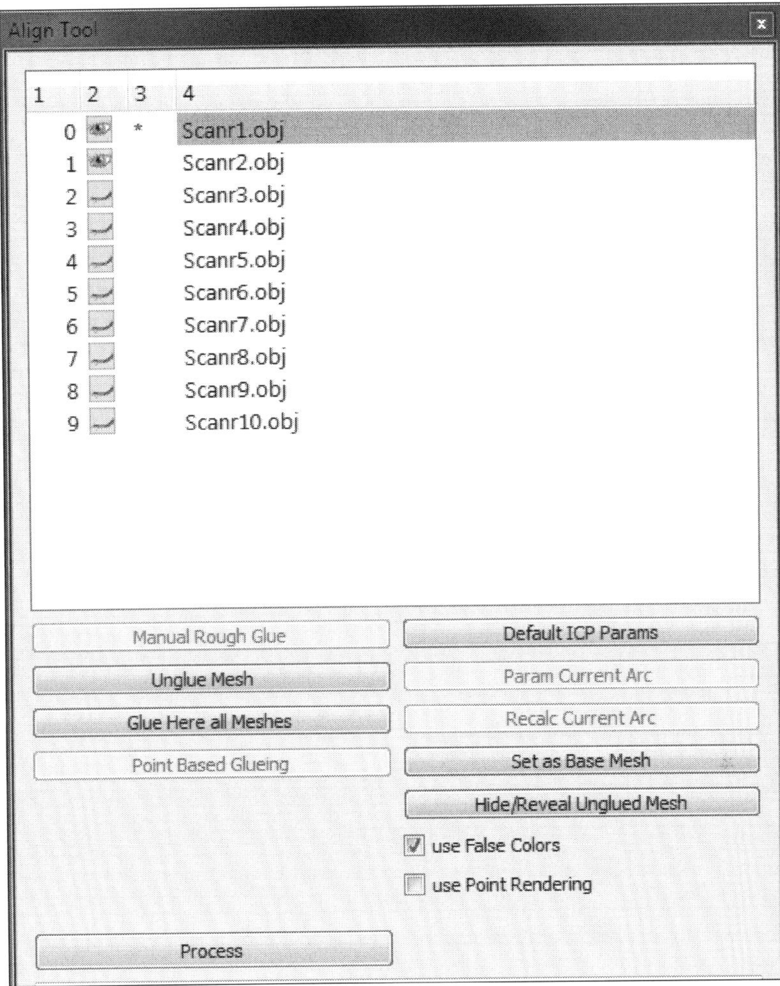

6. Next, select the second file. At the bottom of the window, two new alignment options have become available. Select **Point Based Glueing**. A new pop-up window appears.

7. Now, we see the two selected scans side by side. Use the navigation controls to orient the scans in the same viewing position. This is important so that we can select the corresponding reference points on both scans.

8. Starting with one scan, select a point by double-clicking on it. A tiny red box with a numeral appears. Find the corresponding point on the other scan and double-click on it. A tiny blue box with the same numeral appears. Continue to select points until you have a total of four matching pairs of reference points. Click on **OK**, and the alignment window closes.

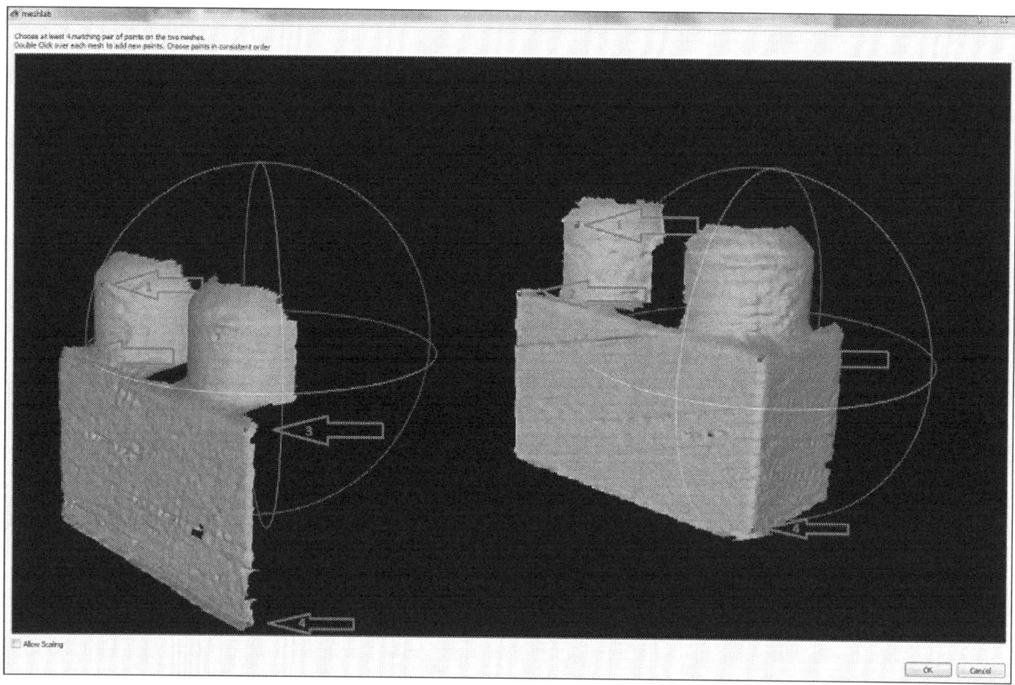

 To delete a point selection, press *Ctrl* on the keyboard and double-click somewhere near the point.

9. In the workspace, the two scans should now be stitched together, forming a more complete model. If the model isn't aligned correctly, then select the **Unglue Mesh** option and start again by choosing an extra pair of points. The more points accurately chosen, the more successful the alignment process.

10. Next, select the third file and then select **Point Based Glueing**. A new pop-up window appears, with the third scan on the left-hand side. On the right-hand side, the two previous scans are shown stitched together. Select four corresponding pairs of reference points and choose **OK**. Make sure that you select the eye icon next to the third scan file in the **Align Tool** window. You should now see all the three scans aligned together.

11. Continue the process of aligning all the scans. When you are finished, choose **Process** at the bottom of the **Align Tool** window. MeshLab now computes a final mesh-mesh alignment.

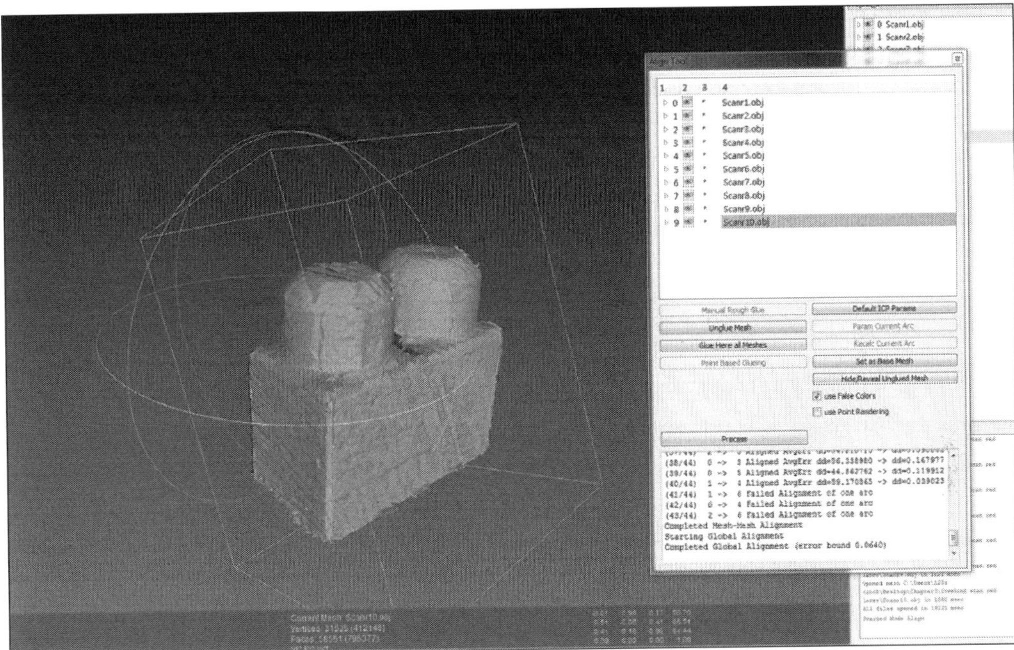

12. It's a good idea to save your project with all the processing information, in case you have a need to modify it. To do this, go to the **Menu** and select **File** and **Save Project**. This will create a MeshLab `.mlp` file.

How it works...

The alignment tool extrapolates the best fit for your scans when you process them, but the scans are still separate layers, even though the program refers to gluing them during the alignment process. If you try to export your aligned model, only the last highlighted scan will save. This is because the alignment has not been fused. Be sure to save the alignment as a project file. In the next recipe, we'll learn how to merge all the scans into one solid shell.

See also

- For a video tutorial, Mister P offers *3D Scanning: Alignment*, which can be seen on YouTube at `http://www.youtube.com/watch?v=4g9Hap4rX0k`

Merging and remeshing the aligned scans in MeshLab

In this recipe, we'll learn how to use filters in MeshLab to prepare our scan for printing. First, we'll learn how to take the layers we merged with the align tool and flatten them into one unifying shell. Then, we'll use another filter to reconstruct the surface and fill holes. The last filter we'll use will decimate the mesh and simplify it for printing.

Getting ready

You'll need your aligned mesh open in MeshLab. If you are opening the mesh from an `.mlp` MeshLab project file, make sure that you have the **Align Tool** window open, and select **Glue Here all Meshes** from the alignment options. One of the quirks of MeshLab is that the alignment meshes are saved unglued.

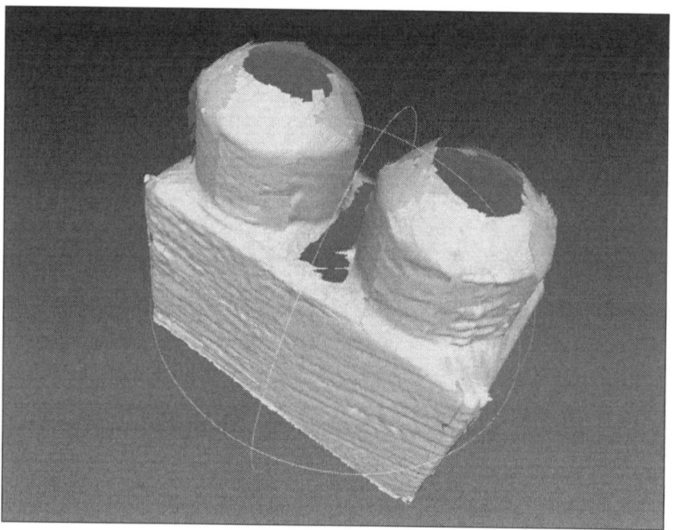

How to do it...

We will proceed as follows:

1. Go to **Menu** and select **Filters**. Scroll down and select **Mesh Layer**. Scroll down the next cascaded window and select **Flatten Visible Layers**.

2. A pop-up window appears. Keep the options at default values and select **Apply**. When the filter is complete, click on the **Close** button. It's a good idea to export the model as an `.obj` file now.

3. Next, go to **Filters** and select the **Remeshing, Simplification**, and **Reconstruction** options. Scroll down the next cascaded window and select **Surface Reconstruction: Poisson**.

4. A pop-up window appears. Start with the default values; only change **Solver Divide** from 6 to 5. Select **Apply**. When the filter is complete, click on the **Close** button.

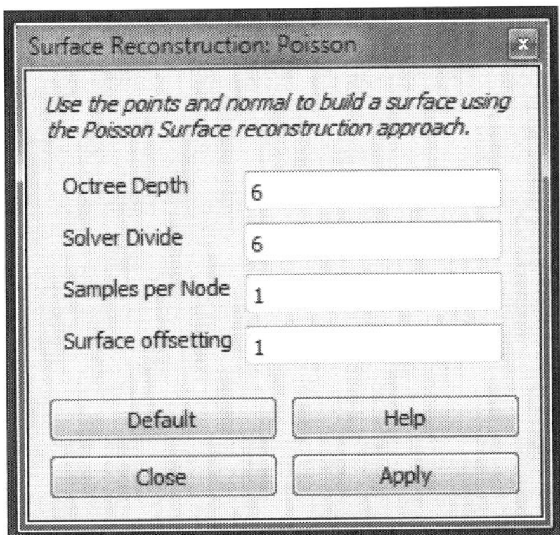

5. Go back to **Filters** and select the **Remeshing, Simplification**, and **Reconstruction** options. Scroll down the next cascaded window and select **Quadric Edge Collaspe Decimation**. Keep the default values and select **Apply**. When the filter is complete, click on the **Close** button.

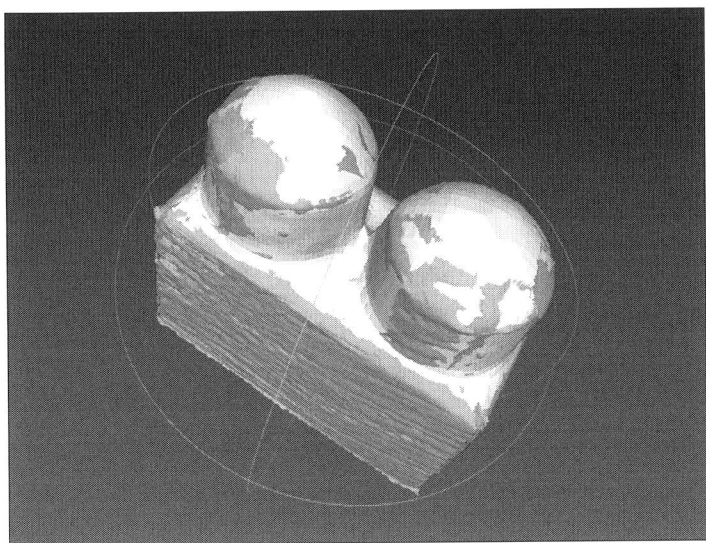

6. Export **Mesh** and save the file.

How it works...

Surface reconstruction with the Poisson filter can be prone to crashing. This is why it's best to start with a lower resolution reconstruction and then try to work up to a higher one. The Octree Depth variable essentially controls the resolution. The default value, 6, can be raised up to 9 or 10. The higher the number, the higher is the resolution. The Solver Divide variable needs to be set either as the same number or one or two less.

The decimation filter simplifies the mesh by decreasing the polygon count. In the case of the example model, the mesh went from 16,816 faces to 8408 faces. We'll learn more about meshes and decimation in *Chapter 5, Manipulating Meshes and Bridges*.

See also

> ▸ For a video tutorial, Mister P offers *3D Scanning: merging with Poisson filter*, which can be seen on YouTube at `http://www.youtube.com/watch?v=dTkiPsNZg_o`

Let's print!

One of the challenges of 3D printing is to make a print with a smooth surface that retains all of its fine details. We're accustomed to our everyday plastic objects having a surface with a glass-like sheen, but these objects have been manufactured with an entirely different process. Recreating the finishes used by traditional plastic molding technologies is impossible with a RepRap machine. However, there are methods to create a finish with higher detail using RepRap-based printers. We'll explore how we can accomplish this by increasing our printer's resolution.

Hot-end nozzle sizes

There are commercial hot ends available that have nozzle sizes varying from 0.2 mm to 0.75 mm. Ideally, each of these nozzle sizes will print layers that are slightly below its bore size. The reasoning behind this is that a print is made of successive layers, which are built upon each other. For each layer to bond, the layer heights must be squeezed against each other. We can see this illustrated clearly in the following figure:

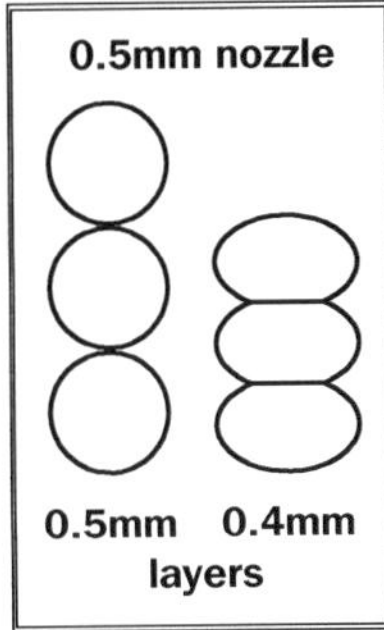

Choosing a print layer that's 20 percent less than its bore is a good starting point. 20 percent of a 0.5 mm nozzle is 0.4 mm, which makes the maximum layer height for the extruded filament bead. However, when printing higher resolutions, all the typical nozzles can work. A 0.5 mm, 0.35 mm, or 0.25 mm nozzle can print 0.1 mm layers.

Then, why have different nozzle sizes? Smaller nozzles will give better results in higher resolutions because of the perimeter width-to-thickness ratio. A 0.5 mm nozzle extruding a 0.5 mm bead will have to flatten the bead to 0.1 mm. This will produce a bead dimension of at least 0.5 mm (nozzle bore diameter) x 0.1 mm (layer depth). A 0.25 mm nozzle will produce, under the same circumstances, at least a 0.25 mm x 0.1 mm bead dimension. In the following figure, we can clearly see the relative differences between the three common nozzle sizes and their respective bead extrusion and why a smaller nozzle will achieve better results for fine detail:

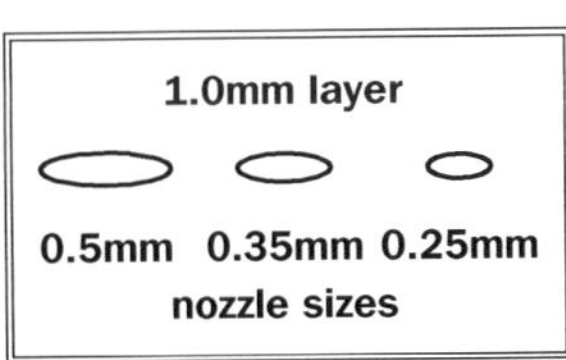

Overall, a 0.5 mm nozzle is a versatile size to own. It can print from at least 0.1 mm to 0.4 mm with good adhering layer thicknesses.

Tuning up the printer

To obtain the best results in high-resolution printing, there are four important tune-ups that we must always keep in mind. They are as follows:

- Make sure that the build platform is at level with the hot end. It's very easy for the build platform to become unleveled by loosening hardware or accidental hot end and build-platform collisions. Taking time to carefully keep the build platform at level with the hot end's nozzle is critical for a successful high-resolution print.

- Adjust the settings of the printer for the first layer height. This is the distance between the hot-end nozzle and the build platform. This distance can vary. The recommended distance set for the first layer should not be more than the diameter size of your nozzle. A 0.5 mm nozzle should be set slightly below 0.5 mm from the nozzle tip to the build platform. What is important is to have a first layer that firmly adheres to the build platform.

- Measure the actual physical diameter of your filament. Using precision calipers, an average of at least five measurements should be made. Enter this data in your slicer.

- Calibrate the extrusion rate. Adjusting the amount of filament that is extruded through the hot end is important for most of the slicer's settings to operate with precision. We do this by calculating a value for **E_steps_per_unit** and uploading this data to the firmware in the controller board. This recipe will show you how to accomplish this task using a command line in the host.

Getting ready

You'll need a metric ruler for this recipe. You'll also need your current **E_steps_per_unit** value, which is located in your firmware settings in the `Configuration.h` file. If your firmware allows, use the `M503` command to echo your printer settings. What you are looking for are two lines similar to the following:

```
echo: Steps per unit:
echo:   M92  X81.00 Y81.00 Z2480.00 E495.00
```

The value you need will be listed after `E`. In this case, it is `495.00`.

For more detailed information about using G-code commands and accessing firmware, see *Appendix A, Understanding and Editing Firmware,* and *Appendix B, Taking a Closer Look at G-code.*

How to do it...

We will proceed as follows:

1. Warm up your printer as you would when making a print. Extrude some filament until it flows freely, using the manual controls on your host.

2. With a ruler, measure 100 mm of the filament from the top of the extruder and make a mark.

3. Extrude the filament.

4. Measure the difference (if any). If the extruder pulled more than 100 mm and you can no longer see your mark, you may have to make a mark at 110 mm or more and adjust the difference.

5. Take your current **E_steps_per_unit** value and divide it by the difference you just measured. Take the sum and multiply it by 100. This is your actual **E_steps_per_unit** value.

6. On the host's command line, enter `M92 Ee`, where `e` is the new **E_steps_per_unit** value.

7. Mark and run 100 mm of the filament again.

8. If the filament measures 100 mm, great! You have finished tuning up the printer. If not, then repeat the steps until you have your extruder pulling exactly 100 mm.

How it works...

Using the command line allows you to make changes while the printer is running. This is far more convenient than making changes to the firmware using the Arduino IDE. However, changes made by the command line are not permanent. If you're using controllers such as Melzi or Sanguinololu that allow changes to be made to EEPROM, then a permanent entry can be made by adding a `M500` command in the command line. This will store the values in EEPROM.

There's more...

When we print at higher resolutions with Skeinforge, we may need to tweak another setting to allow more material to be extruded from a 0.2 mm layer to a 0.1 mm layer. One option is to use a cheat that adjusts the filament length that you configured by your **E_steps_per_unit** setting in the firmware. Under the **Dimension** plugin, adjust the value of the **Filament Packing Density (ratio)** anywhere from 0.95 to 0.9. A value that is lower than the default setting of 1.0 will extrude more filaments.

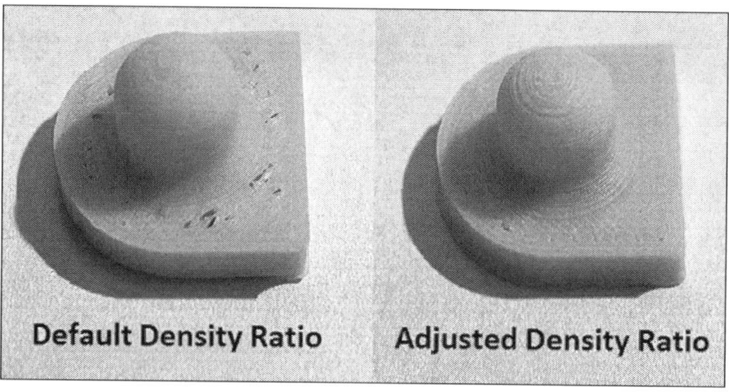

Skeinforge has many plugins that feature variables that work interchangeably by a reciprocal process. It's usually best to keep changes locked in to fewer variables so that the results of a change can be understood better. In this case, it's better to keep to a formula for calculating width over height ratios and then tweak the results by changing the **Dimension** plugin.

A similar problem can also occur with Slic3r. We may need more filaments to be extruded with the lower height layers. In Slic3r, there is a way to cheat the filament extrusion setting. Under **Filament Settings**, adjust the **Extrusion multiplier** by adding to the default value of 1.0. Adjusting the value to 1.1 may be sufficient to provide enough filaments. When the **Extrusion multiplier** value is increased, the amount of extruded filament is increased.

Using Skeinforge with a 0.5 mm nozzle

In this recipe, we will run a series of tests using the 0.5 mm nozzle to print in 0.4 mm, 0.3 mm, 0.2 mm, and 0.1 mm layers.

Registering a bore size in Skeinforge is not a simple task. It requires you to calculate a ratio for each layer of a different thickness. Following the steps in this recipe will help you understand the process and make it easy to make adjustments for any change in the nozzle size or print layer.

 If you don't have a 0.5 mm nozzle, then refer to the following recipe that covers your nozzle size.

Getting ready

The Thingiverse website is a file-sharing site of user-created digital designs. It has many small models that can be used to make quick and efficient print tests. We'll use the one that's designed for surface calibration. It's a good shape for testing resolutions and small enough to print quickly, without much filament waste. It can be downloaded at `www.thingiverse.com/thing:39050`.

How to do it...

We will proceed as follows:

1. Open the **Normal** profile in Skeinforge. Under **Carve**, adjust the **Edge Width over Height (ratio)** to `1.50` and the **Layer Height (mm)** to `0.4`.

2. Under **Inset**, adjust the **Infill Width over Thickness (ratio)** to `1.5`.

3. Click on **Save All** and exit.

4. Print the model.

5. Reopen the **Normal** profile in Skeinforge. Under **Carve**, adjust the **Edge Width over Height (ratio)** to `2.0` and the **Layer Height (mm)** to `0.3`.

6. Under **Inset**, adjust the **Infill Width over Thickness (ratio)** to `2.0`.

7. Click on **Save All** and exit.

8. Print the model.

9. Reopen the **Normal** profile in Skeinforge. Under **Carve**, adjust the **Edge Width over Height (ratio)** to `3.0` and the **Layer Height (mm)** to `0.2`.

10. Under **Inset**, adjust the **Infill Width over Thickness (ratio)** to `3.0`.

11. Click on **Save All** and exit.

12. Print the model.

13. Reopen the **Normal** profile in Skeinforge. Under **Carve**, adjust the **Edge Width over Height (ratio)** to `6.0` and the **Layer Height (mm)** to `0.1`.

14. Under **Inset**, adjust the **Infill Width over Thickness (ratio)** to `6.0`.

15. Click on **Save All** and exit.

16. Print the model.

How it works...

In Skeinforge, the nozzle's bore size data is not registered. The program adjusts to differentiate between a nozzle size using a ratio of the width by the height of the extruded material. We calculate this ratio by taking the nozzle size and adding 20 percent more width to allow more surface contact and thus, a better bond. This has been a common practice with most profile setups.

In this case, adding 0.1 mm (20 percent of 0.5 mm) to the 0.5 mm width of the nozzle bore gives us a total of 0.6 mm for our extruded width, and then, we divide this value with our layer height, 0.4 mm (0.6 mm/0.4 mm = 1.5). This is our ratio. Use the value for both the **Edge Width over Height (ratio)** and the **Infill Width over Thickness (ratio)**. Both of these ratios should be kept consistent (most of the time), as the perimeter wall of the model and its interior should print with the same consistency. Using this formula, we'll get a new ratio for each of our layer heights.

0.5 mm nozzle	Ratio
0.4 mm layer	1.5
0.3 mm layer	2.0
0.2 mm layer	3.0
0.1 mm layer	6.0

The preceding chart provides a good starting point for each layer thickness using a 0.5 mm nozzle.

Using Skeinforge with a 0.35 mm nozzle

In this recipe, we will run a series of tests using the 0.35 mm nozzle to print the 0.3 mm, 0.2 mm, and 0.1 mm layers using a 3 mm filament.

Registering a bore size in Skeinforge is not a simple task. It requires you to calculate a ratio for each layer of a different thickness. Following the steps in this recipe will help you understand the process and make it easy to make adjustments for any change in the nozzle size or print layer.

If you don't have a 0.35 mm nozzle, then refer to the recipe that covers your nozzle size.

Getting ready

The Thingiverse website is a file-sharing site of user-created digital designs. It has many small models that can be used to make quick and efficient print tests. We'll use the one that's designed for surface calibration. It's a good shape for testing resolutions and small enough to print quickly, without much filament waste. It can be downloaded at `www.thingiverse.com/thing:39050`.

How to do it...

We will proceed as follows:

1. Reopen the **Normal** profile in Skeinforge. Under **Carve**, adjust the **Edge Width over Height (ratio)** to `1.4` and the **Layer Height (mm)** to `0.3`.

2. Under **Inset**, adjust the **Infill Width over Thickness (ratio)** to `1.4`.

3. Click on **Save All** and exit.

4. Print the model.

5. Reopen the **Normal** profile in Skeinforge. Under **Carve**, adjust the **Edge Width over Height (ratio)** to `2.1` and the **Layer Height (mm)** to `0.2`.

6. Under **Inset**, adjust the **Infill Width over Thickness (ratio)** to `2.1`.

7. Click on **Save All** and exit.

8. Print the model.

9. Reopen the **Normal** profile in Skeinforge. Under **Carve**, adjust the **Edge Width over Height (ratio)** to `4.2` and the **Layer Height (mm)** to `0.1`.

10. Under **Inset**, adjust the **Infill Width over Thickness (ratio)** to `4.2`.

11. Click on **Save All** and exit.

12. Print the model.

How it works...

When we calculated a width over height ratio for the 0.5 mm nozzle, we added 0.1 mm to our nozzle size to allow swelling of the object. This is an increase of 20 percent. With a 0.35 mm nozzle, we're going to also add an additional amount using the same percentage that was used with the 0.5 mm nozzle. This will give us an extrusion width of 0.42 mm for our 0.35 mm nozzle. We'll use this value to calculate each of our ratios.

0.35 mm nozzle	Ratio
0.4 mm layer	x

0.35 mm nozzle	Ratio
0.3 mm layer	1.4
0.2 mm layer	2.1
0.1 mm layer	4.2

The preceding chart provides a good starting point for each layer thickness using a 0.35 mm nozzle.

Using Skeinforge with a 0.25 mm nozzle

Most RepRap vendors advertise the smaller nozzle sizes (such as the 0.25 mm bore) as being experimental. This is because it requires a finer tuning of the printer and slicer to achieve good results. There's also a higher occurrence in extruder jams with the smaller nozzles. We're going to run a series of tests using the 0.25 mm nozzle to print the 0.2 mm and 0.1 mm layers using a 3 mm filament.

Registering a bore size in Skeinforge is not a simple task. It requires you to calculate a ratio for each layer of a different thickness. Following the steps in this recipe will help you understand the process and make it easy to make adjustments for any change in the nozzle size or print layer.

If you don't have a 0.25 mm nozzle, then refer to the recipe that covers your nozzle size.

Getting ready

The Thingiverse website is a file-sharing site of user-created digital designs. It has many small models that can be used to make quick and efficient print tests. We'll use the one that's designed for surface calibration. It's a good shape for testing resolutions and small enough to print quickly, without much filament waste. It can be downloaded at `www.thingiverse.com/thing:39050`.

How to do it...

We will proceed as follows:

1. Reopen the **Normal** profile in Skeinforge. Under **Carve**, adjust the **Edge Width over Height (ratio)** to `1.5` and the **Layer Height (mm)** to `0.2`.

2. Under **Inset**, adjust the **Infill Width over Thickness (ratio)** to `1.5`.

3. Click on **Save All** and exit.

4. Print the model.

5. Reopen the **Normal** profile in Skeinforge. Under **Carve**, adjust the **Edge Width over Height (ratio)** to `3.0` and the **Layer Height (mm)** to `0.1`.

6. Under **Inset**, adjust the **Infill Width over Thickness (ratio)** to `3.0`.

7. Click on **Save All** and exit.

8. Print the model.

How it works...

To calculate our width over height ratio, we'll adjust our width for a 0.25 mm nozzle by adding 20 percent. This gives us an extrusion width of 0.3 mm.

0.25 mm nozzle	Ratio
0.4 mm layer	x
0.3 mm layer	x
0.2 mm layer	1.5
0.1 mm layer	3.0

The preceding chart provides a good starting point for each layer thickness using a 0.25 mm nozzle.

Using Slic3r to print different resolutions

Slic3r has a much simpler approach when changing resolution settings. Unlike Skeinforge, Slic3r requires the user to input the printer's nozzle size. Along with a preference setting for layer height, Slic3r automatically adjusts the slicer for different resolutions.

Getting ready

The Thingiverse website is a file-sharing site of user-created digital designs. It has many small models that can be used to make quick and efficient print tests. We'll use the one that's designed for surface calibration. It's a good shape for testing resolutions and small enough to print quickly, without much filament waste. It can be downloaded at `www.thingiverse.com/thing:39050`.

How to do it...

We will proceed as follows:

1. Open Slic3r. Under **Printer Settings** in **Extruder 1**, adjust the **Nozzle diameter** to your nozzle size.

2. Under **Print Settings** in **Layers and perimeters**, adjust the **Layer height** to 0.4 mm.

3. Slice the STL file and click on **Save**.

4. Print the model.

5. Repeat the preceding steps, changing the parameters for all layers: 0.3 mm, 0.2 mm, and 0.1 mm. When printing the 0.1 mm layer, adjust **First layer height** from 100 percent to 200 percent in **Layers and perimeters** under **Print Settings**.

6. Save the STL files.

7. Print the models.

How it works...

Slic3r calculates the ratios between nozzle sizes and layer heights internally, without the user having to input anything more than the basic preferences. This makes the slicer easier to adjust than Skeinforge. One of the more useful features of Slic3r is the ability to adjust the first layer height of the print. When printing a 0.1 mm layer, extreme care must be taken in adjusting the nozzle head against the build platform. The perfect distance must be achieved so that the first layer is deposited firmly and evenly. By allowing a greater height to be chosen for the first layer, it's easier to get a good start on an overall finer layer height. Keep in mind that the increment added must not exceed the limits of the nozzle bore. Slic3r has a built-in warning to alert you if your percentage is too high.

Reviewing the print results

If you were ambitious and ran all of the resolution tests along with the three different nozzle sizes with both Skeinforge and Slic3r, you should have 18 surface calibration prints to compare. We are going to take a look at the major differences here.

The most striking difference is between the lowest resolution print and the finest. The lowest possible resolution in our testing utilized a nozzle with a 0.5 mm bore and printed at its maximum height layer of 0.4 mm, as seen in the following image:

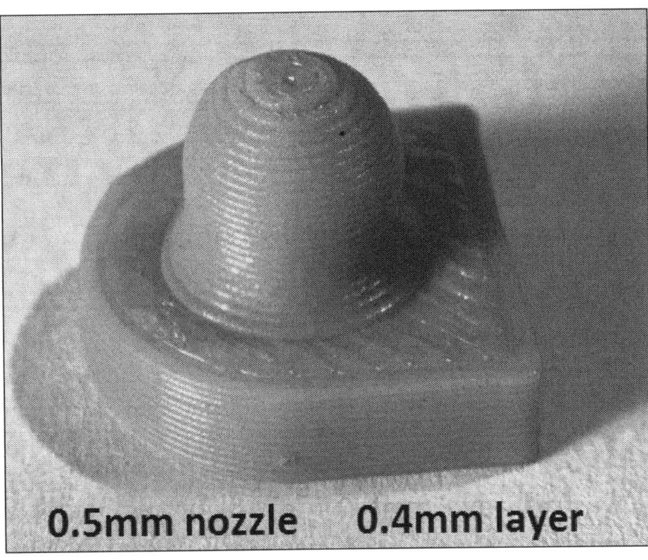

The finest print test utilized a 0.25 mm nozzle and printed at a 0.1 mm layer as seen in the following image. Both of these resolution tests were sliced by Skeinforge.

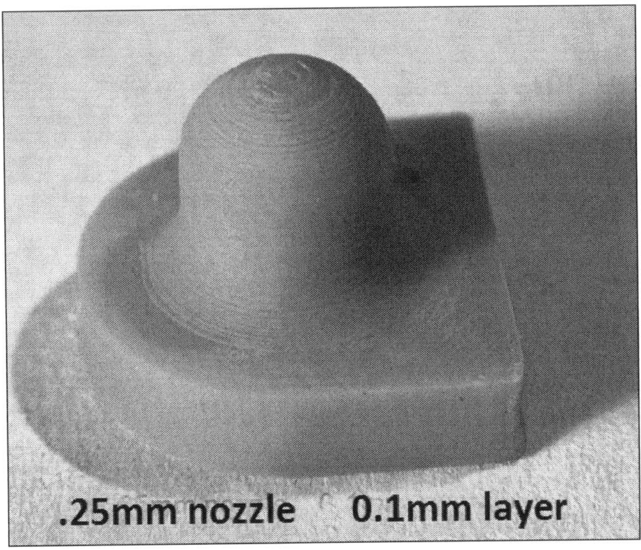

Next we will look at how a 0.1 mm layer is printed using a 0.5 mm, 0.35 mm, and 0.25 mm nozzles. This test was also sliced by Skeinforge.

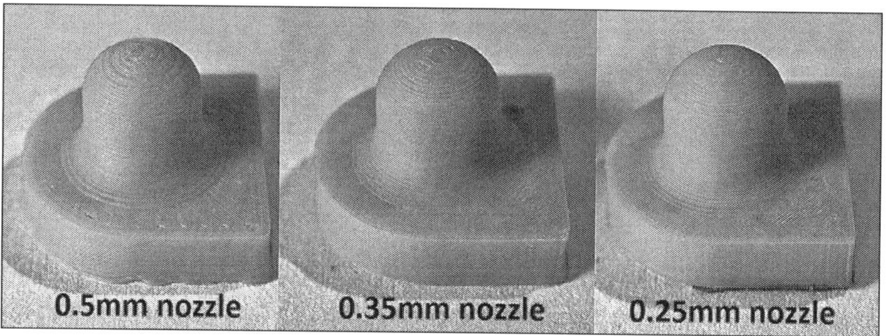

Next, we'll compare the finest print results of Skeinforge and Slic3r.

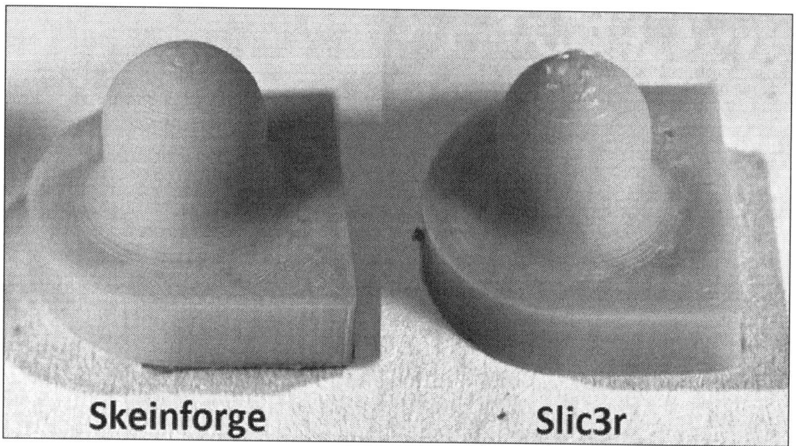

In the preceding image, we can see that the top surface area of the print in Slic3r has a little distortion. This is because the default settings in Slic3r were used. A better print could be achieved by making adjustments with the cooling settings.

Chapter 5, Manipulating Meshes and Bridges, covers the cooling features available with both Slic3r and Skeinforge.

Now, let's look at the printing results of the two models that we didn't specifically print in the recipes of this chapter. However, these are the models that we scanned with DAVID Laserscanner. First up is the coin. How well can a RepRap printer print the fine details of a coin? In the following image, we see a comparison of a Skeinforge-sliced model and the 3D scanned model using the commercial version of DAVID:

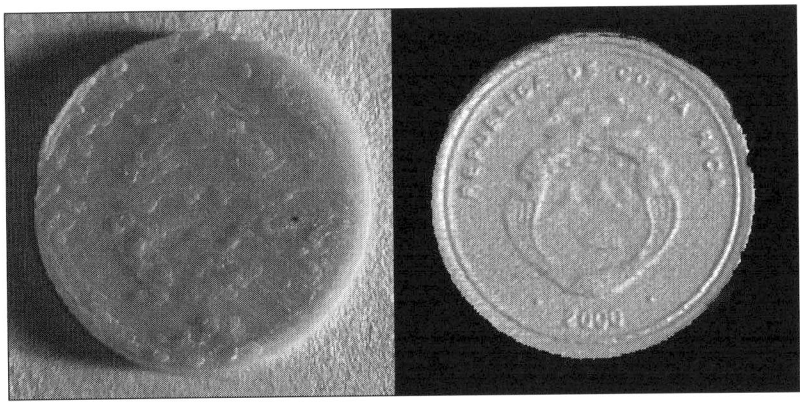

Our last comparison is of the toy block. It's a print comparison between the 3D-scanned models made with the free version of DAVID Laserscanner and its commercial version, as shown in the following image:

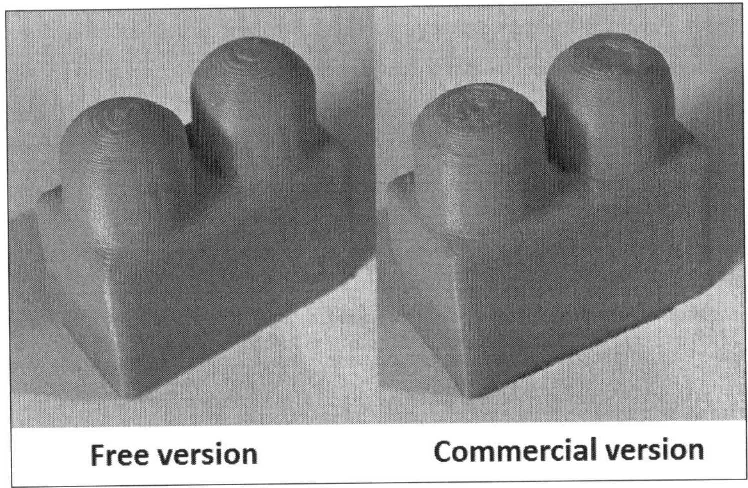

It's easy to see that better results were achieved with the commercial version of DAVID, but remember the initial 3D scan using 123D Catch. The basic setup of DAVID Laserscanner has produced better results!

4

Modeling and Printing with Precision

In this chapter, we will cover the following recipes:

- Warming up with SketchUp
- Using 3D tools from the Extension Warehouse
- Modeling with SketchUp
- Using plugin extensions with SketchUp
- Calibrating the x, y, and z axes
- Controlling the flow rate in Skeinforge
- Adjusting the scale in Skeinforge
- Using Stretch in Skeinforge
- Controlling print warping
- Using brim with Slic3r

Introduction

In this chapter, we're going to use at a 3D CAD program called **SketchUp Make**. What makes this program different from most CAD programs is the ease of its use. SketchUp is not a parametric modeler such as AutoCAD or Solidworks. It doesn't require heavy training and a lot of investment in money. It's an easy, intuitive modeler that allows for direct interaction with the geometry. This provides greater flexibility in making a model on the spur of a moment when creativity sparks.

Later in this chapter, we'll learn how to calibrate the mechanics of our printing by making some changes in the motion of the printer. We'll also examine a variety of solutions for controlling print warping. Controlling warping of prints made with ABS is a very common issue. We'll take a look at different solutions for this problematic issue.

Warming up with SketchUp

SketchUp is a 3D modeling program that's very easy to learn once a few elementary concepts are familiar. We're going to explore how this program works by creating a simple object that will serve as our test model, later in this chapter. First, let's get acquainted with the basic navigation controls of SketchUp.

SketchUp has an easy user interface. At the top of the workspace is a row of icons that contains most of the tools needed for modeling.

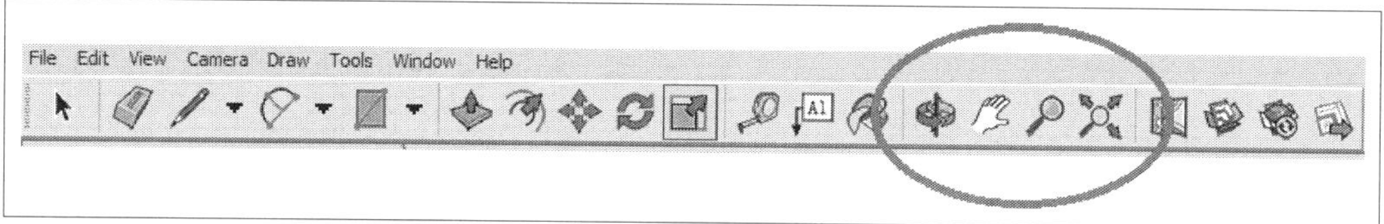

The navigation controls are mentioned in this section. These are circled in the preceding screenshot. By choosing one of the first three icons, movement can be made by clicking-and-dragging with the mouse. The last icon, **Zoom Extent**, will center the model in the workspace. Each of these icons has a keyboard and mouse shortcut. They are as follows:

- **Orbit** (hold down the scroll wheel)
- **Pan** (hold down *Shift* and the scroll wheel)
- **Zoom** (hold down the scroll wheel)
- **Zoom Extent** (*Shift* + *Z*)

Getting ready

You will need to download SketchUp from `http://www.sketchup.com/download` and follow the installation instructions. When you are prompted for a template choice, choose **3D Printing - Millimeters**.

This book uses SketchUp Make v14.0, which is supported on both Windows and Mac operating systems. The initial installation will give you 8 hours of SketchUp Pro features, after which the program reverts to the free SketchUp Make version.

How to do it...

When we open SketchUp, we see a MakerBot build volume. You can choose to use this or hide the box by selecting **Select** (Space bar) in the menu tray. Then, navigate to **Edit** and choose **Hide**.

Let's start off by making a simple shape. This will get us familiar with the basic modeling tools in SketchUp. We will proceed as follows:

1. Navigate to **File** in the menu and select **New** (*Ctrl + N*).

2. Choose the **Rectangle** (*R*) icon [■] and place the pencil cursor on **Origin**. Click, drag, and release a rectangle out at any distance.

3. At the bottom-right corner of the window, there is a command-line tab labeled **Dimensions**. Insert the dimensions, `100, 100`, and press *Enter*. The rectangle will size to 100 x 100 millimeters, as shown in the following screenshot:

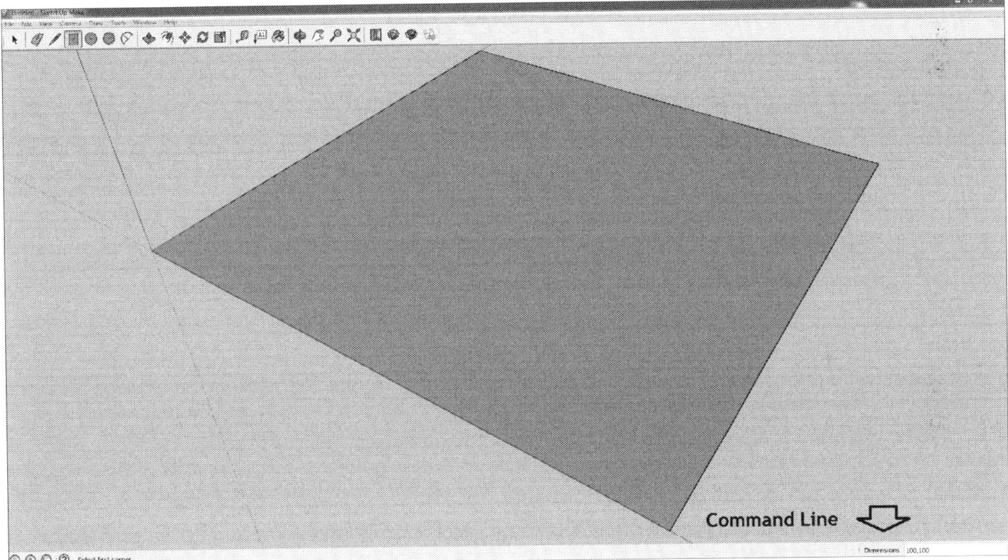

4. Choose the **Zoom Extents** (*Shift + Z*) icon to center the model on the workspace. From the icon bar, choose **Tape Measure** (*T*). Place the cursor on the edge at the bottom-left corner of the square and drag inside a 10 mm-wide guideline.

5. At the top-left corner of the window, drag another guideline inside the square using the **Tape Measure** (*T*). Drop the line at any point and enter `10` in the command-line tab for **Length**.

6. Select **Lines** (*L*) from the icon menu. It is the icon with the pencil image. We are going to follow the guidelines and draw a right angle. Place the pencil cursor at the intersection of the guideline and the bottom-right corner of the square, as shown in the following screenshot:

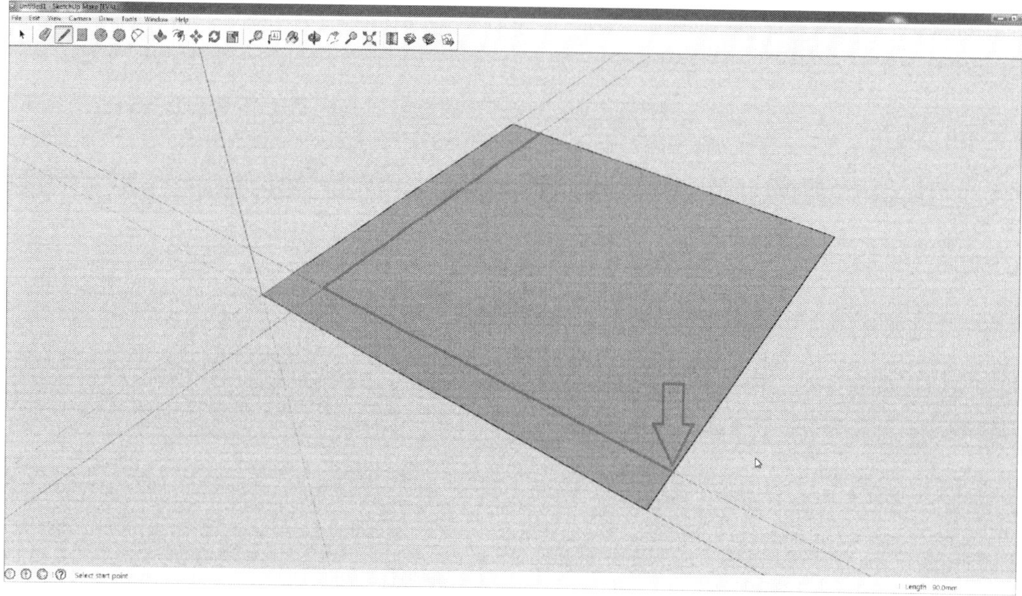

7. Click, drag, and snap the line at the intersection of the other guideline. Repeat and draw a line following the second guideline. You should have a right angle drawn, as illustrated in the preceding screenshot.

8. Choose **Select** in the icon tray (Space bar) and left-click anywhere on the square area. Then, press *Delete* on the keyboard.

9. Choose **Eraser** (*E*) from the icon tray. Click on the remaining lines of the square, creating a right-angle shape.

10. Choose the **Push/Pull** (*P*) tool icon [◆] from the icon tray.

11. Place the cursor on the right-angle and click-drag-release it, pulling the shape up at any distance. We want the height to be 4 mm in this case, so in the command window, enter 4 for **Distance**. Your shape should look like the one shown in the following screenshot:

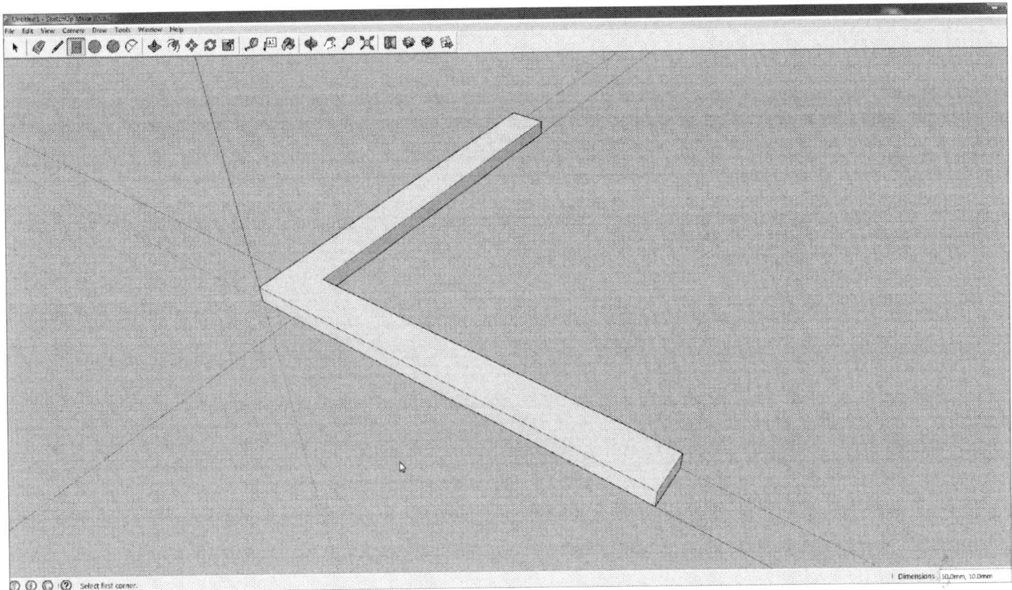

12. Choose **Rectangle** (*R*) and find an endpoint of the right angle's corner. Click-drag-release a square to the opposite endpoint.

13. From the bottom of the right angle, find an endpoint. Draw a square here as well.

14. Choose the **Push/Pull** (*P*) tool and pull both the squares up by 6 mm. You should have a shape similar to the one shown in the following screenshot:

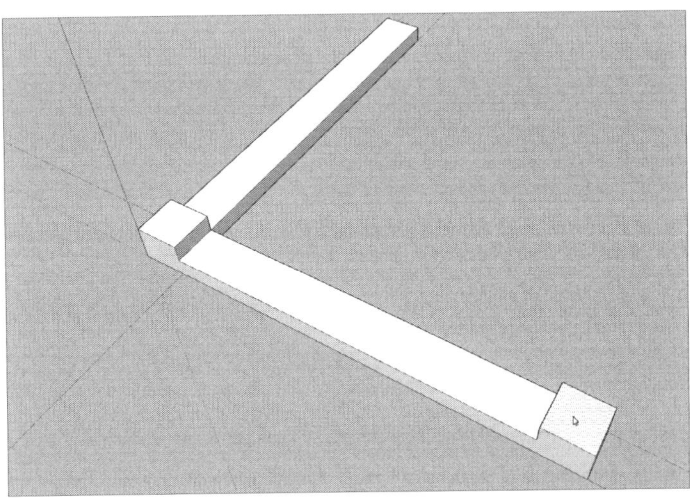

15. Navigate to **File** and click on **Save** (*Ctrl* + *S*). Save the shape as a SketchUp model (*.skp).

How it works...

It's best to think in terms of blocks when building in SketchUp. To do this, it's generally better to start with the largest basic form and work out from it. We do this by first creating a 2D shape (it's better to look at this as a layer) and pulling it into a 3D form. If it is drawn on top of another shape or block, it snaps in place. Then, by pulling it up, it becomes a new feature.

Using 3D tools from the Extension Warehouse

The Extension Warehouse is owned and operated by Trimble Navigation, Ltd., the owners of SketchUp. It is a depository of add-ons that can be used to enhance the features of SketchUp. It continues to grow with the contributions of developers who write small plugins and share them on the site.

In this recipe, we will install SketchUp STL. This is an add-on that will give us the functionality to import and export the `.stl` files.

Getting ready

Go to `http://extensions.sketchup.com/`. Here, you'll find categories of add-ons that are available. Choose the **3D Printing** category. From this page, choose **SketchUp STL**. Download it, and follow the instructions to install it.

How to do it...

Open SketchUp and load the warp-test model we made in the preceding recipe. Then, proceed as follows:

1. We'll export the model as a `.stl` file. Make sure that the MakerBot build volume is unhidden. Go to **File** and choose **Export STL**.

2. A pop up will prompt for information. Choose the **Export Unit** option. We've been working in millimeters; hence, this would be our choice.

3. Choose **File Format**. ASCII allows for easy reading with a text editor, but it is larger than a binary file. A binary file is more compact and faster to read by the slicer. Choose one of the options.

4. Export your model. From the next pop-up window, you'll be able to name your file and click on **Save**.

How it works...

If we open the `.stl` file of the warp test, we'll see that we also exported a mesh of the MakerBot build plate and logo.

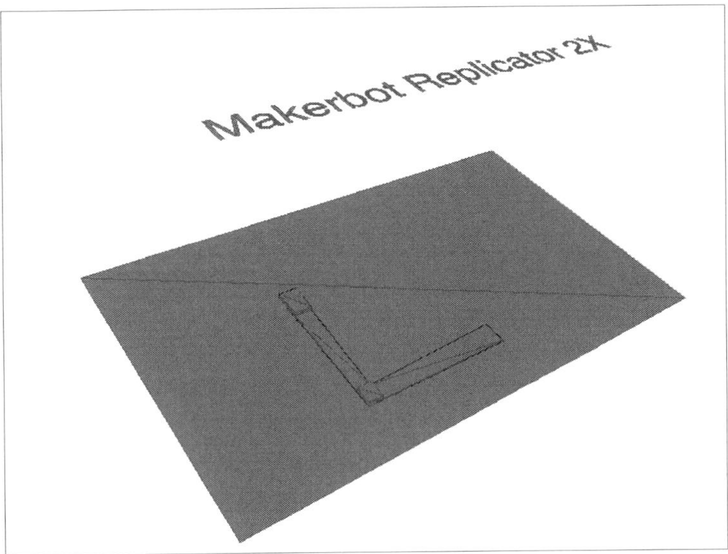

We obviously don't want this to happen, so the point here is to make sure that the build volume is hidden before you export it. Another option is to select the entire model and check mark **Export selected geometry only**.

Modeling with SketchUp

In this recipe, we are going to explore how to use more of the modeling tools in SketchUp by duplicating the toy block we 3D scanned in the previous chapters.

Getting ready

You'll need the toy block and something to measure its dimensions. Digital calipers would be the best tool for this job. Measure all of its basic features and make a note of them.

How to do it...

Open a new workspace in SketchUp and proceed as follows:

1. Choose the **Rectangle** (*R*) tool and draw a rectangle with the footprint dimensions of your block. In my case, the dimension is 31.5 x 63 mm.

2. Choose the **Push/Pull** (*P*) tool. Place the cursor on the rectangle and pull up the height of the rectangular portion of the block. In my case, the height is 38 mm.

3. Choose **Tape Measure** (*T*). Place the cursor on the edge of the object and find the midpoint. The cursor point will turn from red to blue. Drag the cursor along the perpendicular side slowly until you reach the midpoint. Release the cursor and a guideline will divide the rectangle in equal halves. The movements are numbered in the following screenshot:

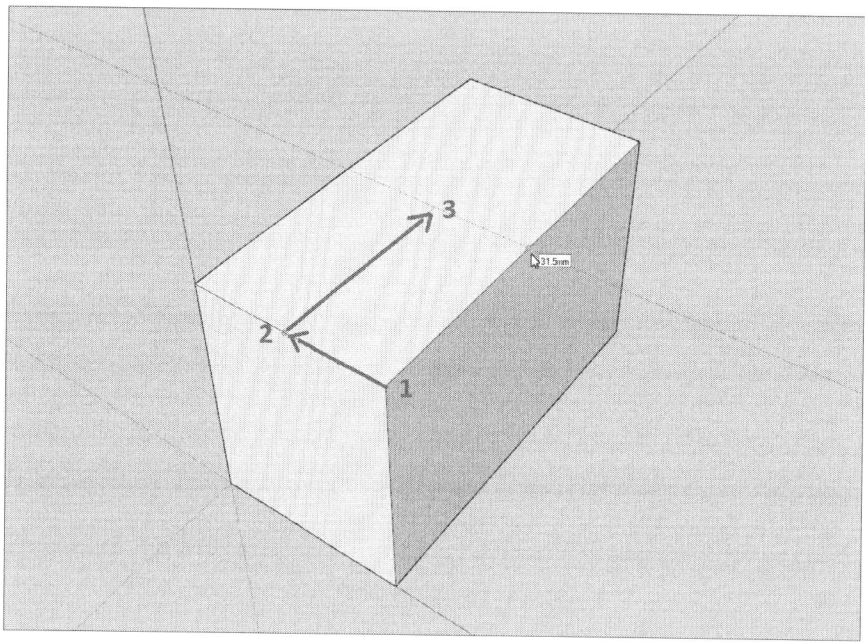

4. Now, we are going to create the two dowels on the block. First, we need to draw some guidelines. From an endpoint, drag out a guideline diagonally across one of the top halves. Repeat the same for the other half.

5. Choose the **Circle** (*C*) icon [●]. It's in the pull-down tray with the **Rectangle** (*R*) icon.

6. The value 24 is in the command window; change this value to 50. This determines how many sides will make up the circle; the higher the number, the finer the resolution.

7. With the circle cursor, find the midpoint of one diagonal. The only indication will be a slight pause at the midpoint and a green line will appear at the intersection. Drag out a circle. In the **Radius** tab of the command window, enter the radius of the toy block's cylinder. In my case, it's 13.5 mm. Repeat this for the other half. You should now have two drawn circles that match the footprint dimensions of the toy block's dowels.

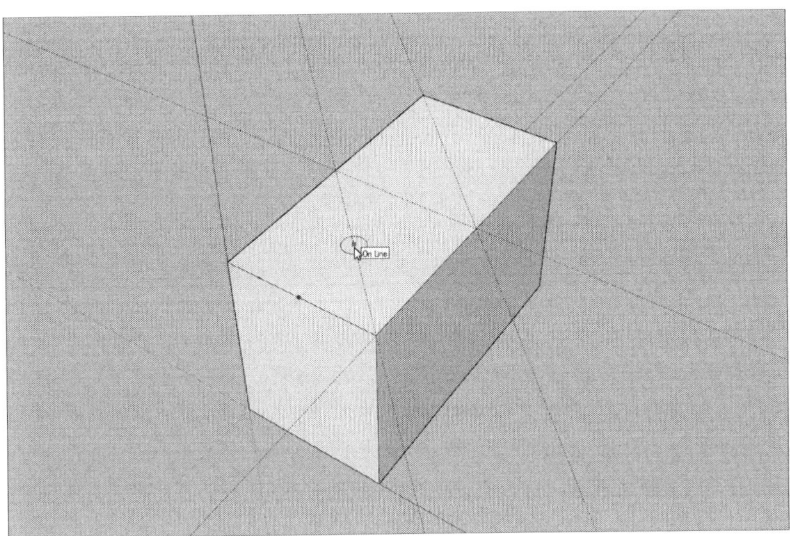

8. Now, we'll extrude the dowels. Choose the **Push/Pull** (*P*) tool. Pull each of the dowels up. In my case, their height is 20 mm.

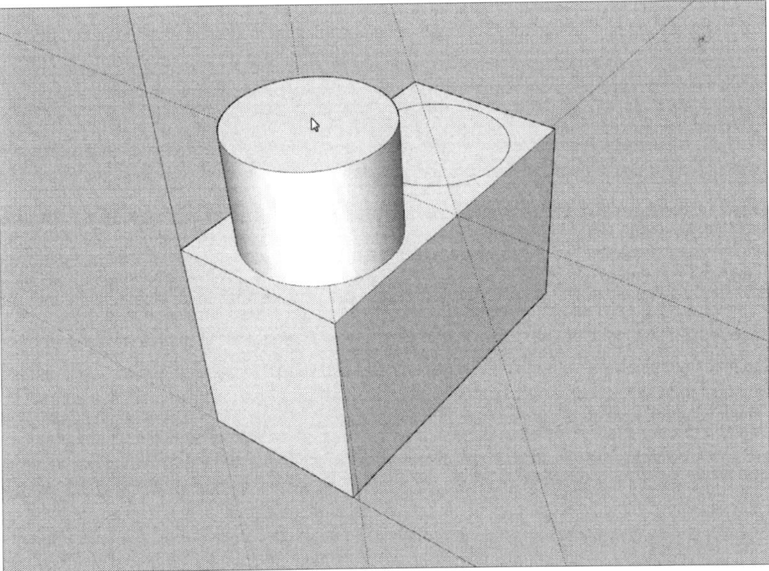

9. The toy block has a small circular indention at the center of each dowel. We'll make these in the same fashion as we did when we made the dowels. Select **Circle** (*C*) and find the center on top of the cylinder. This can be kind of tricky. Slowly, move the circle cursor around the center-point area until the cursor snaps into **Center**. Draw a circle that is the size of the indention. In my case, its radius is 2.0 mm. Repeat the same for the other dowel.

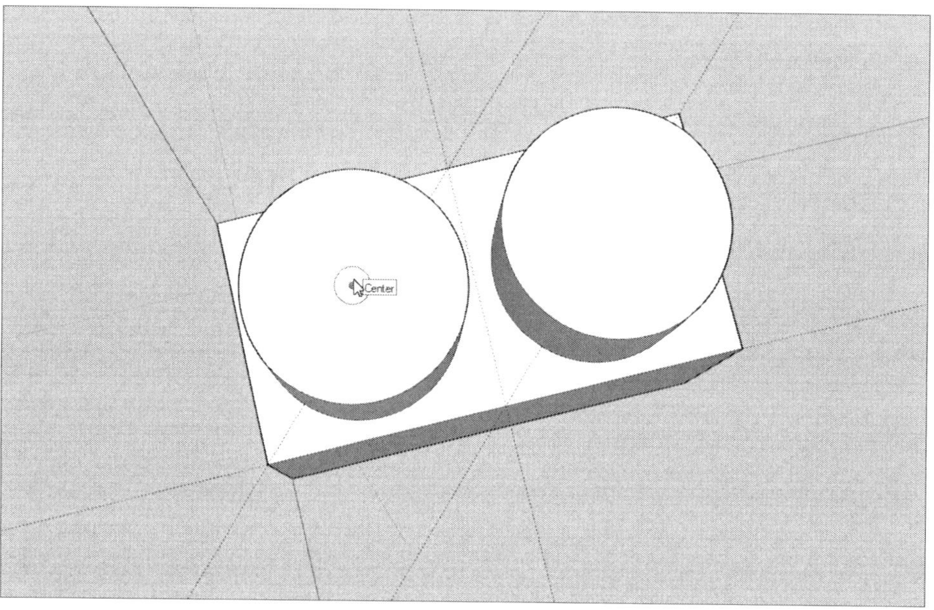

10. Choose the **Push/Pull** (*P*) tool. Push both circles down the length of the indentation. In my case, it is 1 mm.

11. This is a good time to save the model. Go to **File** and click on **Save** (*Ctrl + S*). Save the model as a SketchUp model (`*.skp`).

How it works...

In this recipe, we became familiar to the **Circle** tool. SketchUp is designed to draw circles using polygons. The more sides that make up the polygon, the more refined the circle will be. When we select this tool, the command window displays the number of sides that will be used. The default is 24. In this recipe, we changed this value using a keyboard entry. The following are the two other methods to change this value:

▶   After you draw your circle, the command box will display the radius. Just enter the number of sides using the keyboard and follow the value with an `[s]` extension. Press *Enter*.

- After you draw the circle and progress further along with your project, you may decide to go back and change the number of sides. To do this, select the circle (make sure you haven't changed it by drawing over it) and right-click on it. Choose **Entity Info** from the pop up. Another pop up will give you the option to change the number of sides in segments.

Using plugin extensions with SketchUp

SketchUp has a lot of easy and powerful features, but sometimes, there are hard routes in the modeling process that can be made simpler. Sometimes, using a plugin, the task can be made easier. A few recipes back, we learned how to use add-ons from the Extension Warehouse.

In this recipe, we'll learn how to install plugins from another site, SketchUcation. Then, we'll refine our toy block from the previous recipe and improve it until it's a perfect copy of the original, using the RoundCorner plugin.

Getting ready

Go to `http://sketchucation.com/` and follow the instructions to join this site. Don't worry; it's free. Once you become a member, follow this link: `http://sketchucation.com/forums/viewtopic.php?f=323&t=20485`. From here, you'll be given precise instructions on where and how to install the RoundCorner plugin and its dependencies, **LibFredo6 4.9** or higher and **000-_AdditionalPluginFolders**. Carefully follow Fredo6's installation instructions.

How to do it...

Open your saved `.skp` file of the toy block, which you made in the previous recipe. Then, proceed as follows:

1. We'll start by beveling the two dowels on the block. There should be a floating toolbox for RoundCorner at the top-left corner of your workspace. Choose the **Bevel edges and corners** icon [⊕], and a menu will appear at the top.

2. Select the **Extend selection to curve** icon [❯].

3. Select both the top ends of the dowels. In order to calculate the size of the bevel, measure the diameter of the truncated portion of the dowel (in this case, it is 18 mm). Subtract this amount from the dowel's full diameter (27 - 18 = 9 mm). Enter half of this difference (4.5 mm) for the offset value in the tool menu. It should look similar to the following screenshot:

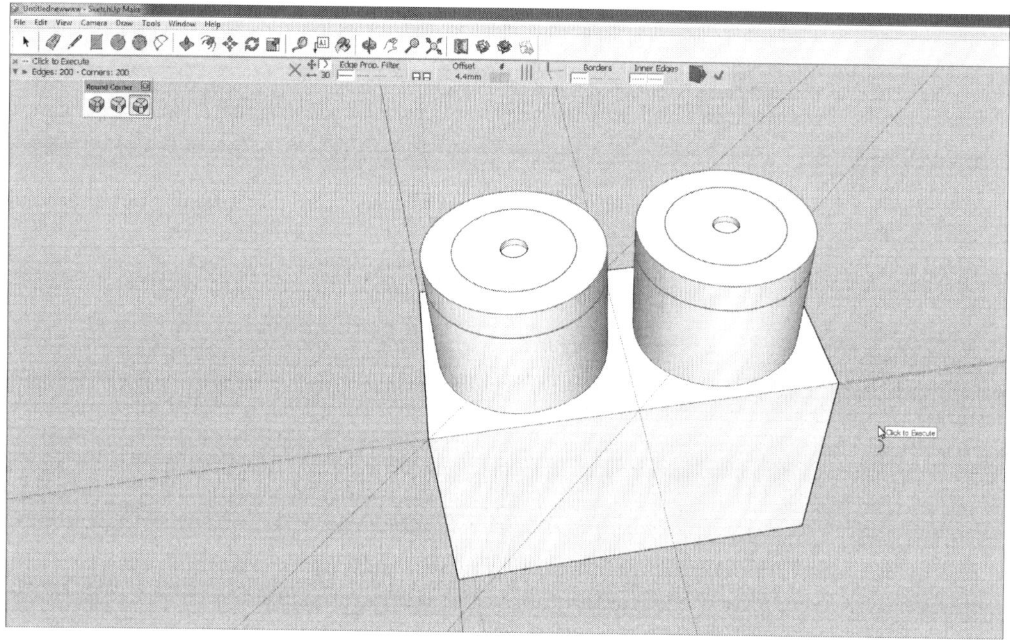

4. The cursor will become a green check mark. Left-click to execute the bevel.

5. Select the **Round corners in 3D** icon [⚙].

6. From the RoundCorner menu, select the **Extend selection to all connected edges** icon [✛].

7. Place the cursor on any edge of the block portion and select an area. Enter roughly 1.6 for the **Offset value** option in the **Tools** menu. This value represents 1.6 mm, and it's determined roughly by a visual guess.

8. Select the icon for **Extend selection to curve**. Left-click on the red guide surrounding the indentations on top of the dowels and the perimeter of the dowel's footprint. These areas should not be rounded; otherwise, this tool will remove the selection. In the left-hand side image of the following screenshot, these areas are shown by the red arrows. The image to the right shows only the edges of the block selected.

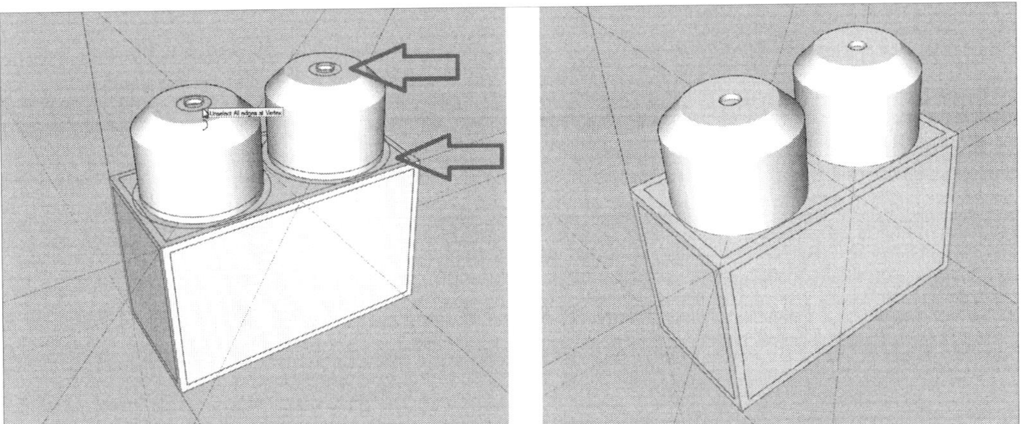

9. Left-click to execute. Your block should look similar to the following image:

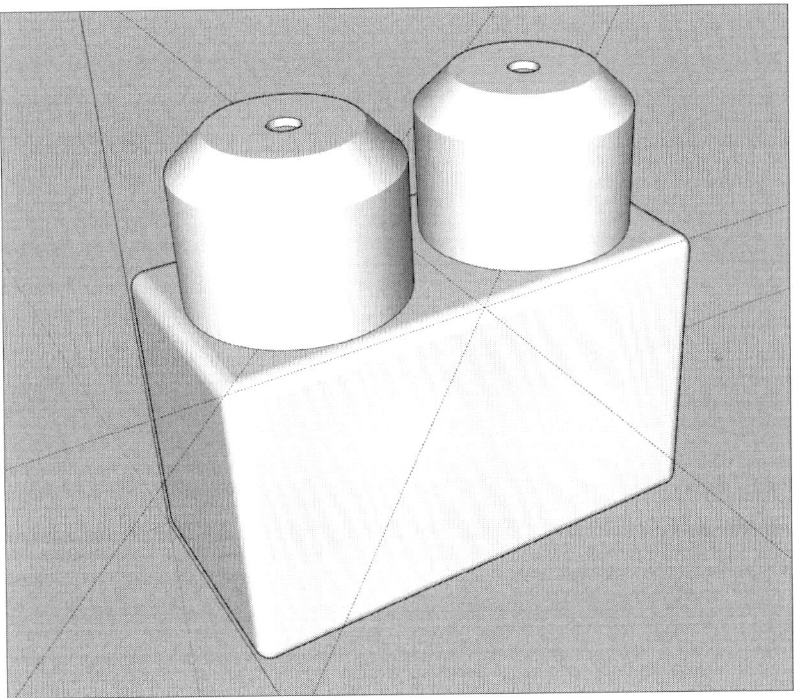

10. Go to **File** and click on **Save** (*Ctrl + S*). Save the shape as a SketchUp model (`.skp`). Export it as a `.stl` file.

How it works...

SketchUp Make works with the addition of plugins based on Ruby scripts. This has allowed users to write a variety of scripts that can be useful, and many are shared on forums such as SketchUcation. When RoundCorner was installed, it created the **Fredo6 Collection** selection under **Tools** in the menu. From here, a variety of tasks, which mirrors the pop-up toolbox, can be chosen. If the pop-up toolbox for RoundCorner is closed and you want it back, it can be found by choosing **View** in the menu and then selecting **Toolbars**. From the pop-up, **Toolbars**, find **RoundCorner** from the list and check mark it.

Let's print!

In the previous recipes, we learned how to make a model with precise measurements. Now, we'll take a look at how we can print a model with better accuracy. We'll start our printing session by first calibrating our x, y, and z axes. This is one of the most important calibrations we can make, if we expect to print a part that is exactly the size of our model.

Then, we'll experiment with some slicer options that will help us tweak the precision of our part. These options are only available in Skeinforge. Conveniently, most of these plugins will have specific functions, and they can be left deactivated until a specific problem is encountered. Some of them are quick cheats to solving a problem, which may be elusive to fix elsewhere. We'll examine these options as we work our way through them.

The recipe named *Controlling print warping* (in this chapter) will cover the methods to solve the warping of the parts printed using ABS. We'll use our warp test model that we made in SketchUp to help us solve this problem. Some of the mechanical tricks can be applied with the use of any slicer, but the Raft plugin option in Skeinforge will be our primary focus.

Slic3r has some limited raft options and another option called **Brim**. We'll look at this feature as well.

Calibrating the x, y, and z axes

Proper calibration of the printer's x, y, and z axes is important if we want an accurate reproduction of a model. This includes both the physical alignment of the axes to each other and the calibration of the firmware, which provides instructions to the stepper motors that drive the axis. For this recipe, we'll assume that you have a 3D printer that's well constructed and has aligned axes. What we'll focus on is finding the correct firmware values for your x, y, and z axes.

Getting ready

You'll need a precision caliper or, at the very least, a metric ruler for this recipe. You'll also need your current **E_steps_per_unit** value, which is located in your firmware settings in the `Configuration.h` file. If your firmware allows, use a `M503` command to echo your printer settings. What you are looking for are two lines similar to the following:

```
echo: Steps per unit:
echo:   M92  X90.00 Y90.00 Z4160.00 E989.00
```

The values you need will be listed after the axis. In this case, they are `x90.00`, `y90.00`, and `z4160.00`.

> For more detailed information about using G-code commands and accessing firmware, see *Appendix A*, *Understanding and Editing Firmware*, and *Appendix B*, *Taking a Closer Look at G-code*.

You'll also need to download the essential calibration kit from Thingiverse at `http://www.thingiverse.com/thing:5573`. In this kit, we'll be using a 20( )mm box calibration.

How to do it...

We will proceed as follows:

1. Print the calibration cube. Measure each dimension, taking care to distinguish the *x* axis from the *y* axis.

2. The cube should print exactly 20 mm x 20 mm. If you don't have the correct size, divide 20 by your test cube's measured size for both the *x* and *y* axes. In this case, I have a measured a size of 19.89 mm for my *x* axis and a measured size of 20.89 mm for the *y* axis. When I divide these values by 20, I get a quotient of 1.005 for the *x* axis and 0.957 for the *y* axis.

3. Multiply the quotient by the value that's stored in your firmware. The firmware value for the *x* axis is 90.000. Multiply 90.00 by 1.005. The product is 90.45 for the *x* axis. The firmware value for the *y* axis is 90.000. Multiply 90.0 by 0.957. The product is 86.13 for the *y* axis.

4. Repeat this process for the *z* axis, keeping in mind that the measured size should be 10 mm.

5. Substitute all the new values for the *x*, *y*, and *z* axes in the firmware. Type the entire command line, `M92 X90.45 Y86.13 Z4240 E989.000`. Press *Enter*.

6. Print another cube and measure. If the size is still not correct, tweak the values by repeating the process.

How it works...

Using the command line allows changes to be made while the printer is running. This is far more convenient than making changes to the firmware using the Arduino IDE. However, changes made by the command line are not permanent. If you're using controllers, such as the Melzi or Sanguinololu controllers, that allow for changes to be made to EEPROM, then a permanent entry can be made by adding an `M500` command in the command line. This will store the values in EEPROM.

Controlling the flow rate in Skeinforge

Flow rate is the speed in which material is extruded from a nozzle. It works proportionally with the feed rate, which is the speed in which the extruder (or the *x* and *y* axes platform) physically moves. If the extruder moves very fast, a higher flow rate will be necessary, and for a slower extruder speed, a lower flow rate would be required.

For a new user of Skeinforge, these adjustments can be confusing. We'll keep the adjustments to a minimum, and we'll only examine how the flow rate affects a model. In this recipe, we'll calibrate a rate that is near perfect to the width of the nozzle's diameter.

Getting ready

For this recipe, we'll be using the thin wall calibration from the essential calibration kit, which we downloaded from Thingiverse. You'll also need precision calipers. Trying to make a precise measurement with a metric rule will not work well with this calibration.

How to do it...

We will proceed as follows:

1. Slice the thin wall calibration model with Skeinforge and print it.

2. Measure its thickness with calipers. In this case, it's 0.97 mm thick and 0.47 mm thicker than the nozzle's diameter.

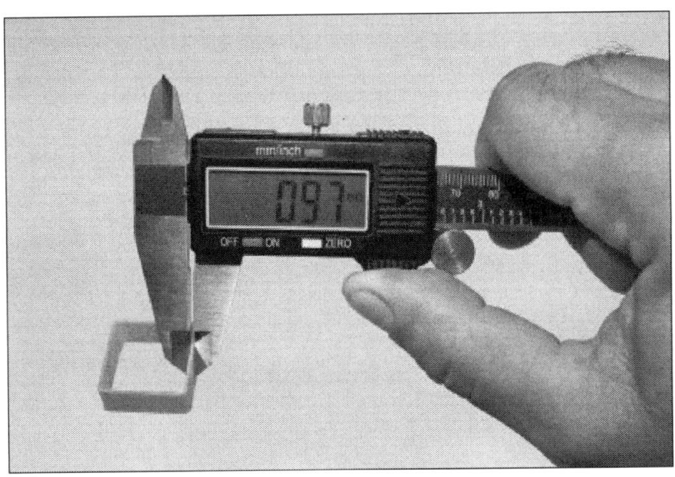

3. Our target wall thickness is 0.5mm. Divide the target thickness by our printed result thickness (0.5/0.97 = 0.5154639). The product is our ratio.

4. In Skeinforge, select the **Speed** plugin. Take the current value in **Flow Rate Setting (float)** and multiply it by the ratio you calculated. In this case, the flow rate is 30.0 (30.0 x 0.5154639=15.463917). Enter this value for the flow rate.

5. Print another calibration wall and measure it with calipers. The wall thickness should be close to or exactly 0.5 mm. If it is not, tweak the values by repeating the process.

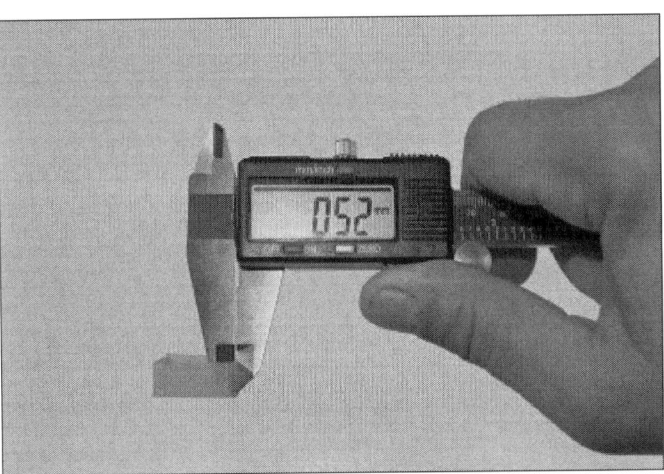

How it works...

The general rule of thumb is to set the extruded width slightly wider than the nozzle's bore size. This isn't the best configuration if higher precision is required. It will be necessary to set an exact extrusion width, but by making this adjustment, we will also create a shorter latitude for error.

If the flow rate drops below its threshold, the extrusion can become thin and irregular. This will produce a weak bond between the layers. We can see an example of this in the preceding image.

There's more...

Adjusting the flow rate with the slicer performs the same task as adjusting the **E_steps_per_unit** value in the firmware. They both determine how much filament will be extruded. If we have a properly calibrated extruder, we ideally wouldn't need to make any adjustments.

With Skeinforge, we calculate a ratio for each nozzle size we decide to use. We do this by taking the nozzle diameter and adding 20 percent more width to allow for more surface contact between the layers and thus, a better bond. This has been a common practice with most profile setups, but what if we want a precise bead width? Making an adjustment in the slicer is a quick way of accomplishing this without changing our normal operating values in the firmware.

Adjusting the scale in Skeinforge

The scale plugin is an option that's available to make small changes in the scale of a printed model. This is accomplished by adjusting the **XY Plane Scale (ratio)** and the **Z axis Scale (ratio)**.

Getting ready

For this recipe, we will use the calibration cube from the essential calibration kit that we downloaded from Thingiverse. You'll also need precision calipers.

How to do it...

We will proceed as follows:

1. In Skeinforge, select **Activate Scale**, keeping the default values.

2. Slice the calibration cube with Skeinforge and print it. We'll use this as a reference to compare with the next print.

3. The default value in **XY Plane Scale (ratio)** is 1.01. This is an automatic increase of 1 percent. For this test, we'll choose an arbitrary 5( )percent increase. This will make 1.05 the new ratio value. Enter 1.05 in the **XY Plane Scale (ratio)** tab.

4. Slice the calibration cube with Skeinforge and print it.

5. The default value in **Z axis Scale (ratio)** is 1.0. This automatically prints the height of the model at 100 percent. We'll use the arbitrary 5( )percent increase again. This will make 1.05 the new ratio value. Enter 1.05 in the **Z Axis Scale (ratio)** tab and click on **Save**.

6. Slice the calibration cube with Skeinforge and print it.

7. Now, measure all the sides of both the cubes and compare them. There should be a 5( )percent increase of all the dimensions when they are compared with the reference cube, which you printed at the beginning of the recipe.

How it works...

It's not recommended that you adjust the z axis more than 5 percent, as this ratio affects many variables related to the layer height; more material will have to be extruded because the layers would be farther apart. The XY plane is not affected in this same manner.

This makes **Scale** a poor option for making large scaling changes in a model, but it does offer a quick solution when a small percentage of scaling is needed.

Using Stretch in Skeinforge

Printing circular holes that are correct in size is problematic for RepRap-based printers. There are a number of issues that can affect the printing of holes with diameters of 2 mm and smaller. One issue involves how the material is laid down while moving in an arc. When a nozzle extrudes while making a circle, more material is deposited on the inside of the circle than on the outside. This is because the inner perimeter of the circle has a slightly shorter radius than the outer perimeter. The difference in the radius size is determined by the width of the extruded line.

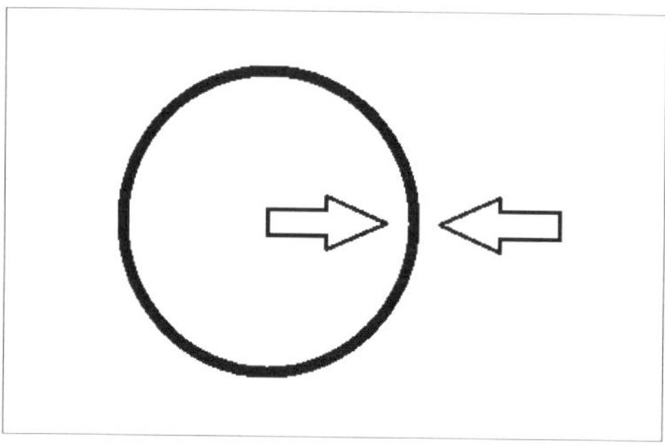

Skeinforge has a means to compensate for this problem by activating a plugin called Stretch. It's not a perfect solution, but it provides better results.

Getting ready

There's a handy hole calibration model that we'll need, and it can be downloaded from Thingiverse. You can find it at `http://www.thingiverse.com/thing:28562`. An assortment of M2, M3, M4, and M5 screws will be helpful in testing the hole gauges of the calibration test, but they are not necessary in order to follow the recipe.

How to do it...

We will proceed as follows:

1. Print the hole calibration test. Test the hole sizes by fitting M2, M3, and M4 screws into the appropriate holes.

2. In Skeinforge, enable **Activate Stretch**. Adjust the **Perimeter Inside Stretch Over Perimeter Width (ratio)** to `1.0`.

3. Print the hole calibration test and retest the hole sizes with the screws.

4. Depending on the results, tweak the **Perimeter Inside Stretch Over Perimeter Width (ratio)** by a small percentage and repeat the process until the screws fit.

How it works...

Let's compare the two prints we made of the hole calibration test. We can see that the smaller holes from the right are filled, as shown in the following image:

Setting the **Perimeter Inside Stretch Over Perimeter Width (ratio)** to 1.0 activates the algebraic expression that calculates the arc compensation.

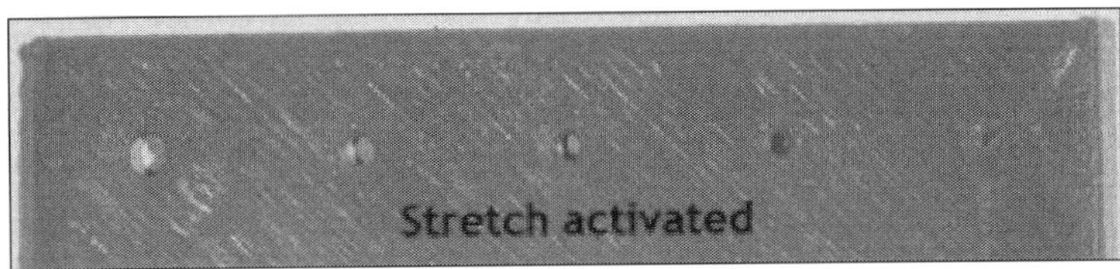

We can see a difference in the preceding example. You may find that increasing the value compared to the existing one will give better results, but you'll have to exercise caution so that other parts of your model are not adversely affected.

Controlling print warping

Print warping is probably the most frustrating issue we will encounter in our printing activities. The damage done by warping can ruin the precision of a model. It can be so severe that the print will curl and catch on the hot end's nozzle, lifting the entire print off the bed.

Print warping is caused by a difference in print temperature and shrinkage along the z axis. This is notably apparent when using ABS filament. ABS cools and shrinks quickly in comparison to PLA. Both can develop warping issues, but ABS is the more problematic of the two.

See *Appendix C, Filament Options for RepRap Printers*, for more information about different filament materials.

The following image demonstrates this by showing two test runs. One is our warp test model printed in ABS and the other is printed in PLA. Both are printed on blue painter's tape and glass (which is a common printing surface that RepRap printer's use) with no heat applied to the bed.

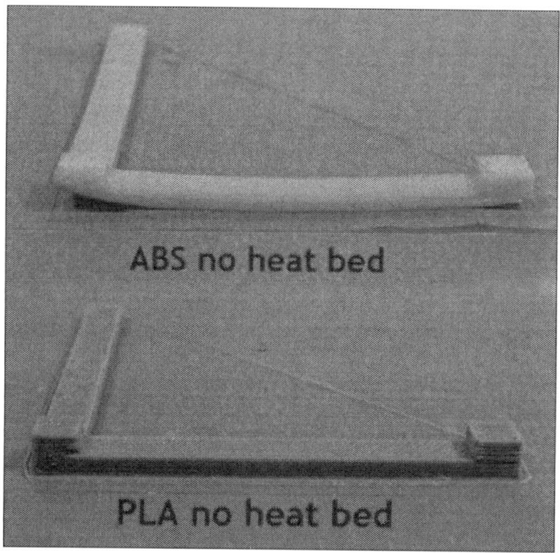

When we use a heat bed with a temperature of 110 degrees Celsius, we solved the problem with warping. We can see this with the ABS warp print test in the following image:

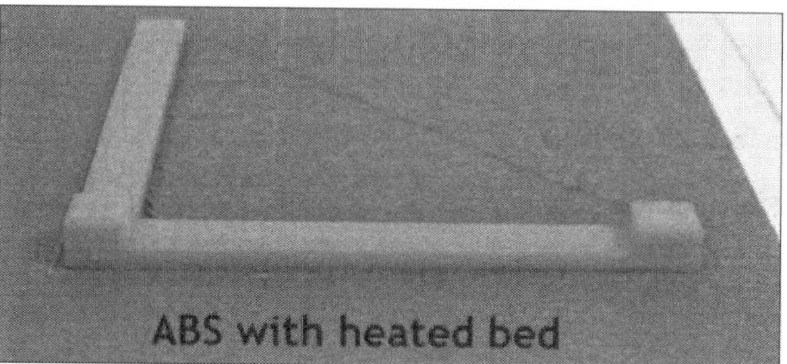

In the following recipe, we'll look at some methods that we can employ to print a warp-free model using an ABS filament, without the use of a heat bed. This will allow us to explore the available options that minimize warping.

One of the benefits of using a PLA filament is its high tolerance to warping issues. There are other filaments that have similar tolerances. You can find these listed in *Appendix C, Filament Options for RepRap Printers*.

Getting ready

You'll need the warp test model we made in SketchUp and Skeinforge to slice the model. Blue painter's tape, Kapton tape, medium-grit sandpaper, and some acetone will also be needed for further testing.

How to do it...

We will proceed as follows:

1. In Skeinforge, open the Raft plugin and check the **Activate Raft** option.
2. Keep the default values, but make sure that in the **Base** section, **Base Layers (integer)** is 1.0. This value determines how many layers of raft will be printed.
3. Under **Interface**, make sure that **Interface Layers (integer)** is 2.0. This value determines how many layers are printed that will allow a better separation from the model during their removal.
4. Under **Raft Size**, make sure that **Raft Margin (mm)** is 3.0. This value determines how wide the raft will be printed.
5. Slice and print the warp test model.

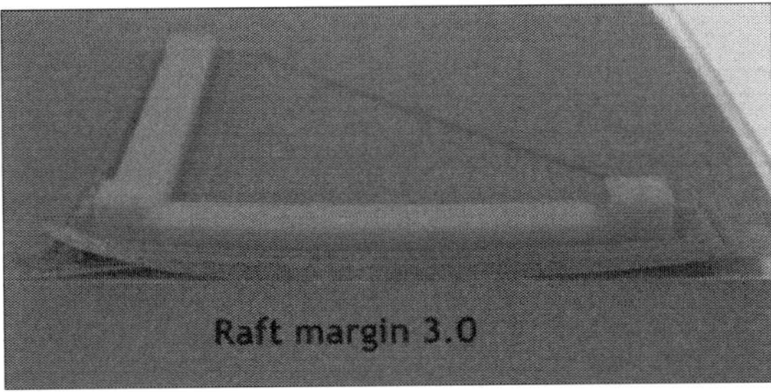

6. If the model is warped, increase the **Raft Margin (mm)** by 25 percent or more and print it.

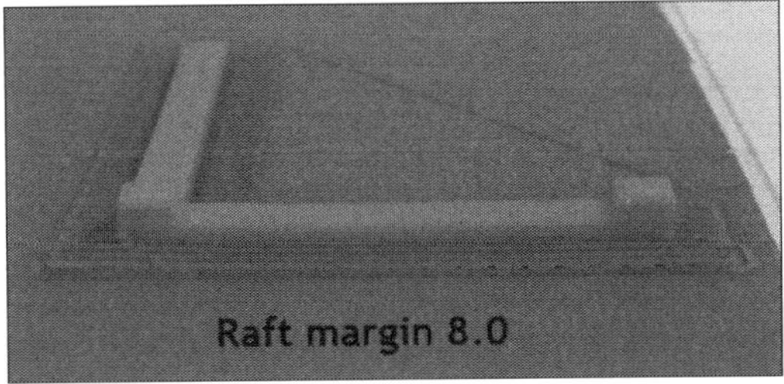

7. Continue to increase the **Raft Margin** until the warp test model prints are perfectly leveled. A raft margin of 8.0 was needed for the preceding example.

How it works...

The Raft plugin has quite a few options, but the most important one that we are examining in this recipe is **Raft Margin**. It controls the size of the raft surrounding your model's footprint. When we increase the value, we increase the raft's width.

The **Base Layer** and **Interface Layers** are kept at a default value of 1 and 2 layers, respectively. The **Base Layer** is extruded slowly and wider than the succeeding layers. This is to provide a better hold on the print bed. The **Interface Layers** are thinner so that the raft is easily removed after printing.

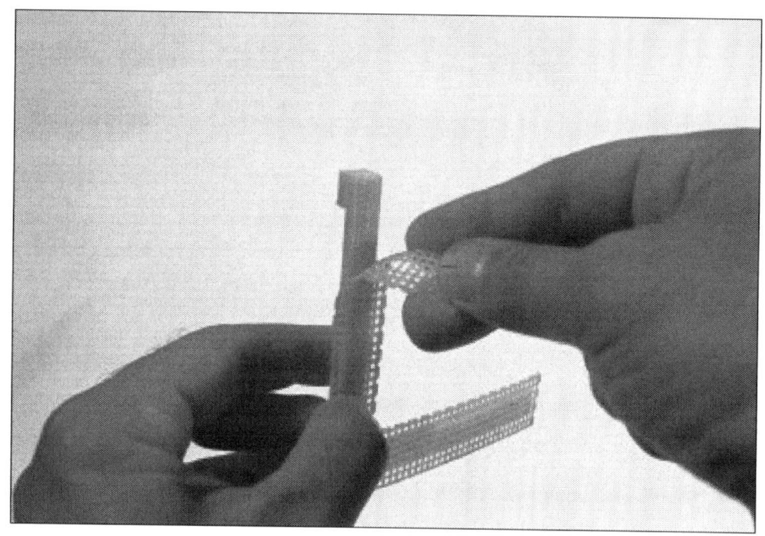

You should be able to print a successful ABS print without any warping on an unheated bed, using the rafting technique. Whether you are able to achieve this with the same **Raft Margin** value as the recipe sample or not will be determined by the ambient temperature of the printer's environment. The recipe sample was printed in a room with a temperature of 23 degrees Celsius. If you printed in a colder room, you might need a larger raft. If you are in a very warm room, you might not need a raft at all!

Drafts and the usage of a cooling fan mounted on an extruder can also affect the print. Remember, ABS cools very quickly. We don't need to accelerate it by keeping an extruder fan running.

Some other factors that can create warping involve a poor calibration of the nozzle and print bed height, inadequate hot-end temperature, and flow settings.

There's more...

One of the most successful tricks to control warping is using Kapton tape on glass and sanding the surface. To increase the holding power of the print even further, a brushing of the ABS glue can be applied. This can be easily made by putting small scraps of the ABS glue in a glass container filled with acetone. The ratio of the ABS glue and acetone is determined more by trial and error. The end consistency should be thin like ink rather than thick like paint. Acetone is a primary ingredient in most fingernail polish removers, but don't let this diminish the fact that it's a toxic chemical. Take care to protect your eyes, lungs, and skin!

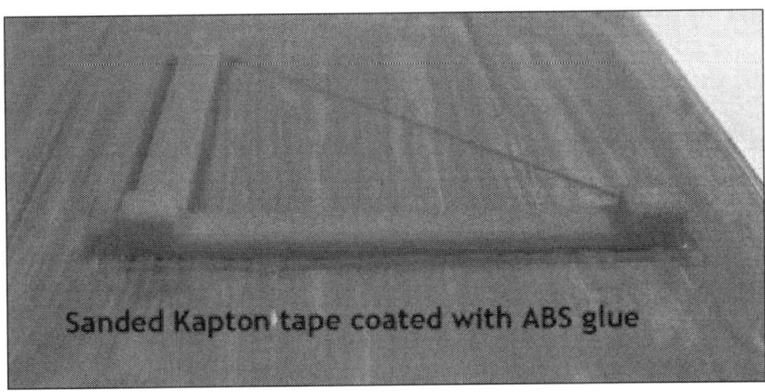

The object in the preceding example was printed without a heated bed. If heat was applied, a raft was activated, and the room was kept at a warm temperature, a properly calibrated RepRap printer would be able to yield some very large prints with minimal warping or, quite possibly, with no warping and cracking at all.

See also

- For more visual information on ABS-warping issues, visit
  `http://www.3dprintedsculpture.com/2012/05/warping-of-abs-prints.html`

Using brim with Slic3r

A form of rafting can be optioned in Slic3r, but it's not as robust as the rafting we can do with Skeinforge. We'll look at how we can use Slic3r's raft option along with brim to create a flange around the model for better adhesion to the build platform.

Getting ready

You'll need the warp test model we made in SketchUp and Slic3r to slice the model.

How to do it...

We will proceed as follows:

1. Open Slic3r. Under **Printer Settings** in **Support Material**, enter the value `1.0` in **Raft Layers**. This value determines how many layers of raft will be printed directly under the model.

2. Under **Options for support material and raft**, enter the value `2.0` in **Interface layers**. This value determines how many raft layers are printed that will allow better separation from the model during their removal.

3. Under **Printer Settings** in **Skirt and brim**, enter the value `8.0` in **Brim width**. This value determines how wide the first layer perimeter will be printed.

4. Slice and print the model.

How it works...

The raft option in Slic3r only generates the raft directly under the model. It doesn't expand outside of the model's perimeter in the same fashion in which Skeinforge's raft option works. However, the interface option in Slic3r does work similarly. It generates a layer that allows for easier removal from the model.

In order to create a form of raft that extends past the model's perimeter, we used an option called brim Refer the following image:.

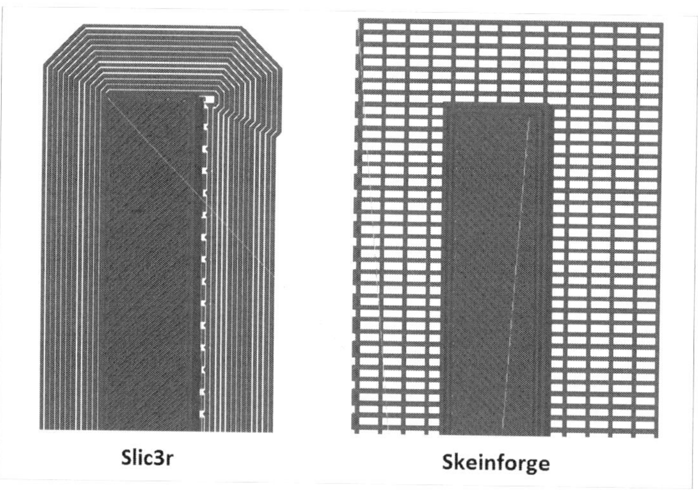

It is a one-layer flange that can be printed at any width outside of the model's perimeter. We can see this illustrated in the preceding image alongside the Skeinforge raft, which was generated in the previous recipe. The primary difference between these two is the strength. The Skeinforge cross hatches a raft with multiple layers. Slic3r can only generate one layer, which is printed with a radial pattern. This does not adhere to the model as well as the Skeinforge system.

Reviewing the print results

Remember all the versions we've made of the toy block? This also includes the toy block we made with SketchUp in this chapter. Here's a comparison of all the prints in the following image:

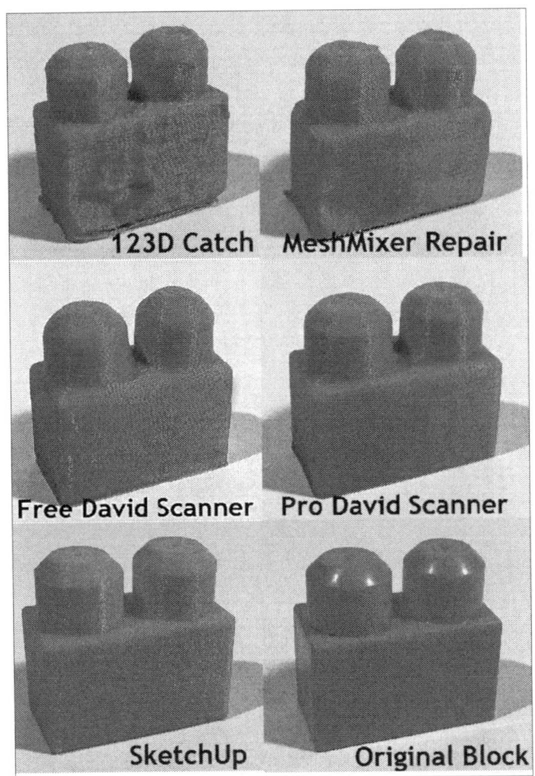

With each successive stage, we have made a better replication of the toy block. Our best result is the model we made with SketchUp. Not only is it better, but it was modeled faster and easier than the others. When mechanical- or geometric-based forms are needed, using a 3D modeling program such as SketchUp is the best solution.

5

Manipulating Meshes and Bridges

In this chapter, we will cover the following recipes:

- Exploring TopMod
- Using TopMod for remeshing
- Using MeshLab for remeshing
- Mesh decimation with MeshLab
- Wireframe modeling with TopMod
- Cooling ABS and PLA with Skeinforge
- Cooling ABS and PLA with Slic3r
- Adjusting speed with Slic3r
- Bridging with Slic3r
- Adjusting speed with Skeinforge
- Bridging with Skeinforge

Introduction

In this chapter, we'll look at some basic concepts about meshes, and how important these concepts can be while dealing with 3D modeling.

Most models that we'll use for 3D printing will have a surface mesh composed of three- or four-sided polygons. The number of polygons necessary to create a model will vary, depending on its detail and complexity. Only six polygons are necessary to create a cube, but for an elaborate organic form, the polygons can number in the millions.

For 3D printing, keeping an eye on the polygon count may be necessary. If the polygon count is too high, some 3D printing services may not be able to process your file. The most popular 3D printing service, **Shapeways,** has a limit of one million polygons for a model.

There may be instances when we may need to increase the polygon count of a model. This typically happens when we want to manipulate the surface of the mesh.

See *Chapter 2, Optimizing the Printing Process,* for surface manipulation using Meshmixer.

If we need to manipulate the surface mesh of a model made with SketchUp, one of the problems we might encounter is illustrated in the following image:

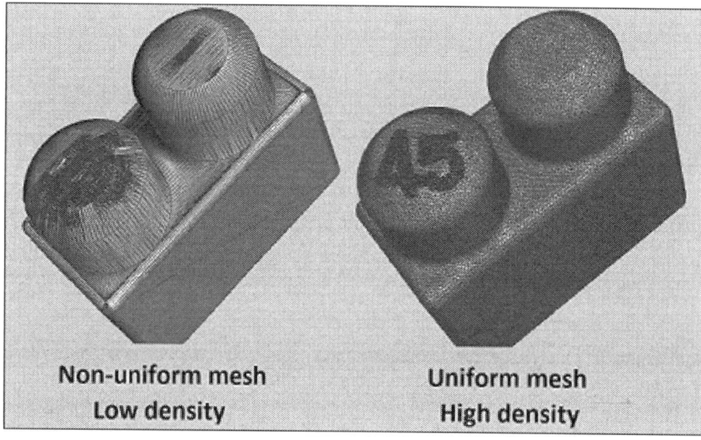

Inscribing the number 45 on the surface of the toy block creates a distorted surface of the non-uniform and low-density mesh. This can be seen in the following image with better clarity when the wire mesh is hidden:

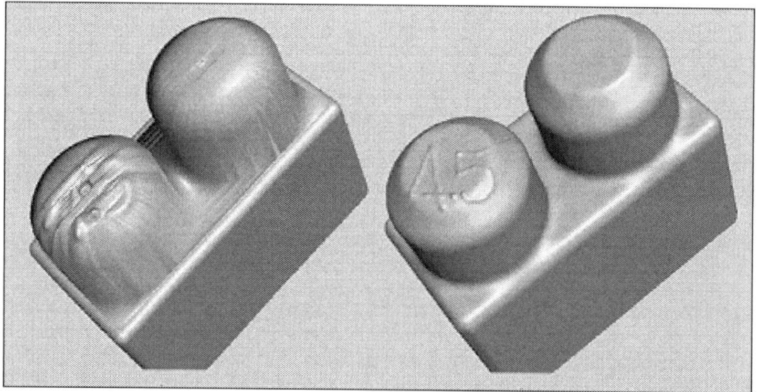

Only by subdividing the SketchUp model as a higher density mesh with more uniformity, was this problem solved. In this chapter, we'll learn how to use subdivision schemes to manipulate a mesh in higher and lower densities.

Exploring TopMod

TopMod was developed by a team at the Texas A&M Visualization Laboratory in the early 2000s. It hasn't been updated since 2007. The program is prone to crashing and you'll discover odd behavior as you work through the recipes. There's also very little information available on its use.

What makes this a program worth learning? You'll find that TopMod has an easy methodology for creating basic and complex forms that can be exported for further manipulation in programs such as Meshmixer and SketchUp. The forms you can create with TopMod will take considerably less effort than what can be accomplished in other 3D modeling programs.

Getting ready

You will need to download TopMod from `http://code.google.com/p/topmod/downloads/list` and follow the instructions for installation.

This book uses the last update of PyTopMod v2.223. It's available for both Windows and Mac operating systems. Information for using TopMod on Linux can be found at `https://code.google.com/p/topmod/issues/detail?id=2#c5`.

How to do it...

We will proceed as follows:

1. When you open TopMod, you'll have a toolbar at the top containing a series of icons. In this recipe, we'll be interested with the **Primitives** tray.

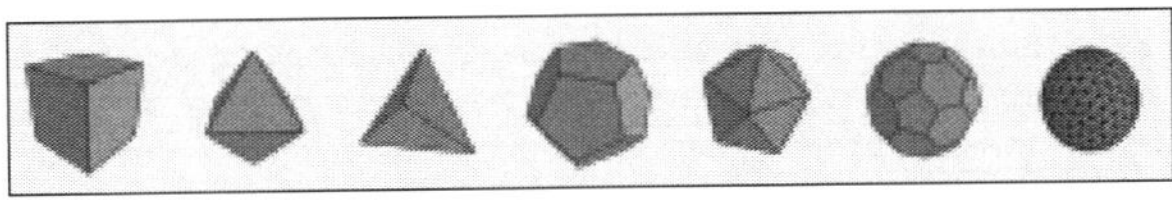

2. Left-click on each one using your mouse. Each icon will load only the primitives that are selected.

3. With one of the primitives loaded on the workspace, move the mouse wheel forward and back to zoom in and out of the model respectively.

4. Press and hold *Alt* on the keyboard and the mouse wheel. Moving the mouse will pan the model.

5. Press and hold *Alt* on the keyboard. By a left-click and hold, the model will orbit by moving your mouse.

6. Now load the cube and position with an isometric view on your workspace. Do this by using the keyboard shortcut (*F*) or go to the menu and select **Display** and then **Reset Camera**. Zoom in on the cube for a comfortable work size, as shown in the following screenshot:

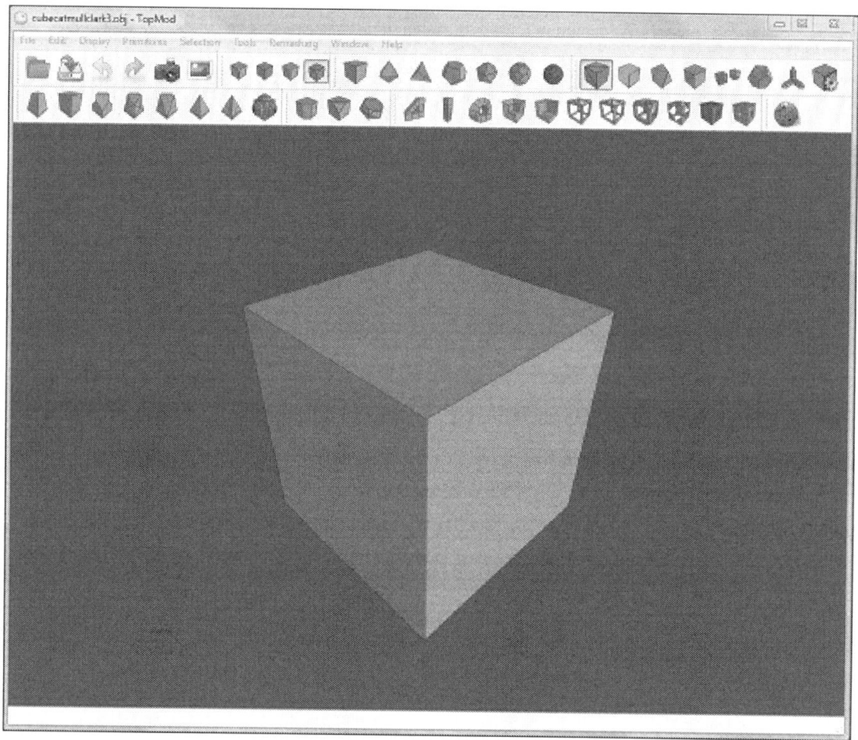

7. To view the model without the wireframe, use the keyboard shortcut (*W*) or go to the menu and select **Display**, and then deselect **Show Wireframe**.

8. Use the keyboard shortcut (*H*) or go to the menu and select **Display** and then select **Show Heads Up Display**. This will bring up a list of pertinent data concerning your model beneath the workspace.

9. Use the keyboard shortcut (*Ctrl + Shift + S*) or go to the menu and select **File** and **Save As**. Name the model cube and from the **Save as type** option, choose **Wavefront OBJ Files** (*obj), and click on **Save**.

How it works...

TopMod has an **Export** function under **File** that will export the mesh as an STL files. Sometimes TopMod is prone to crashing when exporting, and less when saving as an `.obj` file. It's best to save your work before exporting.

Using TopMod for remeshing

TopMod offers 36 different remeshing schemes and this makes the program valuable for this function alone. We're going to explore the most common schemes for subdividing surfaces into higher density meshes.

Getting ready

You'll need TopMod3D open with your cube loaded on your workspace and zoomed to a comfortable work size.

How to do it...

We will proceed as follows:

1. Go to the menu and select **Remeshing** and then **4-Conversion**. From the next tiled window, select **Catmull-Clark**. On the workspace, there is a floating **Tool Options** window. Select **Perform Remeshing**. Save the model with a filename: `cube_catmull_clark_1`.

2. Select **Perform Remeshing** again. Save the model with a filename: `cube_catmull _clark_2`.

3. Select **Perform Remeshing** for a third time. Save the model with a filename: `cube_catmull_clark_3`.

4. Select the undo icon from the toolbar. Continue to undo two more times until the model is reverted back to the cube.

5. Go to the menu and select **Remeshing** and then **4-Conversion**. From the next tiled window, select **Doo-Sabin**. From the **Tool Options** window, select **Perform Remeshing**. Save the model with a filename: `cube_doo_sabin_1`. Repeat two more times, like you did for the Catmull-Clark remeshes.

6. Select the cube primitive icon from the toolbar. Go to the menu and select **Remeshing** and then **3-Preservation**. From the next tiled window, select **Loop Subdivision**. From the **Tool Options** window, select **Perform Remeshing**. Save the model with a filename: `cube_loop_subdivision_1`. Repeat two more times, like you did for the Doo-Sabin remeshes.

How it works...

Catmull-Clark and Doo-Sabin are the first two subdivision schemes developed for polygonal modeling programs. They were developed independently in 1978 and both paved the way towards sophisticated 3D modeling and animation. The Loop scheme was developed later in 1987 and is also a popular subdivision scheme.

These three common schemes and all of the remaining schemes available in TopMod are basically different algorithms that implement a refinement of the mesh into a smoother topography.

By implementing and comparing the different schemes on a primitive, in this case a cube, we can visually observe the differences that different algorithms will produce.

In the following image, we can see three iterations of the Catmull-Clark remesh scheme of a cube composed of six four-sided polygons. This remesh algorithm is generally used when remeshing a model with four-sided polygons and produces more rounded shapes.

In the following image, we can see three iterations of the Doo-Sabin remesh scheme of a cube composed of six four-sided polygons. This remesh algorithm produces shapes that follow the original shape more closely than the Catmull-Clark scheme.

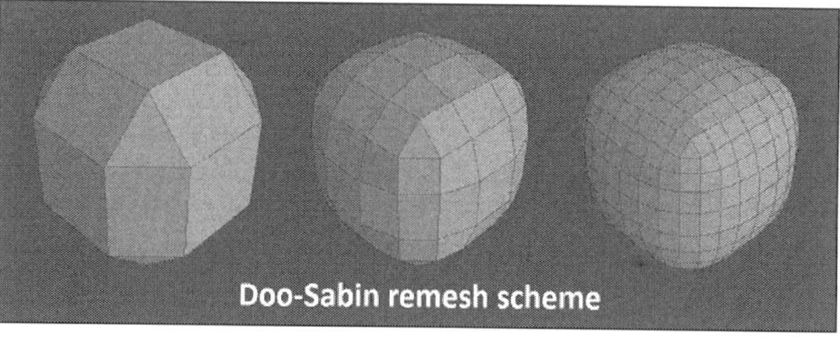

In the following image, we can see three iterations of the Loop subdivision remesh scheme of a cube composed of six four-sided polygons. This remesh algorithm is generally used when remeshing a model with a triangular mesh. It subdivides triangles into smaller triangles with better results than the quad-based schemes. In this example, it even did a better job than the other two remesh schemes in following the mesh of the original shape.

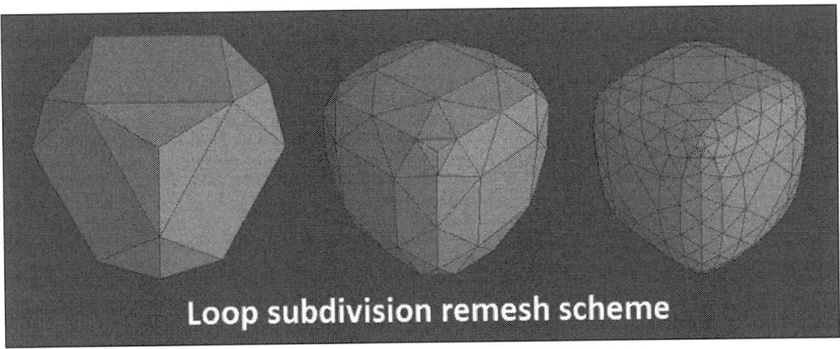

Using MeshLab for remeshing

MeshLab offers a variety of remesh schemes. Some of these schemes offer better control than their counterpart in TopMod. Because of these control options, it's the best program for remeshing 3D models made with SketchUp. In this next recipe, we're going to learn how to subdivide the surface of a SketchUp model into a uniform high-density mesh. This will be important for working through the next two recipes.

Getting ready

You'll need MeshLab. If you didn't download it in *Chapter 3, Scanning and Printing with a Higher Resolution*, then you'll need to from `http://meshlab.sourceforge.net/`. You'll also need the toy block model you made with SketchUp in *Chapter 4, Modeling and Printing with Precision*.

How to do it...

We will proceed as follows:

1. Select the **Import Mesh** icon on the toolbar. Open the model of the toy block you made in SketchUp Make, as shown in the following screenshot. The default view is **Flat**. Choose the **Flat Lines** icon on the toolbar.

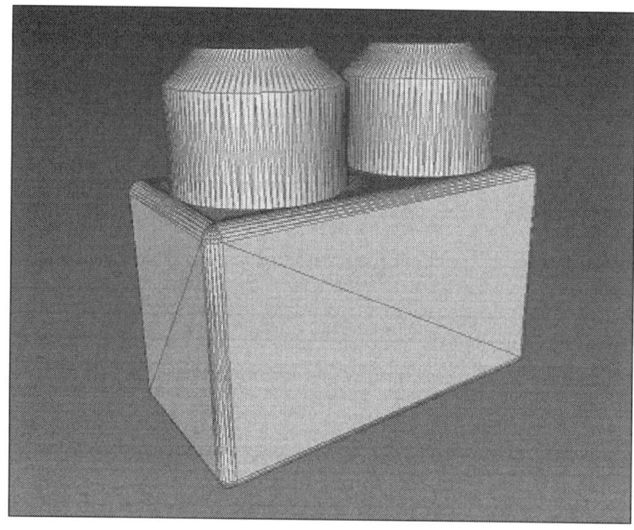

2. Go to **Filters** and select **Remeshing, Simplification,** and **Reconstruction**. Scroll down the next cascaded window and select **Uniform Mesh Resampling**.

3. A pop-up window appears. Start with the default values and select **Apply**. When the filter is complete, close the window.

4. Select **Export Mesh** and save it as an `.obj` file. Keep the model loaded on your screen.

5. Go back to **Filters** and select **Remeshing, Simplification,** and **Reconstruction**. Scroll down the next cascaded window and select **Subdivision Surfaces: LS3**.

6. A pop-up window appears. Start with the default values, except change **Weighting scheme** from **Loop** to **Enhance regularity**. Select **Apply**. When the filter is complete, close the window.

7. Select **Export Mesh** and save it as an `.obj` file.

How it works...

When we remeshed the toy block with **Uniform Mesh Resampling**, we took the SketchUp model, which consisted of 13,738 faces and created a uniform mesh consisting of 10,708 faces. By doing this, we also lost some of the detail of the model and created distortion along the circumference of the cylinders, as shown in the following image:

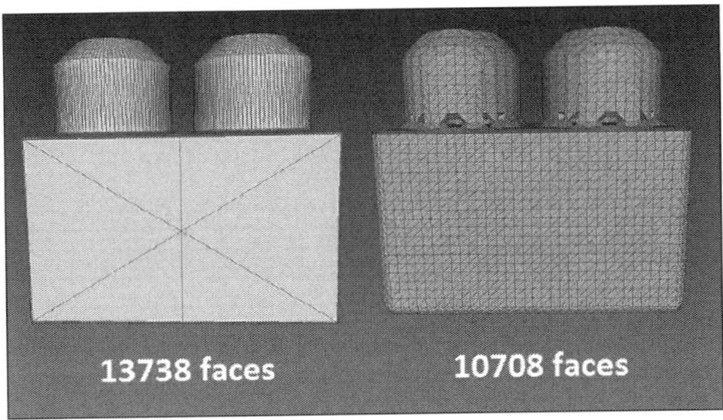

If we want a higher resolution without distortion, we will have to increase our mesh density. We can do this by lowering the default value `2.000` in **Precision (abs and %)** to `0.250`. This will increase the total number of faces to 6,45,696.

In the following image, we can see that our mesh still has polygons with unequal proportions:

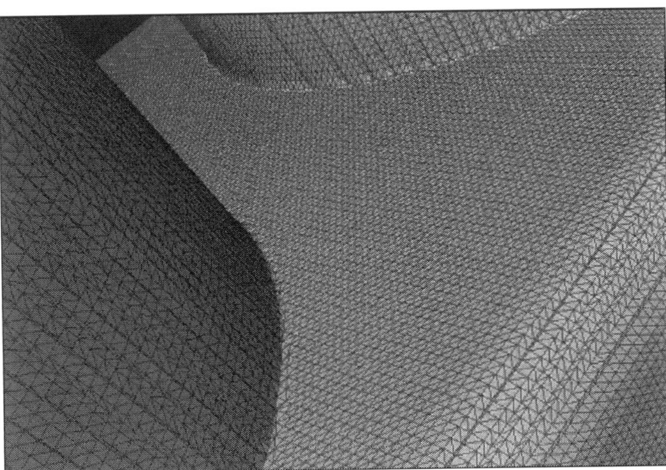

To equalize the mesh even further, we used **Subdivision Surfaces: LS3** and changed the **Weighting scheme** from **Loop** to **Enhance regularity**. This gave us an even better mesh with uniform polygons as shown in the following image:

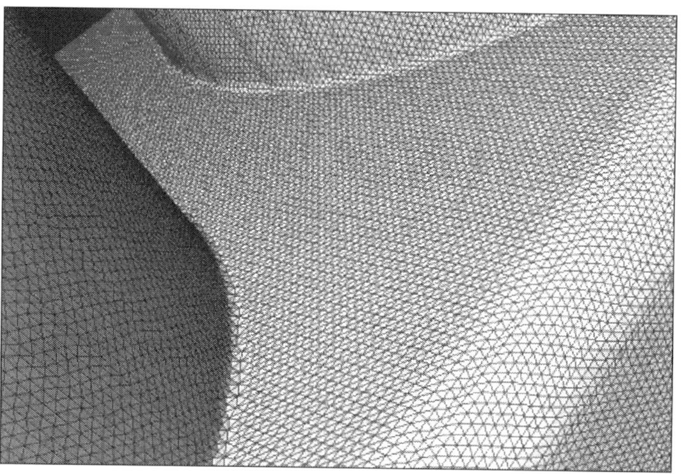

There's more...

MeshLab is prone to crashing when multiple schemes or filters are used sequentially in a workflow. Because of this, it's best to save the model after each filter is applied and reopen the saved model for further manipulation. Sometimes, this method is the only approach to observe a visual change on the workspace.

In the following example, a model has been remeshed, but the visual representation on screen has been superimposed with both old and new meshes. Only by reloading the 3D file will the superimposition disappear. Occasionally, selecting the **Reload** icon will make this task easier, but it's not always dependable.

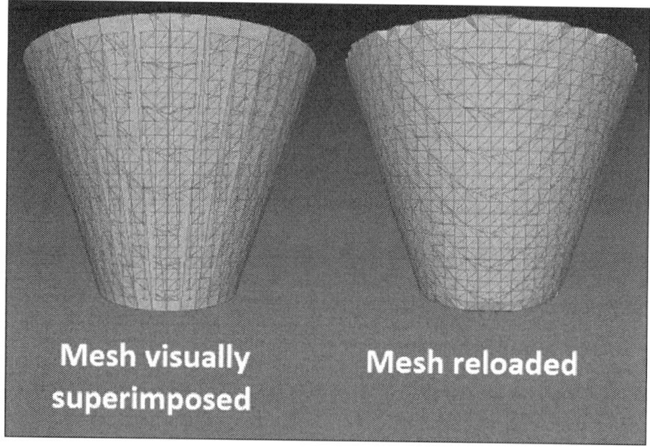

Mesh decimation with MeshLab

In the preceding recipe, we learned how to increase the density of our mesh. Sometimes, we need to do the exact opposite. We're going to learn how to decimate a high-density mesh to a uniform low-density mesh in this recipe.

Getting ready

You'll need MeshLab. You'll also need the `.obj` file of the toy block. This is the model with a uniform mesh that you made in the last recipe.

How to do it...

We will proceed as follows:

1. Select the **Import Mesh** icon on the toolbar. Open the `block_uniform_remesh_LS3.obj` file and choose the **Flat Lines** icon on the toolbar.

2. Go to **Filters** and select **Remeshing, Simplification, and Reconstruction**. Scroll down the next cascaded window and select **Quadric Edge Collapse Decimation**.

3. A pop-up window appears. Check mark **Planar Simplification** and change the **Quality threshold** to `1.0`. The target number of faces for this model is 59,791. The default value is always half of the model's total face count. Select **Apply Export Mesh** and save the file as `block_decimation_59791.obj`.

4. Select the **New Empty Project** icon and then the **Import Mesh** icon on the toolbar. Also choose the **Flat Lines** icon to observe the mesh. Open `block_decimation_59791.obj`. The default target number of faces is 29,895. Select **Apply Export Mesh** and save the file as `block_decimation_29895.obj`.

5. Continue decimating the block until you reach about 950 to 1,000 faces and save your files.

How it works...

When you first open the **Quadric Edge Collapse Decimation** filter, the default value in **Target number of faces** is half of the number of faces of your loaded model. For our recipe experiment, we started with this number and continued to decrease our mesh by half. Each time we saved and reloaded our model. Once again, MeshLab is prone to crashes and continually saving the model is simply a measure of good habit.

For this particular model, we checked **Planar Simplification**. This added constraints to the simplification, which helped in keeping the large planar surfaces of the model intact from distortion. This may not be good for other type of models.

We can see a comparison between two mesh decimations in the following image:

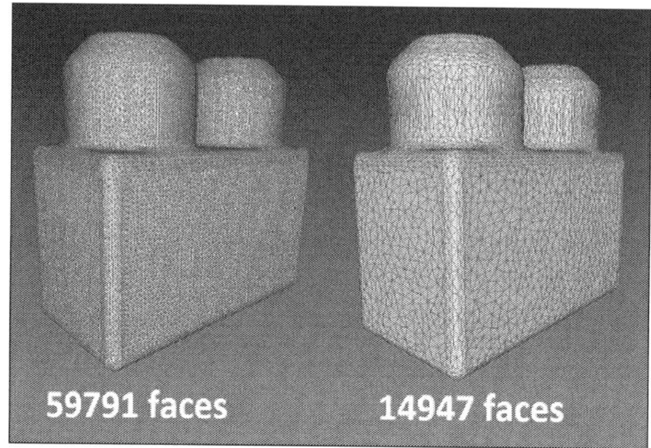

In the following image, we can see a continuation of the mesh decimation. The final toy block has 934 faces and the faces are fairly even, weighted by size:

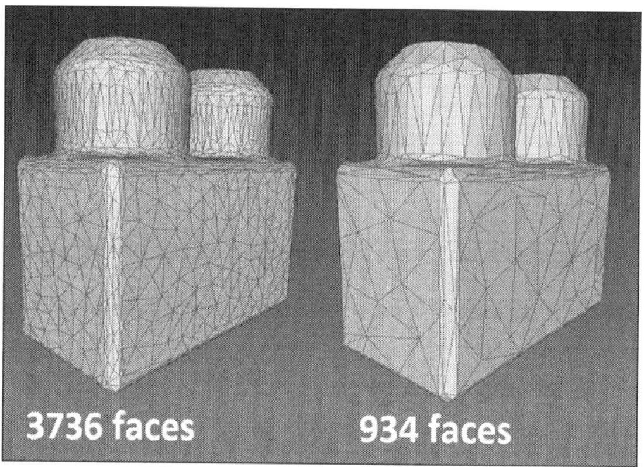

There's more...

Saving and reloading our model was a safe method to avoid a possible loss of work, but there is also another factor to consider. By making a direct reduction to the smallest polygon count, we might end up with a model that is slightly inferior in quality in comparison to a model that's decimated with a gradual reduction.

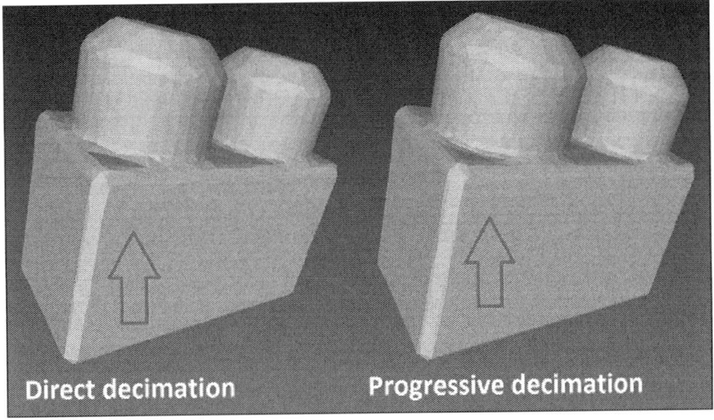

You can see some distortion in the edge of the toy block from the directly applied decimation.

Wireframe modeling with TopMod

Two of the exciting features of TopMod are the wireframe and column modeling modes. With these tools, we can make a 3D model by converting each edge of a polygon mesh into a 3D pipe. This will translate the structure of our mesh into a fully formed 3D model that's watertight and is possible to 3D print.

In the past two recipes, we did a lot of work increasing and decreasing the number of polygons in a model. We'll see how this is important when we use the wireframe modeling tool with the model of the toy block.

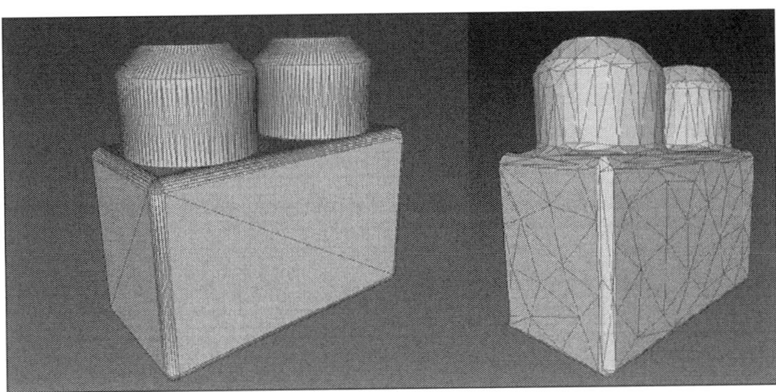

It's fairly easy to see in the preceding comparison, what would happen if we were to make a 3D pipe with each polygon edge in the toy block on the left. The edges of the block and the two dowels on top would be a jumbled mass of 3D pipes. The model we manipulated with subdivision schemes will make a more uniform structure of 3D pipes.

In this recipe, we will use wireframe and column tools to make some test models to test the concept of bridging, later in this chapter.

Getting ready

You'll need to open a workspace in TopMod. You'll also need to load the lowest-decimated block file you made in the last recipe.

How to do it...

First, we'll create our test models from a cube and then proceed as follows:

1. Go to the menu and select the **Cube Primitive** icon. Once you have it sized on your workspace, choose the **Wireframe Modeling Mode** icon [⬦]. There are two similar icons. Choose the one on the left. At the floating **Tool Options** window, keep the default value `0.250`. Select **Create Wireframe** and save the model as `wireframe _model_default.obj`. Keep the model loaded on the workspace.

2. Select **Undo** from the menu.

3. Choose the **Wireframe Modeling Mode 2** icon. This time, choose the one on the right. At the **Tool Options** window, keep the default value `0.250` for **Width** and change the default value `0.250` in **Thickness** to `0.740`. Select **Create Wireframe** and save the model as `wireframe_model_thick.obj`. Keep the model loaded on the workspace.

4. Select **Undo** from the menu.

5. Choose the **Wireframe Modeling Mode 2** icon. At the **Tool Options** window, change the default value `0.250` for **Width** to `0.750` and change back the **Thickness** value to the default value `0.250`. Select **Create Wireframe** and save the model as `wireframe_model_wide.obj`.

6. Now, we'll work with our toy block. Go to the **File** icon and open the `.obj` file of your lowest decimated saves of the toy block.

7. Go to the menu and select **Remeshing** and then **3-Conversion**. From the next tiled window, select **Vertex Truncation**. On the workspace, there's a floating **Tool Options** window. Change the default value `0.250` in **Offset** to `0.500`. Select **Perform Remeshing** and save the model with a filename (maybe use a name such as `block_vertex_truncated.obj`). Don't close out the model from your desktop.

8. Go to the menu and select the **Wireframe Modeling Mode** icon from the **Tool Options** window and change the default value 0.250 in **Width** to 1.0 Select **Perform Remeshing**, save the model, and close out.

How it works...

When we used the wireframe-modeling tool, we made a three-sided polygon of each edge of our mesh. As we can see with our recipe experiments, we have a lot of control over the shape of this polygon by controlling the dimension of its width and thickness. The following image shows the different shapes of the polygon:

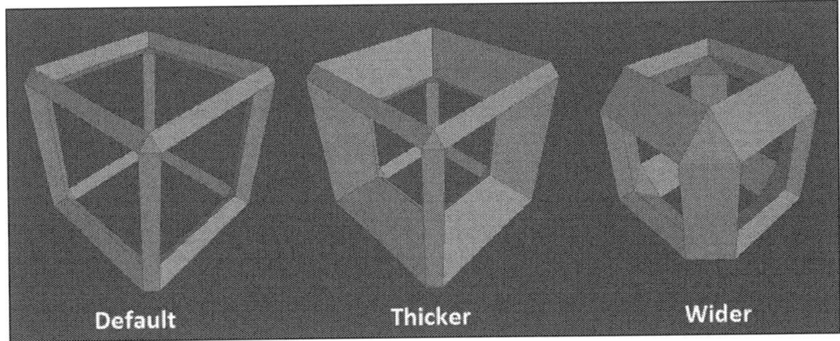

There are varieties of mesh schemes that can give us interesting mesh patterns. Sometimes the results can be very subtle, for example, when we compare the vertex truncation and honeycomb schemes. On the toy block, if you follow the diagonal line from the bottom-left corner moving up to the top-right corner on both meshes, you can see that the vertex truncation mesh is smoother in comparison to the honeycomb mesh, as shown in the following image:

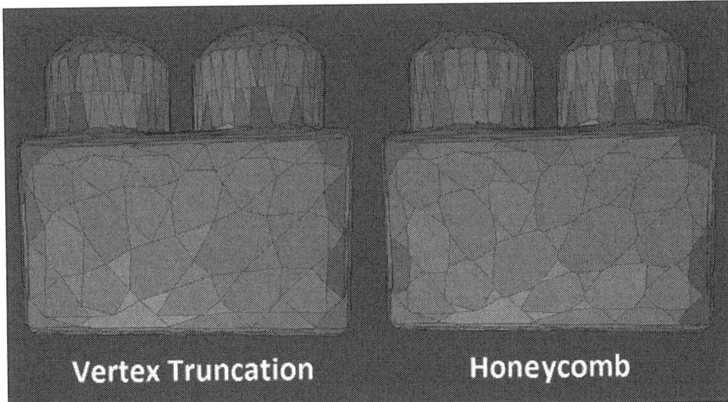

Sometimes the choice of mesh can be instrumental in giving us a structure that works well with the wireframe mode, or simply be for aesthetic reasons, as shown in the following image:

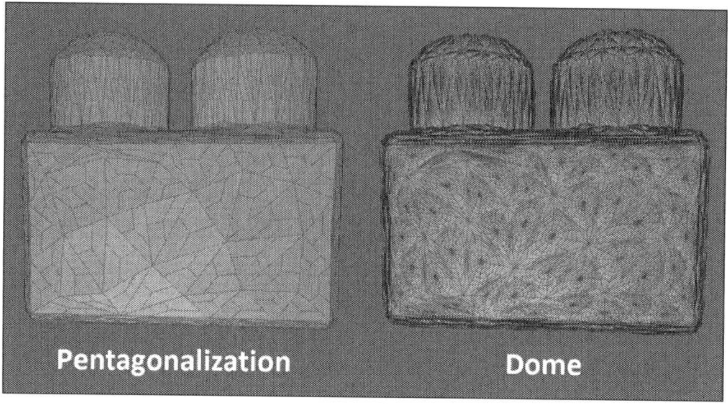

The choice to use the vertex truncated mesh for the toy block was made because it created an interesting pattern that would translate well with the wireframe modeling tool. The following image shows the comparison between the loop and vertex truncated mesh:

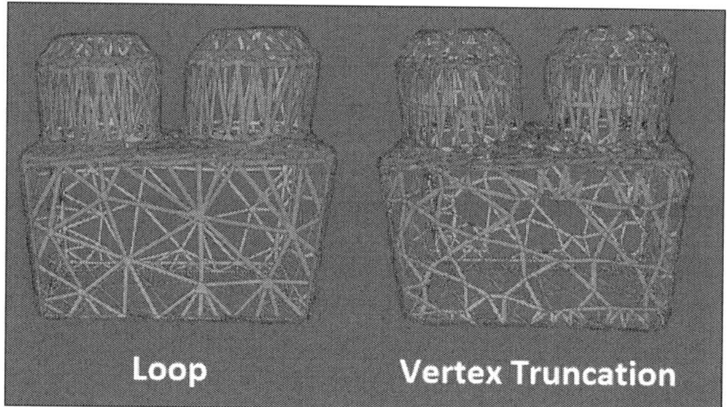

There's a lot of room for exploring here. Depending on the form of the model and the manner in which the mesh is structured, there are many possibilities for very interesting results.

There's more...

The **Column Modeling** mode, displayed by the icon [◉], is another way to create a 3D pipe of each edge of a polygon-based mesh. The wireframe gave us a three-sided polygon, whereas the column mesh gives us four sides or more. With this tool, by generating a high number of sides, we can create a cylinder from each edge.

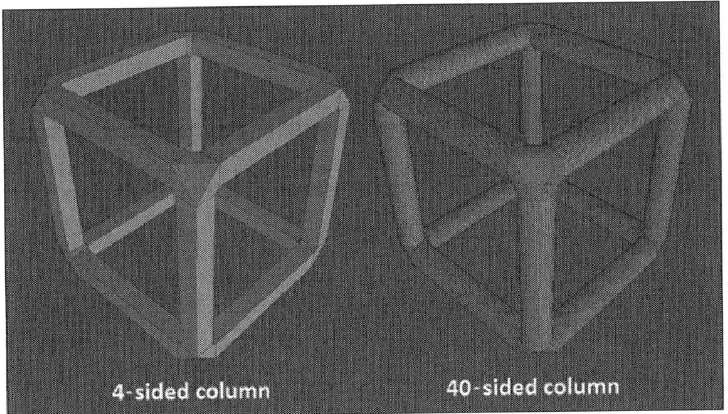

Let's print!

In the following recipes, we are going to experiment with a printing technique called bridging. Bridging is a term that is used to describe a situation when a printer extrudes filament over a gap by spanning two points. The wider the two sides, the harder it is to maintain a layer that does not droop or fall when successive layers are placed on top. We can see this illustrated in the following image:

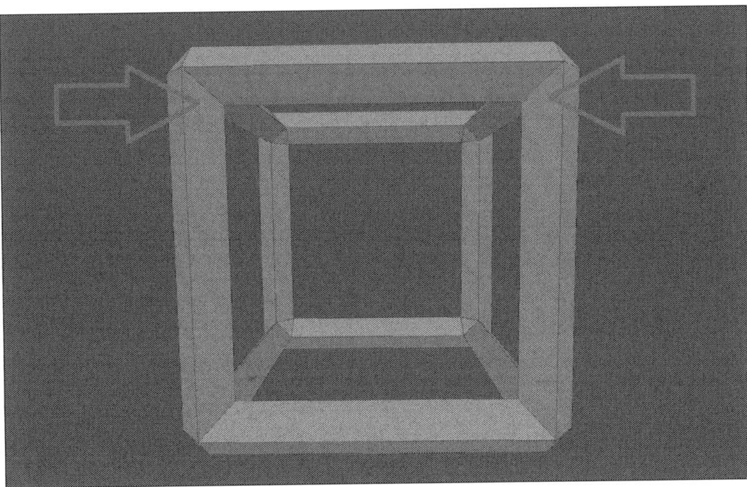

The cube we made in TopMod using the wireframe tool has an area to bridge from each post. The first layers must span this distance without sagging and also with enough strength to carry the load of successive layers.

Controlling speed is an important function of bridging. In Skeinforge and Slic3r, there are options that control the general speed of the printer and more specialized options that adjust the printer's speed for areas that require bridging. We'll take a look at some of these options in the following recipes.

For bridging to be successful, we first must have a good control of the cooling process of our printing. We'll look at cooling procedures with both Skeinforge and Slic3r before we move onto bridging techniques.

Cooling ABS and PLA with Skeinforge

Before we begin this recipe, let's first look at what happens with a test model when we don't use cooling methods. Keep in mind, that the rate of cooling is also affected by the ambient temperature of the build environment, and also how well you set your extrusion temperature for the material you are using.

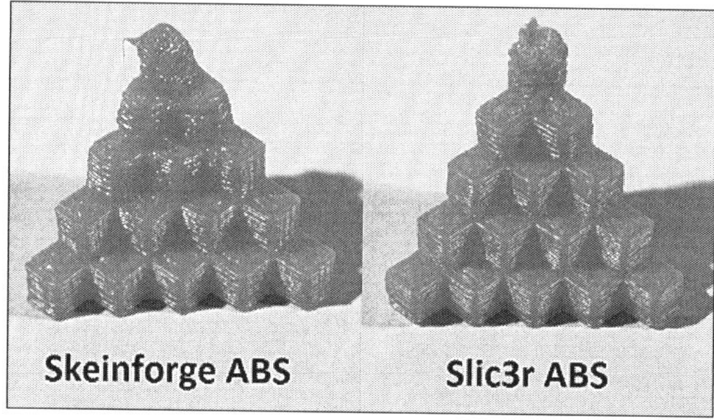

In the preceding and the following image, we can see the result of using ABS and PLA filament to print the model without any cooling setting with the slicer:

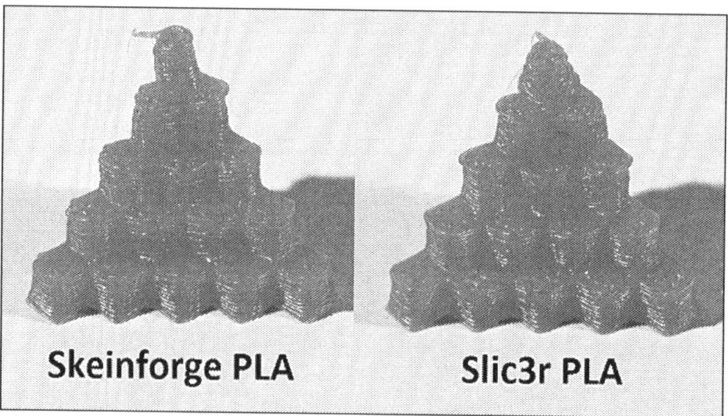

We can clearly see that with both slicers, we have a problem with cooling at the top with both ABS and PLA filament. When printing with PLA, it's common to utilize a fan to cool the extrusion. We can see how much effect adding a fan can produce by keeping the cooling features OFF on slicer and printing with only a fan blowing.

There's a slight distortion of the last step on the model, but it's almost perfect. With all of the following recipes, we'll use a fan when printing with PLA, unless noted in the recipe.

Getting ready

You'll need Skeinforge and ABS and PLA filament. You'll also need two calibration models that you can download from Thingiverse. They are as follows:

- **5mm Calibration Cube Steps** (`www.thingiverse.com/thing:24238`)
- **Small Calibration Pyramid** (`www.thingiverse.com/thing:22340`)

How to do it...

We'll start by running a few tests with the cube step calibration model and proceed as follows:

1. Slice and print the **5mm Calibration Cube Steps** using the default settings.
2. In Skeinforge, open the **Cool** plugin under **Craft**. Change the **Minimum Layer Time (seconds)** from the default value `15.0` to `5.0`. Slice and print the model in ABS.
3. In Skeinforge, change the **Minimum Layer Time (seconds)** back to the default value `15.0` and change the **Cool Type** to **Orbit**. Slice and print the model in ABS.

4. Now we'll slice a quick test using the small pyramid. In Skeinforge, change the **Minimum Layer Time (seconds)** from the default value 15.0 back to 5.0. Slice and print the pyramid calibration in ABS.

5. Repeat the previous steps using PLA. Keep all the same values, but check mark the box for **Turn Fan ON** in the beginning.

How it works...

Both ABS and PLA models printed well when we activated the default settings of the Cool plugin; this is shown in the following image:

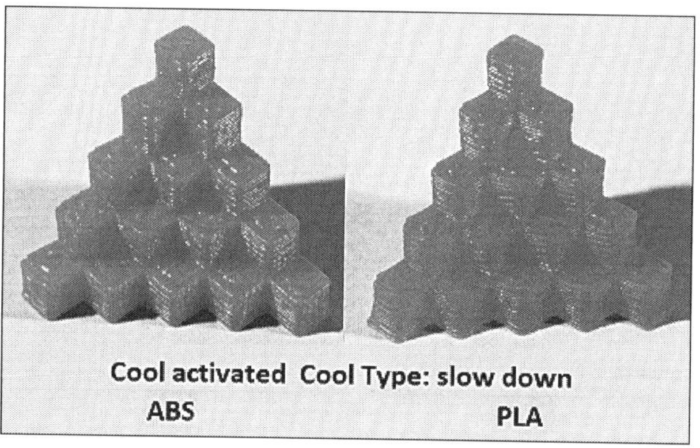

Cool activated Cool Type: slow down
ABS   PLA

Orbit is a cooling type that utilizes the time it takes the extruder to orbit around a layer from a slight distance to give the layer more time to cool down. When we changed the cool type to orbit, we developed a problem of the filament ooze creating a distortion on the model. The final result of using orbit is not worth the effort in creating a profile that will work well with this method, as shown in the following image:

Skeinforge cool activated
Cool type: orbit
ABS

In the recipe, we can adjust the time when the slowdown will activate by adjusting the minimum layer time. In this case, we lowered the default setting of 15 seconds to 5 seconds. This will activate the slowdown starting with any layer that takes 5 seconds or less to print.

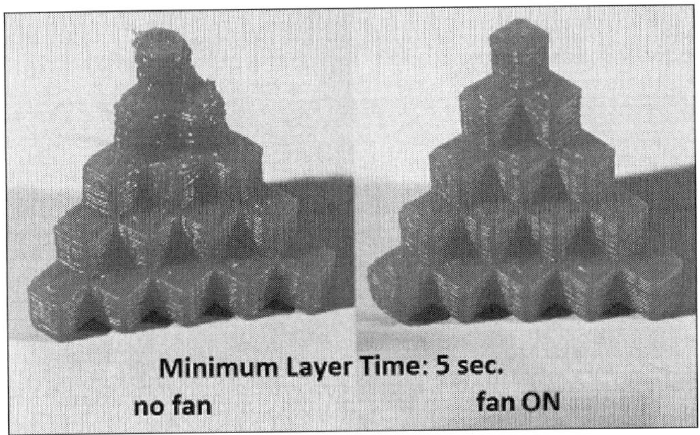

The result didn't work well with ABS unless we activated a fan. In this case, why bother? The main reason is to save time. The default ABS model took 18 minutes 14 seconds to print. When we set the minimum layer time lower, we saved time; it took only 11 minutes and 20 seconds to print.

Unfortunately, Skeinforge only allows a fan to be turned ON at the beginning of a print run and OFF at its end. For ABS printing, this wouldn't be good in most cases.

There's more...

There is a method of controlling when a fan is commissioned during a print run by editing the G-code. This can be accomplished by using a text editor and opening the G-code that Skeinforge created.

```
G1 X16.891 Y52.804 E16.85589
G1 X16.891 Y53.739 E16.92783
G1 X18.761 Y55.609 E17.13132
G1 X17.826 Y55.609 E17.20326
G1 X16.891 Y54.674 E17.30502
G1 X16.891 Y55.609 E17.37697
M106 S255
G1 F1800.000 E16.37697
G92 E0
G1 Z0.750 F7800.000
G1 X19.992 Y52.508
G1 F1800.000 E1.00000
G1 X19.992 Y47.492 F600.000 E1.34678
G1 X25.008 Y47.492 E1.69355
G1 X25.008 Y52.508 E2.04033
G1 X20.070 Y52.508 E2.38171
```

By adding `M106 s255` (the `s` value can be from `1` to `255`; it determines the fan's speed) towards the last quarter of the code, this will turn the fan ON much later in the print run.

> For more detailed information about using G-code commands, see *Appendix B, Taking a Closer Look at G-code*.

Cooling ABS and PLA with Slic3r

In this recipe, we'll run some tests to see how well Slic3r works with cooling procedures.

Getting ready

You'll need Slic3r and ABS and PLA filament. You'll also need the same calibration models that you downloaded in the previous recipe.

How to do it...

We'll start by running a few tests with the cube step calibration model and proceed as follows:

1. Slice and print the **5mm Calibration Cube Steps** using the default settings.

2. In Slic3r, go to **Filament** under **Filament Settings** and change the **Extrusion multiplier** from the default value `1` to `0.8`. Slice and print the model in PLA.

3. In Slic3r, go to **Cooling** under **Filament Settings** and change the **Slowdown if layer print is below** from the default value of `30` to `5.0`. Slice and print the model in PLA.

4. Now we'll slice a quick test using the small pyramid. Slice and print the calibration pyramid in PLA with the current settings.

5. Repeat the previous steps using ABS, except change the default value `1` in **Disable fan for the first** to `100`.

How it works...

Enabling cooling in Slic3r helps, but still falls short when using default settings for printing ABS. There's still slight distortion on the PLA model, as shown in the following image:

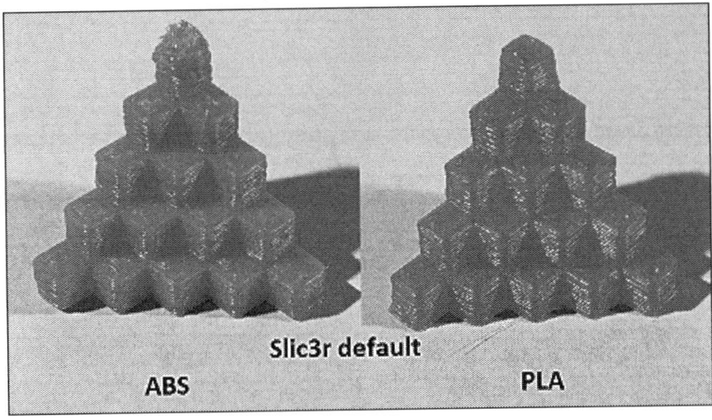

As we've seen in the past few chapters, decreasing the extrusion multiplier from its default value down to 0.8 helps in making a better print.

Slic3r utilizes a slowdown method of cooling. Like Skeinforge, the time when the slowdown activates can be controlled by the length of time it takes to print a layer.

There are better fan control options with Slic3r. This is useful when the continuous use of a fan is undesirable. For example, when printing with ABS, the fan can be disabled for the first printing layers by designating a layer count in the **Disable fan for first** option. This will keep the fan OFF for the initial print layers and activate ON when cooling is needed at the top of the print.

Adjusting speed with Slic3r

In this recipe, we'll test how far you can push your printer's speed before it affects the quality of the print. We'll do this by adjusting parameters in Slic3r.

Getting ready

Using a small cube as a test object will be an efficient method for this recipe. You can make a cube 20 mm x 20 mm x 20 mm in SketchUp or download the calibration cube collection from Thingiverse. This can be found at http://www.thingiverse.com/thing:56671.

How to do it...

We will proceed as follows:

1. Go to **Print Settings** and select **Speed**. Make sure the **Perimeters** speed is set at 30 mm/s.

2. Now set the **Infill** speed to 60 mm/s. Slice and print the 20 mm cube.

3. Go back to **Speed** in the **Print Settings** option. Change the **Infill** speed from 60 mm/s to 180 mm/s. Slice and print the 20 mm cube.

4. Now keep the **Infill** at 180 mm/s and change the **Perimeters** speed from 30 mm/s to 60 mm/s. Slice and print the 20 mm cube.

5. Go back and change the **Perimeters** speed from 60 mm/s to 120 mm/s. Slice and print the 20 mm cube.

How it works...

The ability to increase the infill speed helps in reducing the overall print time. Even with degradation of the interior infill, we're able to increase the infill up to 180 mm/s and maintain a good exterior surface of the print. We can see this illustrated in the following image:

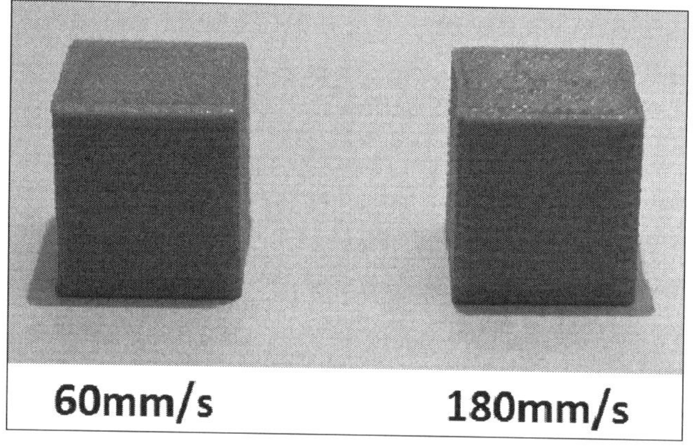

Keep in mind though, that the default speed for the perimeter was kept at 30 mm/s.

When we increase the perimeter speed, we can see a severe degradation of the model's surface. We can see this illustrated in the following image:

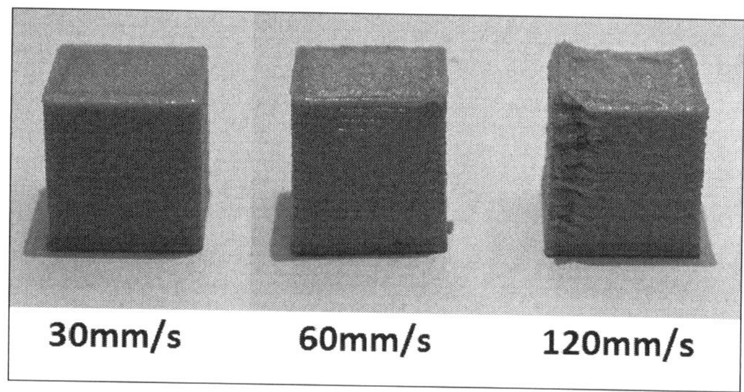

By adjusting both infill and perimeter speeds, the overall print time can be decreased, but it's best to keep the speed on the low end, if a finer surface detail is required. In the next recipe, we'll see how speed can be adjusted for only specific areas that require bridging.

Bridging with Slic3r

Slic3r is generally known to perform better bridging methods than Skeinforge. As we'll see in the following recipes, this holds true. We'll see how easy it is to achieve decent results printing a bridge 50 mm across!

First, we'll look at layer height. As we can see in the following example, a lower-print layer will generally give a better result:

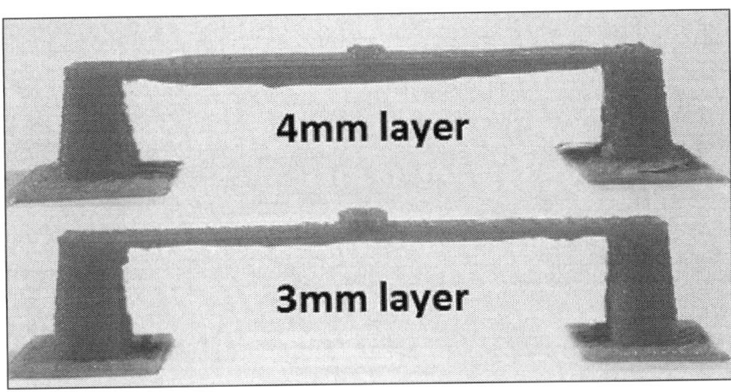

For this reason, we'll be printing the following tests in this recipe with a 3 mm layer.

We'll also be experimenting with both ABS and PLA filament. Keep in mind that the filament isn't consistent in grade and the results may vary.

Getting ready

You'll need Slic3r and ABS and PLA filament. You'll also need to download the **Bridge Torture Test** from `www.thingiverse.com/thing:12925`. You'll also need the cube you made in the *Wireframe modeling with TopMod* recipe.

How to do it...

We will proceed as follows:

1. Slice and print the **Bridge Torture Test** and cube using PLA and the default settings with your best cooling settings.

2. Under **Print Settings** in **Speed**, change the default value 60 in **Bridges** to 30 mm/s. Slice and print **Bridge Torture Test**.

3. Under **Print Settings** in **Speed**, change the value 30 in **Bridges** to 10 mm/s. Slice and print **Bridge Torture Test**.

4. Under **Print Settings** in **Speed**, keep the present values and change the value 60 in **Infill** to 30 mm/s. Slice and print **Bridge Torture Test**.

5. Repeat the previous steps using ABS, except, in **Cooling**, change the default value 1 in **Disable fan for the first** to 100.

How it works...

Slic3r works well with default settings. When we slowed the bridging speed, we actually worsen the results. By slowing the infill speed, we gained back some of the good quality. This is a good example of how changing the speed of different aspects of the printing process can make a significant change in the results. Every model will have a unique signature that will require a tweaking of slicer profiles to obtain perfect results, as shown in the following image:

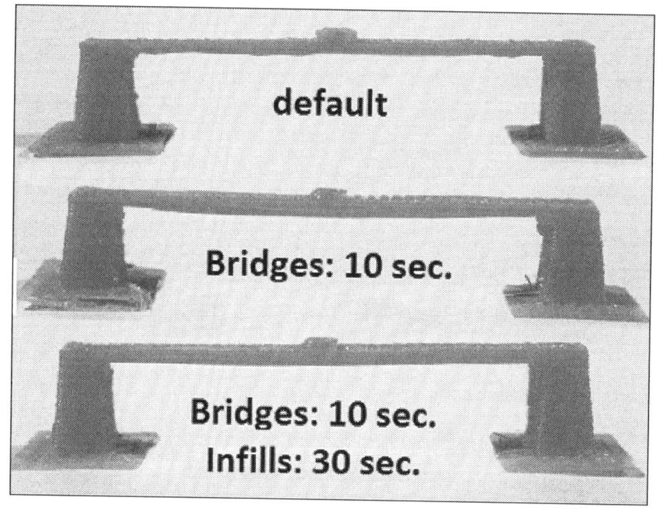

Adjusting speed with Skeinforge

In this recipe, we'll make the speed adjustments in both infill and perimeter. We'll find the similar results that were achieved with Slic3r are possible with Skeinforge as well. However, the slicer control settings are different. Skeinforge uses a feed and flow rate ratio to determine a speed. We'll find this isn't that difficult to master in this recipe.

Getting ready

You'll need the same test cube we use for the Slic3r recipe.

How to do it...

We will proceed as follows:

1. First, we'll set the overall printing speed. In the **Speed** tab, make sure the value in both **Feed Rate mm/s** and **Flow Rate Setting (float)** is set at 32.0. Slice the cube and print.

2. Go back and change **Feed Rate mm/s** and **Flow Rate Setting (float)** value from 32.0 to 64.0. Slice and print.

3. Go back and change **Feed Rate mm/s** and **Flow Rate Setting (float)** value from 64.0 to 120.0. Slice and print.

4. Now we're going to change the perimeter print speed. Keep the feed and flow rates at 120.0 mm/s and change **Perimeter Feed Rate Multiplier (ratio)** and **Perimeter Flow Rate Multiplier (ratio)** from the default value 0.8 to 0.4. Slice the cube and print.

5. Go back and change the perimeter feed and flow to 0.2. Slice the cube and print.

How it works...

The following image shows the amount of distortion that can generate by increasing the speed two times and three times the original value in Skeinforge:

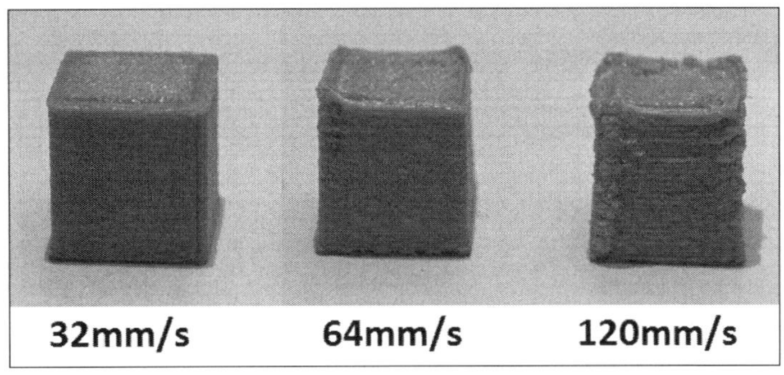

As with Slic3r, a method of retaining surface resolution is to keep the infill speed high and the more important perimeter lines at a lower print speed. We can see the results illustrated in the following image:

The default perimeter feed to flow ratio is 0.8, which is a 20 percent reduction in speed. By decreasing the ratio value, we decreased the perimeter speed even more.

Bridging with Skeinforge

Skeinforge is more difficult to build a profile for bridging. We'll discover this first hand in this recipe. However, let's look at how temperature can affect the quality of a bridge. In the following example, we have an ABS series of bridges printed with a default temperature and 15 degree Celsius higher and lower:

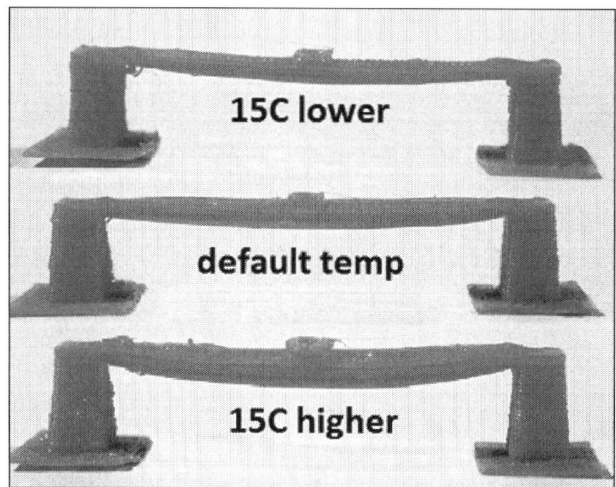

As we can see, by lowering the temperature, we gained a better bridge. Caution must be exercised when lowering the temperature. Outside of the obvious reasons, such as extruder jamming, we also have to take into consideration the bonding quality of the layers. If the filament is too cool when bridging, the first layers may not bond together. This can be seen in the following image:

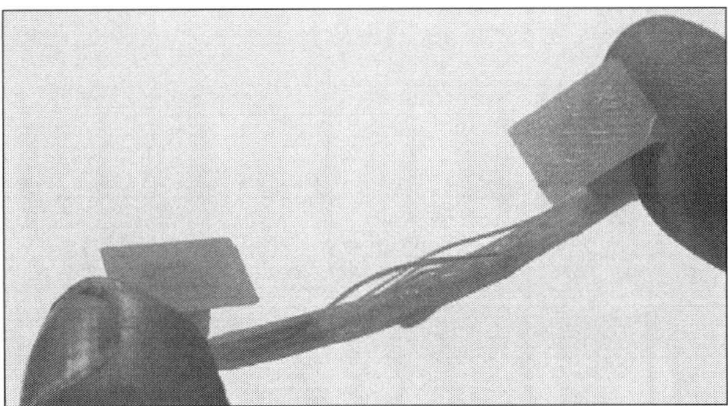

In the following recipes, the temperature will be lowered by 15 degree Celsius from its normal operating temperature.

Getting ready

You'll need Slic3r and ABS and PLA filament. You'll also need to download the **Bridge Torture Test** from www.thingiverse.com/thing:12925. You'll also need the cube you made in the *Wireframe modeling with TopMod* recipe.

How to do it...

We'll proceed as follows:

1. Slice and print **Bridge Torture Test** and cube using PLA and the default settings with your best cooling settings.

2. Select the **Speed** plugin, change the default value 1.0 in **Bridge Flow Rate Multiplier** to 0.8. Slice and print **Bridge Torture Test**.

3. Select the **Speed** plugin, change the value 0.8 in **Bridge Flow Rate Multiplier** to 0.6. Slice and print **Bridge Torture Test**.

4. Repeat the previous steps using ABS, except, in **Cooling**, make sure the fan is set to **OFF**.

How it works...

Skeinforge has the ability to change both, the speed of the bridge and the amount of filament extruded by changing the feed rate (speed) and the flow rate (amount) with a ratio. The lower the number entered, the slower and fewer the filaments extruded.

In this recipe, we are concerned with lowering the amount of extrusion. As we can see in the following image, by limiting the amount of filament we have made a better bridge:

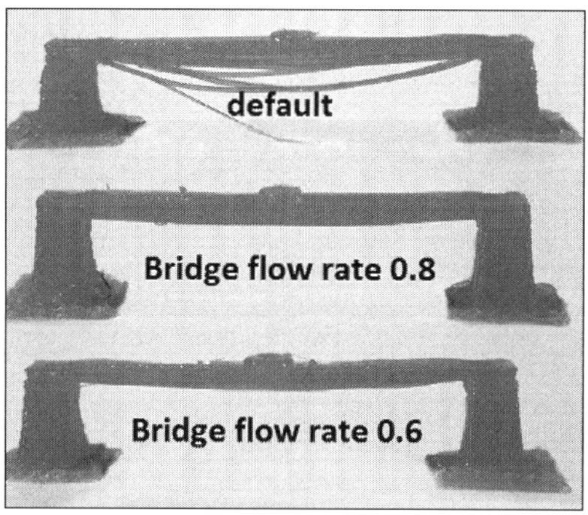

Reviewing the print results

Let's take a look at the best prints and compare the results of both Skeinforge to Slic3r and ABS to PLA.

With the tiny pyramid (which measures 5 x 5 x 5 mm), it appears that Skeinforge has done a better job in making a good print in both materials, as shown in the following image:

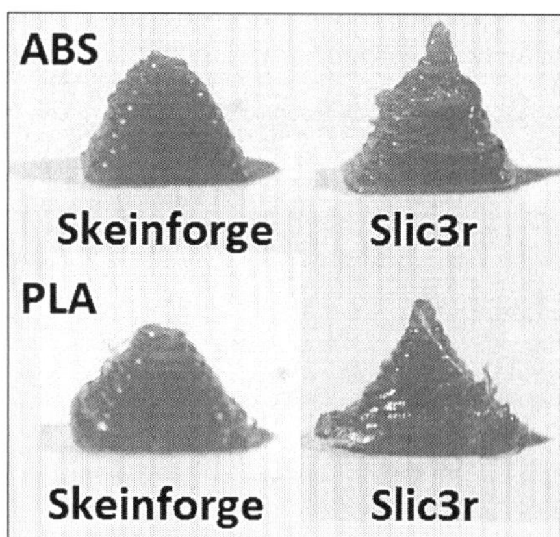

In the following image, we'll see a comparison of Slic3r and Skeinforge using ABS filament for the bridging test:

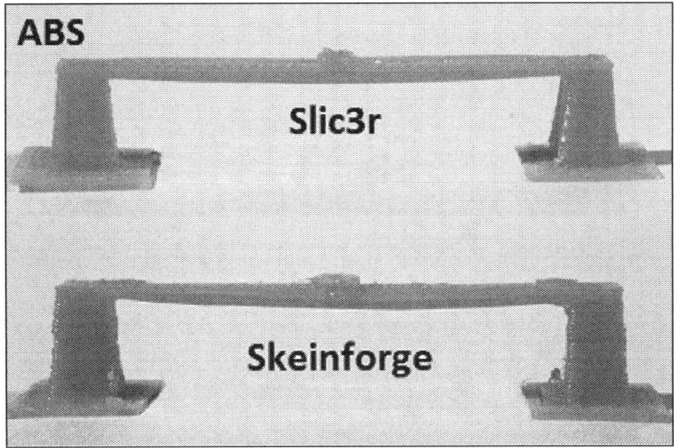

In the following image, we'll see a comparison of Slic3r and Skeinforge using PLA filament for the bridging test:

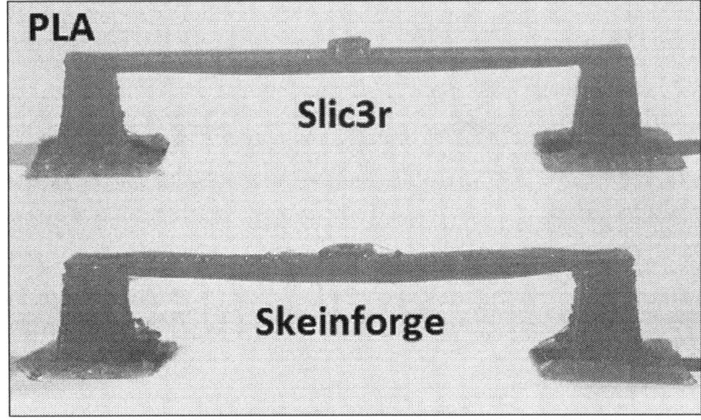

With these results, it appears that Slic3r does work much better for bridging and that equal results can be obtained with ABS and PLA.

Let's look at the following image that shows the results of the wireframe cube we made with TopMod:

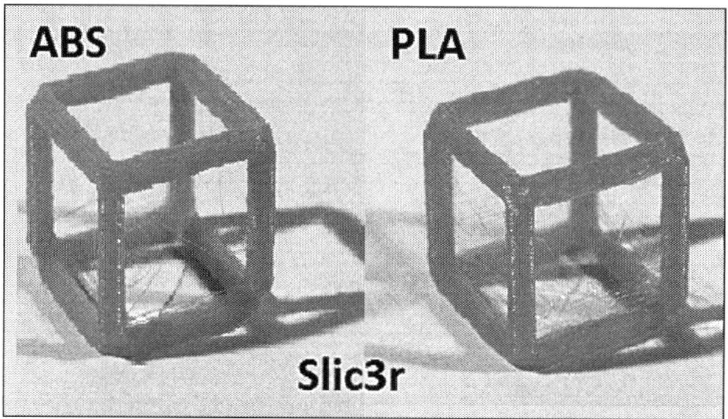

Both slicers did an adequate job with printing the cube. Skeinforge has a little sagging with the PLA printed model as shown in the following image:

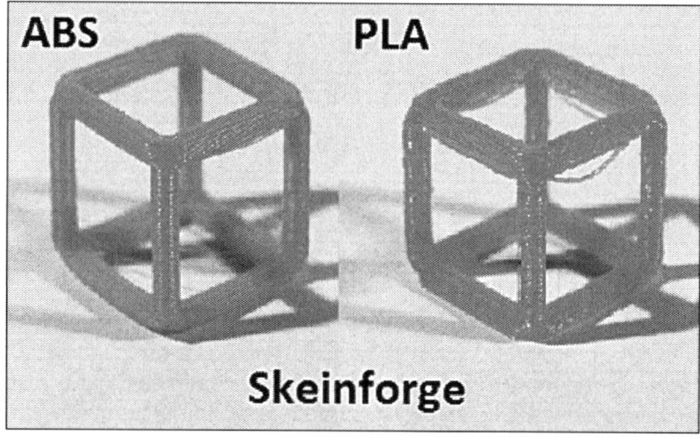

The following image is the toy block we modified using MeshLab and TopMod:

This isn't a good example for showing bridging techniques. While the pattern may seem to require the need to successfully print an open span, the pattern is more like a spider web. There are very few open spans from post to post. Most of the lines in this model were printed by successive layers building upward in an angle. Yet, the best profiles for cooling and bridging in Slic3r were used for printing it.

6

Making the Impossible

In this recipe, we will cover the following topics:

- Using extruding options in TopMod
- Using cutting options in TopMod
- Working with edges in TopMod
- Creating handles in TopMod
- Making a starfish in TopMod
- Creating support with Meshmixer
- Creating support with Skeinforge
- Support options with Skeinforge
- Creating support with Slic3r
- Support options with Slic3r

Introduction

TopMod is a powerful program for making exotic forms. Once you have a basic understanding of how the program works, you'll find that it can be a quick and easy solution to generate a finished model or a model to export into another program for further manipulation.

TopMod operates in a manner similar to SketchUp; it works by building a model from shapes that are extruded into forms. However, TopMod has a different approach. It constructs a model by starting with a primitive; the faces of the primitive are then extruded in order to build a form. With the addition of cutting and connecting tools, the faces, edges, and vertices of a model can then be manipulated. With some planning, a complex form can be generated quickly and then remeshed into an interesting organic model.

In this chapter, we'll examine TopMod's basic set of tools by making some models that we can use to test support structures. A printed support structure is added to a model when there are areas where the filament will sag in normal printing situations. This will be important if we wish to print objects with overhangs, with angles greater than 45 degrees, or encounter areas that are too extreme for bridging techniques.

Using extruding options in TopMod

TopMod provides a library of seven different primitives. They are a series of geometric forms that are the simplest objects a 3D program can produce.

In this recipe, we're going to make some interesting forms by building them from a dodecahedron. We'll use two extrude tools: the Doo Sabin Extrude and Dome Extrude Modes. They can be seen respectively in the following circled icons:

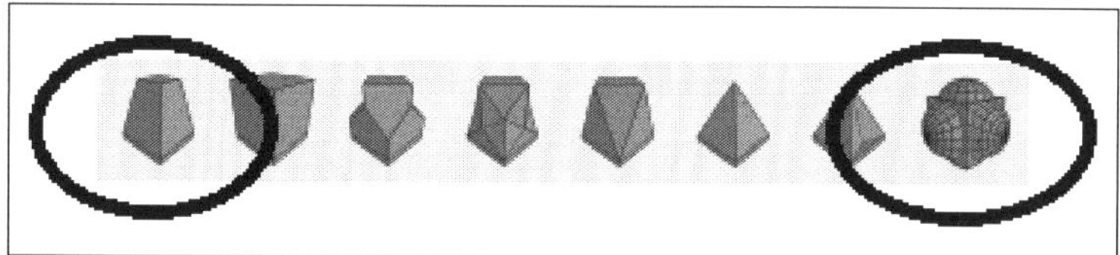

Getting ready

You'll need to select the dodecahedron from the primitive's icon tray. Zoom to a comfortable work size.

Before we get started, let's look at the selection tools. These are called Selection Masks. We'll be using three out of the four available masks that are located in the icon tray under the program's menu. They can be seen in the following image:

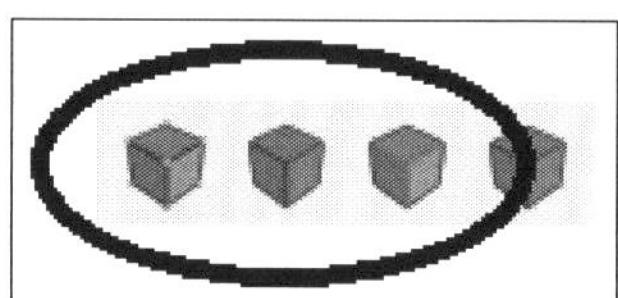

From here, we'll be able to select three of the major components of a polygon mesh: vertices, faces, and edges, as show in the following image:

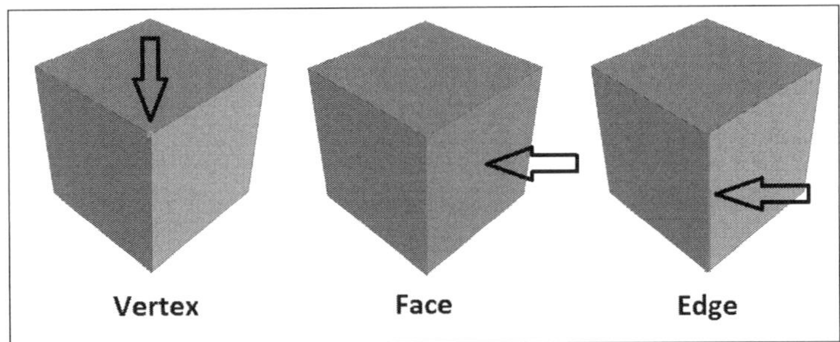

Click on any part of the model to select it and click and hold *Ctrl* to deselect it.

By choosing **Selection** from the menu, we'll be able to choose the options that control and refine our selection process.

How to do it...

We will proceed as follows:

1. Choose the **Select Faces** icon [▩].

2. Then, select one face as shown in the following image:

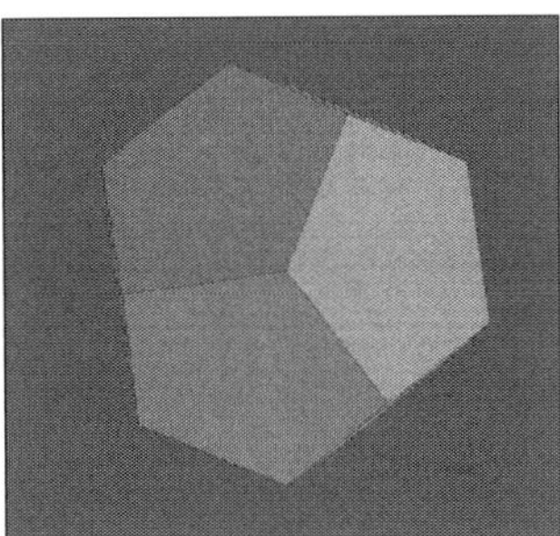

3. Go to the **Extrusions Tools** tray and select the **Dome Extrude Mode** icon. Take note of the floating **Tools Options** window. For now, we'll leave the defaults alone. Click on **Perform Extrusion**.

4. Now, go to the menu and choose **Selection**. From here, choose **Select Multiple** from the selection menu. Examine the following image. We can see the results of dome extrusion in the image on the left-hand side. Select the faces as shown in the image on the right-hand side.

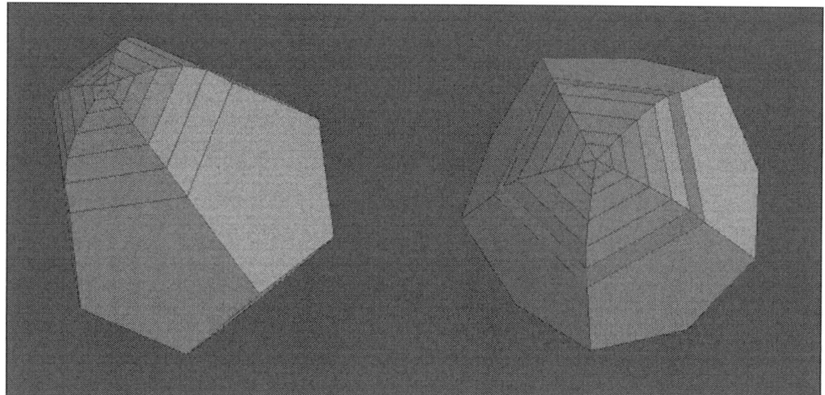

5. Go to the **Extrude Mode** tray and choose the **Doo Sabin Extrude Mode** icon [▮]

6. From the **Tool Options** window, choose **Extrude Selected Faces**, keeping the default values. You should have a model similar to the one shown in the following image:

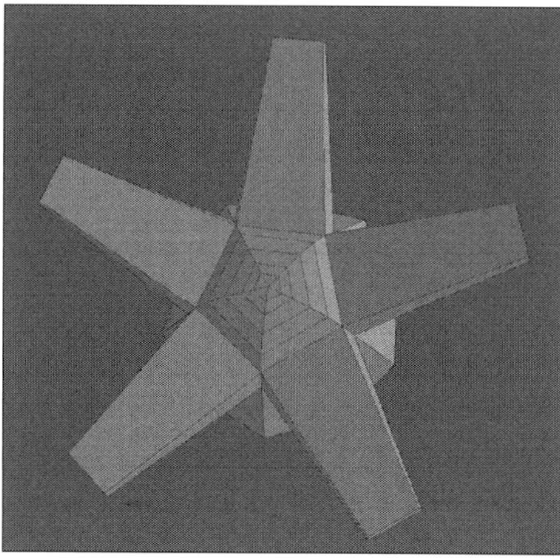

7. Save the model. Let's label the file as base, as we'll be using it several times in this recipe.

8. Now, select the tips of all of the five arms. The tip is shown in the following image on the left-hand side. Change the **Length** field in the **Tool Options** window from `2.000` to `.800`.

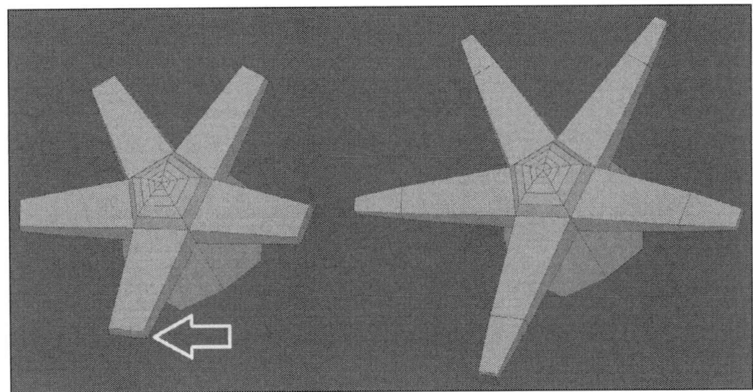

9. Click on **Extrude**. The results should look like the preceding image on the right-hand side. Save the model. We'll be using it later in this chapter.

10. Now, reload the base model and select all the five tips again.

11. Set the **Length** field to `.400` and select **Extrude**. Save the model. We'll be using it later.

12. Now, reload the base model again. We'll remesh the geometry to make it smoother. Go to the menu and select **Remeshing**. From **4-Conversion**, choose **Catmull Clark**. Click on **Perform Remeshing** from the **Tool Options** window.

13. Repeat the remeshing two more times. Now, your model should look like the one shown in the following image:

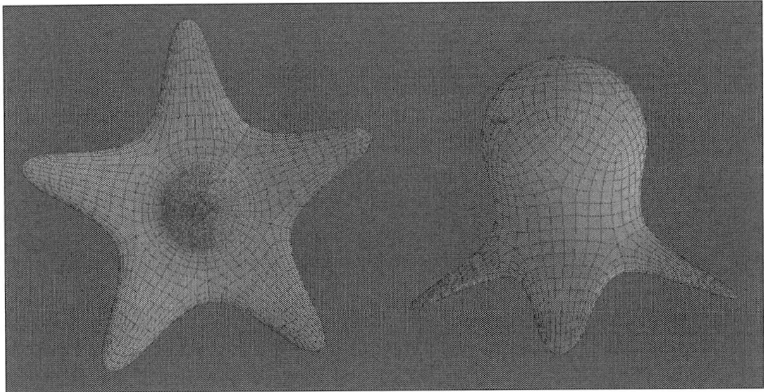

14. Save the model for printing. We'll be using it as a test model later in this chapter.

How it works...

There are eight different types of extrusions available. Each of the extrusion modes may have an adjustment for **Length, Twist, Rotate, Scale,** and **Segments**. The **Icosahedral Extrude Mode** and **Dodecahedral Extrude Mode** have additional extrudes for **Length** and also an additional adjustment for **Angle**.

For example, let's examine **Icosahedral Extrude Mode**. We can see the default setting in the object at the center of the following image. By changing the default extrusion angle's value from 50.0 to a lower and higher angle, the extrusion will change.

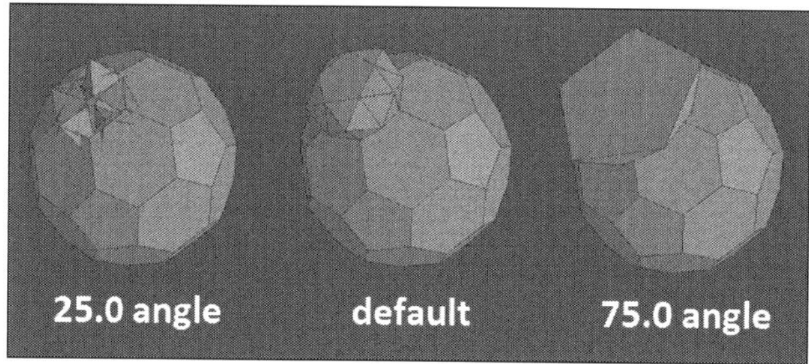

More modifications can be made by changing the length value to 5.000 in **Length 1** (the default is .5000), **Length 2** (the default is .7000), and **Length 3** (the default is .8000). We can see the results in the following image:

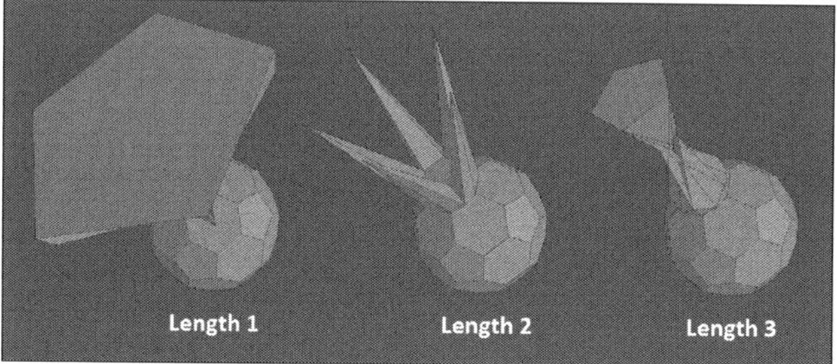

Making extrusions with some settings may produce forms with intersecting triangles and create other nonmanifold issues. The preceding image on the right-hand side has nonmanifold issues as well as the model that was extruded with a 25.0 angle extrusion.

These models will require repair if they are to be 3D printed; we'll learn how to fix these types of issues in *Chapter 8, Troubleshooting Issues in 3D Modeling*.

Using cutting options in TopMod

TopMod has three cutting options that can be used to shave off portions of a model. They work by making cuts based on a selection of an edge, vertex, or face. These tools are selected from the **Conical** icon tray that is shown in the following image:

Getting ready

If you still have the program open from the previous recipe, save your work and reload TopMod. Open the first model we labeled as `base` on the workspace.

If you want to revert to the default settings, then save your model and reload TopMod. To revert to the default view settings, select **Reset Camera** from the menu under **View**.

How to do it...

We will proceed as follows:

1. Go to the **Conical** icon tray and choose the **Cut by Face Mode** icon [●].

2. Select the face on the model, as shown in the following image, set the offset to 2.0 in the **Tool Options** window, and click on **Perform Cutting**:

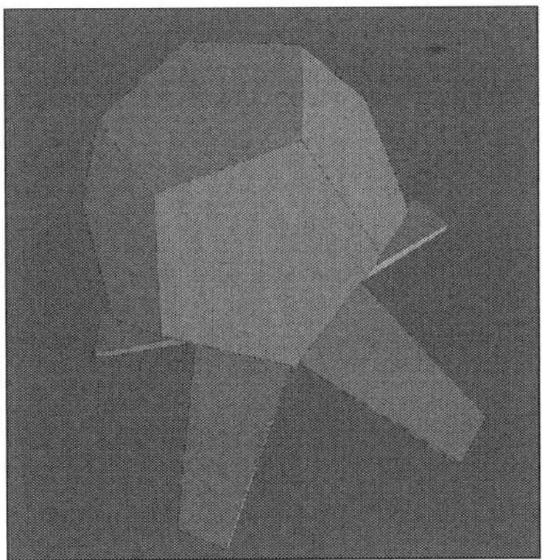

3. Select the face and cut it one more time. The model should look like the one shown in the following image:

4. Go back to the **Conical** icon [ ] tray and choose **Cut by Edge Mode**.

5. From the **Selection** menu, choose **Select Multiple**. Select the edges, as shown in the following image:

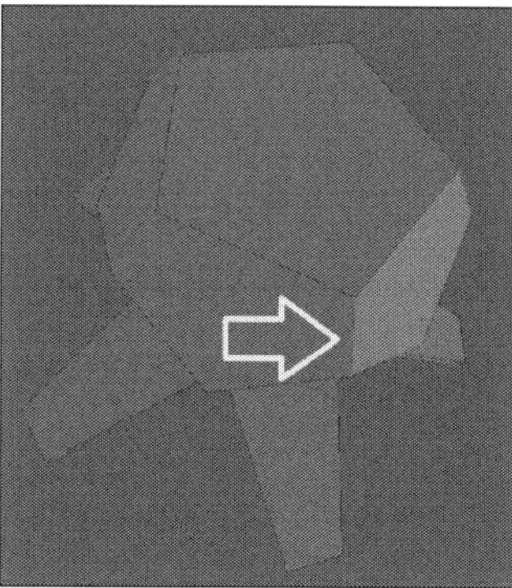

6. In **Tool Options**, adjust the offset from 0.250 to 2.0. Now, click on **Perform Cutting**. The model should look like the one shown in the following image:

7. From the **Conical** icon tray, choose the **Cut by Vertex Mode** icon [⬡].

8. Select the vertex as shown in the following image. In **Tool Options**, the value should be set to `2.00`. Click on **Perform Cutting**.

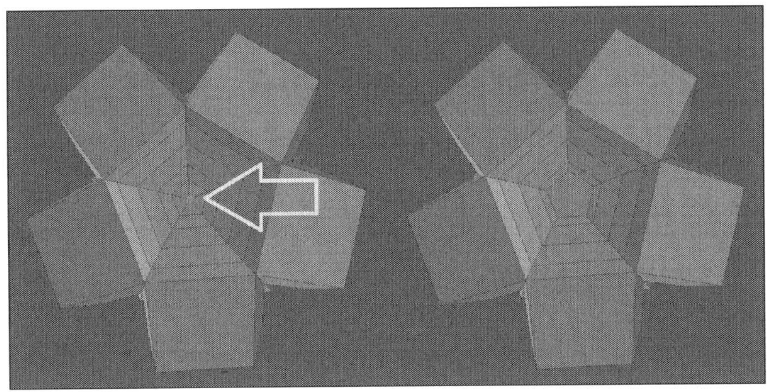

The model should look like the one on the right-hand side in the preceding image. Save the model as a `.obj` and `.stl` file. We'll be using it again in *Chapter 8, Troubleshooting Issues in 3D Modeling*.

How it works...

The **Cutting By Face Mode** option offsets only a default value of 25 percent for each cut. Changing the offset has no effect.

However, changing the offset does affect both **Edge Cut Mode** and **Vertex Cut Mode**. The following illustration shows the different offset values and their corresponding effects:

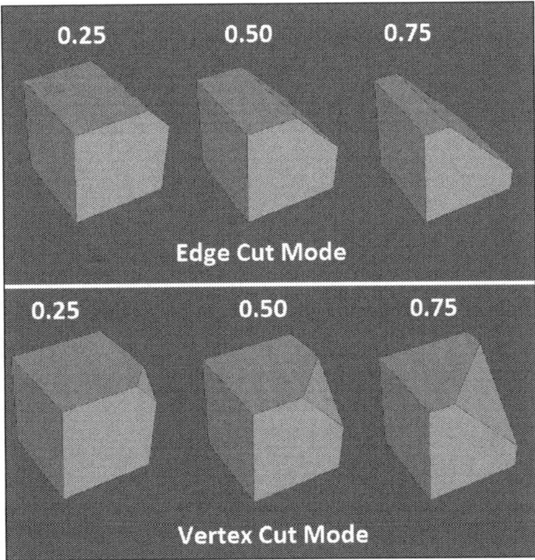

The following image illustrates how the cutting plane works:

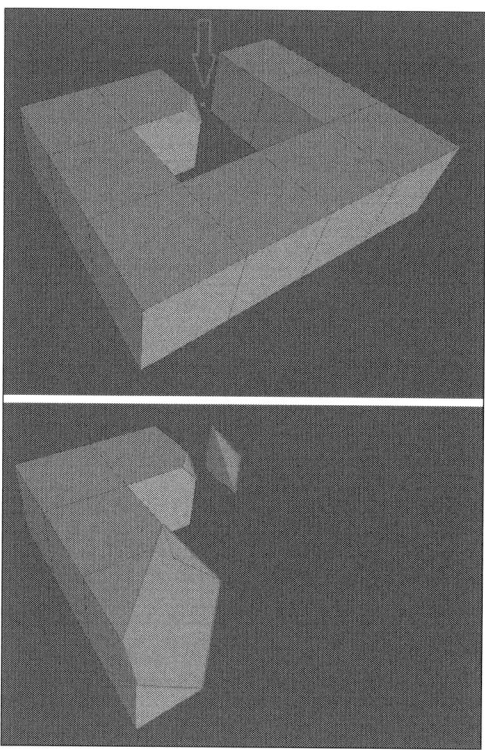

When any of these cut modes are applied, the cut is not limited to the immediate polygon component of the mesh. The cut extends throughout the model's mesh.

Working with edges in TopMod

In this recipe, we'll learn how to edit the individual polygons of a mesh. This will be an important task to model the primitive in more detail. We'll do this by manipulating the edges of the polygons.

There are five tools we'll be using; they are **Insert Edge**, **Delete Edge**, **Collapse Edge**, **Subdivide Edge**, and **Connect Edge**. They are circled in the same order in the following **Tools** icon tray:

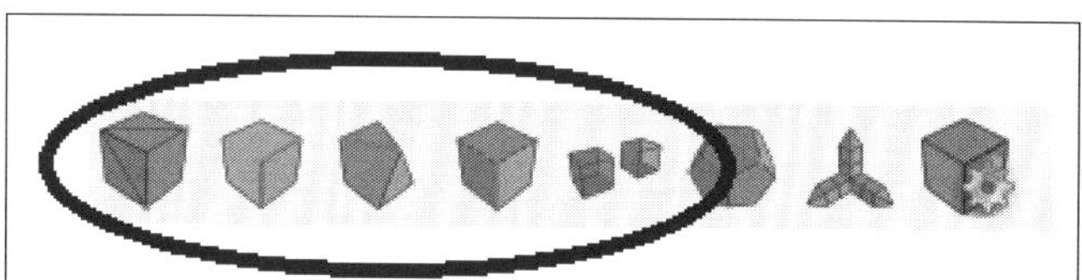

Getting ready

Open TopMod. Load the base model with the additional Doo Sabin `.800` length extrusion from the first recipe. It should look like the model shown in the following image:

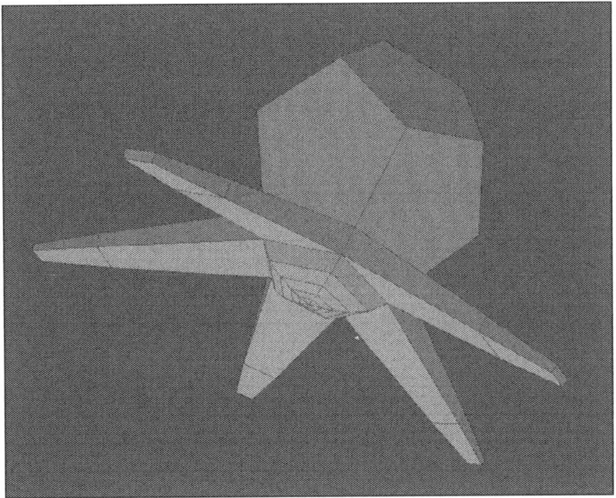

How to do it...

We will proceed as follows:

1. From the **Tools** icon tray, choose the **Delete Edge Mode** icon [⬡].

2. Left-click on the edge, as illustrated in the following image. By clicking on the edge, it's removed without further action. The model should now resemble the model on the right-hand side.

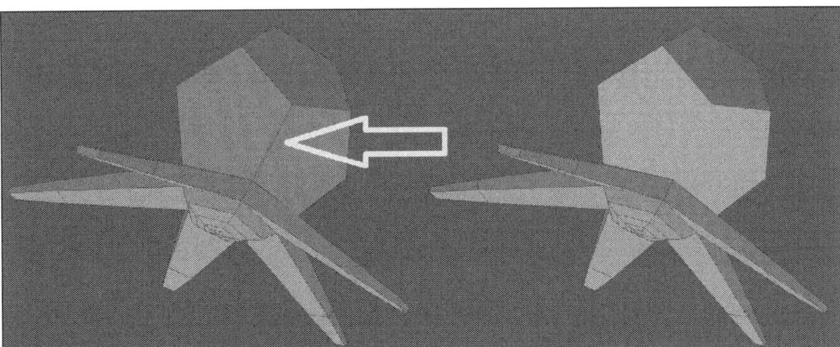

3. We're going to separate the dodecahedron from the body of the starfish shape. We'll do this by continuing to remove all of the similar edges around the dodecahedron, until your model is similar to the one shown in the following image:

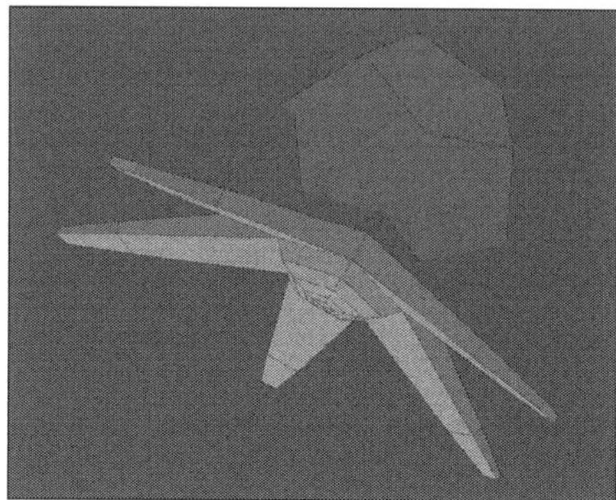

4. In the **Tools** tray, choose the **Connect Edges Mode** icon [ ].

5. Now, we're going to connect the edges of the pentagons on the separated object. Select one edge and then left-click on the adjacent edge to connect the two. The two edges are shown in the following image on the left-hand side:

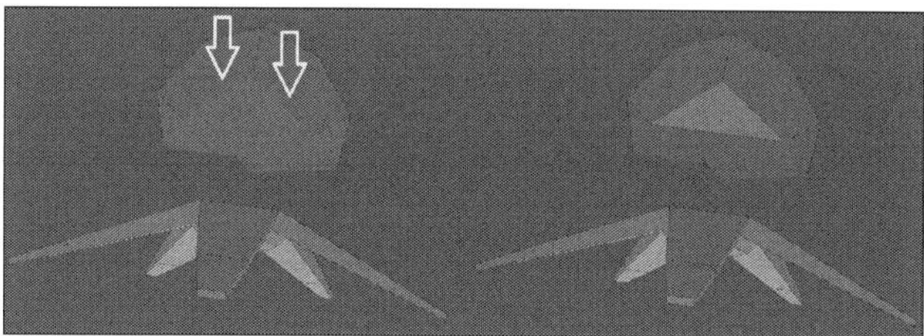

6. With the release of the mouse button, an edge is formed, creating a triangle. This can be seen in the preceding image on the right-hand side.

7. Continue to connect all the similar edges around the object until it's similar to the one shown in the following illustrated model:

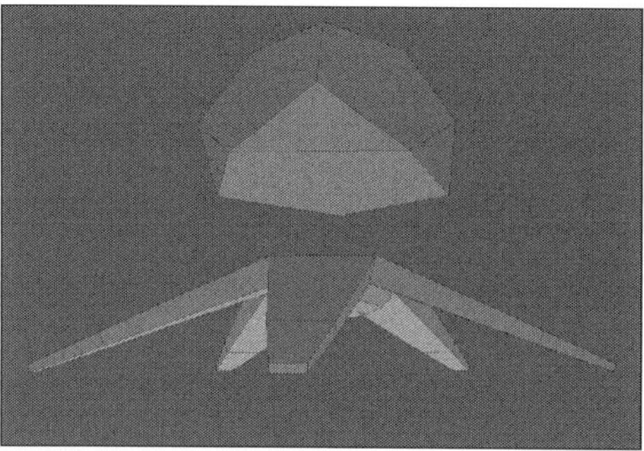

8. Let's now look at how the insert and subdivide edges work. Orient your model similar to the one shown in the following image:

9. In the mode icon tray, choose the **Insert Edge Mode** icon [⬡].

10. Select the inside of corner **1**, as seen in the following image. Left-click on the adjacent corner **2** to connect. We now have separated the four-sided polygon into two triangular parts, as seen in the following image on the right-hand side:

11. Now, let's divide one of the triangles into halves. To do this, we'll need to divide the diagonal edge into two separate parts. From the **Tool** tray, choose the **Subdivide Edge Mode** icon [⬡].

12. Left-click on the center of the diagonal edge, as illustrated in the following image:

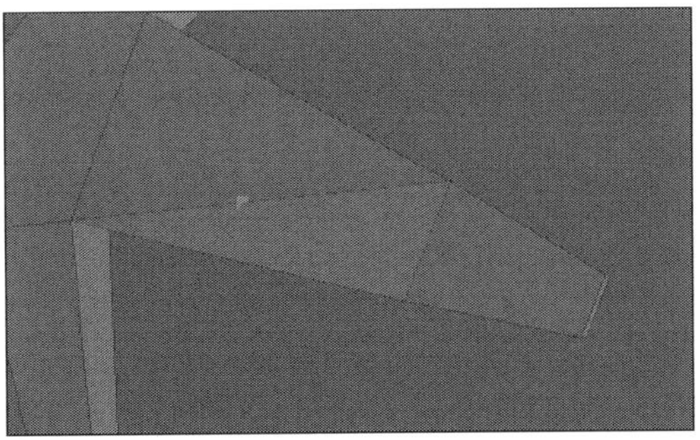

13. The edge will momentarily flash red. This is the only visual indication that something has happened.

14. Go back to the **Tool** tray and select **Insert Edge Mode**. Select the midpoint **1** of the diagonal and then click on the corner **2**, as shown in the following image:

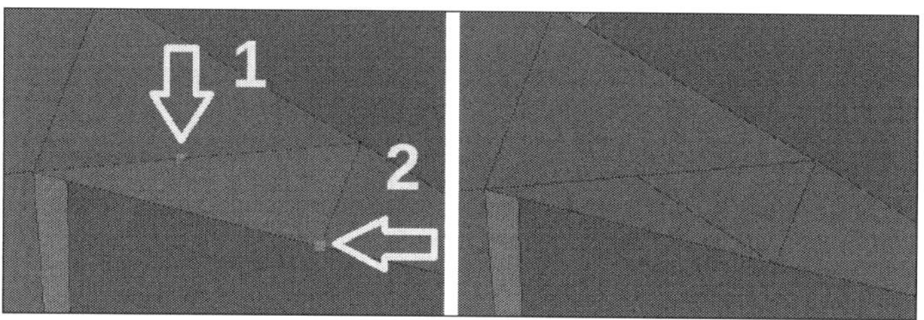

15. We can see in the preceding image on the right-hand side that we now have subdivided the triangle. We'll discover why this is important in the next recipe. Make sure that you save this model before going any further.

16. We have one more tool to examine. It's the **Edge collapse Mode**.

17. Select the icon [●] from the **Tool** tray.

18. We'll use this tool to remove the partial dodecahedron from the starfish shape. Left-click on the edge as shown in the following image on the left-hand side. The result on the right-hand side shows how we reduced the five-sided polygon into a four-side one.

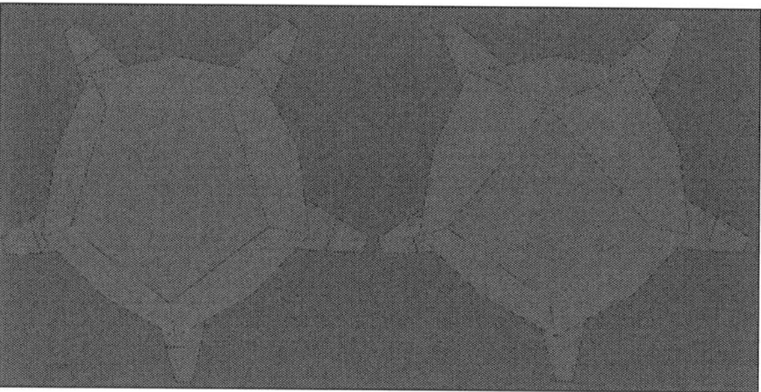

19. Continue to left-click on the edges, collapsing the part into smaller pieces.

20. Beware of stray edges! If you try to collapse one, the program will crash. An stray edge can be seen in the following image:

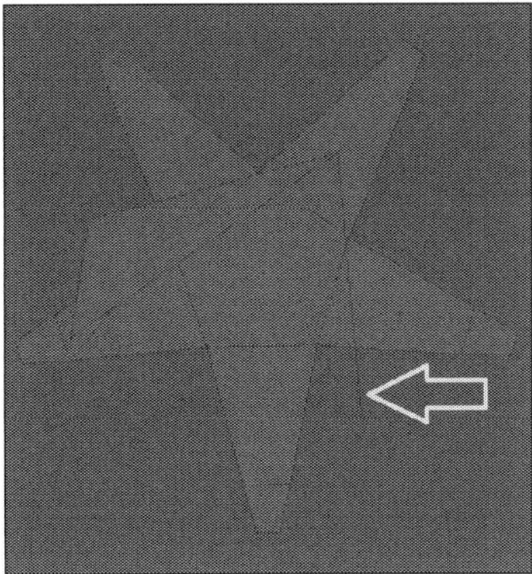

21. Use **Delete Edge Mode** to remove stray edges that are attached to only one vertex. Continue to remove the part using both the collapse edge and delete edge tools until only the starfish shape remains. Save the model. We'll be using it later.

How it works...

By allowing direct access to the geometry of the mesh, just about any kind of form can be made with these editing tools. Unfortunately, TopMod doesn't allow the import of more than one primitive at a time in a workspace. However, working with separate parts can be achieved by dividing a primitive, as we've seen illustrated in this recipe.

Models created in other programs such as SketchUp can be imported into TopMod for further manipulation. If a solid model consisting of more than one part is imported, all parts must be saved as a single component before importing into TopMod.

Creating handles in TopMod

The creation of a handle or hole between two faces of a model's mesh is generally referred to as high-genus modeling. TopMod produces a watertight two-manifold model when these tools are used to make multiple connections. What this basically means is that we'll be able to create objects with intersecting loops and holes. We'll see how this works in this recipe.

We'll be using two tools from the **High Genus** tray: **Add Handle/Hole** and **Add Handle (Shape Interpolation)**. These are circled in the same order in the following image:

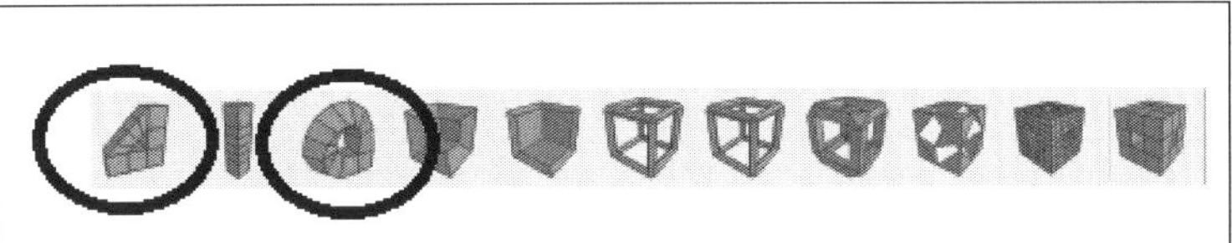

Getting ready

You'll need the model we worked with from the earlier recipe. It's the `base` model with the separated partial dodecahedron.

How to do it...

We will proceed as follows:

1. Orient your model similar to the one on the left-hand side in the following image. Choose the **Add Handle/Hole Mode** icon [ ].

2. Select the vertex shown by the number **1**.

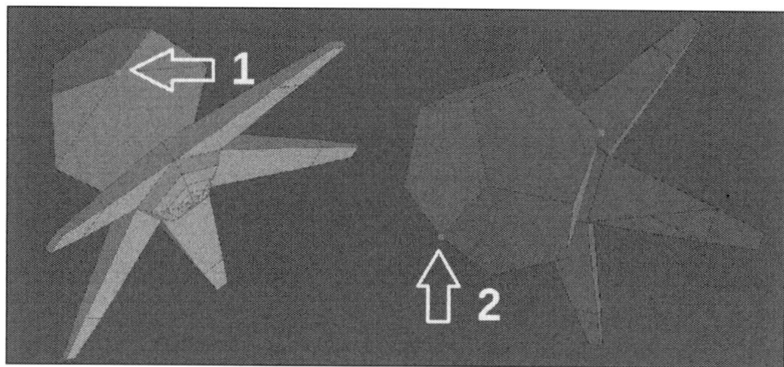

3. Now, reorient your model similar to the one on the right-hand side in the preceding image. Left-click on the vertex shown by the number **2**.

4. The model should now have a spiraling hole through the partial dodecahedron, as shown in the following image:

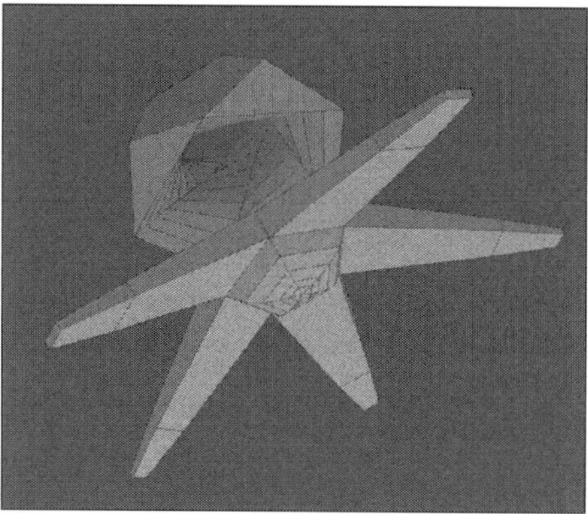

5. Next, choose the **Add Handle (Shape Interpolation)** icon [ ].

6. Select the vertex shown by the number **1** on the starfish shape in the following image. Then, left-click on the vertex shown by the number **2**.

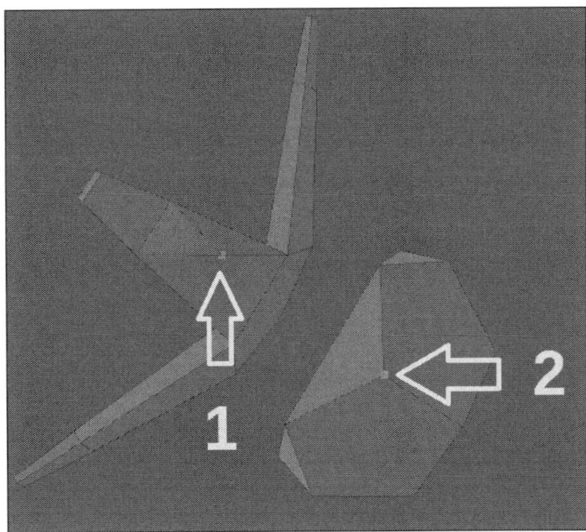

7. Your model should look like the one at the top of the following image:

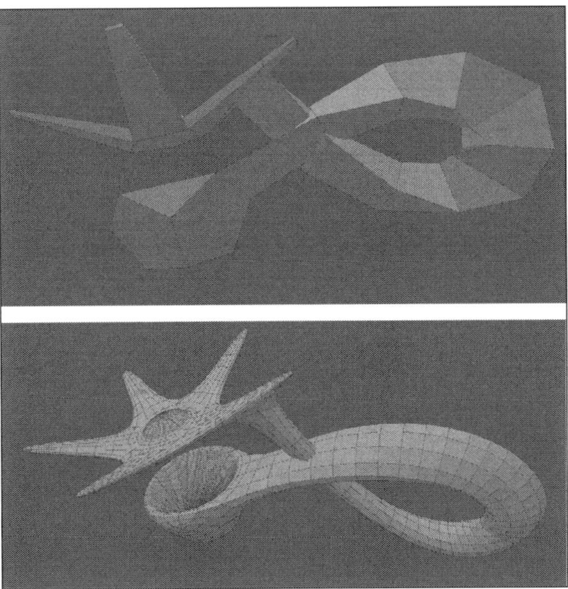

8. Now, we'll remesh it to give a more organic feel. Go to **Remeshing** and choose **Catmull Clark** from the **4-conversion** options. Remesh twice. It should look like the model at the bottom of the preceding image. Save the model for printing.

How it works...

Choosing the correct vertex is important when using the handle/hole tool. Each vertex will loop the handle differently, depending on which face is selected.

Keep in mind that when you select the vertices, the two polygons that are highlighted during the selection process will help visualize how the handle or hole will form. This is easily imagined by visualizing the two selected polygons positioned at the ends of a looped connection. Then, think of the two selected vertices as the line that makes the connection in a loop that the tube of the handle follows.

Keep in mind that when a loop makes an intersection, we'll be creating manifold issues that will have to be corrected if they are to be 3D printed effectively. We'll be examining how to fix these issues in *Chapter 8, Troubleshooting Issues in 3D Modeling*.

Making a starfish in TopMod

In this recipe, we'll use the tools we've learned to use in this chapter to make a more complex starfish shape.

Getting ready

Open TopMod. Load the base model with the additional Doo Sabin `.400` length extrusion. It should look like the model shown in the following image:

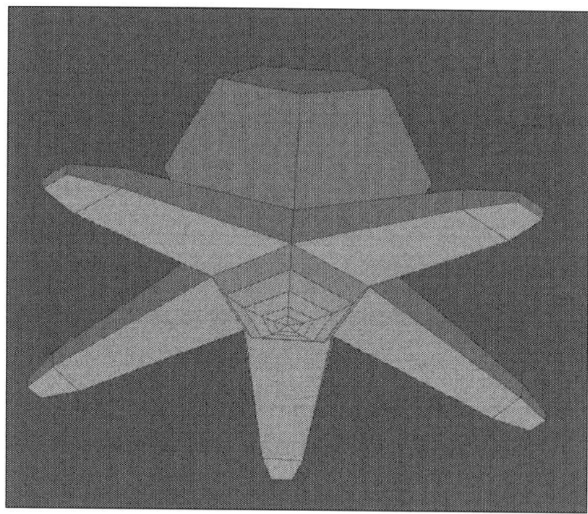

Make sure that you save your model frequently. Not only is TopMod3D temperamental and may crash, there are only 21 undo steps available.

How to do it...

We will proceed as follows:

1. First, we need to remove the dodecahedron from the starfish shape.

2. Once the dodecahedron is removed, center the exposed back of the starfish on your workspace. Then, select all the edges on the back, as shown in the following image on the left-hand side. There are a total of 10 edges; when they are removed, the model should look like the one on the right-hand side in the following image:

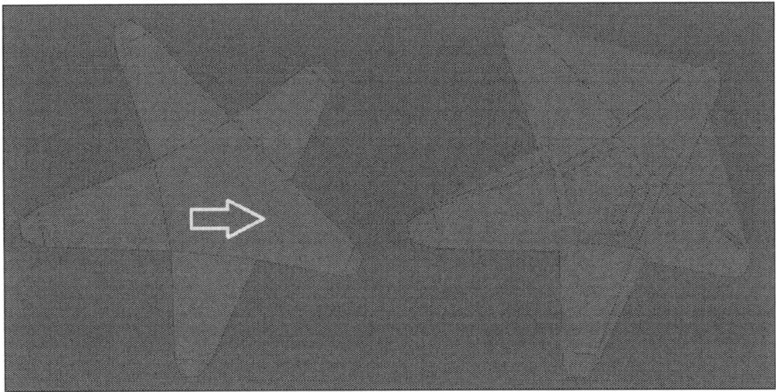

3. Select **Dome Extrude Mode**. Set the height to 1.6 in the **Tool Options** window. Select the back of the starfish, as shown in the following image on the left-hand side. The result should look like the one on the right-hand side in the following image:

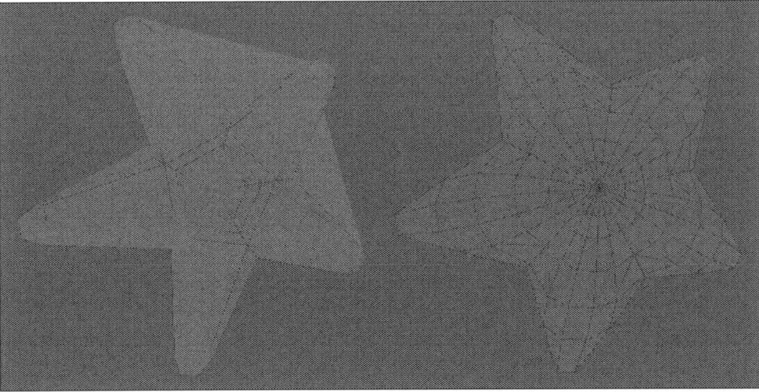

4. Flip the model over. Remove all the edges that make up the shape of the pentagon in the center of the starfish, as shown in the following image on the left-hand side. The model should look similar to the following one on the right-hand side when finished:

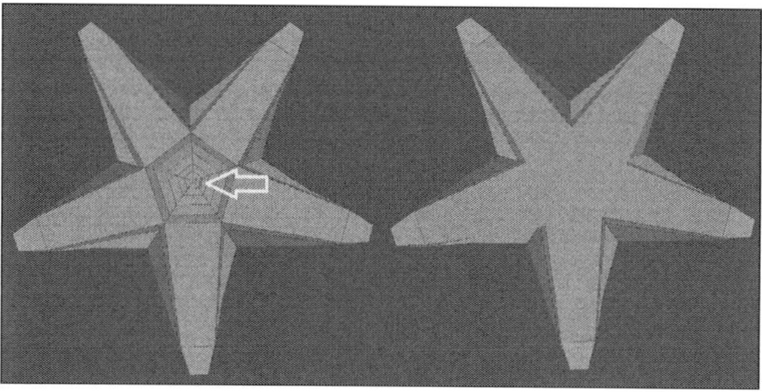

5. Select the star shape as shown in the following image on the left-hand side. Set the **Dome Extrude Mode** to a height of .400. Extrude the model as shown in the following image on the right-hand side:

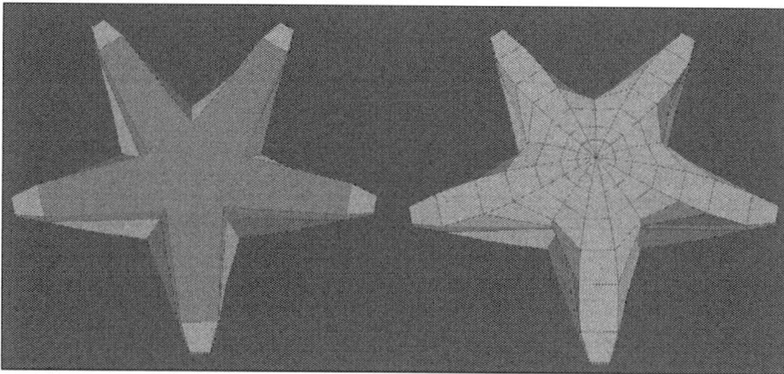

6. Now, we're going to make a series of spikes circling the center of the starfish, but first, we need to remove some edges in order to create a shape to extrude. There are seven edges that need to be removed to make each shape. This can be seen as the dark area of the starfish in the following image on the left-hand side. Remove all the edges to make a ring of five shapes as seen in the following image on the right-hand side:

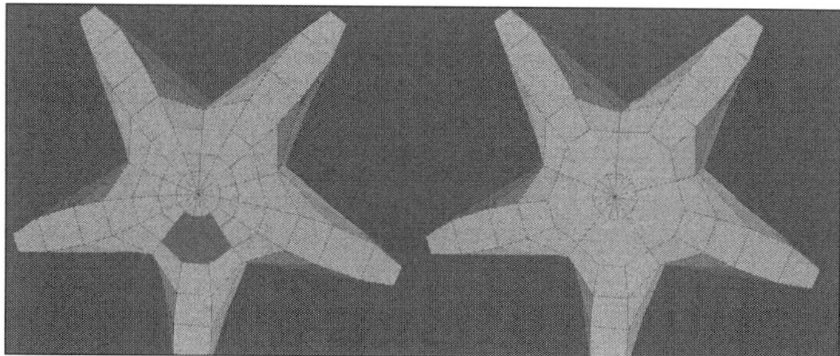

7. The ring of shapes can now be extruded. Choose **Dome Extrude Mode** and set the **Height** field to .600 and **Scale** to .800. Select the five shapes as seen in the following image on the left-hand side, and then extrude them. The result should look similar to the starfish on the right-hand side in the following image:

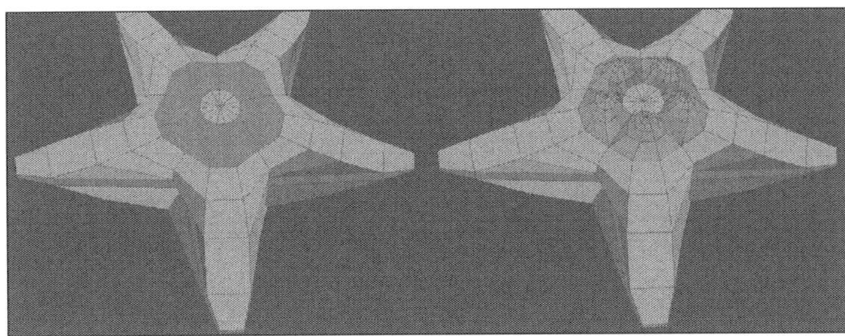

8. Let's add some protrusions on the ends of the arms. Choose **Doo Sabin Extrude Mode** and set the **Height** field to 0.100. Select the ends as seen in the following image on the left and extrude. The result of extruding can be seen in the following image on the right:

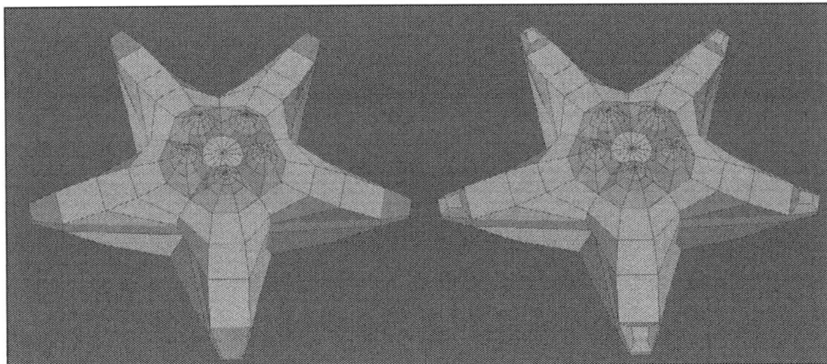

9. Now, let's soften the extrusion by removing a single edge from the side of each extrusion. This edge is shown in the following image on the left-hand side. When all of the images are removed, the starfish should look like the one shown in the following image on the right-hand side:

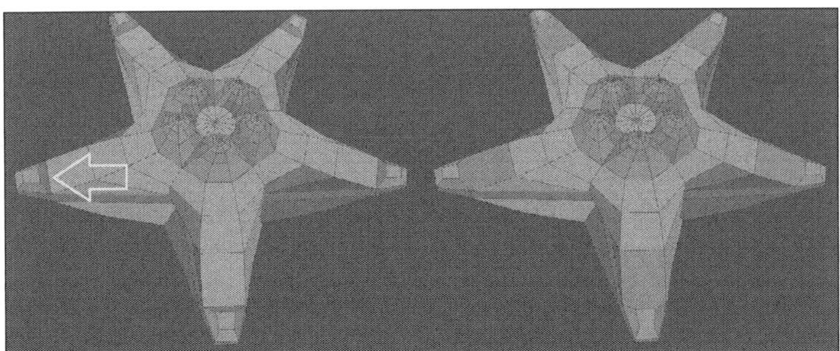

10. The basic form of the starfish is finished, but we have one last step to perform. To give the starfish an organic feel, we'll remesh it. Go to the menu and select **Remeshing**. From **4-Conversion**, choose **Catmull Clark**. Click on **Perform Remeshing** from the **Tool Options** window.

11. Remesh the starfish one more time. After two remeshes, you should have a starfish that appears similar to the one in the following image:

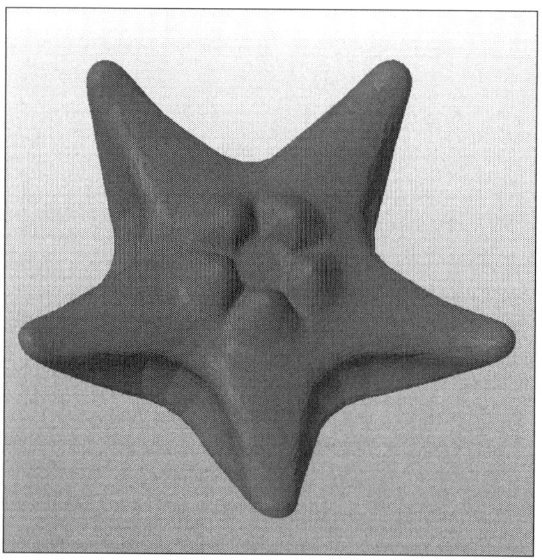

How it works...

By now, you should have a clear understanding of how to utilize the tools in TopMod to make a model. With a little planning (and lots of file saving), many concepts can be potentially constructed with more ease using TopMod rather than with other 3D modeler, such as SketchUp or Meshmixer.

However, we'll see that the real power behind 3D modeling lies in utilizing the strengths of all of the tools at our disposal. In the next chapter, we'll continue to modify our starfish for more realism using Meshmixer.

Creating support with Meshmixer

Many complex models will have a structure consisting of areas that have sharp angles and layers, which have little or no contact with the build platform surface. We can see this illustrated in the following jellyfish shape.

By printing this model in several different positions, there would be issues with drooping filaments in the areas marked as **1** in the following image. There would be insufficient surface contact on the build platform in areas marked as **2**.

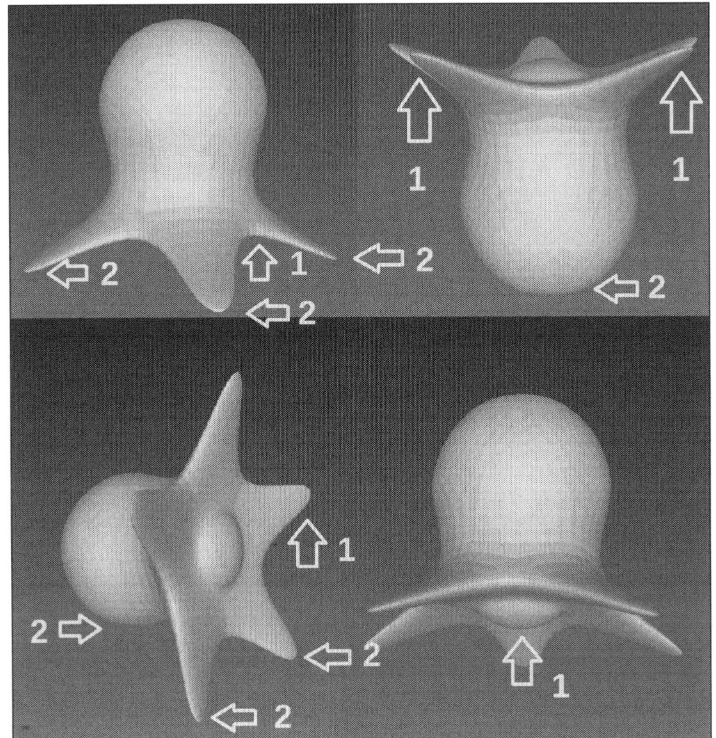

Let's look at another model that we made in this chapter. In the following image, we can easily see that severe support issues would occur. There is minimal surface contact, and there are areas where print layers would print in open space without underlying support.

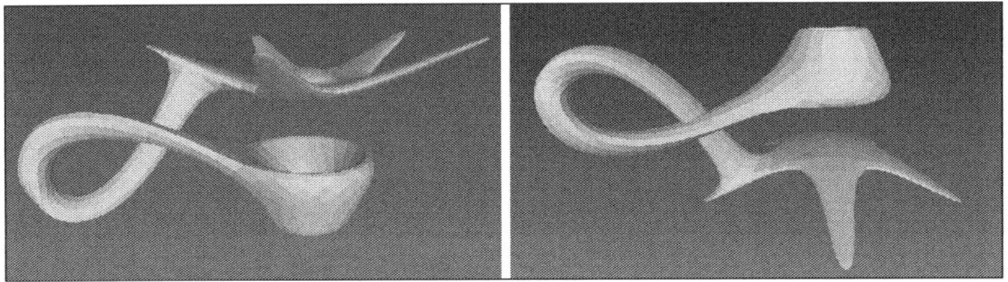

In this recipe, we'll learn how to use Meshmixer to create a temporary support structure for these models.

Getting ready

Open Meshmixer and import the starfish/handle model.

How to do it...

We will proceed as follows:

1. From the toolbar on the left-hand side, choose **Analysis**. From the pop-up window, choose **Overhangs**. The model is now outlined with a blue line, as shown in the following image:

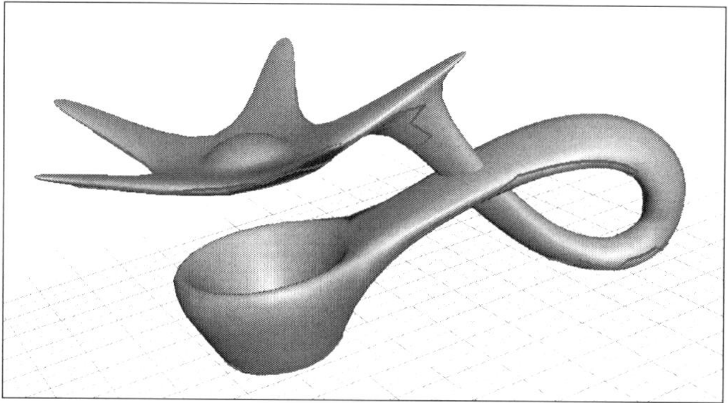

2. Now, go back to the pop-up window. It has now changed to a list of support properties. Left-click and drag the slider back and forth for **Angle Thresh**. The blue outline is adjusted according to the angle of support that is chosen. However, when the angle increases, the support will max out with a calculated angle. Moving the slider past this point will not create any more support.

3. Set the **Angle Thresh** field to 40 and then choose **Support All Overhangs**. You should have a model that looks similar to the one shown in the following image:

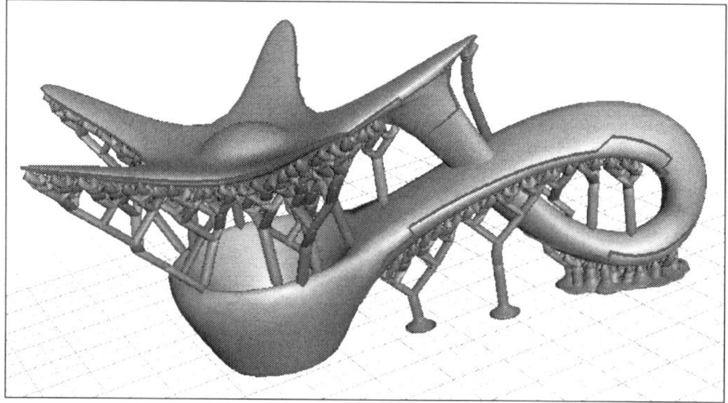

4. Features of this support can be altered. Left-click on the small arrow next to **Support Generator**. A roll-out box with more support properties appears.

5. Let's increase **Post Diameter** from 2 mm to 4 mm and **Base Diameter** from 6 mm to 12 mm.

6. Select **Remove all Supports** and then redo **Support All Overhangs**. You should have a model similar to the one shown in the following image:

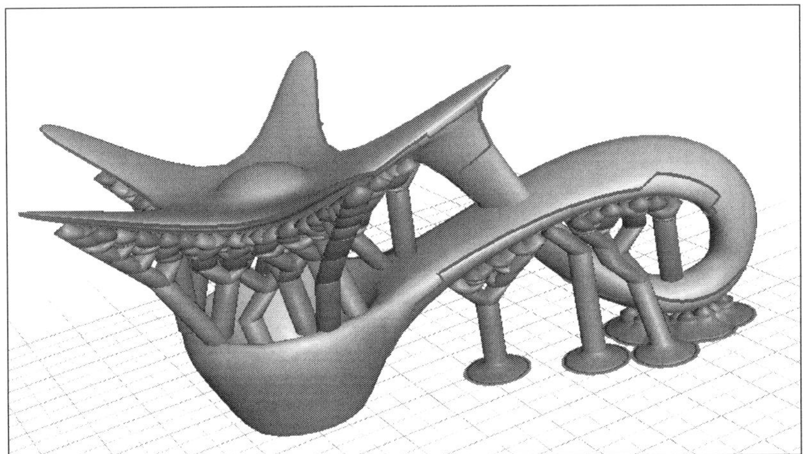

7. Go back to the properties window and change **Density** from 75 to 100.

8. Select **Remove all Supports** and then redo **Support All Overhangs**. You should have a model similar to the one shown in the following image:

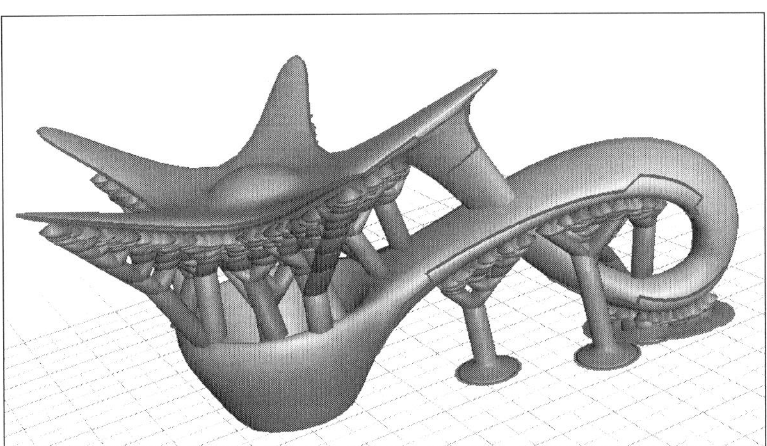

9. Manual supports can be added as well. Hold the *Shift* key and left-click on an area that requires more support. Drag and hold the post down to the platform. When the mouse is released, a fully formed post is generated. This can be seen illustrated in the following image:

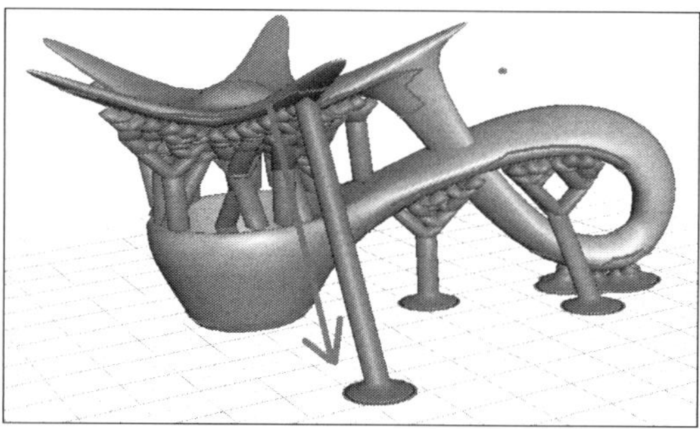

10. Save the model.

How it works...

There are other support properties that are worthy of experimentation as well. The **Tip Diameter** property is one of them. This value adjusts the size of the contact point at the model's surface. This is important for two reasons: too little contact, and the post will fall during printing and too much contact, and the support material will be difficult to remove.

There's more...

Check your saved model with the Meshmixer Inspector. You should have a model with manifold issues like the model in the following image:

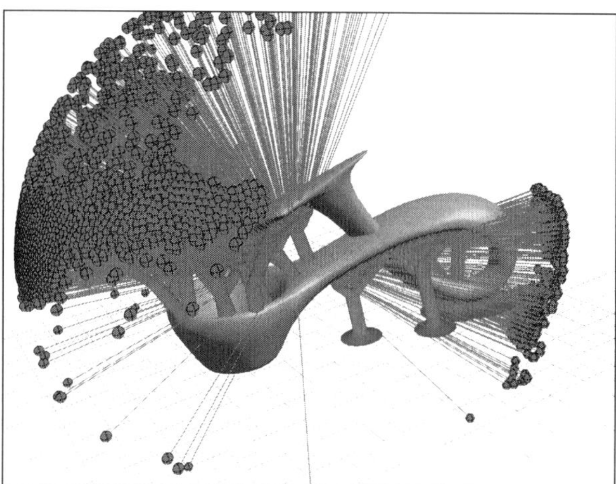

The support isn't viable unless you make the model solid. Do this by selecting **Convert** to **Solid** in the **Support properties** window.

Let's print!

Support structures can be generated with both Skeinforge and Slic3r. We'll experiment with them using the jellyfish model we made in this chapter and a new model shown in the following image:

This model will be good to illustrate some issues that can occur when generating support and how they can be solved by making adjustments in the slicer.

We'll also save the different G-code files that we generate when we run our tests and view them with a G-code viewer. This will save the time and expense of printing multiple copies.

Creating support with Skeinforge

In this recipe, we're going to explore the different adjustments that can be made for determining where and how much support is added.

Getting ready

You'll need to make the soccer ball wireframe model. You can do this easily with TopMod by importing the soccer ball primitive and then applying **Wireframe Modeling Mode**. You'll also need a G-code viewer. You can use the one that's part of Repetier-Host or check *Appendix B, Taking a Closer Look at G-code*, for more options.

How to do it...

We will proceed as follows:

1. Select the **Raft** plugin. Make sure that **Activate Raft**, **Add Raft**, **Elevate Nozzle**, and **Orbit** are check marked. Scroll down the page to the **Support At Support Material Choice** section and change the default setting from **None** to **Everywhere**.
2. Deselect the **Support Cross Hatch** option.
3. Slice and save the G-code.
4. Go back to **Support Material Choice** and change the setting to **Exterior Only**.
5. Slice and save the G-code.
6. Go to **Support Minimum Angle (degrees)** and change the default value from 60 to 80.
7. Slice and save the G-code.

How it works...

When we initiated support everywhere, Skeinforge generated support for both the exterior and interior of our model. We can see this in the following image:

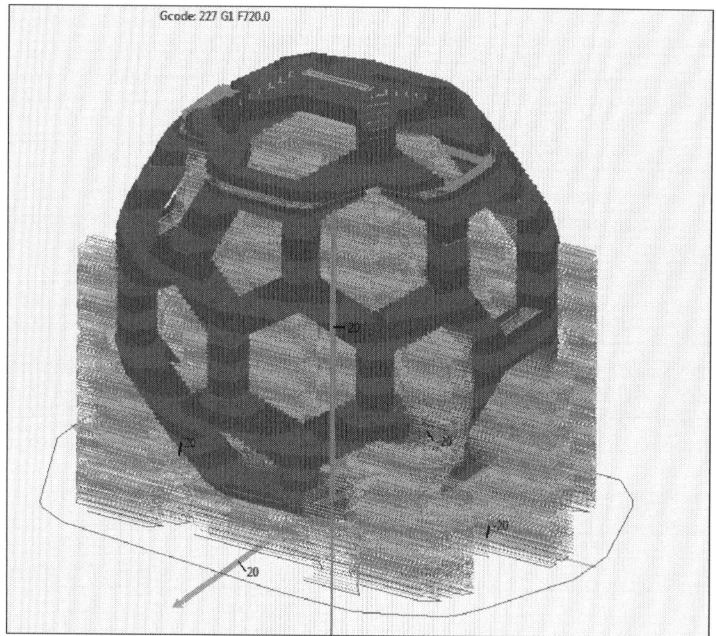

This may be fine for some situations, but in this case, it would be better to keep the support outside of the model. To accomplish this, we set the support material choice to **Exterior Only**. As we can see in the following image, the results are better, but there is still support material inside the model:

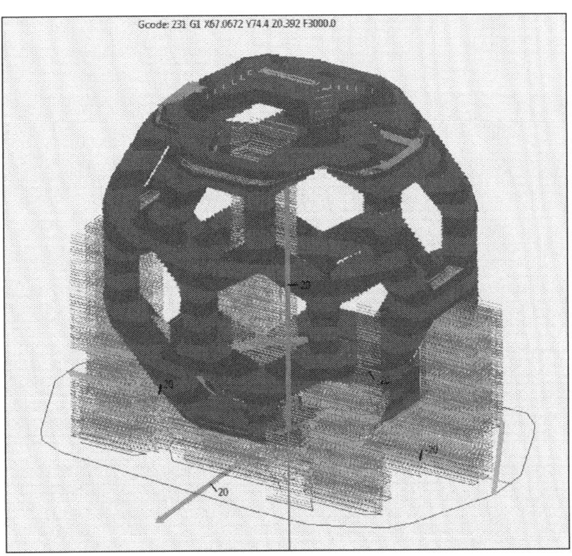

By changing **Support Minimum Angle** from the default setting of 60 degrees to 80 degrees, we lost some exterior support but kept our interior clear.

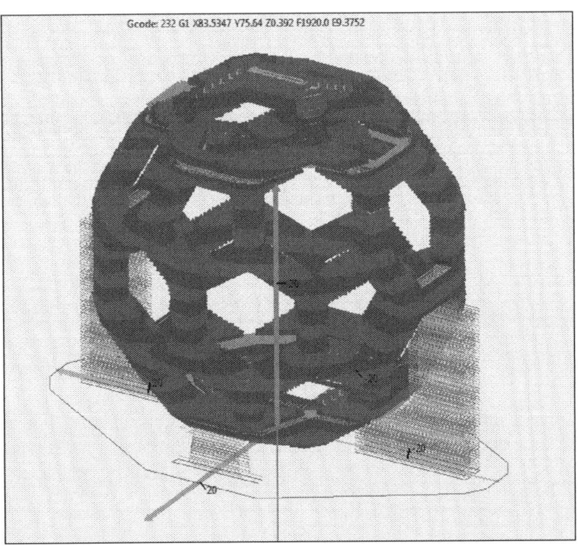

This is the best that we can get in this particular situation with Skeinforge.

There's more...

Setting **Support Minimum Angle** to 80 with the **Material Choice** support set to **Everywhere** doesn't give us the same results as the **Exterior Only** setting. Skeinforge certainly considers the interior and exterior of the sphere differently but still doesn't completely interpolate the interior of the sphere as we would assume.

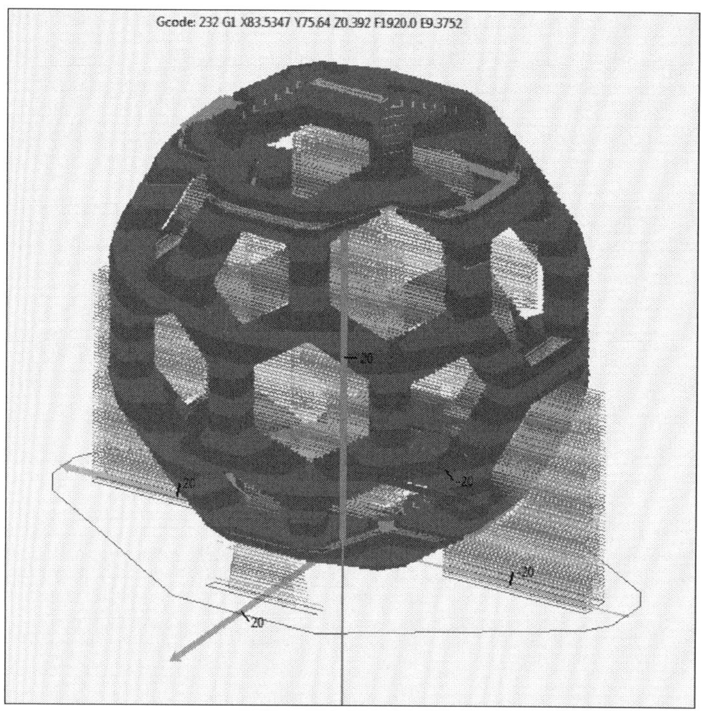

We would expect that the interior would be completely clear of support with any angle setting when **Exterior Only** is chosen. This is one reason to check your model with a G-code viewer before printing. The results are going to always be dictated by the uniqueness of your model.

Support options with Skeinforge

In this recipe, we're going to examine some support options in Skeinforge that will adjust the physical contact of the support material to the model. This is important for tuning a profile that will provide not only a good support but also a support material that can be easily removed.

Getting ready

You'll need the jellyfish model.

How to do it...

We will proceed as follows:

1. Select the **Raft** plugin. Scroll down the page to the bottom section **Support At Support Material Choice** and set it to **Everywhere**.

2. Make sure that you keep **Support Cross Hatch** deactivated.

3. We'll test the default support values now. Save the G-code and print the model.

4. Under the **Interface** heading, go to **Interface Density Infill (ratio)**. Change the default value `0.5` to `0.1`. Slice and save the G-code.

5. Print the model.

How it works...

In order to have support material that works successfully, we need to consider the following two primary factors:

▸ First, we need a support structure that adequately provides a prop for the filament layer extrusion.

▸ Second, we need a support structure that can be easily removed.

Both of these factors affect each other. The stronger we make the support, the more difficult it will be to remove it. Another method of decreasing the amount of support material is by increasing the space between the support walls.

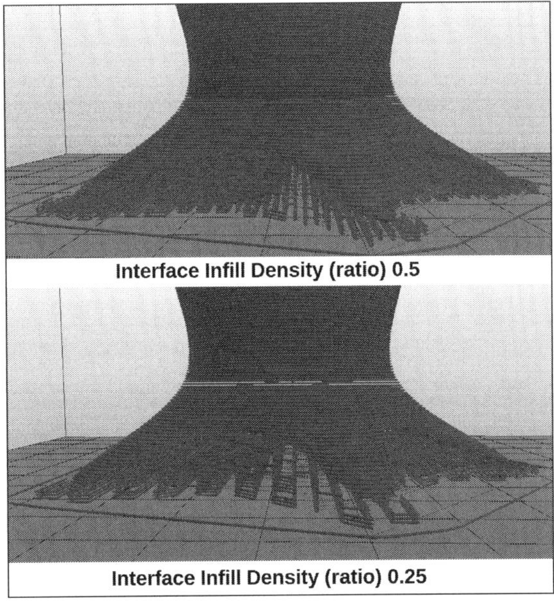

In the preceding example, we can see the results of changing **Interface Density Infill (ratio)**. Depending on the structure of the model, the minimal amount of support material is preferable. This allows for more ease in the removal of the support material with the added benefit of decreasing the print time and print material costs.

There's more...

By adjusting **Support Flow Rate over Operating Flow Rate (ratio)** and **Support Gap over Perimeter Extrusion Width (ratio)**, we can fine-tune the support material to work with the best of both worlds. By lowering **Support Flow Rate over Operating Flow Rate (ratio)**, we can instruct Skeinforge to decrease the flow rate of the support material. This produces a thinner and weaker filament wall that is easier to remove. By lowering **Support Gap over Operating Flow Rate (ratio)**, we can instruct Skeinforge to decrease the distance between the support material and the model.

By activating **Support Cross Hatch**, a stronger support structure can be generated. This is, in many cases, difficult to remove from the model. It's best to keep this feature deactivated.

Creating support with Slic3r

In this recipe, we're going to explore the different adjustments that can be made for determining where and how much support is added. We'll be using similar options that we used in Skeinforge.

Getting ready

You'll need the soccer ball wireframe model.

How to do it...

1. Under **Print Settings**, select **Support material**. Check the box for **Generate support material**. Slice and save the G-code.

2. Go to **Overhang threshold** and change the default value from 0 to 80. Slice and save the G-code.

3. Go to **Overhang threshold** and change the default value from 0 to 95. Slice and save the G-code.

4. Go to **Overhang threshold** and change the default value from 0 to 140. Slice and save the G-code.

5. Reset the default value 0 in **Overhang threshold** and uncheck **Generate support material**.

6. Go to **Enforce support for the first** and change the default value from 0 to 60. Slice and save the G-code.

How it works...

Keeping the default value 0 in **Overhang**, the threshold will set the automatic detection of the overhang angle, which is generally 45 degrees. With this particular model, we have the problem of keeping the interior clear of support material. We can see the differences in support generated by changing the angle in the following image:

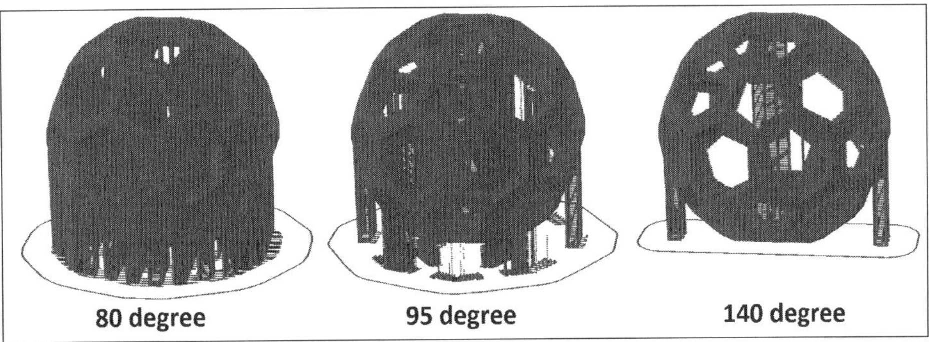

Here, we don't have an option for choosing **Exterior Only** support as we do with Skeinforge but we can make another adjustment. The option to reinforce the support for a specified number of layers is intended to help keep models with a smaller footprint attached to the print bed. In the case of the following model, a very small portion of the model actually bonds to the print bed.

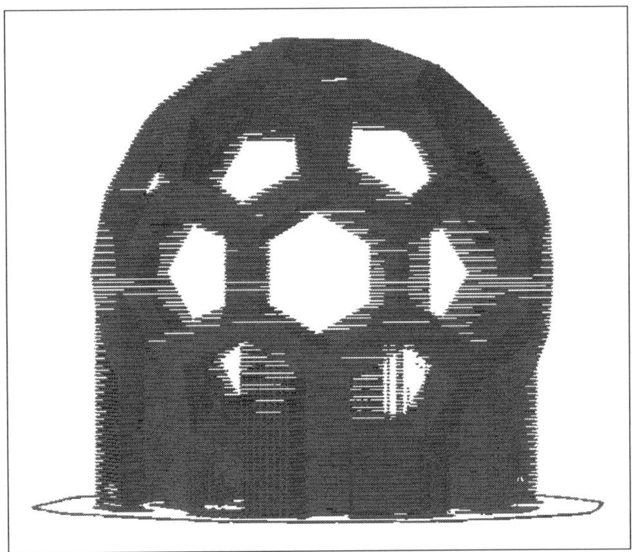

Oddly enough, it's this feature that helps us solve the problem of keeping the interior of the model clear of support. The **Enforce** support option is available whether **Support material** is enabled or not. By turning **Support material** off and selecting a layer count to print, which rises to the middle of the sphere, we can print a stable model without interior support.

Support options with Slic3r

In this recipe, we're going to examine some support options in Slic3r that will adjust the physical contact of the support material to the model. This is important in order to tune a profile that will provide not only good support but also a support material that will easily be removed.

Getting ready

You'll need the jellyfish model.

How to do it...

We will proceed as follows:

1. Under **Print Settings**, select **Support material**. Check the **Generate support material** box.
2. Change the default setting for **Pattern** from `honeycomb` to `rectangular`.
3. Now, choose **Pattern spacing** and change the default value from `0` to `2.5`.
4. We'll test the other support settings at the default values. Slice and save the G-code.
5. Print the model.
6. Now, choose **Pattern spacing** and change the value from `2.5` to `5.0`. Slice and save the G-code.
7. Print the model.

How it works...

With **Pattern spacing**, we're making the same adjustment we made in Skeinforge with **Interface Density Infill (ratio)**. We increased the space between support walls. This is clearly represented in the following image:

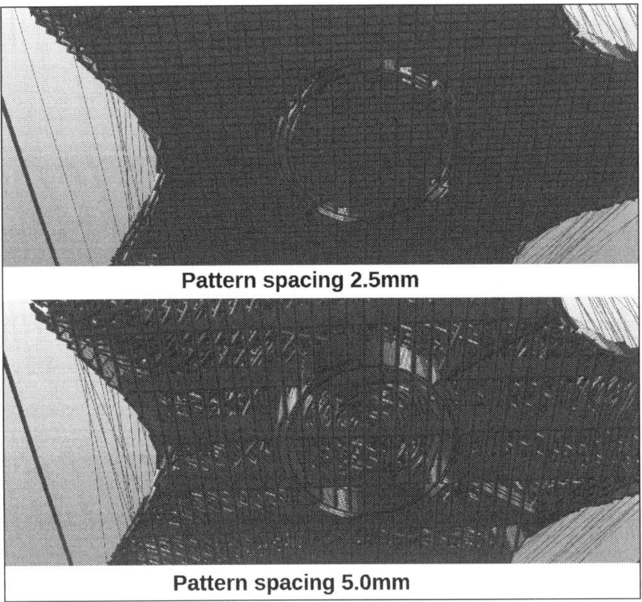

We changed the honeycomb pattern to rectangular because it's generally too difficult to remove. The rectangular pattern is similar to the pattern that Skeinforge generates (when cross hatch is deactivated).

There's more...

Slic3r also has a method of weakening the bond between the support material and the model by creating an interface layer.

By changing the default value from 0 to 1 or more in interface layers, we can activate the function and instruct the slicer to add one or more interface layers. By increasing the interface pattern spacing, we can even make it weaker between the support material and the model by spreading the extrusion further apart.

Reviewing our print results

Generating good support material is a balancing act between fabricating enough layers that will prevent the drooping of the filament and creating layers that are weak enough that they can be removed. In the following image, we can see the support structure under the model of the jellyfish form:

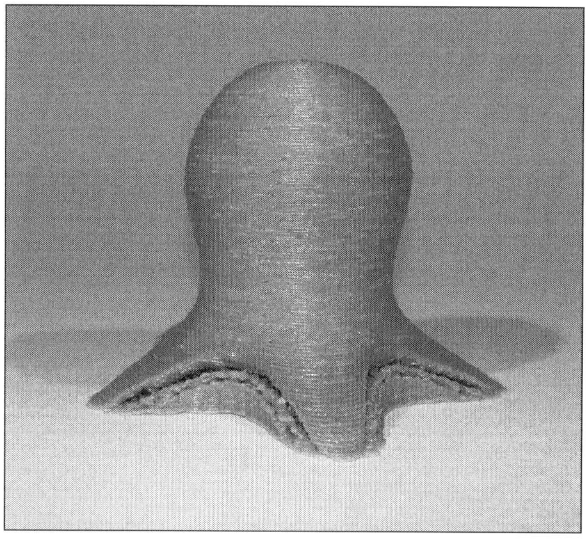

In the following image, we can see the partial removal of support that was generated with the default values in Skeinforge on the left-hand side and Slic3r on the right-hand side:

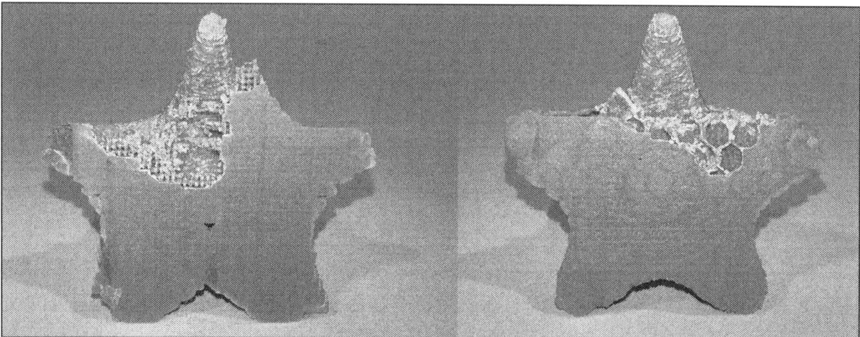

Both of these slicers produced a support that was difficult to remove. By changing the pattern's shape to rectangular and increasing the pattern spacing, both slicers generated a support that was easier to remove. This can be seen in the following two images:

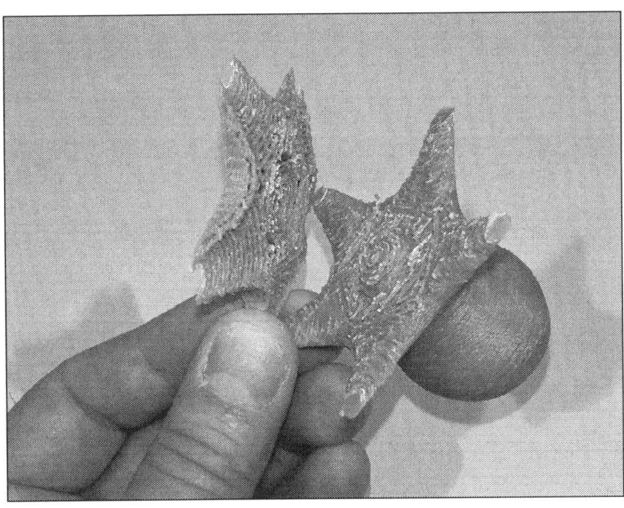

In the preceding image, Skeinforge generated a support that was removed in one piece.

In the preceding image, Slic3r generated a support that was easily removed with a pair of pliers.

A fine finish typically cannot be achieved in areas where support has been generated. There will be a "loose" appearance of the individual filament lines. There will also be marks left by the areas where the support was in contact with the model. We can see a comparison of the two bottoms of the model in the preceding image. On the left-hand side, Skeinforge was the slicer utilized, and on the right-hand side, Slic3r was used.

Overall, we can see in the following image that both slicers did well in printing the jellyfish form:

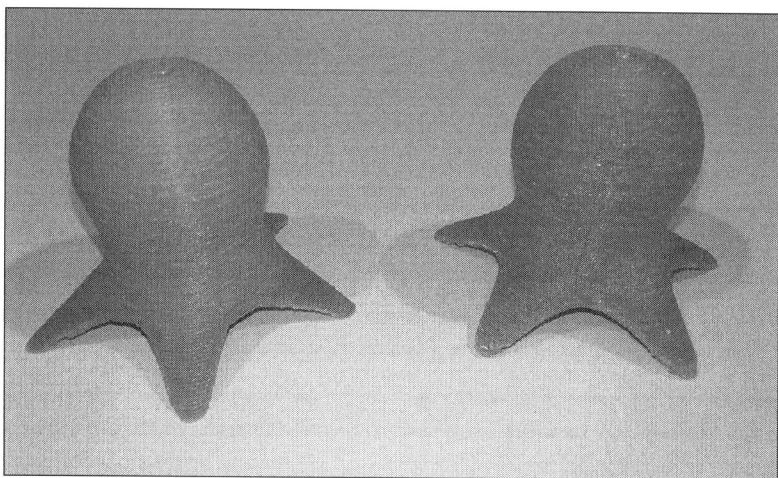

The following is the starfish shape to which we attached a looped handle:

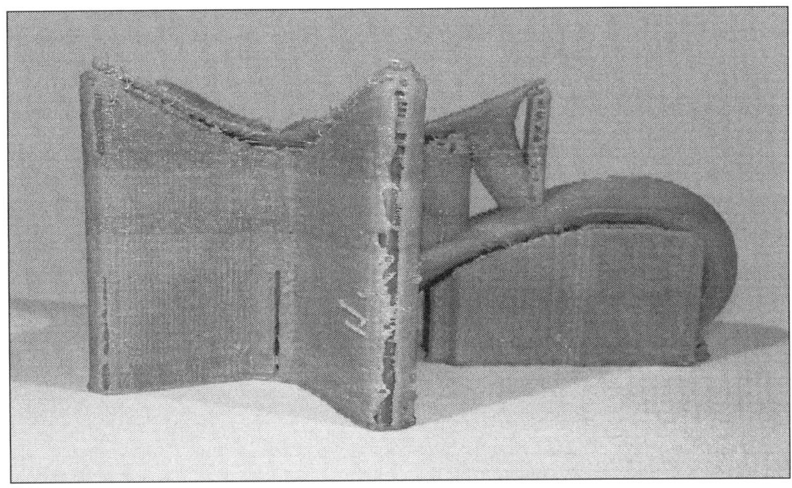

Slic3r was used to generate the support material with the same settings as the jellyfish.

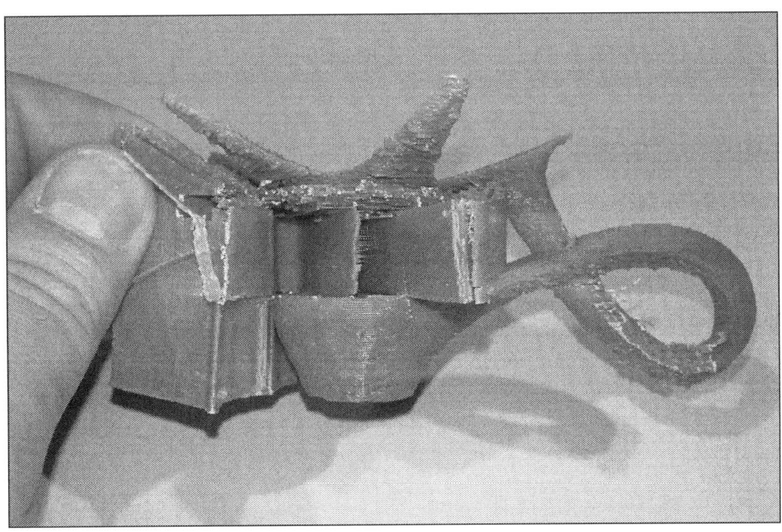

The support material was removed with ease, but there are many areas on the model that are defaced by the contact points of the support material.

Under the starfish shape, there is heavy distortion of the filament layers.

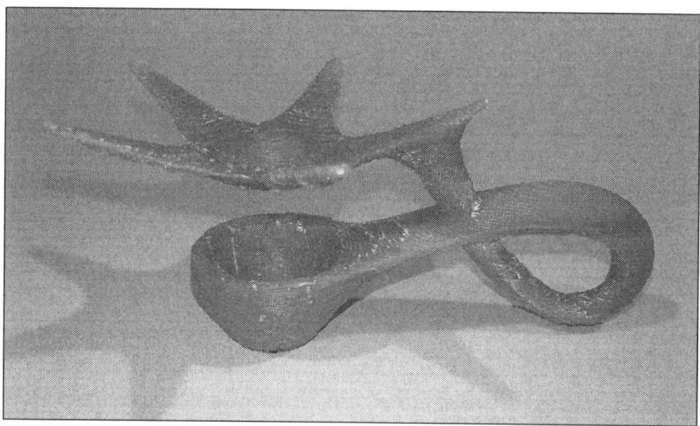

Overall, the model printed successfully. Without a support structure, it could not have been printed.

The slicer profiles that we created in the preceding recipes are a good start for creating support material. Always use your G-code viewer to check the generated support for issues.

However, it is more difficult to gauge the interface values using a G-code viewer. Only by printing the model will you have a good idea of how well the support will release and how well it will support the layers.

7
Texture – the Good and the Bad

In this chapter, we will cover the following recipes:

- Making textures with Meshmixer
- Making stencils with Paint.NET
- Stamping stencils with Meshmixer
- Making patterns with Meshmixer
- Making more patterns with Meshmixer
- Making textures with MeshLab
- Adjusting the travel speed with Skeinforge
- Adjusting retraction with Skeinforge
- Adjusting Jitter with Skeinforge
- Adjusting the travel speed with Slic3r
- Adjusting retraction with Slic3r
- Randomizing the starting points with Slic3r

Introduction

In this chapter, we're going to learn how to make some interesting surface textures. Modeling programs such as SketchUp and TopMod are great for creating smooth geometric forms, but how would we create a model with realistic organic textures? Meshmixer makes available a set of stencils that can create interesting textures, which can be either stamped or brushed. We'll learn how to customize our own stencils and use them on the starfish shape we made earlier with TopMod.

Later in this chapter, we're going to find that some textures are undesirable. During the process of 3D printing, some imperfections may occur. These imperfections will leave bumps, holes, and stringing filaments on the model. We'll look at how we can avoid these imperfections by making calibrations with the slicer.

Making textures with Meshmixer

Meshmixer offers a great set of sculpting brushes. One powerful feature is the ability to stamp or drag a pattern. These tools allow a variety of textures to be applied to the surface of a model with stencils. In this recipe, we're going to look at how this works using the three default stencils.

Getting ready

You'll only need Meshmixer for this recipe.

How to do it...

We will proceed as follows:

1. Open Meshmixer and select **Import Sphere**.
2. Go to the toolbar and select **Sculpt**. At the top in the pop-up menu, toggle to **Surface**.
3. From the new menu selection, choose **Stencils**. From the pop-up row on the right-hand side of the window, choose the **Stencil** icon [■].
4. Your drawing brush will now use this stencil to draw with. You can make changes to the brush characteristics from the **Properties** window.

5. Using the following sphere, change some of the properties of the stencil to experiment with how it can make textures:

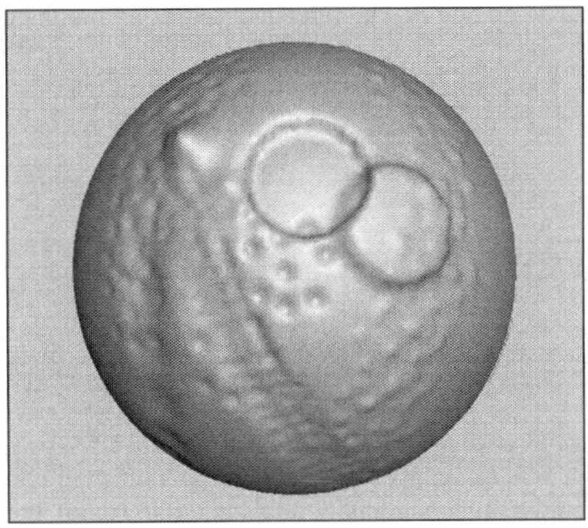

6. Select the remaining two stencils and experiment with how they work and compare the results.

How it works...

The stencils work with any of the brush types that are available in the **Brushes** menu. The control of the brush is adjusted in the same way as any of the other brushes that function using the parameters available in the **Properties** window. The use of the *Ctrl* key also works with the brush texture.

By holding down the key, the stencil will be inverted, thereby making an indentation on the surface similar to what a physical stamp tool would make on a ball of clay. Changing the **Falloff** will adjust the walls of the shape.

There's more...

Models loaded in Meshmixer appear to have the color and lighting of a chrome material. This can be changed. By selecting **Shaders** in the toolbar, a pop-up window displays an assortment of materials that can be selected to shade your model. It works by clicking, holding, and dragging the sphere of your choice to your model and dropping it. The model then takes on the material's characteristics.

Making stencils with Paint.NET

There aren't many stencils available to choose from in Meshmixer, but fortunately, it's easy to add custom stencils to your palette. This makes for a powerful feature that has unlimited potential. In this recipe, we're going to look at how we can make some simple stencils using a freeware program called Paint.NET. Refer to the following screenshot:

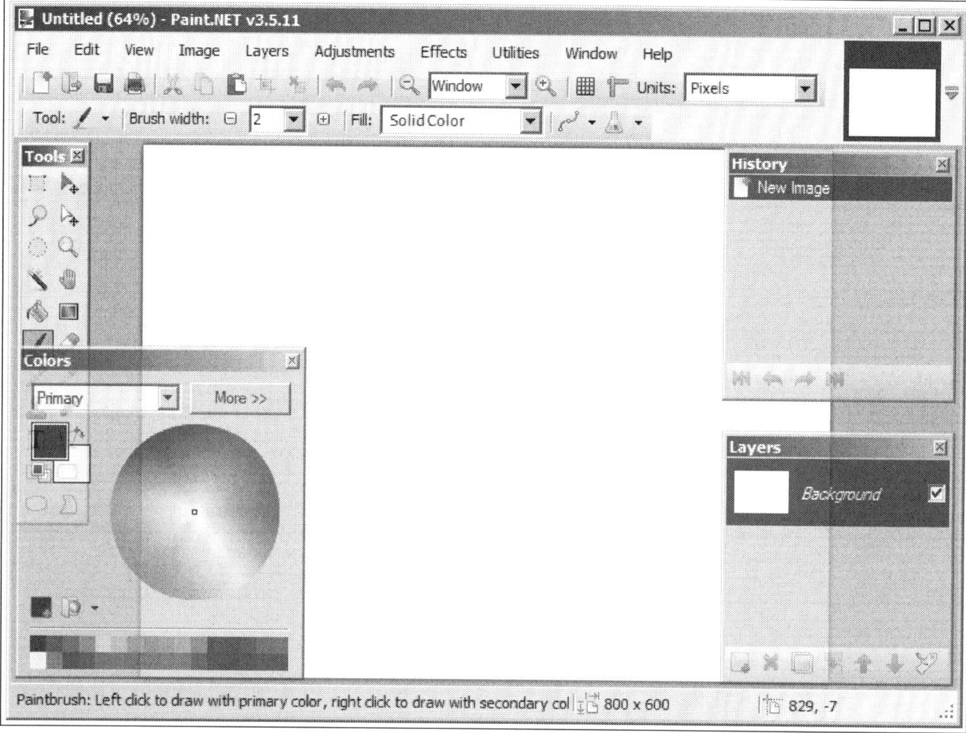

In the preceding screenshot, we can see the interface of Paint.NET. You'll find that it has some features that are similar to the Windows Paint accessory, but with a lot of additional features, such as Photoshop, that expensive photo editors will have.

Getting ready

You'll need to download Paint.NET from `http://www.getpaint.net/download.html` and follow its installation instructions.

This book uses Paint.NET v3.5.11 for Windows. It's not available for other OS platforms.

How to do it...

We will proceed as follows:

1. Go to **File** and select **New**. From the pop-up window, change the **Width** and **Height** to 100 x 100 pixels. Left-click on **OK**.

2. First, go to the menu at the top and adjust the brush width from the default value 2 to a width of 9.

3. Now, select the paintbrush icon from the **Tools** palette (*B*).

4. Draw the following shape using the **Ellipse** (*S*) and **Line/Curve** tools (*O*) from the **Tools** palette:

5. Now, go to the menu and select **Effects**. From the drop-down menu, select **Blurs** and then **Gaussian Blur**.

6. From the **Gaussian Blur** pop up, adjust the **Radius** to 10. Left-click on **OK**. You should have the following image:

7. Go back to the menu and select **Adjustments**. Choose **Invert Colors**.

8. Save the texture image with whichever common image format you would like to use.

9. Continue to make more textures until you have a series similar to the following set:

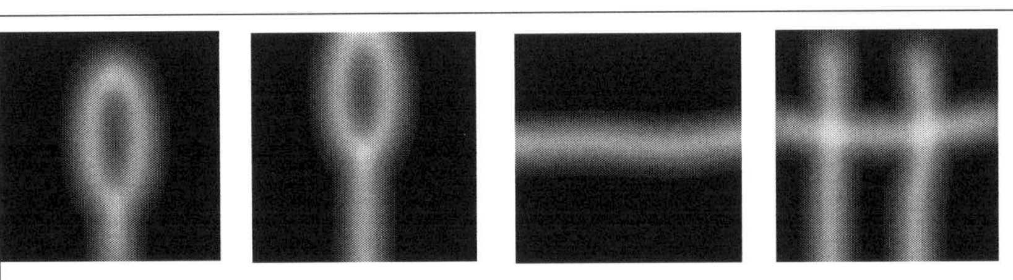

How it works...

Paint.NET is a great program for creating stencils, but any graphics program that has at least a blur filter and the ability to invert an image will suffice. Paint.NET has a nice collection of artistic filters and fractal-generating tools, which would be worth exploring for creating textures.

When we create a grayscale image for use as a texture, it's important to keep in mind that the black areas are null areas. They will not affect the model's surface with or without the *Ctrl* key pressed. The tonal quality of the image will determine the strength of the brush texture, with the white areas creating the strongest affect.

Stamping stencils with Meshmixer

In this recipe, we're going to work through an exercise using the stencils we made with Paint. NET. We'll use the starfish model we made in *Chapter 6, Making the Impossible*, as our work example. We'll find that stamping stencils with Meshmixer is an easy solution for making a realistic organic form using patterns and textures.

Getting ready

You'll need the starfish model that we made in TopMod.

First, we'll need to do a little work with the model before we start. Let's take a look at the following image of real starfish:

We'll need to model some more features of the starfish before we can add a texture.

The starfish on the left-hand side of the following screenshot is what we made in TopMod. The starfish on the right-hand side has been modeled in more detail using the sculpting brushes in Meshmixer. You should be familiar with these tools from the Meshmixer recipes in *Chapter 2, Optimizing the Printing Process*.

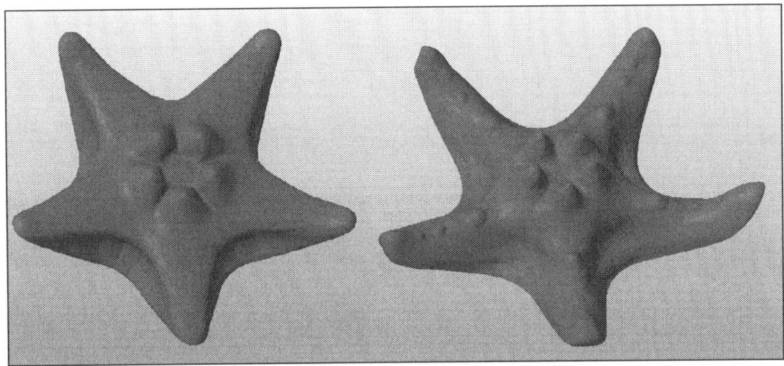

How to do it...

We will proceed as follows:

1. First, we need to load the brush textures into Meshmixer. We do this by selecting **Stencils** in the **Sculpt** menu. Click on the large **+** icon and locate your stencil image. Click on **Open** and repeat this process for all the texture images.

2. Now, your stencils are available in the palette. Choose the following texture:

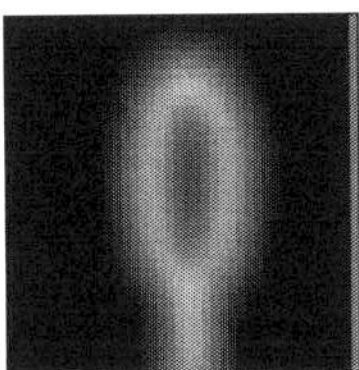

3. We're going to use the **Draw3** brush from the **Sculpt** menu.

4. In **Falloff**, select the **Bubble** icon (it's the last one in the row).

5. Now, we need to set a few parameters in the **Properties** window. Set **Strength** to `100` and keep the other default settings.

6. Under **Refinement**, set **Refine** to `100` and keep the other default values.

7. Hold the *Ctrl* key as you left-click on the object. This will stamp the stencil along the bottom of the starfish, as illustrated in the following image:

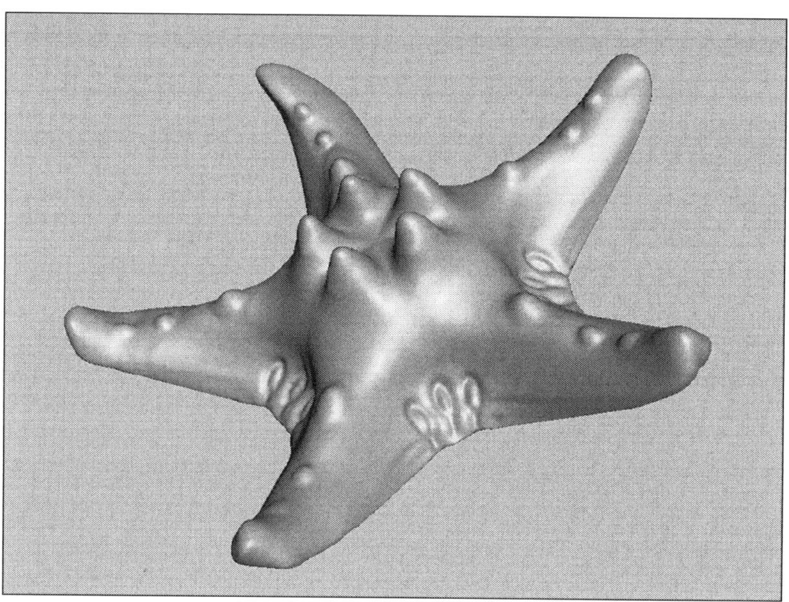

8. In **Properties**, change the value in the **Size** tab from 38 to a lower value to reduce the size of the stencil as you move out towards the tip. Stop when you reach slightly past the midway point.

9. Now, choose the following stencil:

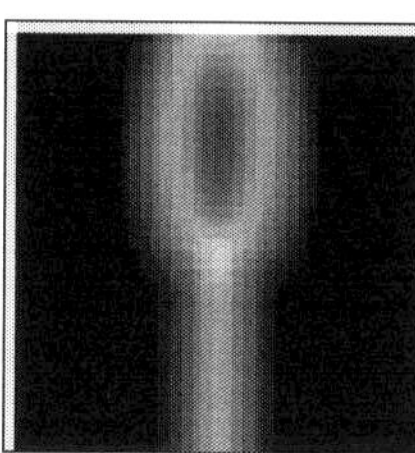

10. Continue the stamping along the arms, reducing the size as you go, until you have a pattern similar to the one illustrated in the following image:

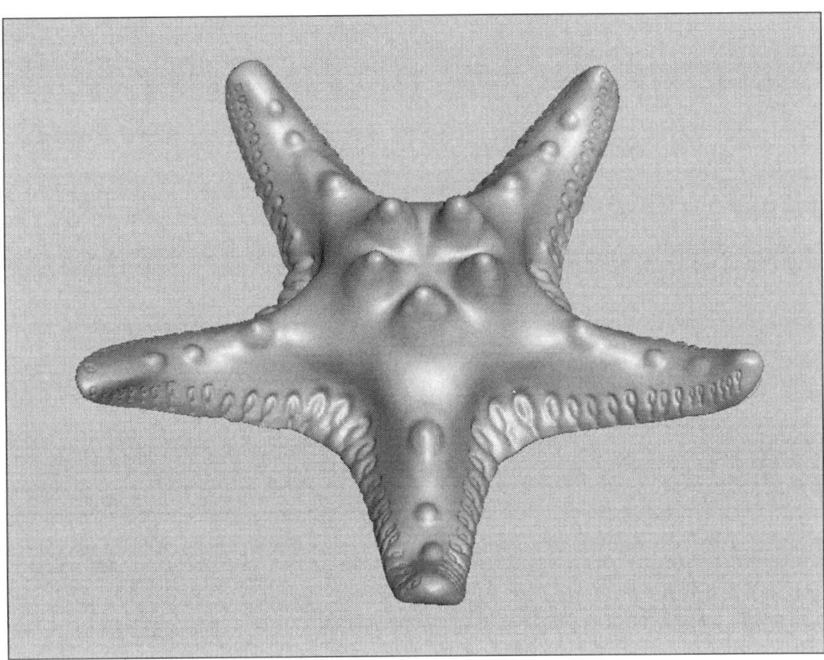

11. Now, choose the following stencil:

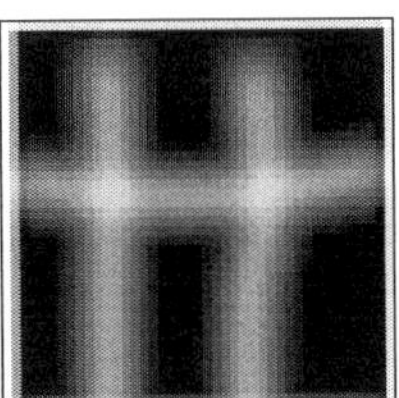

12. Increase the brush size back to 50. Create a series of crosshatchings along the broad open areas of the arms, as illustrated in the following image. Reduce the brush size in the narrow portions when needed.

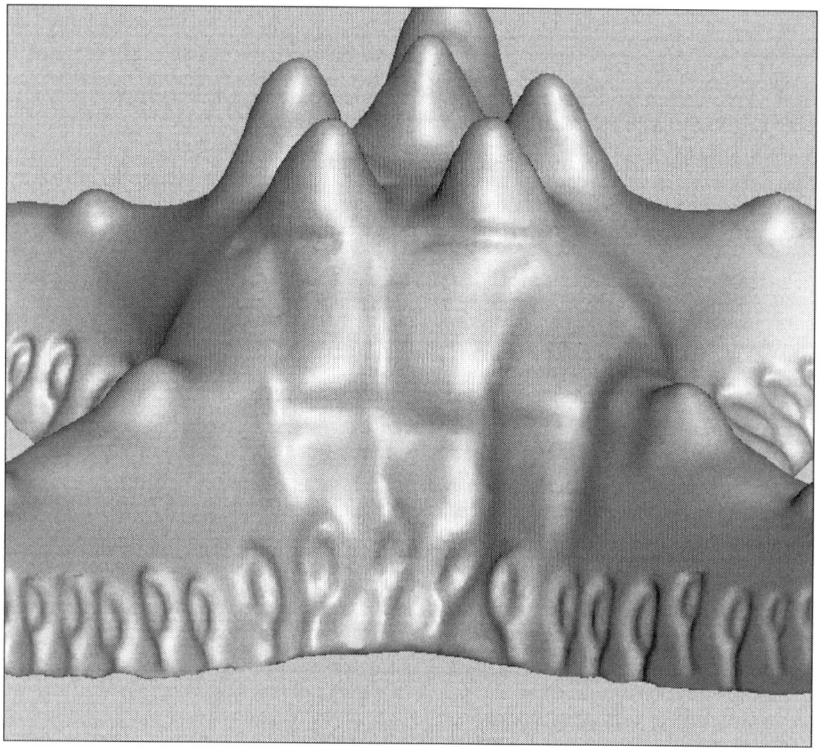

13. Now, we'll add a final detail. Choose the following stencil:

14. Use this stencil to indent around the horns and anywhere else that seems appropriate.

How it works...

In the following image, we can see how well these tools work in creating a model with organic qualities:

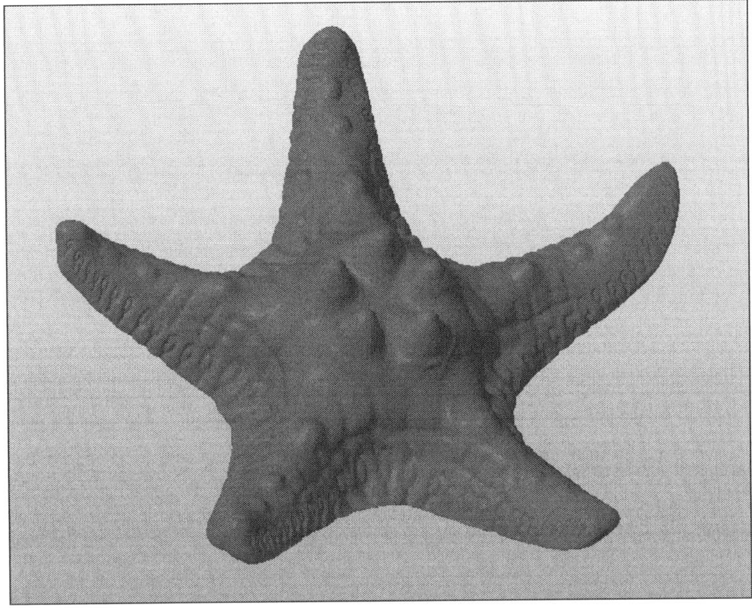

With practice, it shouldn't take long to create interesting textures or surface details using these tools. It would have taken a considerably longer time if we had modeled the starfish with the standard sculpting brushes.

Making patterns with Meshmixer

Some really cool texture effects can be made with the pattern tool. We'll now take a look at the three basic patterns that can be used to carve or build up a model using the model's form.

Getting ready

For this recipe, we'll use the Meshmixer bunny. Import it from the **Import Bunny** icon at the welcome screen or from **File** in the menu.

How to do it...

We will proceed as follows:

1. To access **Make Pattern**, go to the toolbar on the left-hand side and choose **Edit**. It's located at the end of the pop up. When you select **Make Pattern**, you'll see the following image:

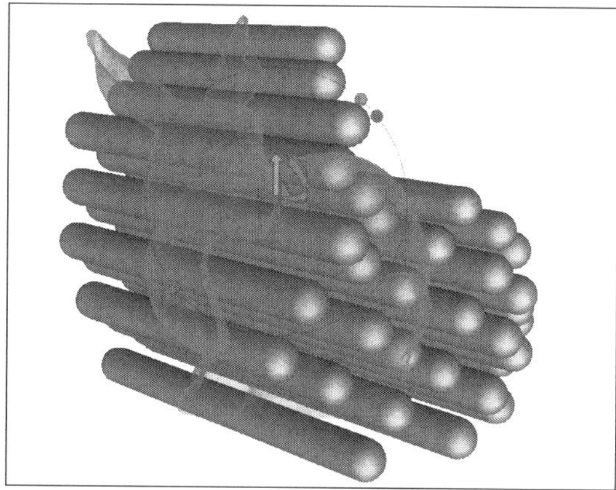

2. There are three pattern choices: tube, sphere, and lattice. The **Tiled Tubes** pattern is the default setting. It creates a pattern by filling the object with tubes and then subtracts them from the original object. The orientation of the tubes can be adjusted by the red, blue, and green axes controls. Different orientations are illustrated in the following image:

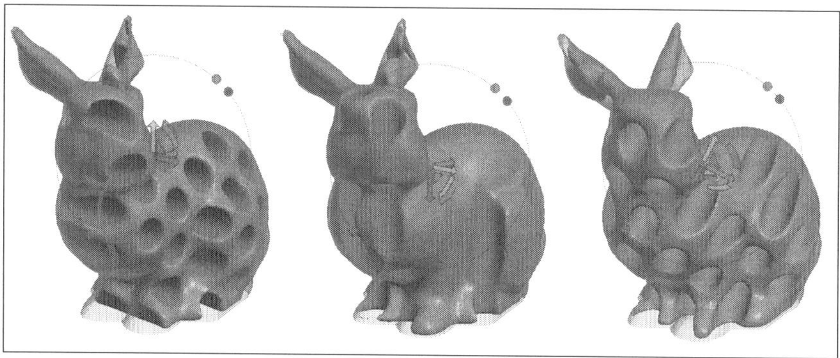

3. Choose how you want the tubes to be positioned by clicking, holding, and dragging the axes. Select **Update** when you've made your choice. During this time, you can go back and readjust the axes without making permanent changes. Just be sure you update the position of the tubes each time to see the results.

4. Select **Accept** when you've made your choice to save the pattern. After the pattern has been saved, the bunny will appear solid again on the screen. To see the pattern result, close the eye icon in the **Object Browser** window by clicking on it (**Object Browser** is a small floating window at the bottom-right corner of the workspace).

5. Explore the other patterns using spheres and lattices. Be careful when using the lattice pattern. Meshmixer will change **Subtract** to **Intersect** in the **Properties** window. Make sure you choose **Subtract** for this recipe.

How it works...

A variety of patterns can be made by adjusting the **Element Dimension** and **Element Space** properties. The following images illustrate the changes in dimension:

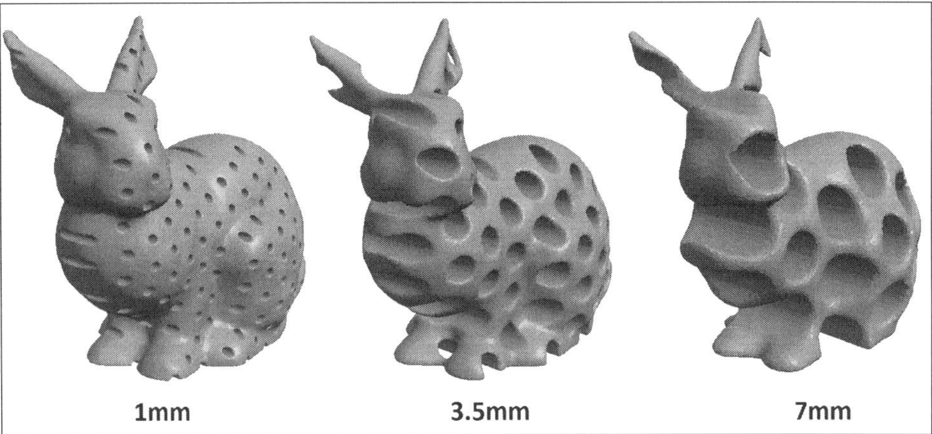

The following images illustrate the changes in space:

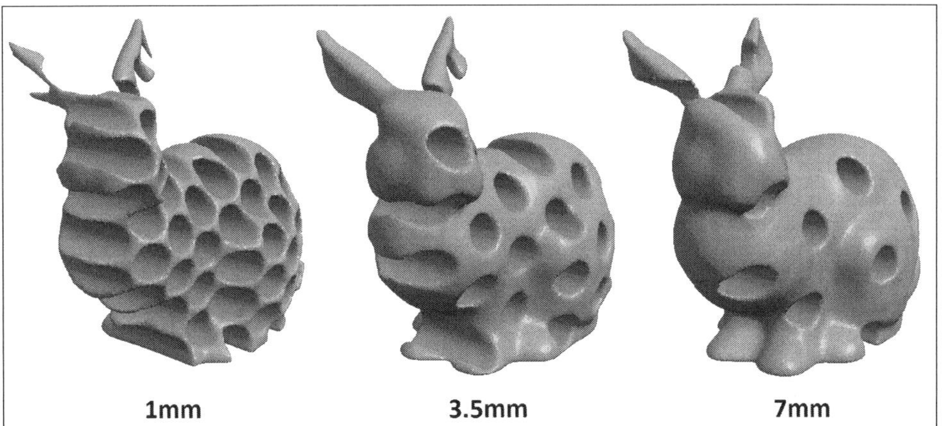

When both of the pattern properties are changed, more options are available. In the following image, the dimension was changed to `1` mm and space was changed to `0.3` mm:

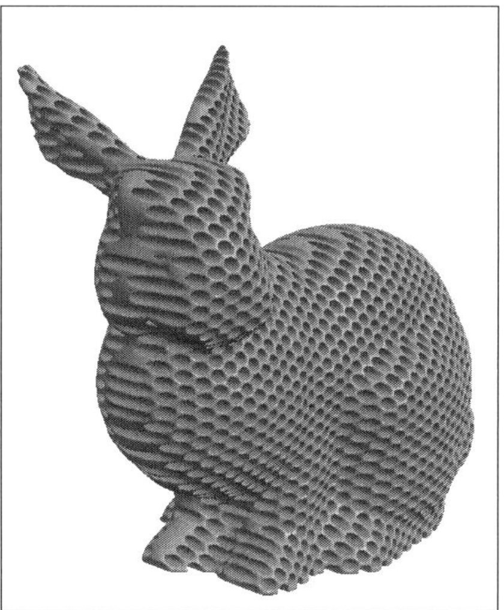

There's more...

When the lattice pattern is chosen, Meshmixer changes the default setting from **Subtract** to **Intersect**. What this does is inverts the way in which the shape is interpolated. Instead of creating a negative space of the pattern, it creates a solid. Refer to the following image:

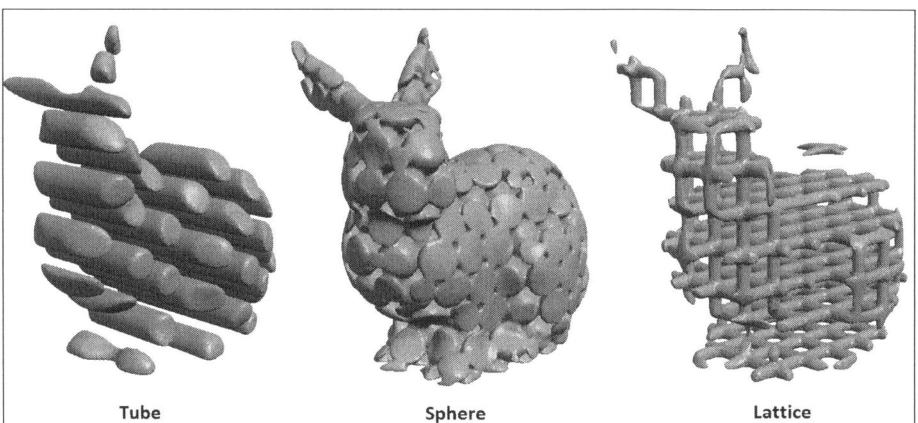

We can see what happens to the bunny when we choose **Intersect** for all three patterns. With all the values at default settings, only the sphere pattern generates a model that will print well. By experimenting with the dimension and space elements, interesting textures can be generated with all three patterns.

The default activation of **Clip to Surface** in **Properties** also generates a different output. It'll work in different ways depending on which pattern you select and whether you use **Subtract** or **Invert**. Deactivating and experimenting with the results is the best way to get results.

Making more patterns with Meshmixer

The pattern tool can also create interesting surfaces using the model's mesh as a template. This is very similar to what we did in *Chapter 5*, *Manipulating Meshes and Bridges*, when we used TopMod to make 3D pipes of a wireframe. In this recipe, we'll discover how Meshmixer can be utilized to create an interesting texture.

Getting ready

For this recipe, we'll use the Meshmixer bunny again. It's a good form with lots of curves and it's not a solid, so that'll give us an opportunity to see what happens inside the model. First, we'll need to make a quick modification. We need to reduce the bunny's polygon count.

We can do this easily using the keyboard shortcuts. The shortcut *Ctrl + A* will select the entire model and *Shift + R* will bring up the **Reduce** window. Reduce the bunny to **96%** and save the model.

How to do it...

We will proceed as follows:

1. Load the reduced bunny mesh. Go to **Edit** and choose **Make Pattern**.
2. Change **Tiled Tubes** to **Dual Edges**. Accept the changes and save the model.
3. Reload the reduced bunny mesh.
4. Change **Dual Edges** to **Mesh + Delaunay Dual**. Accept the changes and save the model.

How it works...

The mesh pattern tools work best with polygons that are large. The polygon edge must have enough space to be inflated to the width that's specified in **Element Dimension**. The default value is 2 mm, so the mesh polygons must be sized appropriately for the effect you wish to achieve. The following image is a comparison of the default bunny mesh with the dimension set at 0.5 mm. The reduced bunny mesh is generated with the default dimension setting of 2.0 mm.

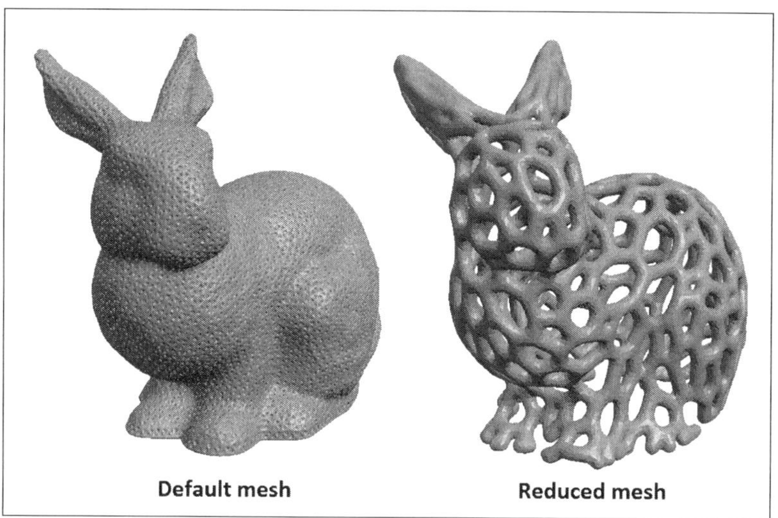

Default mesh   **Reduced mesh**

The primary difference between the **Dual Edges** and **Mesh + Delaunay Dual Edges** options is what happens inside the model. Let's look at the bottom of both of these models in the following illustration:

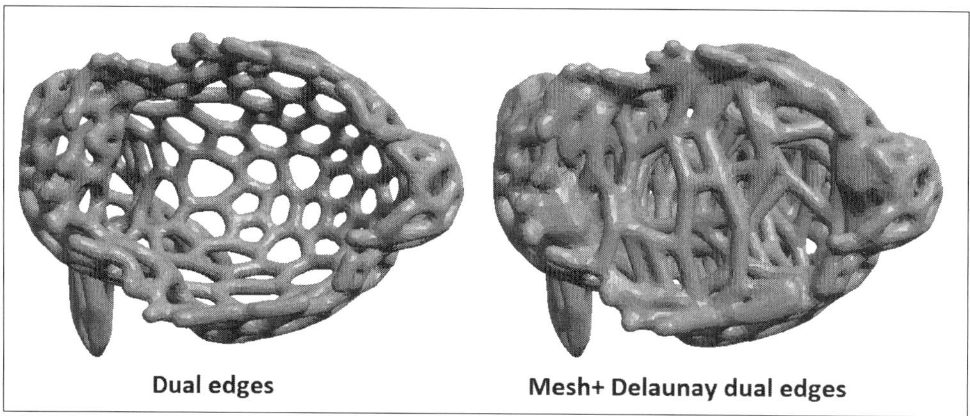

Dual edges   **Mesh+ Delaunay dual edges**

We can see that the interior of the Delaunay option will generate a mesh-like support structure within the model, whereas the dual edge option generates a clean interior.

There's more...

Interesting texture effects can be made by combining the original model with the generated mesh model, as shown in the following image:

This is achieved by starting with the original bunny. Append **Import** to the dual edge bunny mesh so that both meshes are added together. To make this a permanent composite, you'll need to combine them. From the **Object Browser** window, hold *Shift* and click on the unselected file.

This will select both the bunny files and also bring forth a pop-up menu. From this pop up, select the **Combine** option. Now, the model can be exported as one file.

Making textures with MeshLab

MeshLab has a variety of options for creating random patterns and textures on a model. We're going to look briefly at a couple of these options in this recipe.

Getting ready

You'll need MeshLab open and ready.

How to do it...

We will proceed as follows:

1. Go to **Filters** in the menu and select **Create New Mesh Layer**. From the cascaded window, select **Sphere**. Choose **Apply** from the pop-up window and click on **Close**.

2. Go back to **Filters** and select **Remeshing, Simplification, and Reconstruction**. From the cascaded window, select **Subdivision Surfaces: LS3 Loop**. Choose **Apply** from the pop-up window and click on **Close**. Save the remeshed sphere.

3. Go back to **Filters** and select **Smoothing, Fairing, and Deformation**. From the cascaded window, select **Fractal Displacement**. Choose **Apply** from the pop-up window and click on **Close**. Save the model.

4. Load the remeshed sphere. Go to **View** in the menu and choose **Show Layer Dialog**.

5. Go to **Filters** and select **Sampling**. From the cascaded window, choose **Montecarlo Sampling**. Change the **Number of samples** option to 10. Choose **Apply** and click on **Close**.

6. Go back to **Filters** and select **Smoothing, Fairing, and Deformation**. From the cascaded window, select **Craters Generation**.

7. In the pop-up window, we see **Montecarlo Samples** listed in both **Target mesh** and **Samples layer**. Change the **Target mesh** to **Sphere**.

8. Adjust **Min crater depth** to 0 and **Max crater depth** to 0.04.

9. Choose **Apply** from the pop-up window and click on **Close**. Save the model.

How it works...

A simple method for creating a variety of textures is using fractal displacement. In the following image, we can see the results using the default settings:

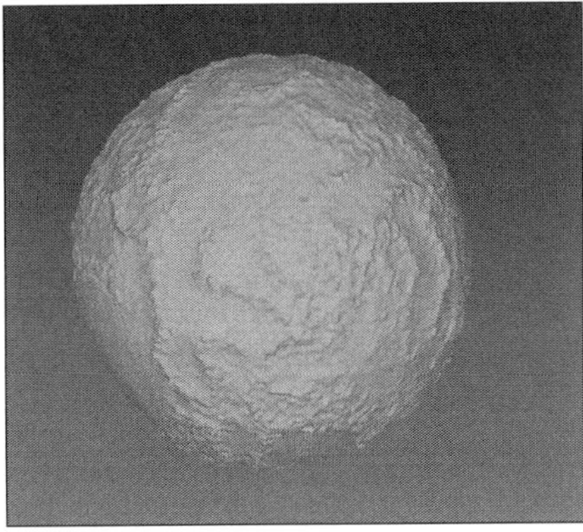

A nice variety of effects can be made using this filter. Try experimenting with the suggested parameter values that are listed at the top of the **Fractal Displacement** window.

Another method to create textures is by sampling and using the crater-generation filter. There are a variety of sampling algorithms to choose from; these sampling algorithms will create different effects. In the following image, only 10 samples were chosen in the Montecarlo sampling instead of the default 40482 samples (this value will change depending on the polygon count of the model sampled):

You'll gain a much better understanding of the texture possibilities if you experiment with all the parameters. There are different sampling options and many variables within the filters that will produce different effects.

Let's print!

We've spent a lot of time learning how to create surface textures, but how do we get rid of unwanted textures that are a result of the printing process? We'll now look at how printing calibrations can improve the surface quality of a model.

We'll do this by running some tests with a model that can be easily made with SketchUp. We can see it in the following image:

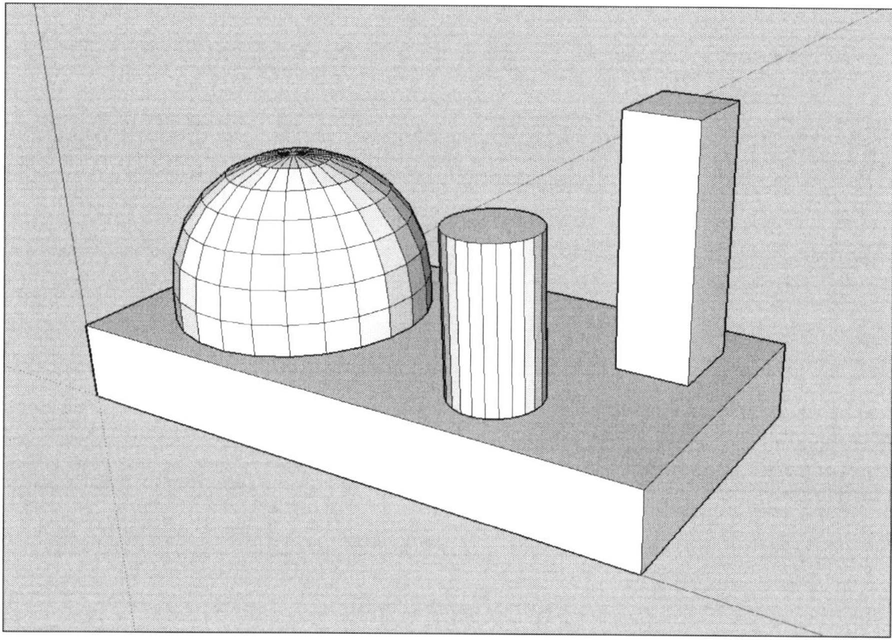

It's a simple construction consisting of different shapes that'll help us with the calibration of different slicer controls.

Before we get started, let's review what we know about temperature control and how it can have an effect on the surface texture.

Temperature control of the extrusion is one of the most important variables that should be determined for your particular system. Every 3D printer will have its own unique signature, and it is in your best interest to take the time to figure out the optimum temperature to operate the printer for the specific filament that you're using. Unfortunately, this variable will probably change with each new roll of filament and invariably with each different color. In the following example, we can see this illustrated with a series of ABS prints, which are printed with different temperatures. We can also see how this can affect the surface quality of the model.

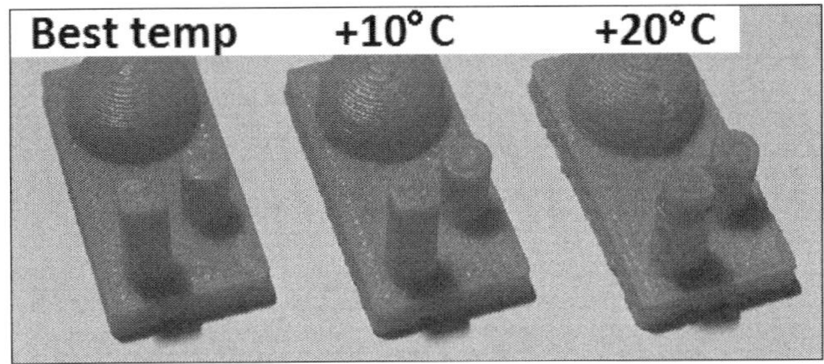

In the next series of images, we can see a more dramatic consequence of variable temperature extrusion when we print with PLA:

Temperature isn't the only variable we should review. There are others such as infill. Infill can also affect the surface quality of prints, especially when we increase the resolution of the print. In the next image, we can see distortion on the flat surface of the test model when we print with a 0.1 mm layer using the best temperature setting:

By increasing the infill and also by adding additional print layers, we can improve the surface quality of the print, as shown in the following image:

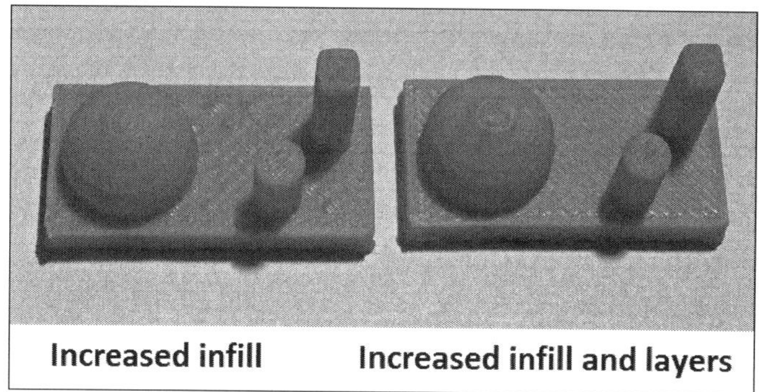

Printing speed is also a variable that will affect surface quality. Even a subtle change in the printing speed, activated by a cool plugin, will create an undesirable surface texture. In the following image, we can see this illustrated in the upper portion of the tallest column:

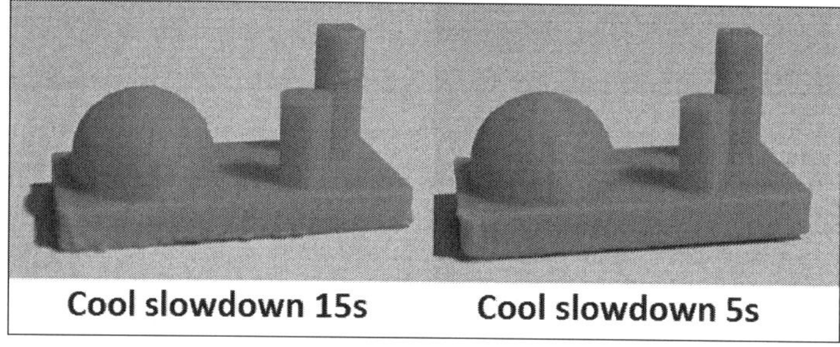

When you change the slowdown speed in Skeinforge's cool plugin, it not only decreases the protuberance in the column, but also creates a slight ripple from the vibration of the increased speed in the lower portion of the image.

We've examined these variables in greater depth in the previous chapters, but we didn't place an emphasis on controlling surface texture. We'll focus now on how we can make adjustments with the slicer that will help us improve our surface quality.

Adjusting the travel speed with Skeinforge

The travel speed is how fast your printer's hot end moves through an open space between sections of your model for each layer. For example, the amount of time it takes for the hot end to transverse between the two columns and dome might allow enough time for your hot end to ooze a minimal amount of material. This excess extrusion will transfer to the next section of the model, creating an unwanted buildup.

Getting ready

You'll need to test the model made with SketchUp. If you would rather download the model, it's available at `http://www.thingiverse.com/thing:152695`. This recipe is also better illustrated if the PLA filament is used.

How to do it...

We will proceed as follows:

1. In Skeinforge, open the **Speed** plugin. Scroll down to the bottom to **Travel Feed Rate (mm/s)** and change the default value `50.0` to `25.0`.

2. Print the surface test model.

3. Go back and change the **Travel Feed Rate (mm/s)** to `15.0`.

4. Print the surface test model.

How it works...

In this recipe, we actually degraded the results by changing the default value to a slower speed. In most cases, we normally wouldn't do this, but it works to better illustrate the effect of this calibration.

In the following image, we can see the buildup from two different travel-speed settings. This is not an uncommon problem, and we'll see how this will help us make decisions with retraction adjustments in the following recipe.

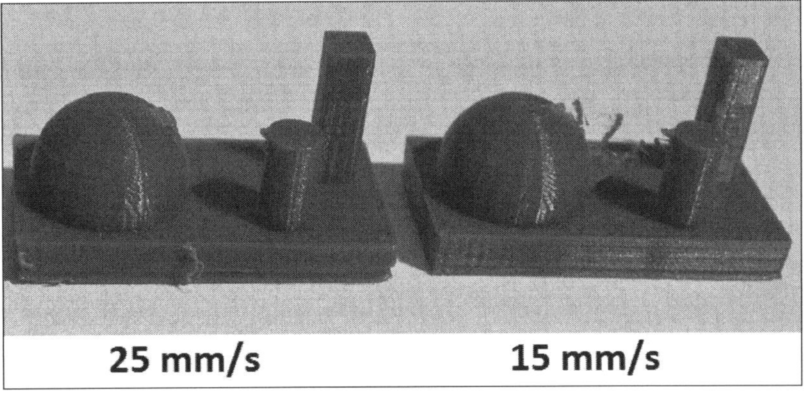

Adjusting retraction with Skeinforge

Our best Skeinforge plugin for eliminating ooze and stringing is the retraction setting in **Dimension**. This plugin allows for adjustments that control how much filament is fed to the hot end.

In this recipe, we're going to make adjustments with retraction speeds and distances to better refine our printing results.

Getting ready

We'll use the SketchUp model for this recipe as well. An extruder using a Bowden cable system would be great for testing these parameters. Bowden cables have a tendency to ooze and string a filament.

How to do it...

We will proceed as follows:

1. In Skeinforge, open the **Dimension** plugin. Go to **Extruder Retraction Speed (mm/s)** and change the default value `12.0` to `32.0`.

2. Print the surface test model.

3. Go back and change **Extruder Retraction Speed (mm/s)** to `85.0`.

4. Print the surface test model.

5. Keep **Extruder Retraction Speed (mm/s)** at `85.0` and scroll down to **Retraction Distance (millimeters)** to change the default value from `0.0` to `1.2`.

6. Print the surface test model.

7. Go back and change **Retraction Distance (millimeters)** to `2.4`.

8. Print the surface test model.

9. Go back and change **Retraction Distance (millimeters)** to `4.8`.

10. Print the surface test model.

How it works...

Ooze and stringing isn't the only cause of unwanted texture on a model; another cause is created by the tool path of the hot end. For each section on each layer, the hot end will begin and end from the same point before it travels to the next section of the model. When this happens, there'll be a minimal discharge of the filament; this will create a buildup of unwanted material. The best method for reducing this discharge is to instruct the extruder to pull back a specified amount of filament when the hot end reaches these points of change. This is called retraction.

At the beginning of the recipe, we made adjustments to the retraction speed. As we can see in the following image, there was very little difference between the speed changes:

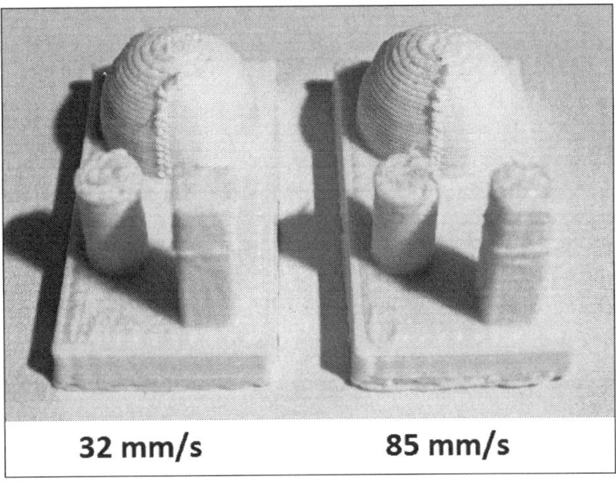

In the latter half of the recipe, we made changes to the retraction distance of the filament, keeping the highest retraction speed, which we made earlier. We can see how this improved the ridge created by the buildup from the following image:

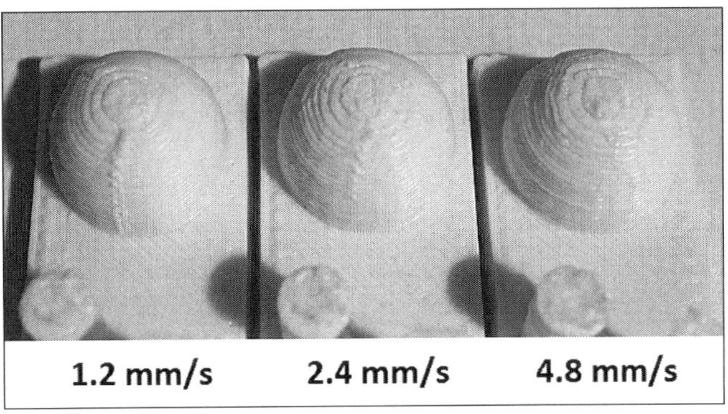

Even though there seemed to be no visible effect on the model's surface when we adjusted the retraction travel speed, we can see a dramatic affect with the next image:

When the travel speed was returned back to the default setting of 16 mm/s and the model was printed with only the adjusted retraction distances, the model printed with severe problems. It is really important to remember that most of the controls in Skeinforge are affected by each other. As a result of this, it is always best to make note of all the default values and the changes made.

Adjusting Jitter with Skeinforge

When the extruder begins with each print layer, it loops back to its starting position and then lifts to the specified layer height for the next layer. As it continues to do this layer by layer, a ridge begins to form.

This is caused by oozing. No matter what we try to prevent oozing, there will always be a continual release of filament. As the hot end remains momentarily stationary in the x and y axes, when it lifts, a fraction of this ooze is noticeable.

Using the Jitter plugin in Skeinforge, you can control where the hot end lifts for each layer. This will eliminate the ridgeline. In the next recipe, we'll see how well the plugin works.

Getting ready

You'll need the SketchUp model. A magnifying glass may help for examining the surface.

How to do it...

We will proceed as follows:

1. In Skeinforge, open the **Jitter** plugin. Check the **Activate Jitter** option. Keep the default values, but make sure **Jitter Over Perimeter Width (ratio)** is 2 . 0.

2. Print the surface test model.

3. Go back and change **Jitter Over Perimeter Width (ratio)** to 8 . 0.

4. Print the surface test model.

How it works...

The Jitter plugin works by changing the starting position for each layer in a different position. This separates any imperfections caused by a layer change throughout the model, as shown in the following image:

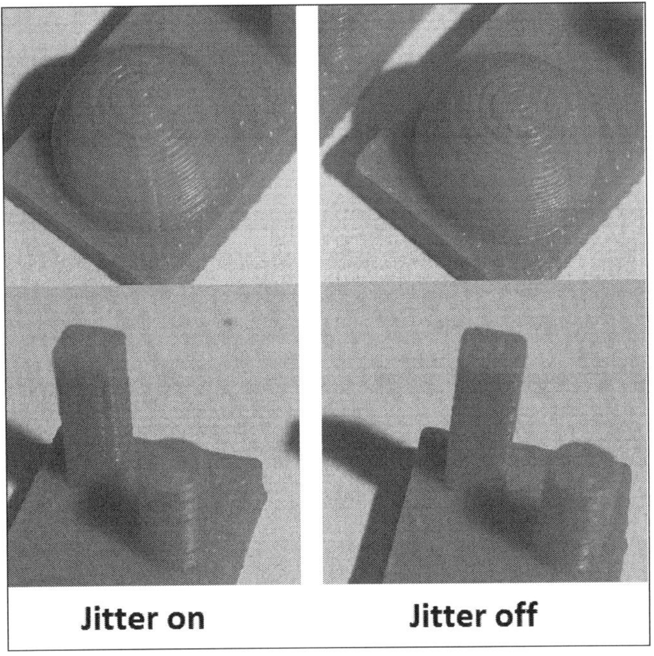

If you look closely at the preceding image, the model in the left-hand side has an indentation along the corner of the column and the side of the dome. This has disappeared on the model in the right-hand side. One of the disadvantages of using Jitter is that sometimes, this will create a random spotting of bumps or indentations all over the model. Depending on the final finishing you desire for the model, this may not be acceptable.

Adjusting the travel speed with Slic3r

Adjusting the travel speed in Slic3r is similar to Skeinforge's approach. By setting a speed based on how many millimeters is transversed in a second, the speed of the hot end can be adjusted when it moves through nonprinted areas.

Getting ready

We'll be using the same SketchUp model that we used in the previous recipes. This will be good, because we'll be able to compare the results between Slic3r and Skeinforge.

How to do it...

We will proceed as follows:

1. In Slic3r, under **Print Settings**, select **Speed**. Scroll down to the middle and select **Travel under Speed for non-print moves**. Change the default value from `130` to `25.0`.
2. Print the surface test model.
3. Go back and change **Travel** to `15`.
4. Print the surface test model.

How it works...

The setting for travel speed works identical to the setting in Skeinforge. Slic3r has a much higher default value for travel; this value works well for most prints.

Adjusting retraction with Slic3r

Slic3r also has retraction settings that can be adjusted for eliminating ooze. In this recipe, we're going to make adjustments with retraction speeds and distances to better refine our printing results.

Getting ready

You'll need the SketchUp model and, preferably, a PLA filament for this recipe. It would also be best if you have a Bowden cable system for printing the tests.

How to do it...

We will proceed as follows:

1. Print the test model using the default settings of the PLA filament.
2. In Slic3r, under **Printer Settings**, go to **Speed** and change the default value from `30` to `45`.
3. Print the surface test model.
4. Go back and change the **Speed** value to `80`.
5. Print the surface test model.
6. Keep the **Speed** value at `80` and scroll up to **Length** to change the default value from `1` to `2`.
7. Print the surface test model.
8. Go back and change **Length** to `3.2`.
9. Print the surface test model.

How it works...

Overall, the default settings for Slic3r work well. Remember that every machine is going to work with its own unique characteristics, sometimes with subtle differences, and at other times, the characteristics are vastly different. Finding a spot where the calibration works well will take a little time in testing out your machine's signature.

In the following image, we can see what happens when we go too far with retraction:

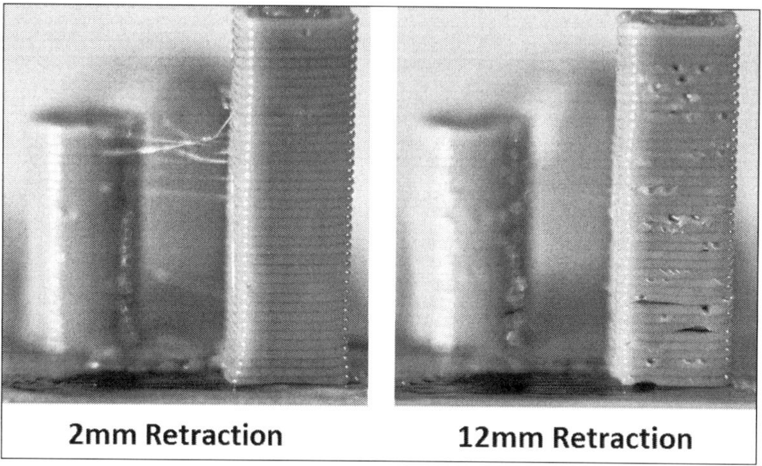

If we instruct the slicer to retract too much filament, we'll end up with layers that are broken up and spotted with holes.

Randomizing the starting points with Slic3r

Like Skeinforge's Jitter, Slic3r has a method of alternating Z-lift points.

Getting ready

You will need the SketchUp model. A magnifier would also be good for looking closely at the surface results.

How to do it...

We will proceed as follows:

1. In Slic3r, under **Print Settings**, select **Layers and perimeters**. Scroll down to the middle and check the **Randomizing starting points** box.
2. Print the surface test model using your best setting.

How it works...

Slic3r only allows for one setting to randomize the Z-lift points. Skeinforge, on the other hand, allows for a degree of choice by adjusting **Jitter Over Perimeter Width (ratio)**. The option to randomize is really the most valuable feature.

Reviewing the print results

Let's look at the following image to see how our starfish is printed:

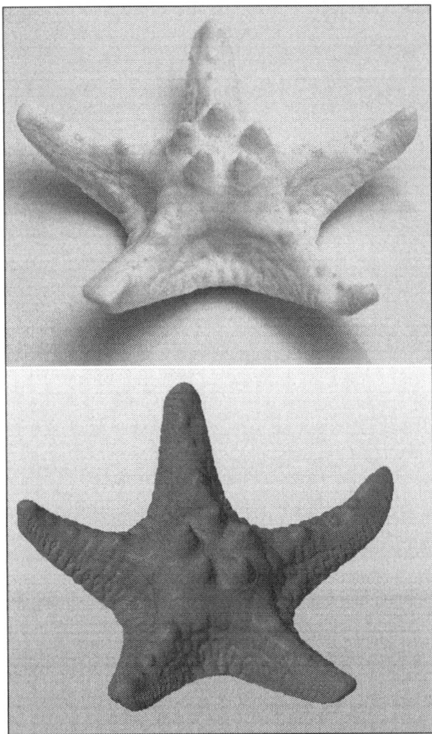

There are two important variables that we need to consider for a successful interpretation of a model with texture detail; they are as follows:

- ▶ Printing resolution
- ▶ The scale of the model

We can see in the close-up in the following image that the stamping is a little softer than the digital model. By increasing the print resolution, we'll gain a little more sharpness in the form. If we were to print the model even larger, this would clarify the texture even more.

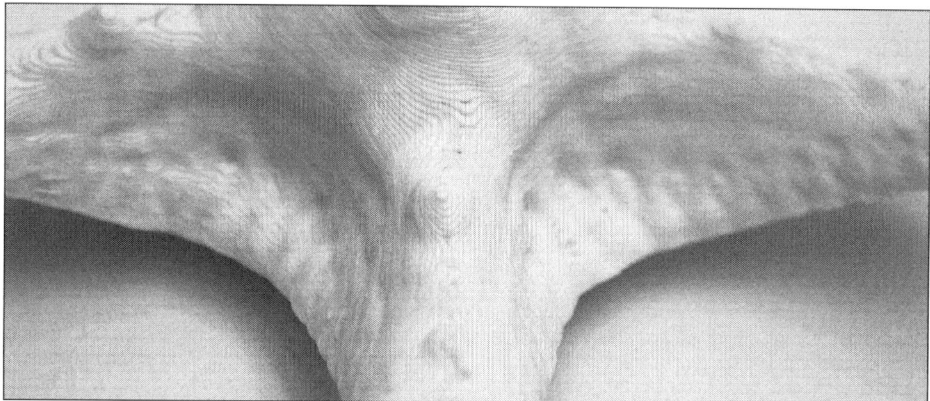

8

Troubleshooting Issues in 3D Modeling

In this chapter, we will cover the following recipes:

- Using Repetier-Host for analysis
- Repairing mesh geometry issues
- Using SketchUp for editing meshes
- Using MeshLab for fixing normals
- Using MeshLab for cleaning meshes
- Creating a hollow model with MeshLab
- Creating a drain hole with Meshmixer

Introduction

Throughout the course of this book, we have examined many issues that affect the 3D printing of a model. We learned how to solve some of these issues by making adjustments with the slicer. However, many problems can occur by way of poor modeling. Modeling for 3D printing utilizes a different approach than what other applications such as 3D rendering and animation may require. A 3D model designed to be 3D printed must have a finished mesh that is triangulated and manifold.

What exactly is a manifold mesh? Simply put, it is a watertight form consisting of a contengous surface of polygons that completely forms a skin of the model. This is illustrated in the following image:

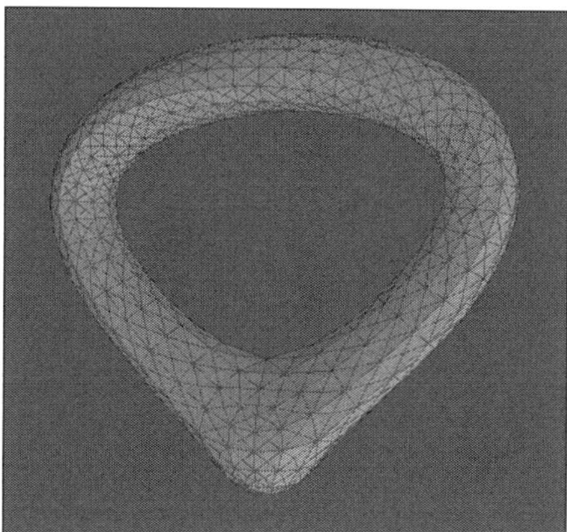

Even though there is a hole through the object, the mesh is manifold. It abides by the following four basic conditions:

- Each edge is shared by two faces. Here are some examples of non-manifold connections:

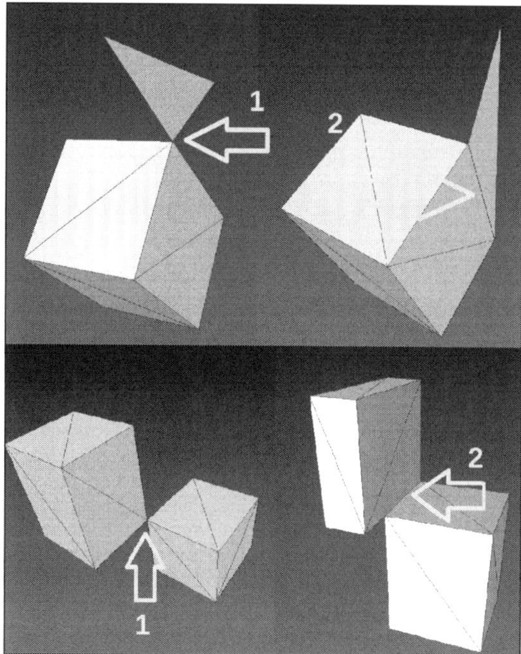

There is only one connection point (by way of vertices) between the faces that are marked as number **1**. The faces connected by more than two edges are shown marked as number **2**. Even though all of the polygons are part of the logical body of the mesh, this model cannot exist in physical space. It would not be possible to manufacture these models with 3D printing.

- There are no self-intersecting faces. Here is an example of self-intersecting faces:

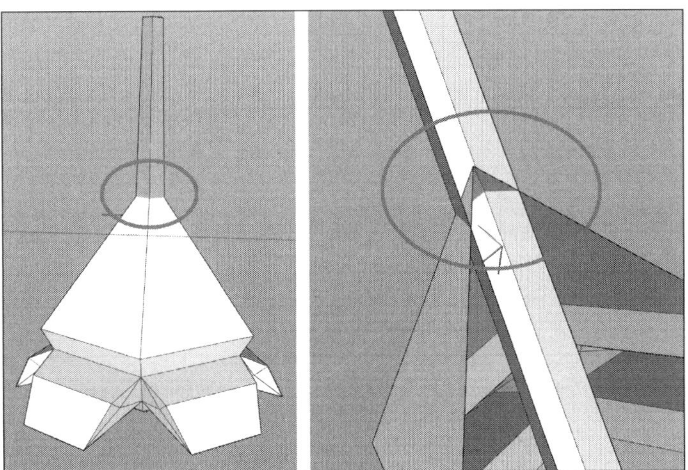

In the preceding image on the left-hand side, there doesn't appear to be a problem. However, inside, we can see that the top faces that form the pyramid shape have been extruded by the faces of the shaft. This creates a series of self-intersecting faces as seen in the image on the right-hand side. Self-intersecting faces often occur when using extrusion tools during modeling. Care must be taken when extrusions pass through another part of the model's surface.

- The mesh is a watertight body. Here are two examples of a mesh with holes:

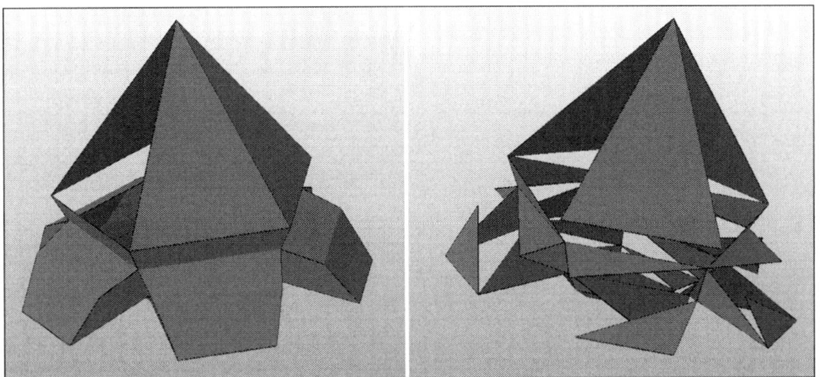

In the preceding image on the left-hand side, we have a model with missing polygons. The image on the right-hand side is an extreme example. It's obvious that neither of these models have a watertight mesh. Most of the time, it's not quite so obvious, and it may require deeper analysis using software tools.

- The normals are oriented coherently. Normals define the exterior and interior of a mesh. Each polygon has a centroid. This is a midpoint created by the intersection of its medians. This is illustrated in the following image on the left-hand side:

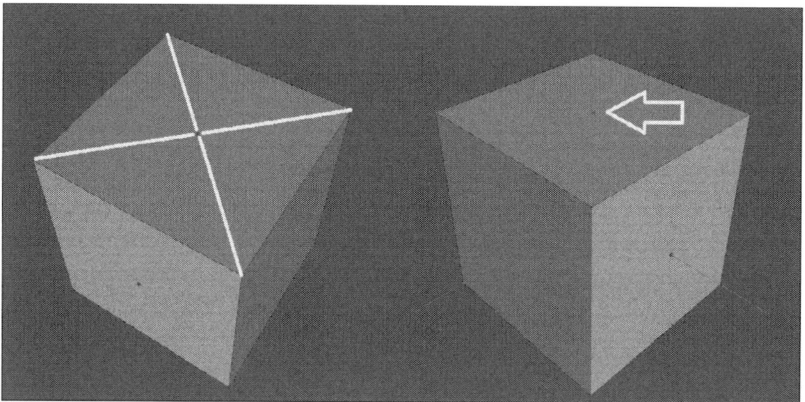

The outside face of a polygon, that is, the normal (that is represented by a line), projects out from the centroid. This can be seen in the preceding right-hand side image. If it's projecting inside, the normal is inverted. This would reveal the interior face on the exterior surface of the mesh. It is understandable how this would be confusing for a slicer when trying to create layers of a model with mismatched normals.

An example can be seen in the following image. The arrow points to a centroid where the normal projects back into the shaft of the model.

All of these non-manifold issues must be repaired for a model to be successfully 3D printed. In this chapter, we will learn how to accomplish this using the programs we used in the preceding chapters and a new freeware program called **netfabb Basic**. We'll also use a free online repair service offered by Microsoft; this service is powered by netfabb.

At the chapter's end, we will learn how to hollow a model and create a drain hole in its shell. This is important if we decide to have the model printed by a 3D printing service such as Shapeways.

Using Repetier-Host for analysis

Repetier-Host is a popular host software package which contains a lot of useful features. The object analysis tool is one of these features. Not only does Repetier-Host analyze the imported model, but it will attempt to make basic repairs.

More information about Repetier-Host can be found in the *Preface*.

In this recipe, we'll use this program to analyze a model saved in both `.obj` and `.stl` formats.

Getting ready

You'll need the `.stl` and `.obj` files of the model that we made in *Chapter 6, Making the Impossible*. It looks similar to the one shown in the following image. From this point on, let's refer to it as the capsule.

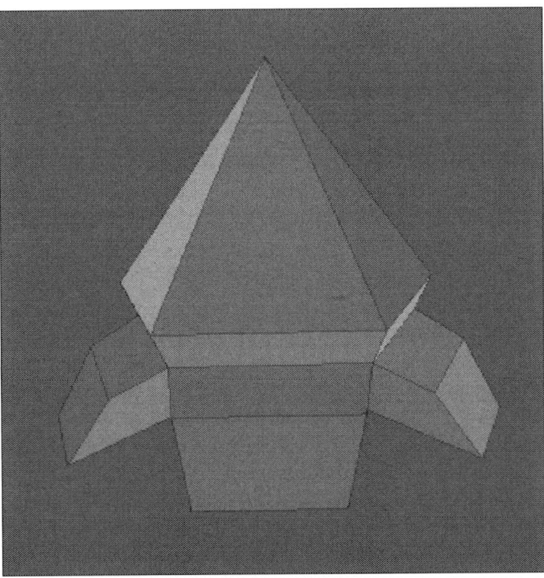

You'll also need to modify it with TopMod for a second model. Do this by selecting the pentagon face as shown in the following image on the left-hand side and extruding it with **Doo Sabin Extrude Mode** with a **Length** of `-4.000`:

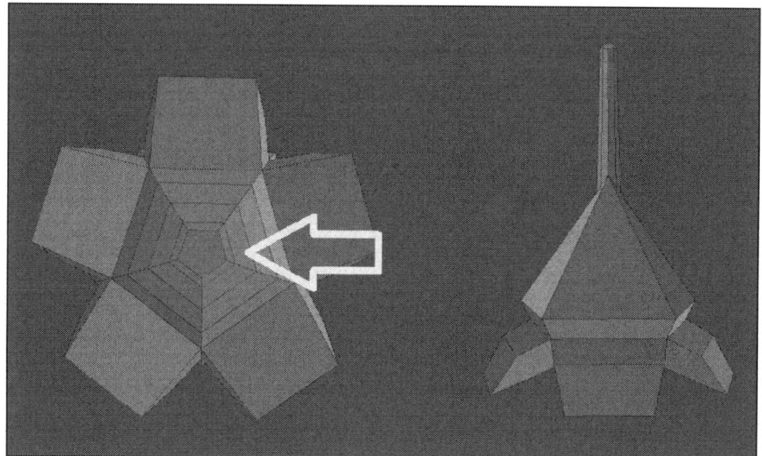

The finished result should look like the preceding image on the right-hand side. We'll refer to it as the extended capsule. Save it as a `.stl` file.

Open Repetier-Host. There's a window with a build plate on the left-hand side and a series of tabs on the right-hand side. Make sure the **Object Placement** tab is selected.

How to do it...

We will proceed as follows:

1. Take the capsule `.stl` file and drop it on the build platform. Let's look at the compiled information displayed on the right-hand side under **Object Analysis**. Take note of all the information here. It should look similar to the following screenshot:

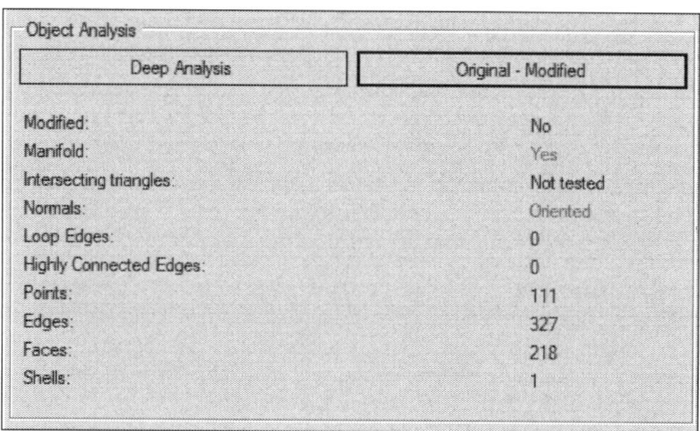

Object Analysis	
Deep Analysis	Original - Modified
Modified:	No
Manifold:	Yes
Intersecting triangles:	Not tested
Normals:	Oriented
Loop Edges:	0
Highly Connected Edges:	0
Points:	111
Edges:	327
Faces:	218
Shells:	1

2. We'll take a look at how Repetier-Host modified the model (if any modifications were made) by exporting a `.stl` file. Do this by selecting the disc icon as shown circled in the following screenshot. After exporting the model, clear the build platform.

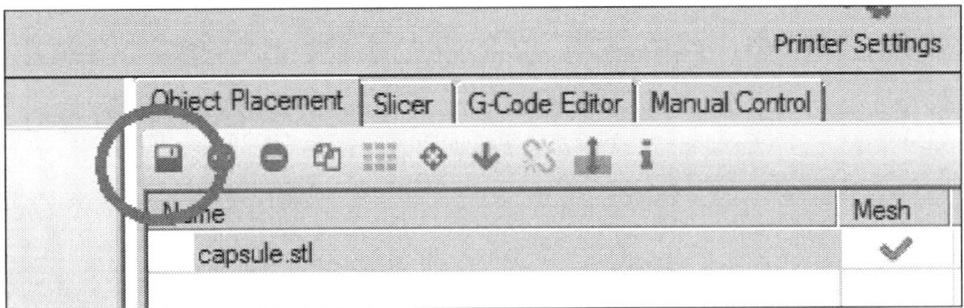

3. Left-click on the **Deep Analysis** button. The result should look like the one shown in the following screenshot:

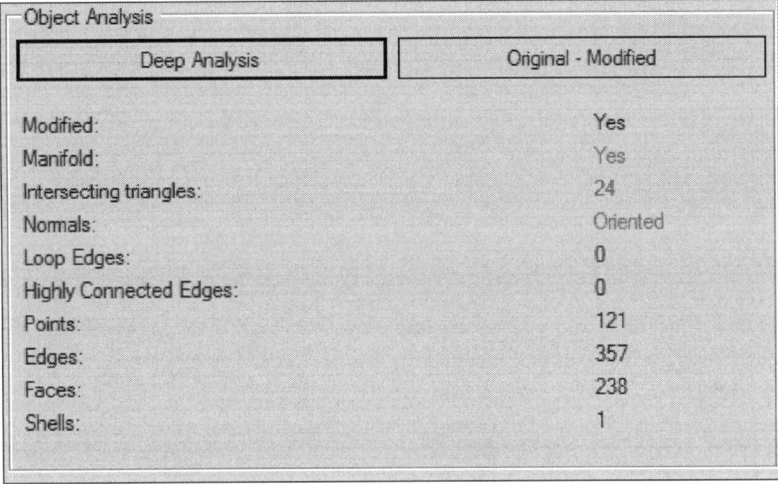

4. Export the `.stl` file and clear the build platform.

5. Now, we'll test the capsule `.obj` file. Drop the file on the build platform. The analysis that you see should be like the one in the following screenshot. Export the model as a `.obj` file.

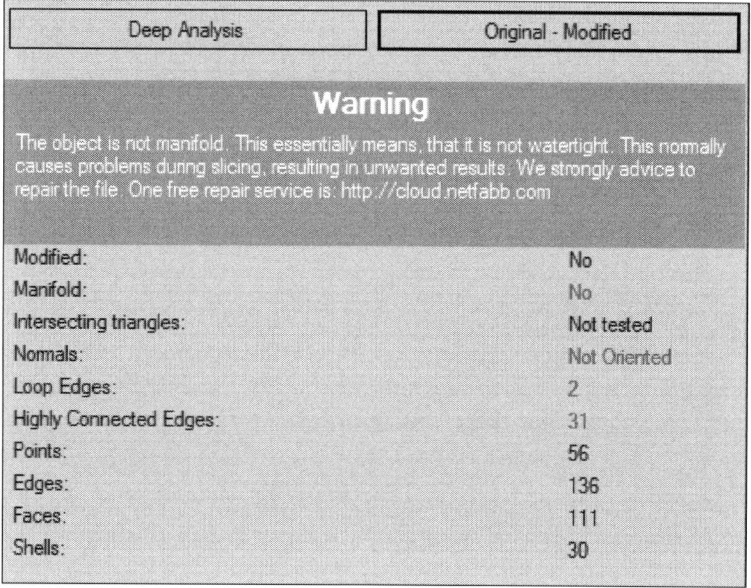

6. Now, left-click on the **Deep Analysis** button. The results should be similar to the following screenshot. Export the model as a `.obj` file.

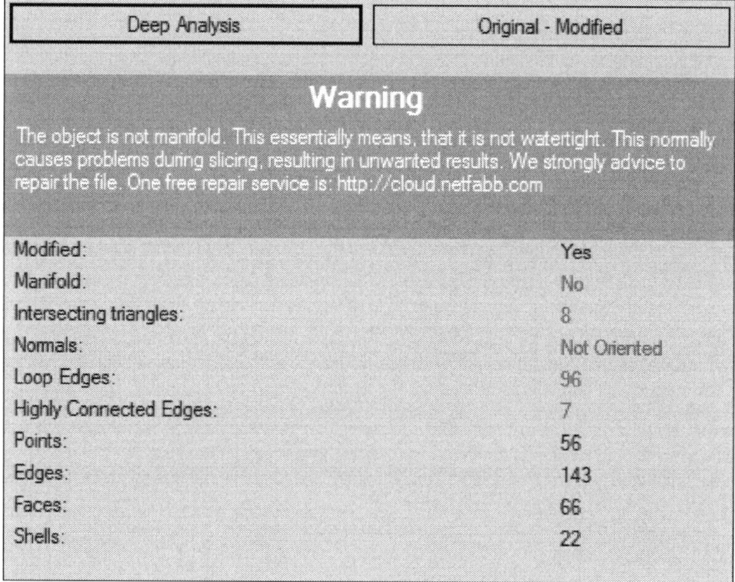

7. Repeat the analysis with the extended capsule `.stl` file.

How it works...

The first test, utilizing the capsule model in `.stl` format, tested manifold and ready for printing. After a deep analysis was executed, there was an indication of intersecting triangles.

Repetier-Host gave an initial analysis that the capsule model in the `.obj` file format has many mesh errors. More issues surfaced after a deep analysis. This can be seen in the following image:

The image on the left-hand side is the capsule model in the `.obj` file format as seen in MeshLab before it was imported into Repetier-Host. In the center, there is the model after loading it in Repetier-Host. Automatic repairs were performed, but the results were worsened. A deep analysis was made with the model, as seen on the right-hand side. The results are even worse. The faces have collapsed onto each other.

Repetier-Host provides a good analysis of a mesh, but it's not very competent in making repairs. We'll learn how to solve these issues in the next recipe.

Repairing mesh geometry issues

In this recipe, we're going to work through the process of repairing non-manifold issues with the following tools:

- netfabb Basic
- Microsoft Repair Service
- Autodesk 3D Print Utility
- Meshmixer

Getting ready

You'll need to download netfabb from `http://www.netfabb.com/downloadcenter.php?basic=1`.

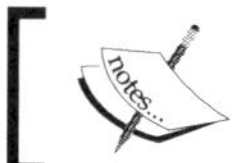

> This book uses netfabb Basic Version 5.1.1. It supports Windows XP/7/8, Linux, and Mac OS.

Follow the installation instructions and register the program. The netfabb interface is shown in the following screenshot:

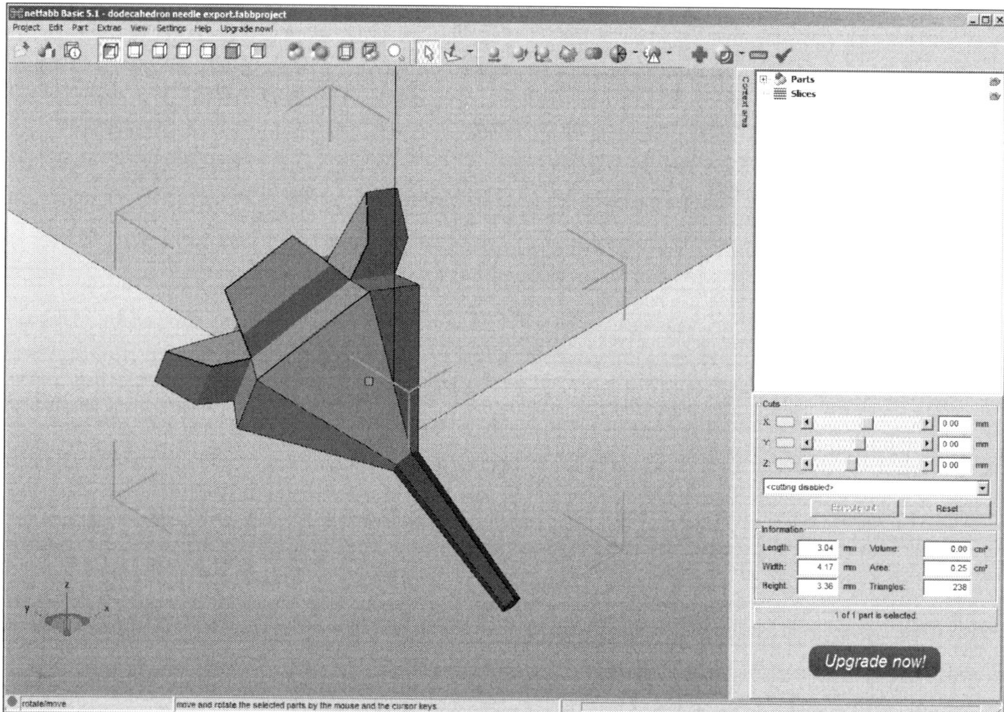

The basic functions are similar to other 3D modeling programs. They are as follows:

- To import a file, you can drag-and-drop it on the build platform.
- To freely orbit around the model, right-click on it and drag.

- To pan the model, hold down on the scroll wheel and drag. If you don't have a scroll wheel, hold *Shift*.

- To zoom, turn the scroll wheel or hold *Alt*.

You'll also need a connection to the Internet to access the Microsoft Repair Service. The programs we used earlier, Autodesk 3D Print Utility and Meshmixer, will be needed in addition to the extended capsule `.stl` file we made in the previous recipe.

How to do it...

We will proceed as follows:

1. Load the extended capsule `.stl` file into netfabb. It should look like the previous screenshot.

2. First, let's look at how netfabb analyzes the model. Any portion that is highlighted in red is considered a problem area. The netfabb software will also use a red exclamation mark within a triangle to warn us of errors. This generally appears at the lower-right corner of the workspace. In this case, the problem is in the extended part of the model and is the result of inverted normals. To make a repair, go to **Extras** in the menu and select **Repair part**.

3. Now, choose **Automatic repair** at the bottom-right corner of the workspace.

4. A pop up will inquire about the type of repair. Keep the default repair and then select **Execute**.

5. Go back and select **Apply repair** and then select **Yes** in the **Remove old part?** option.

6. Save the model by going to the menu and choosing **Part** and then **Export part**. Save it as a `.stl` file. The netfabb software will attach a **(repaired)** tag to the filename.

7. Now, let's go online to the Microsoft Repair Service. This is located at `https://netfabb.azurewebsites.net/`. Sign up for the free service and log in.

8. Drop the extended capsule `.stl` file on the **Upload** icon. In a short time, the system will repair it. Download the file. Microsoft will add a **_fixed** tag to the filename.

9. Now, open Autodesk 3D Print Utility. Load the extended capsule `.stl` file and repair it. Label the `.stl` file appropriately for future reference so that we know that A3DP Utility made the repair.

10. Now, we'll make one last repair. Open Meshmixer and load the extended capsule `.stl` file. Go to **Analysis** and then select **Inspector**. You should see numerous problems as illustrated in the following image:

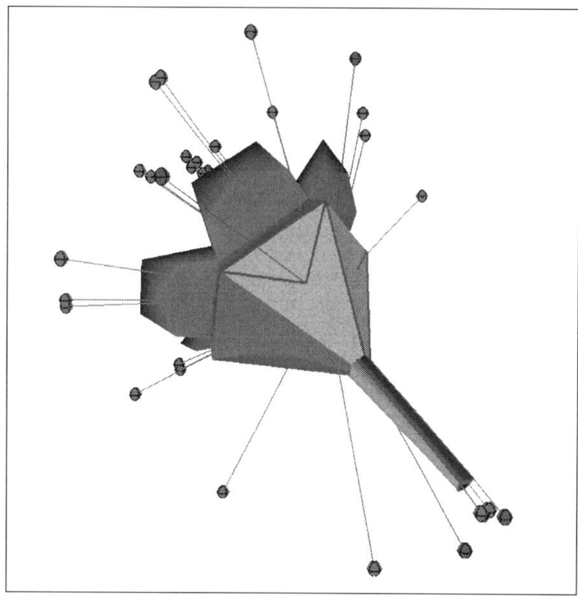

11. Select **Auto Repair All** and then click on **Done**. Export the model as a `.stl` file that is appropriately labeled for future reference.

How it works...

The following is a visual survey of the results of each repair tool we used in this recipe:

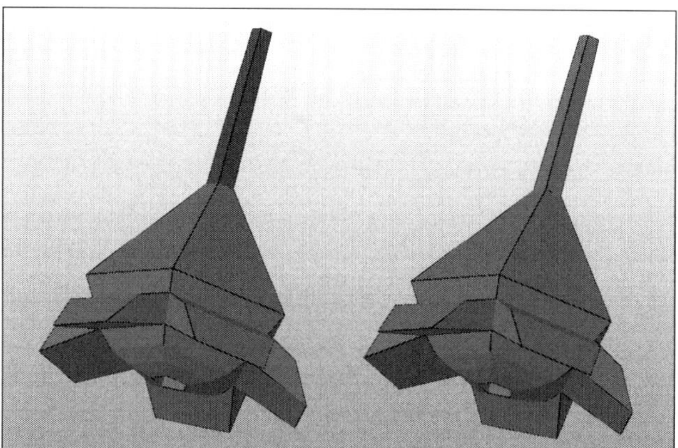

The preceding image on the left-hand side was repaired using netfabb Basic. It indicates that there is still a problem in the shaft of the model. The highlighted red areas indicate a problem in the mesh. By checking the analysis in Repetier-Host, we find that there are inverted normals.

The image on the right-hand side is the model repaired with the Microsoft Repair Service. It visually appears to be manifold. After checking the analysis, we find no issues, after deep analysis, we find that there is an issue with the self-intersecting faces.

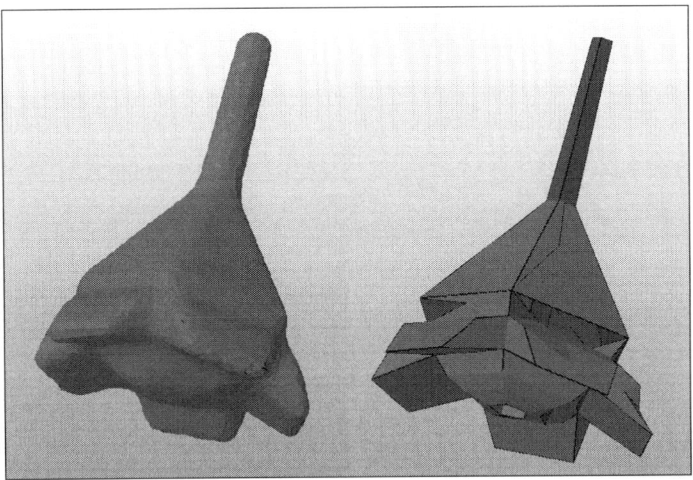

The preceding image on the left-hand side was repaired with Autodesk 3D Print Utility. The model appears to be manifold, but the model has been distorted.

The image on the right-hand side is the model repaired with Meshmixer. The model has developed more issues after the repair.

Using SketchUp for editing meshes

In this recipe, we're going to repair the self-intersecting triangles in the extended capsule model. We'll do this by editing the mesh with SketchUp Make. SketchUp is the only program that we've reviewed in this book which will allow us the access we need to make this repair.

Getting ready

You'll need SketchUp Make and the extended capsule `.stl` file. Use the original file that hasn't had repairs from the previous recipes.

How to do it...

We will proceed as follows:

1. Open SketchUp and import the extended capsule `.stl` file. Select the model. You should see a blue boundary box surrounding the model. This signifies that the model is a solid component.

2. We need to edit the individual components of the model. To do this, go to **Edit** and choose **Solid Component** at the bottom of the screen. Then, choose **Edit Component** from the cascaded menu.

3. Now, we're going to create edges along the perimeter of the extrusion. Choose the **Lines** icon and move from vertex to vertex. This is illustrated in the following image:

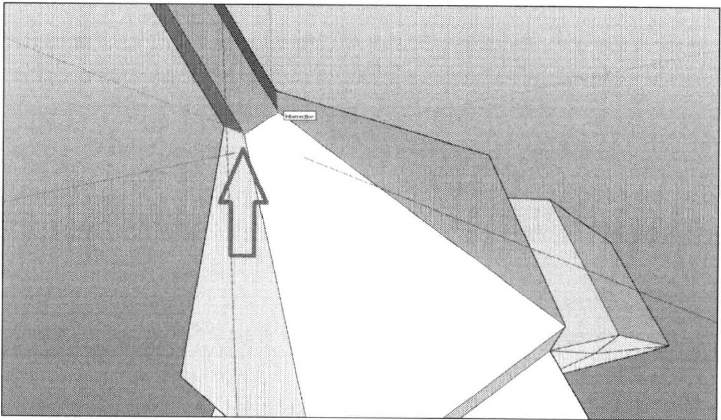

In this case, SketchUp will indicate the vertex as an **Intersection** or **endpoint** when selected.

4. Now, we need to temporarily remove a face of the extrusion so that we can see inside. Select the eraser icon and remove one edge of the extruded part.

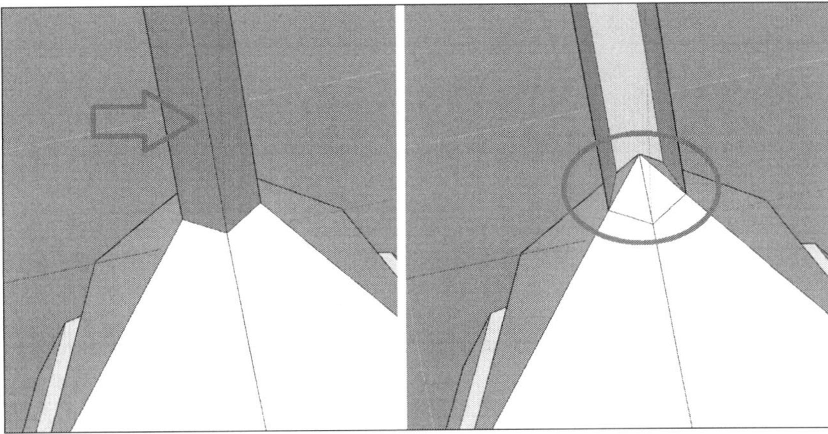

Now, we can determine with certainty that we've made a separation of the extruded part with our added edges.

5. Export the file as `.stl` and label it appropriately for future use.

How it works...

By creating edges around the shaft at the point of intersection, we've been able to make a separation in the geometry. We can confirm that this repaired the model of self-intersecting triangles by using the Repetier-Host analysis. However, there is still a problem with the normals. We'll take care of this with MeshLab in the next recipe.

Using MeshLab for fixing normals

In this recipe, we're going to learn how to use MeshLab to visually inspect and correct the face normals of a model. MeshLab has a good collection of tools to repair and modify face normals. Using the selection tools, we'll be able to choose the faces we want to repair.

Getting ready

You'll need MeshLab and the extended capsule file model that you modified with SketchUp in the previous recipe.

How to do it...

We will proceed as follows:

1. Load the model in MeshLab. MeshLab indicates inverted normals by displaying the faces in black. We can see this in the following image:

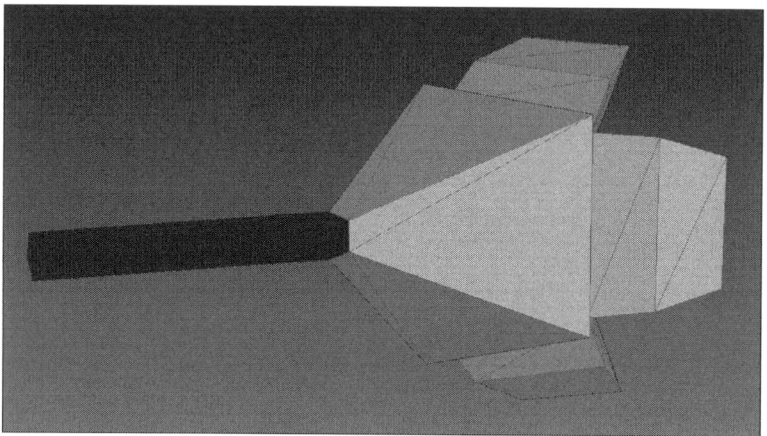

2. Let's take a look at the normals. We can do this in MeshLab by selecting **Render in the menu** and then **Show Normal/Curvature** from the list. Not only does MeshLab display the face normals (blue lines), but it also displays the vertex normals (violet lines).

3. Go to the icon tray and select the **Flatlines** view.

4. The inverted normals are difficult to see, so choose **Wireframe** for the view. We can see the inverted normals in the circled area of the following image:

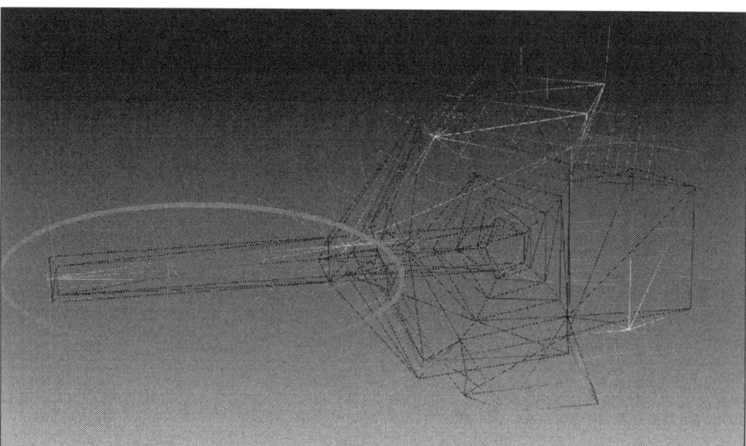

5. In order to correct their orientation, we need to select the part. Do this by choosing the **Select faces in a rectangular region** icon. Drag it over the extruded part. Most of the part will be highlighted in red, as shown in the following image:

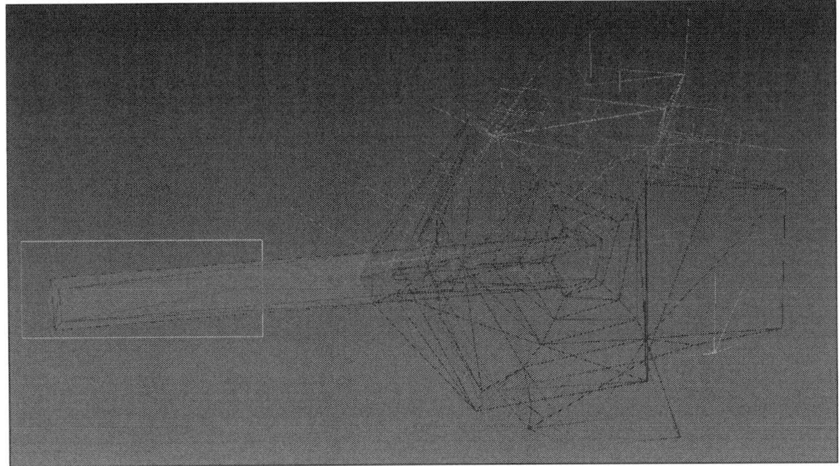

6. Now, we're ready to make the repair. Go back to the menu and select **Filters**. Choose **Normals**, **Curvature**, and **Orientation** and choose **Invert Faces Orientation** from the cascaded window. From the pop up, select **Flip only selected faces**. Left-click on **Apply** and then select **Close**. Now, the normals are facing properly.

7. Now, let's check the model carefully. There is still an area that has inverted faces. This is shown in the following image:

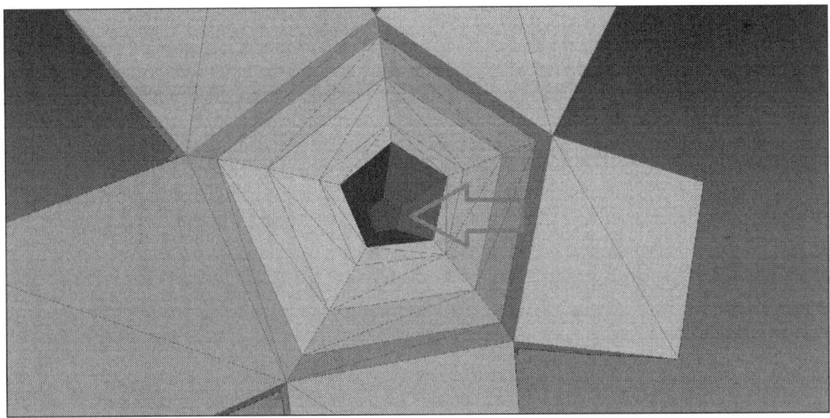

8. Select it using the **Select faces in a rectangular region** icon while holding the *Alt* key. This will allow only a selection of polygons that are visible on screen. This function is indicated by a small eye icon attached to the cursor.

9. Now, go back to the menu and select **Filters**. Choose **Normals, Curvatures, and Orientation** and then select **Invert Faces Orientation**. All normals should be oriented in the same direction now.

10. Now, export the model as `.stl`; it should be appropriately labeled for future reference.

How it works...

MeshLab is the best tool for visually inspecting and repairing face normals. There are a variety of options in the **Normals, Curvatures, and Orientation** filter sets. Only by experimenting with these filters will you gain a better understanding of how they work. However, you'll find that the **Invert Faces Orientation** filter will usually be the best solution for most problems.

How successful was our repair of the extended capsule? If we use the Repetier-Host analysis, we'll find that the model has not improved. However, we'll take the model and make another repair using the A3DP Utility.

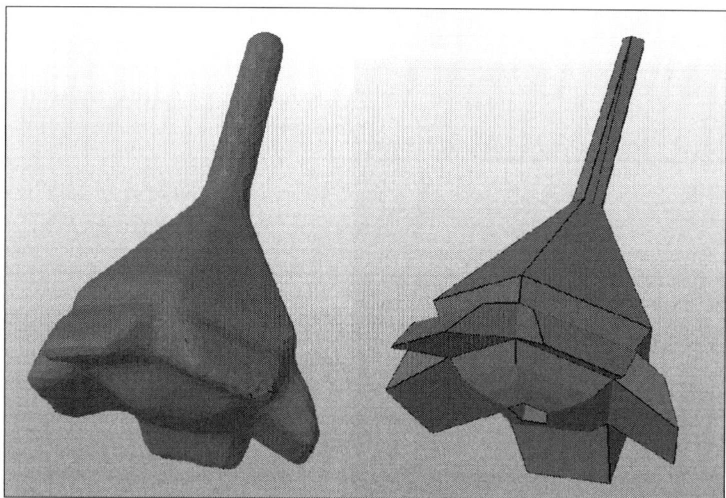

In the preceding image on the left-hand side, we have the original model repaired with the A3DP Utility without modifications. The model on the right-hand side is the model we repaired using SketchUp and MeshLab and then repaired it with the A3DP Utility. It took more work, but a successful repair was made by combining the tools of three different programs.

Using MeshLab for cleaning meshes

MeshLab has a collection of filters that can aid in the repair of a model. In this recipe, we'll attempt a repair using the capsule model.

Getting ready

You'll need the original capsule `.obj` file that hasn't been repaired. You'll also need MeshLab open and ready.

How to do it...

We will proceed as follows:

1. Load the capsule file and take a look around it. There appears to be only three faces missing. These areas are shown in the following image:

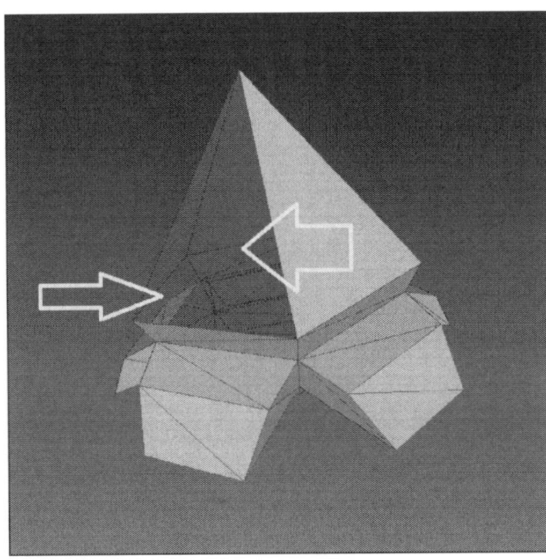

2. Before we begin making repairs, let's open the **Layer Dialog** box by selecting **Show Layer Dialog** in the menu. This will give us a record of our repairs.

3. Now, let's get started by closing up the open areas of the model. Go to **Filters** and select **Remeshing, Simplification**, and **Reconstruction**. Scroll down to the next cascaded window and select **Close Holes**. Keep the default values and select **Apply**. When the filter is complete, click on **Close** to close the window.

4. MeshLab has successfully closed the two openings of the model; however, in the dialog box, we can see that MeshLab has closed only one hole and added seven new faces. This isn't what we observed visually. We'll check for geometry errors by going to **Filters** in the menu. Scroll down and select **Cleaning and Repairing**. In the next cascaded window, choose **Select Self Intersecting Faces**. Click on **Apply** from the pop up.

5. In the following image, we can see that we have a problem with self-intersecting faces. The faces are highlighted in red, as shown in the following screenshot:

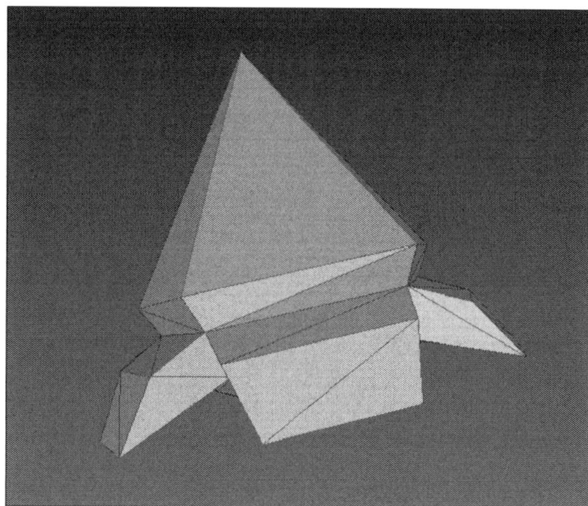

6. Now, we'll check for another potential issue. Go back to **Filters**. Scroll down and select **Cleaning and Repairing**. In the next cascaded window, choose **Select non Manifold Edges**. Click on **Apply** from the pop up.

7. We can see that there are no highlighted areas that signify problems.

8. Now, let's try to repair the issue of self-intersecting faces. We'll attempt to make some repairs that will not remove the surface geometry of the model. Go back to **Cleaning and Repairing** and select **Snap Mismatched Borders**. Keep the default values and select **Apply**. When the filter is complete, click on **Close** to close the window.

9. From the dialog box, we can see that nothing was achieved.

10. Go back to **Cleaning and Repairing** and select **Merge Close Vertices**. Keep the default values and select **Apply**. When the filter is complete, click on **Close** to close the window.

11. From the dialog box, we can see that seven vertices have been merged.

12. Go back and test the repair by choosing the **Select Self Intersecting Faces** filter. It now appears to be free of self-intersecting faces.

13. Export the model as a `.stl` file.

How it works...

Checking the repair with MeshLabs tools and Repetier-Host confirms that the model is now manifold. We can experiment with many other filters that we didn't use in this recipe however, you'll find that the filters we did use will generally be the most useful.

Let's examine Meshlab's analysis even deeper by taking a look at the extended capsule model that we successfully repaired in the previous recipe. The Repeteir-Host analysis shows a good manifold model without errors, but is this correct?

By examining the model with MeshLab, we can see that there is still an issue with self-intersecting faces. In the following image on the left-hand side, we can see areas that MeshLab has highlighted red, detecting the intersecting faces:

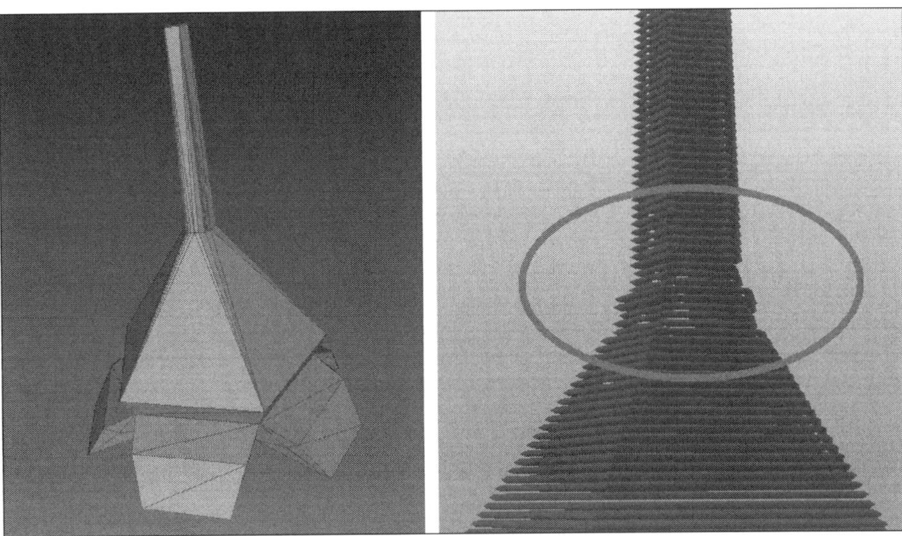

In the model on the right-hand side, we can see that after slicing, there is distortion in the model where the model's shaft is connected. This is a result of the unrepaired intersecting triangles.

We can attempt more repairs, but the time involved will be better served by practicing good modeling techniques.

Creating a hollow model with MeshLab

Creating a hollow model with MeshLab is not about repair issues, but it is about the modifications necessary for proper preparation of a model that is intended for a commercial 3D printing service. Most of these services charge by calculating the volume of material required to print the design. In this case, by making a model hollow, it will decrease the volume of material necessary and greatly decrease the cost of the print job.

Getting ready

You'll need MeshLab and the support test model we made in *Chapter 6, Making the Impossible*. It looks like the following image:

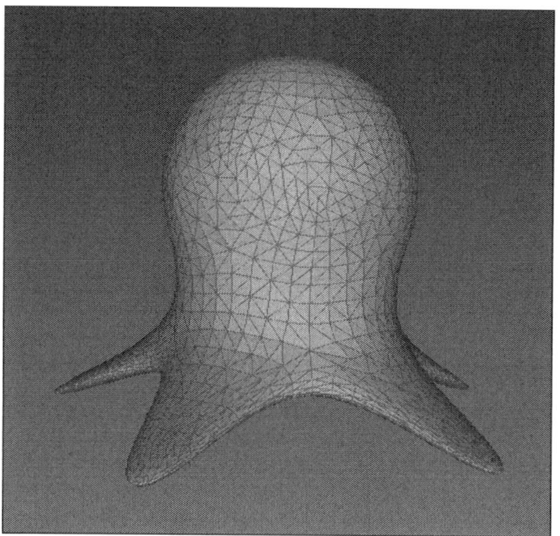

How to do it...

We will proceed as follows:

1. Select the **Show Layer Dialog** icon.

2. Go to **Filters** and select **Remeshing, Simplification,** and **Reconstruction**. Scroll down to the next cascaded window and select **Uniform Mesh Resampling**.

3. From the pop up, change the **Precision (abs and %)** field to 1.0 in **World Unit**. Change **Offset (abs and %)** to -3.0. Check **Clean Vertices** and **Multisample**. Click on **Apply**.

4. Change the view to Wireframe. Toggle the view of the two layers from the layer box (remember that by clicking on the green eye icon, it shows/hides the layer). We can see the results in the following image:

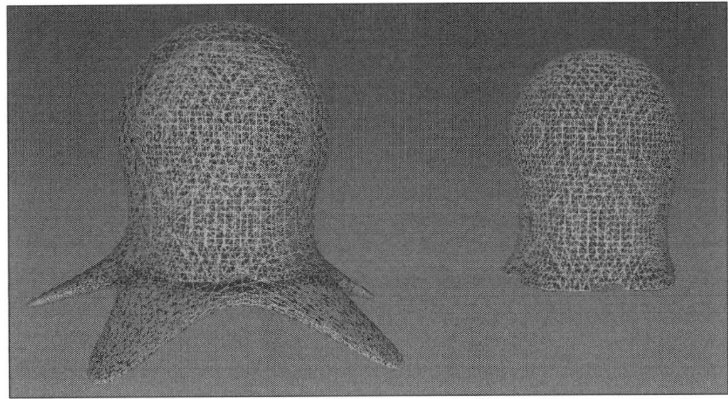

The image on the right-hand side is the new interior wall we made. We can see it nested within the model on the left-hand side.

5. Now, let's check the normals. Go to the menu, select **Render**, and choose **Show Normal/Curvature** from the list. Hide the outer layer. We can see the new part in the following screenshot:

6. All of the normals are facing outward as we normally would want them to. In this case, we want them pointing inward for this model to be understood as a hollow object. We'll do this by keeping the first layer hidden and making sure that the second layer is selected in the layer box. Then, go to the menu and select **Filters**. Choose **Normals, Curvatures**, and **Orientation** and choose **Invert Faces Orientation** from the cascaded window. From the pop up, keep the default settings. Click on **Apply** and then on **Close**. Now, the normals are facing inward. Refer to the following image:

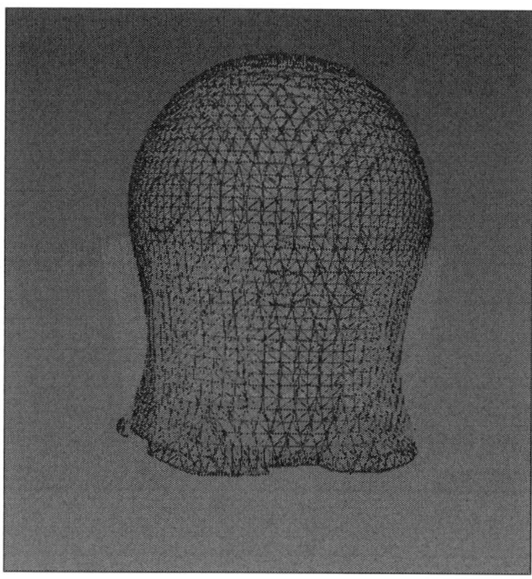

7. Now, we have to merge the two layers together to make a complete model that is hollow. Go to **Menu** and select **Filters**. Scroll down and select **Mesh Layer**. Scroll down to the next cascaded window and select **Flatten Visible Layers**.

8. A pop-up window appears. Keep the options at default and select **Apply**. When the filter is complete, click on **Close** to close the window. The model can now be exported as a `.stl` file.

How it works...

By setting the **Offset (abs and %)** field to `-3.0`, we essentially determined that the inset would begin 3 mm from the outer shell. This creates a shell that is 3 mm thick. The offset variable can be set as a negative or positive integer. For instance, by setting the value to `3.0`, we can increase the model's size by 3 mm from the original shell. Refer to the following image:

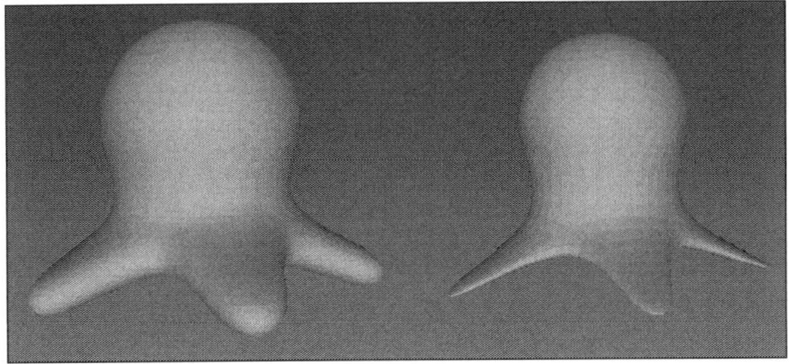

However, when we create a shell extending outward from the original surface, the model becomes distorted.

Creating a drain hole with Meshmixer

One of the most popular 3D printing services is **Shapeways**. It can be found at `https://www.shapeways.com/`. This service requires the model to have a drain hole if it is hollow or else it will be considered a solid. This is to allow the support material that's utilized to be removed.

In this recipe, we'll learn how to do this using Meshmixer and a fabricated part using SketchUp.

Getting ready

You'll need to make a small part with SketchUp. A dowel with a 3-mm diameter and a length of about 20 mm will suffice. It should resemble the following image:

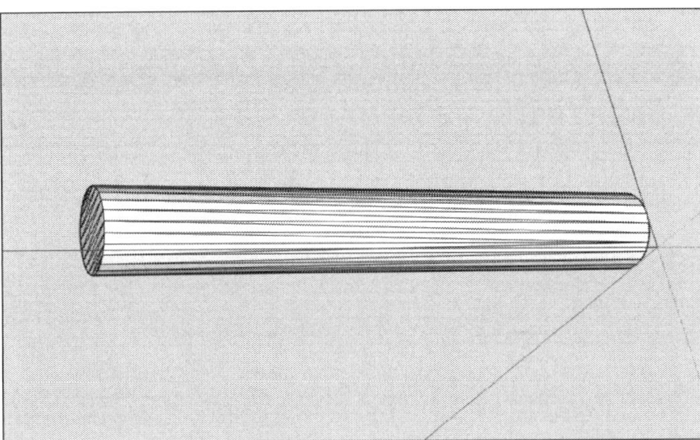

You'll also need Meshmixer and the hollow support model you made in the previous recipe.

How to do it...

We will proceed as follows:

1. Import the hollow support model. Adjust the orientation of the model with a good view of its bottom. The least obtrusive area for a small hole would be at the bottom. This is marked in the following image:

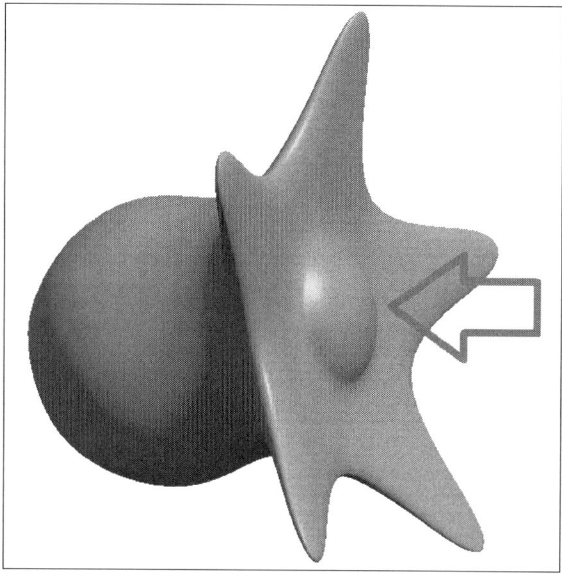

2. Now, go to **File** and select **Import** and then **Append**. Choose the dowel model.

3. In this particular case (it may be different in yours), a warning may appear. The imported dowel is too far away from the current scene. Meshmixer prompts that an automatic repair can be made. Choose **Yes**.

4. Initially, after loading the dowel, only the support model can be seen. At the bottom-right corner, there is an **Object Browser** window. It shows that the dowel has been imported. Click on the eye icon of the support model. We can now see the dowel as shown in the following image:

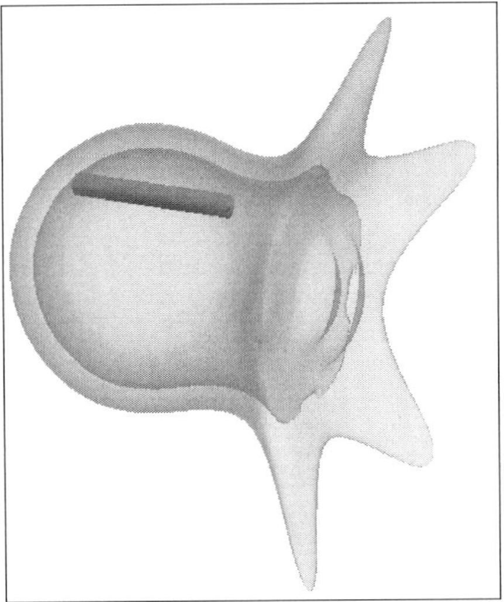

5. Now, we want to position the dowel where it extrudes halfway between the shells of the model at the future hole's position. We do this by selecting the dowel layer at the **Object Browser** window. We'll need to see the outer surface of the model, so unhide the support model layer. Go to **Edit** and choose **Transform**. You should see a set of navigation controls, as seen in the following image:

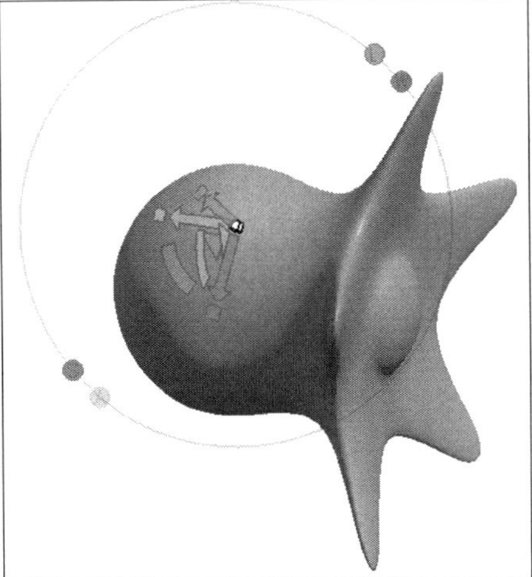

6. By left-clicking and dragging any of the three axes' arrows, the dowel can be positioned accurately. This is illustrated in the following image:

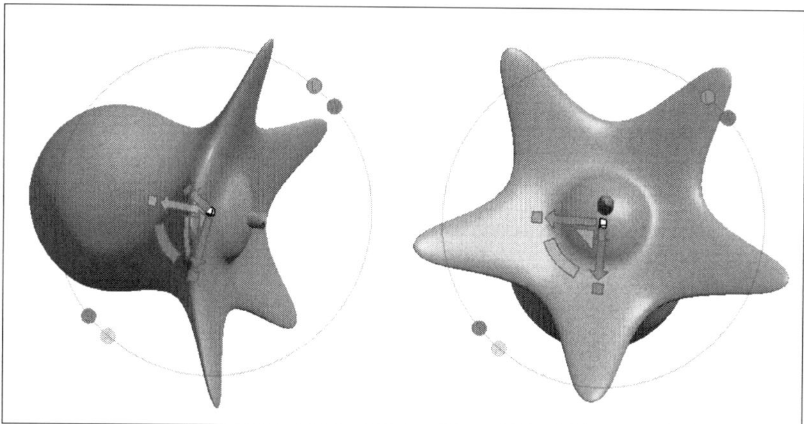

7. Now, we need to subtract the dowel in order to make a hole in its place. Before we do this, it's very important to make sure that the mesh between the two parts is fairly uniform in density. Go to **View** in the menu and select **Toggle Wireframe**. In the following image on the left-hand side, we can see that the mesh between the dowel and model is not uniform.

8. We can make the two components more uniform using a sculpting brush. Go to **Sculpt**. In **Volume selected**, choose **Brushes**. Choose the **Refine Brush** (it's a triangle with a plus symbol). Make sure that only the dowel part is selected in the **Object Browser** window. Refer to the following image:

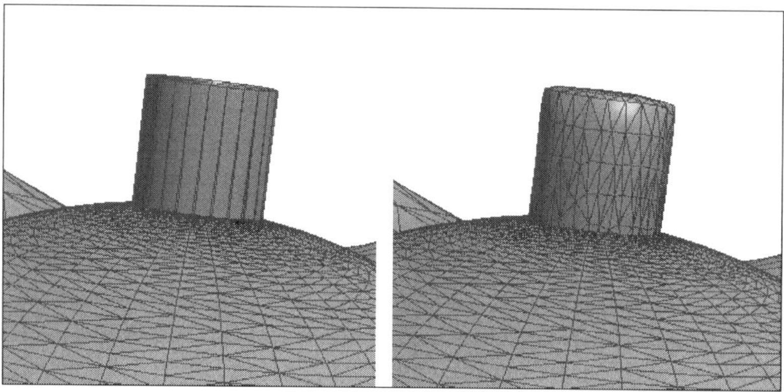

Adjust the size and strength by trial and error, moving the brush over the dowel. The end result should be similar to the preceding image on the right-hand side.

9. Now, we're ready to remove the dowel. Press *Shift* and select both parts in the **Object Browser** window. Make sure that the model is selected first, and then the dowel. A new menu with Boolean functions appears. We want to select **Boolean Difference**. Once the selection is made, the dowel disappears and a hole is created. This can be seen in the following image:

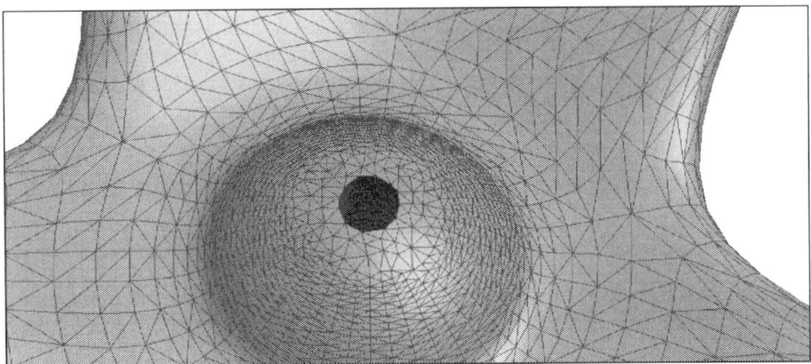

10. Choose **Accept** and the model is ready for export.

How it works...

Using the Boolean functions in Meshmixer can be a little quirky, so it's a good idea to save your model before performing the Boolean difference. The trick is to make sure that the mesh of the two parts is relatively uniform. In most cases, this will ensure a good cut.

There's more...

How successful was the modification of the support model? How much does it save in material costs?

In the following image, we can see that by Shapeways' calculations, we essentially saved half the cost by printing a hollow object rather than a solid:

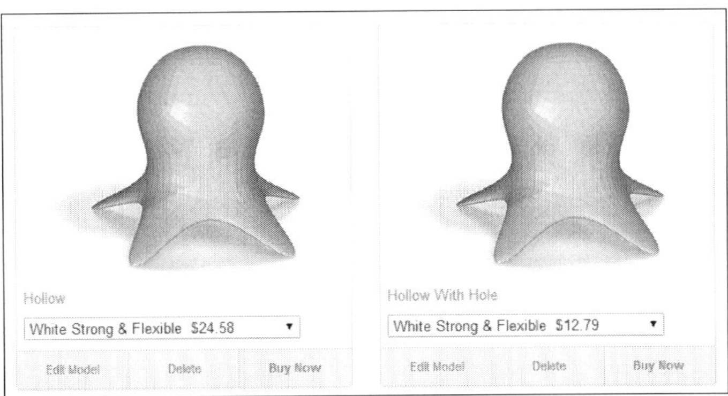

9

Troubleshooting Issues in 3D Printing

In this chapter, we will cover the following recipes:

- Leveling the build platform
- Taking proper care of the build platform surface
- Troubleshooting issues with the heat bed
- Troubleshooting issues with the extruder
- Troubleshooting issues with the hot end
- Troubleshooting issues with the x, y, and z axes
- Troubleshooting issues with the motor system

Introduction

If you have experience with 3D printing using a RepRap printer, it will come as no surprise that occasionally, something will go wrong. You may find that it's not the result of a poor slicer profile or a poorly modeled object but a failure of the mechanical function of your printer. You might observe some strange behavior that quite possibly degrades the results of your print, or your printer may not work at all.

Usually, this is the result of a part or connection wiggling loose or the tension of a belt becoming slack. Sometimes, it's as simple as a screw or bolt falling off. If the printer is moved about often, there's a chance for it to be knocked out of alignment, or even worse, a part might be unknowingly damaged. After all, if you're using a true RepRap-designed printer, it's a bare-bones contraption, without the shielding of a hard case. It's very easy to have a wire snag on something and in turn, create a possible malfunction in the printer's activities.

This chapter will focus on the basic components of a 3D printer system that is constructed with the *x*, *y*, and *z* axes, which move using belts and threaded rods. Many of the concepts can be applied to printer systems that are different but have similar mechanical operations. For example, there are many different hot end extruder designs available in the 3D printer market today, but most operate with similar mechanical and electronic systems. Even most of the new and popular delta printers use belts and pulleys.

There are too many different 3D printer designs for this book to cover any particular problem in specific detail. This book is a RepRap Cookbook. Its focus is on one of the most prolific designs called the **Prusa Mendel**. This was the type of printer that was used for printing the recipe exercises in this book.

The two basic variations can be seen in the following image:

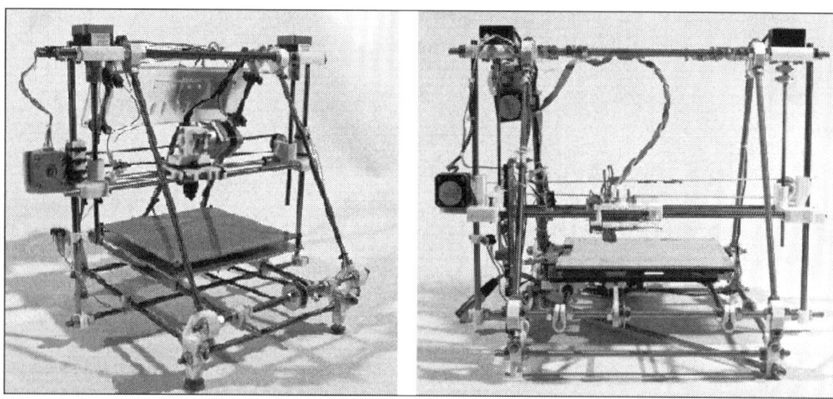

On the left-hand side of the preceding image is a classic Prusa Mendel 3D printer designed by Josef Průša. It was constructed by sourced parts, and it follows the build instructions written by Gary Hodgson. The printer on the right-hand side of the preceding image is a RepRapPro Mendel. It was designed by Adrian Bowyer and his team, and it was purchased as a kit from his online store.

A list of suppliers for the Prusa Mendel can be found at `http://www.reprap.org/wiki/Prusa_Mendel_Buyers_Guide`.

The Prusa Mendel build manual can be found at `http://garyhodgson.com/reprap/prusa-mendel-visual-instructions/`.

The RepRapPro Mendel kit is sold at `https://reprappro.com/`.

This chapter's focus is not intended to be an overview of the basic problems arising from printing flaws due to poor slicer adjustments. Neither will this chapter focus on the printing flaws encountered by poor modeling. The previous chapters in this book offer most of the information needed for these types of problems. This chapter will focus on the common issues that tend to recur over and over again in regards to the mechanical functions of the printer.

More troubleshooting information can be found at `http://reprap.org/wiki/Print_Troubleshooting_Pictorial_Guide`. It surveys not only the mechanical issues, but also the issues that can be corrected by firmware or slicer adjustments.

Leveling the build platform

Let's take a look at the most common issue that can affect the printing of the first few layers: an unleveled build platform. The following are some very important reasons to keep your build platform leveled:

- To keep a print adhered to the build plate. A level bed will allow an even first layer to be applied.

- To keep the first print layers from becoming distorted. In areas where the distance is too far from the nozzle tip, filament layers will be weak. In areas where the nozzle tip is pressed against the build surface, the filament will be squished too thin.

- To reduce the risk of an extruder jam. If an area of the build plate is too tight against the hot end nozzle, internal pressure can build within the hot end and cause stripping of the filament at the extruder.

- To reduce the warping of the print. In areas where the nozzle tip is spaced too far from the build plate, the poor adhesion of the filament layer will be prone to warping.

The following recipe will demonstrate a simple way to level the build platform.

Getting ready

Every RepRap 3D printer has a build platform. It's typically constructed of aluminum, acrylic, or wood, and its size can vary. On a Prusa Mendel, the plate is about 220 mm x 220 mm. A heated bed and a sheet of glass are usually on top of this plate. It's with this system combination that we'll be focused.

Familiarize yourself with your specific build platform. Determine where the screws and springs (if any) are located, and be prepared to have the proper tools to make adjustments.

How to do it...

We will proceed as follows:

1. Place a sheet of paper on the platform. It doesn't necessarily need to cover the entire surface, as it can be shifted around during the calibration.

2. Place the hot end nozzle at the center of the platform and slightly above the paper. It's preferable that the nozzle tip appears to be touching the paper but doesn't dig into the paper. You'll want to move the paper freely (with some drag) against the nozzle.

3. Move the extruder using the manual controls in the host software. Move the nozzle to one corner of the platform. If the travel is uneven across the paper surface, adjust the build platform until it's equidistant from the nozzle placement at center.

4. Repeat the extruder moves for the other three corners. Adjust the build platform, if necessary.

5. Move the nozzle back to the center and inspect its distance from the build plate closely. It is always important to make sure that the area around the center portion of the build platform is kept leveled. This is where most of the printing activity takes place. Repeating the preceding steps may be necessary to finalize the calibration. A YouTube video demonstrating a bed leveling can be seen at `http://www.youtube.com/watch?v=5bzAE5-QgUY`.

How it works...

It cannot be stressed enough how important it is to keep your build plate leveled. This alone will save much frustration in the long run. This is usually a tedious calibration, and to be honest, really not that much fun at all.

However, there have been recent advances in DIY autoleveling systems. One system uses a retractable probe constructed with a micro switch. By adding some instructions in the firmware, the probe's data can be interpreted. Information on its construction can be found at `http://reprap.org/wiki/Kossel`.

Another DIY system uses **Force Sensing Resistors** (**FSR**) in-between the glass plate and the build platform. When the hot end's nozzle presses against the glass, it acts as a probe and sends data that's interpreted by the firmware. Unfortunately, this system does not work in conjunction with a heat bed. The FSR components are not heat tolerant. Information about this system can be found at `http://reprap.org/wiki/FSR`.

It's worth keeping an eye on the different systems that may become available in future.

Taking proper care of the build platform surface

Most DIY 3D printers work on the surface of a glass plate. This makes the surface of the glass a very important substrate of the build platform. How well the print adheres to this surface will determine the success of the printing.

In this recipe, we'll follow some suggestions on how to care for the glass plate and how to optimize the surface for the ABS and PLA filaments.

Getting ready

You'll need rubbing alcohol, tape, and soft rags for cleaning. You will also need straight-edge razors designed for scraping windows and hairspray. The following recipe will explain the supplies needed, in greater detail.

How to do it...

We will proceed as follows:

1. Keeping the glass secured to the build platform is an important first step! Sometimes, a shift in the x and y axes may occur between print layers because of an unsecured glass plate. It's been a popular trend for RepRap printers to utilize metal clips to hold the glass plate against the heat bed. Make sure your glass plate is firmly attached by these clips. It's an easy oversight that can quickly lead to a print failure.

2. Cleaning the build plate regularly is very important! A buildup of finger grease, old adhesives from tape, and added glues should be removed. Rubbing alcohol or denatured alcohol works well for this. For heavy deposits, a straight-edge razor designed for scrapping windows works very well.

3. Coating the glass with a layer of tape helps in keeping the print adhered. Choosing the proper kind of tape is important. Make your choice by referring to the following two suggestions:

   - The PLA filament should be printed on a blue painter's tape. A coat of heavy-duty hairspray will help to adhere to the print as well.

   - The ABS filament should be printed on a Kapton or PET tape. A fine tooth sanding of the tape will help adhere to the print as well.

4. Applying the tape with a slight gap between the strips is preferable to an overlapped tape

How it works...

Using a glass plate is a very convenient method for keeping the build platform flat and protecting the delicate surface of a PCB heat bed. It's important to keep in mind the fragility of this material, especially, if the typical windowpane glass is utilized.

Most 3D printers (if shipped with a glass plate) will utilize the Borosilicate glass. It's the best for use as a build surface for a number of reasons. It has higher thermal tolerances and is stronger than regular windowpane glass. It is less likely to break, and if it's purchased specifically from a 3D printer supplier, it will have soft grounded edges. It's far less likely that you'll break the glass or cut yourself with it!

There's more...

A removable plate makes it convenient to remove a difficult print from the build platform. After a print has cooled, it may be necessary to apply some aggressive removal tactics, and you may want to do this away from your printer.

My favorite tool for removing prints is an artist's palette knife. This is shown in the following image:

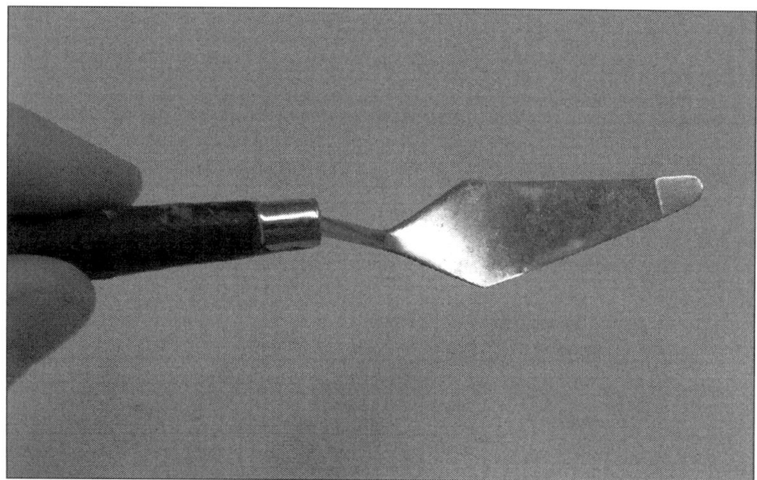

A print can be loosened by wedging the thin blade under an edge. By slowly working around it, you should be able to pull the print off without difficulty.

Troubleshooting issues with the heat bed

There are different methods for generating heat for a build platform. The most common component used for a RepRap printer is a PCB bed. This is a printed circuit board, which has etched copper traces running throughout one side of the surface. This creates the heating element. On the other side is a silkscreen surface with hot zone warnings. This is the side that is used to print on. Some 3D printers, such as the RepRapPro Mendel, have a sheet of aluminum sandwiched between the PCB heat bed and the glass plate.

In this recipe, we'll look at solving some common issues with this system.

Getting ready

A basic set of tools is always useful. I would speculate that if you own a 3D printer, you at least have a small collection of tools. A multimeter should be added to this collection. The instrument's function for testing voltages and resistance will be invaluable for troubleshooting the electronic systems in your printer. To measure the heat sources of your printer, such as the heat bed, you'll need a thermometer. However, investing in these tools may be an expense that some may not want. Inexpensive thermometers can be purchased, but their reliability may be suspect.

How to do it...

We will proceed as follows:

1. First, we need to make sure that the bed is operating with the correct temperatures. The recommended temperatures are as follows:

    - ABS should have a bed temperature between 80 and 120 degrees Celsius

    - PLA should have a bed temperature between 40 and 50 degrees Celsius

2. To test the temperature, a thermometer can be used. This is typically a gun-shaped device that is guided by laser. It's a handy tool for troubleshooting the heat elements of your 3D system. It can be seen demonstrated in the YouTube video at `http://www.youtube.com/watch?v=sCOUFC3m3nk`. However, the temperature is not likely to match the setting you have made with your host, but an average can be taken from different areas of the PCB bed. You'll get a good idea whether the heat bed is in the general temperature-operating range.

3. If the bed is not generating enough heat or it's not heating up at all, the first check should be with the power supply. Check to make sure that all the connections in the system are secure.

4. Next, check your system specifications for the correct voltage reading. Most RepRap printers are based on a 12V system. This is the voltage that is also applied to the hot bed. The best device to check the voltage is a multimeter. If you're unfamiliar with this device, visit `https://learn.sparkfun.com/tutorials/how-to-use-a-multimeter` for more information.

5. If the heat bed temperature is erratic, the problem may be with the heat sensor. Depending on your system, a thermistor or thermocouple may be used. These are electronic components that are placed against the heat bed to monitor the temperature. Sometimes, this sensor can become loose against the bed and give false or erratic temperature readings. Make sure that this system is secured and all wires and connections are intact.

If you believe that the heat sensor component is malfunctioning, test the resistance of the unit with a multimeter. In an ambient room temperature of 25 degrees Celsius, the resistance of the device should read around 100k ohms. If the resistance fluctuates greatly from this, such as 0 ohms for a short circuit or infinity for an open circuit, the heat sensor is faulty.

How it works...

Using a heat bed is essential for printing with an ABS filament. Make sure you preheat your build platform to its maximum temperature. This will help prevent print curling and possible print disengagement. Using the heat bed for a PLA filament can also be beneficial for the first initial layers, but it is not usually necessary.

It's best to limit the use of the heat bed when possible. The amount of heat that's generated from a lengthy print job can affect the plastic components of the 3D printer. This is especially true for RepRap printers that have parts made of PLA. This material has a lower melting point, and it can be more easily warped by too much heat.

Troubleshooting issues with the extruder

Generally, the extruder for a RepRap 3D printer is referring to both the device that drives the filament (the cold end) and the hot end that melts it. In this recipe, we'll take a look at some issues that arise from the cold end of the extruder.

Getting ready

Extruder designs have become so prolific that a book could be written about this mechanism alone. However, most of them are quite simple and work with a common principle; a filament is sandwiched between an idler bearing and a toothed gear or bolt (called the drive gear from here on) that's motor driven.

Familiarize yourself with your specific extruder system. Yours may be attached directly to the hot end, or it may be separated by a Bowden Cable system. In either case, the following recipe will be useful.

Be prepared to make some adjustments that will require basic tools. Precision digital calipers or a micrometer would be ideal for measuring.

How to do it...

We will proceed as follows:

1. Difficulty in passing the filament to the hot end is a common issue. Most of the time, this is due to incorrect idler pressure. Many extruders have a combination of screws and springs to exert idler pressure. Some extruders, such as the RepRapPro design, do not use springs to apply pressure. The mechanism uses two screws that compress the extruder's body, which contains an idler bearing against the filament. This can be seen in the following image:

2. A variation of Brutstruder used on MakerGear extruders utilize two spring loaded screws to apply pressure to the idler. This is shown in the following image:

3. When making adjustments to the idler tension, make sure that the filament is held firmly against the drive mechanism. Keep the following two basic points in mind:

- You'll want it tight enough so that it will not be possible to pull the filament out of the system; yet it should not be so tight that it distorts the filament. It's not uncommon for the filament to become squished and lose its round shape. This can cause problems as it travels further down the extruder system.

- If the idler tension is too loose, the filament may slip against the drive mechanism and not travel precisely. It might also shave pieces from the filament. This can be seen on a Hyena hobbed drive gear in the following image:

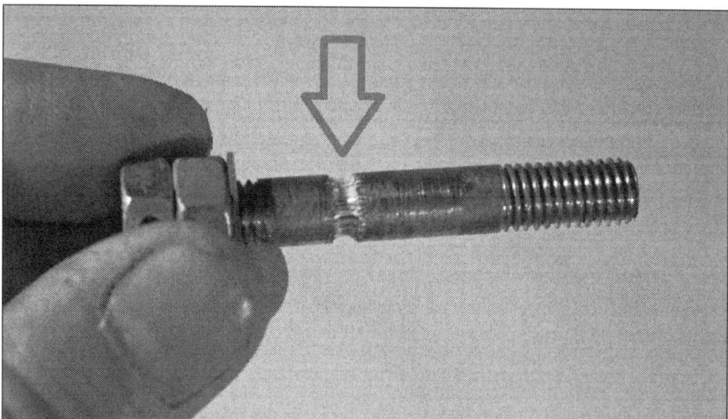

4. These particles will collect and also pose problems in the system.

5. If you are using a Bowden Cable system, make sure that both ends are firmly attached. If a connector becomes loose, this will prevent the filament from travelling. Refer to the following image:

6. Check the mechanism that feeds the filament. Make sure that the spool is moving well without obstruction.

   A 1.75 mm filament becomes more easily tangled on a spool and can tie itself into a knot, as shown in the following image:

7. Check the filament for abnormalities, as shown in the following image:

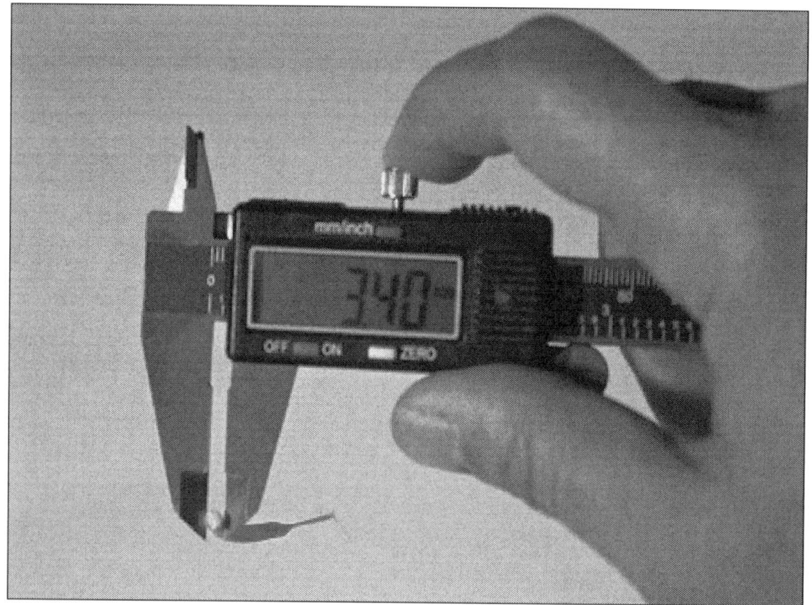

The filament in the preceding image jammed the extruder system when its diameter went from 2.74 mm to 3.40 mm. Diameter fluctuations can be fatal, but abnormalities in shape, can also become the cause of an extruder jam.

How it works...

Adjusting the idler is one of the most difficult adjustments to make. There is generally no consistent means of marking a good adjustment, since the filament can vary in size and consistency. It's more common for someone to under tighten rather than over tighten an idler. A lot of pressure needs to be applied to the idler. A sweet spot is found by trial and error, and in time, experience will help determine future adjustments.

Refer to the last recipe to check the extruder's motor system. The same troubleshooting method used for electronics is relevant here as well and can be a primary cause of the extruder not working.

Troubleshooting issues with the hot end

There are a lot of hot end designs out there, but they all operate with one underlying principle: a filament is melted in a chamber and extruded through a tiny hole. Temperatures up to 240 degrees Celsius are typical, with some hot ends capable of 300 degrees Celsius or more.

The hot end is the work dog of the 3D printer. When it stops working, the printing process fails. This is probably one of the most frustrating problems that's encountered, and it can be a painful issue to resolve.

We'll look at some of the problems that can occur with the hot end in this recipe.

Getting ready

For this recipe, a basic toolkit is required. A soldering iron or crimpers may be necessary for making connection repairs. To test the wire leads and the heating element, a multimeter is necessary. There are more specialized tools mentioned throughout the recipe.

How to do it...

We will proceed as follows:

1. First, it's a good idea to determine whether the hot end or cold end of the extruder is at fault. Do this by manually pushing the filament through the hot end while it's at the operating temperature. If you can extrude the filament through the hot end in this fashion, the system is operating.

2. If you are unable to extrude the filament, it's quite possible that the nozzle and/or heating chamber needs to be cleared. You'll have to refer to the breakdown schematic for your hot end design, but generally, most hot ends have a nozzle that can be screwed off.

3. A nozzle may need to be heated in order to clear it of filament. This is generally done using a flame. Care must be exercised if you are using a butane torch. The nozzle can be warped by too much heat. Have a look at the following YouTube video, `http://www.youtube.com/watch?v=6bTfl35zlHE`, which shows the process.

4. If you're using ABS, you can also soak the nozzle in acetone. This is a strong solvent, and if you're unfamiliar with it, you should refer to a **material safety data sheet** (**MSDS**). This can be found at `https://www.google.com/#q=msds+acetone`. This will take a long time to dissolve the filament and may require picking away at sections as they weaken.

5. If you're using PLA, you can use a solution of lye (sodium hydroxide) and water with an ultrasonic cleaner. This can be helpful in breaking up and dissolving the PLA inside the hot end. Care must be taken when using this chemical! Eye protection and chemical gloves are required. Lye is a common ingredient in many drain cleaners and clog removers. A **safety data sheet** (**SDS**) can be found at `https://www.hip-petrohemija.com/upload/documents/engleski/25_SDS_Sodium_hydroxide_eng.pdf`.

6. If the hot end appears to be heating up with unusual temperature readings, you may need to check the thermistor or thermocouple. This device is the sensor that reads the temperature of your hot end. A thermistor and MakerGear hot end is shown in the following image:

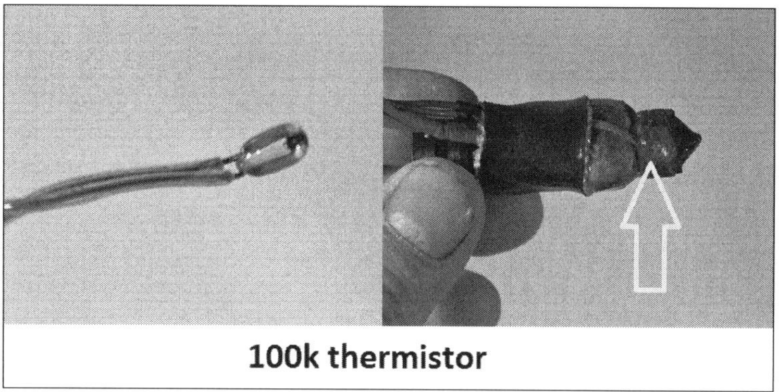

7. Sometimes, this sensor can become loose against the heat barrel of the hot end and give false or erratic temperature readings. Make sure that this system is secured and all wires and connections are intact.

8. If the hot end is not warming up, you'll have to troubleshoot the electronics. Using a multimeter, check first that you are getting the proper voltage to the hot end heating element. Check your system specifications for the correct voltage reading. Most RepRap printers are based on a 12V system. This is the voltage that is also applied to the hot end.

9. If the voltage readings are adequate, you'll need to check the resistance of the heat resistor or heat core. Two common heaters are shown in the following image:

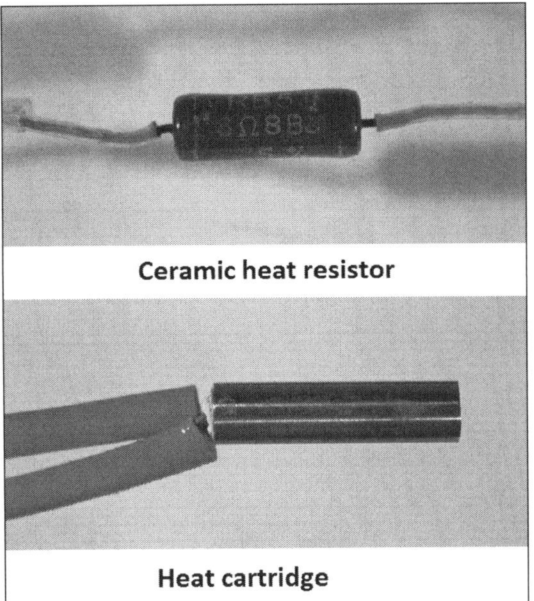

Ceramic heat resistor

Heat cartridge

10. The preceding image shows the heating elements of the hot end. They can vary greatly in design, but all will have a resistance around 6 ohms for a 12V system. In the following image, a DIY fabricated heat core using nichrome wire is shown:

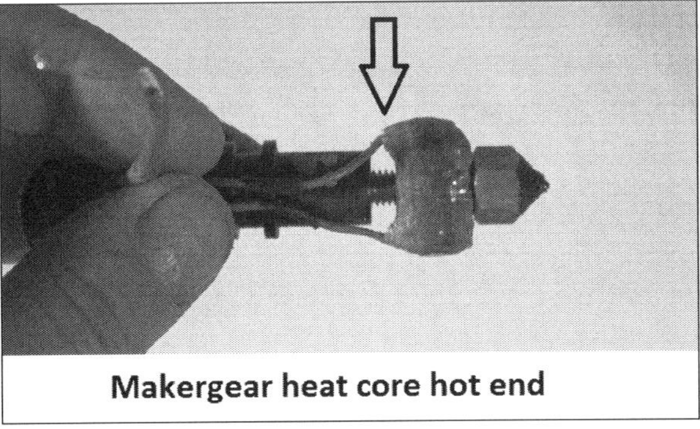

Makergear heat core hot end

It's a very reliable MakerGear design. You'll need to refer to the specifications of your own hot end design for deviations.

How it works...

There's a lot of vibration in a RepRap 3D printer when it's in operation. Coupled with the addition of extreme heat generated by the hot end, it's very common for wire connections to loosen, erode, and fall off. When a heating problem is encountered with a hot end, always check first that there is adequate voltage supplied and all connections are secured. Most of the time, issues occur in these areas.

Troubleshooting issues with the x, y, and z axes

The RepRap Mendel design is a basic Cartesian robot. It positions the extruder using three axes to calculate a point in space. There are many different frame designs that can achieve this. The Prusa Mendel design moves the build platform along the *y* axis and the extruder across the *x* axis. The entire *x* axis assembly is raised and lowered along the *z* axis. Belts, pulley bearings, and rods are necessary to achieve this movement. The primary visual difference between most 3D printers is what holds it all together. This is the frame, and it should be sturdy and well maintained.

In this recipe, we'll look at some issues that can affect this system and how we can keep it well maintained.

How to do it...

We will proceed as follows:

1. The frame is what holds it all together. If the nuts and bolts loosen, the square of the frame may shift; circles will become ellipses, and precision parts might not fit together. It's very important to keep all of the fittings tight. Check your printer regularly, especially before a long print run.

2. Check the XY pulleys on the stepper motors. Tighten the set screw (also called a grub screw) on the pulley if it's loose on the motor shaft. A slipping pulley can create a misalignment between print layers. An example of a pulley and its set screw is seen in the following image:

3. Check for a slipping *z* axis coupler. This can vary visually, but they all serve the same purpose. It's a connector between your stepper motor's shaft and the threaded rod that it drives. It's usually a flexible device that allows some play between the shaft and rod so that any slight misalignment can be smoothed out. This will help keep the vertical layers smooth on your print. The coupler on the RepRapPro Mendel is a combination of PLA print clamps and flexible PVC tubing. This can be seen on the left-hand side in the following image:

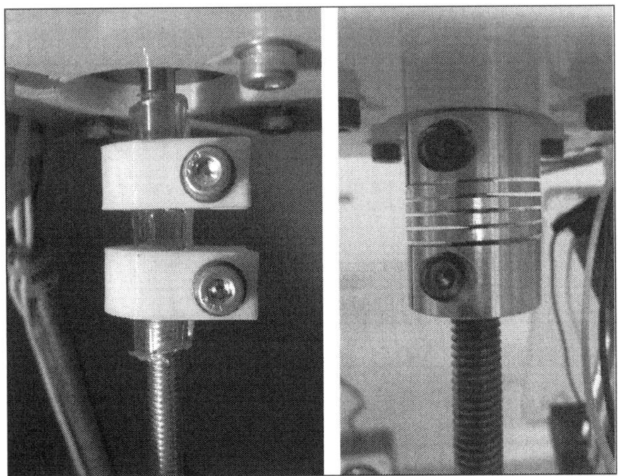

4. On the right-hand side is a flexible aluminum coupler that is commonly used on a Prusa Mendel design.

5. The *z* axis is driven by a threaded rod on a Mendel design. Clean and lubricate the threaded rod regularly with a nonpetroleum lubricant (don't ever use WD-40) such as silicon- or lithium-based products (lubricants used for skateboard bearings is an option).

6. Check the tension of your belts. Make sure that the tension is tight when you press down on the middle of the belt. You can see the belt tension in the following YouTube video, `http://www.youtube.com/watch?v=Uoa8XAwTYFc`.

7. If the belt needs tightening, loosen one anchor and pull the belt tighter, securing the belt before it releases. This can be a rather difficult procedure. If the belt only needs to be tightened slightly, a tensioner can be added without readjusting the belt anchor, as shown in the following image:

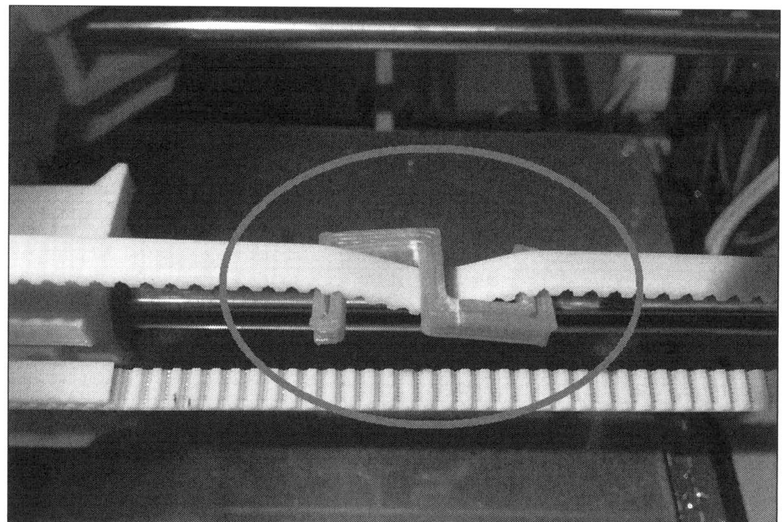

8. In the preceding image, you can see a small plastic device that can be downloaded from Thingiverse at `http://www.thingiverse.com/thing:10082`.

9. Check your smooth rods and bearings. Make sure that all the parallel rods are true and wipe them down regularly to keep them clean from debris. Make sure that all of the bearings are firmly seated in their housings and not binding at points along the travel of the axis. If you're machine uses the common LM8UU bearings, you can lubricate them with white lithium grease. However, unless you get the lubricant inside the bearing, it won't be very effective. By placing the lubricant on the rod, the bearings will just wipe it off.

How it works...

Most of the points covered in this recipe can be applied as a regular maintenance routine on a monthly cycle. However, it's probably a good idea to always give your printer a good visual check with some tweaking if a very long print job is anticipated. It's a very frustrating situation when you find that a bolt or nut needs tightening half way through a 20-hour print run!

Troubleshooting issues with the motor system

All RepRap printers use stepper motors to drive the movement along the x, y, and z axes. These kinds of motors operate by moving in set intervals, by a way of pulses generated by a stepper driver. With this system, a precise and continuous movement can be achieved. Without this precision, we wouldn't be able to control the precise position of our extruder.

In this recipe, we'll look at solving some common issues with this system.

Getting ready

A basic toolkit consisting of a micro screwdriver set and long needle nose pliers would be helpful.

How to do it...

We will proceed as follows:

1. A motor that's not moving at all is a major issue. The first step in resolving this situation is to make sure that all the connections for the motor are firmly attached. In the following image, there are two different connection points for the stepper motor on the controller:

2. A typical RepRap stepper motor will have four leads that are connected to the controller. If one wire becomes loose or detached, the motor will stall or vibrate without rotating. The standard black Molex pin connector can sometimes wiggle free out of the housing. This can cause a poor intermittent connection. This is illustrated in the following image:

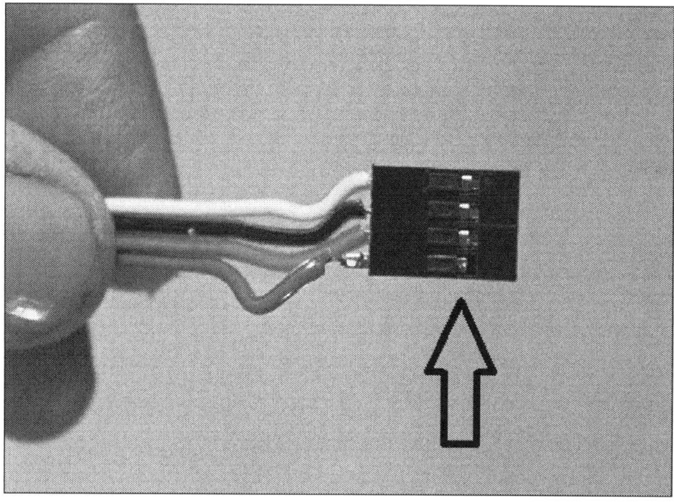

3. If the connector has been accidentally reversed on the controller, the motor will still work, but in reverse. This is a good reason to mark the connector in case of an accidental detachment, even if the wire leads are color coded.

4. Some stepper motors have connectors at the body. Make sure that the connections are firmly attached. This is illustrated in the following image:

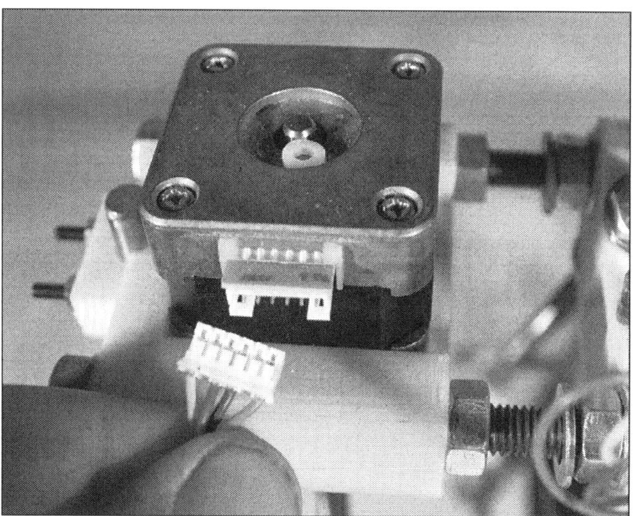

5. Make sure that none of the wire leads that attach to the Molex connector are loose or have become unattached. You can do this by making sure that the crimp is good on the individual connectors. A YouTube video outlining the crimping process can be seen at `http://www.youtube.com/watch?v=sr9zE9aRTJc`.

6. The endstops are another part of the stepper motor system. These devices are basically microswitches that are monitored by the firmware. A typical microswitch is shown in the following image:

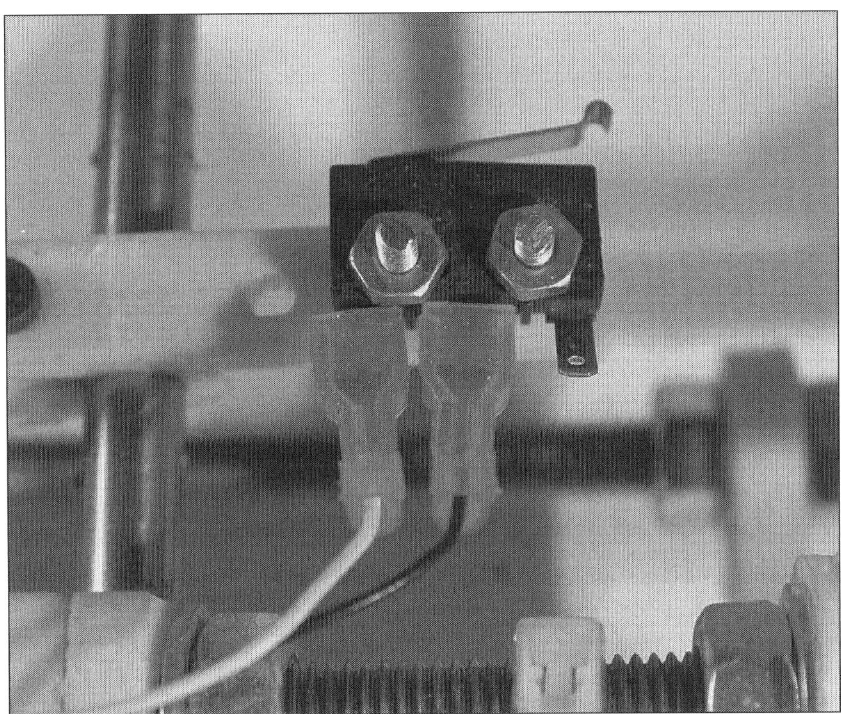

7. It alerts the controller when an axis reaches its limit (these are often referred to as limit switches as well). Most configurations have the endstop set to ON until the switch is triggered. Check both sides of the endstop connection. If there's a loose or detached connection, the controller will think that the axis has been triggered and remain OFF. The stepper motor will not move.

8. Erratic behavior of the stepper motor's movement can also be caused by the stepper driver. The stepper driver is the controller that sends a single pulse to the stepper motor and in turn, rotates it by one micro-step. If these pulses are interrupted, the stepper motor skips a step, and the axis position is altered. The most common cause for this type of issue is an inaccurate current setting. First, let's locate your stepper drivers. They should be components that are attached to your controller or built into the controller board. The Melzi controller has three drivers built into the board. This can be seen in the following image:

9. Overheating is caused if too much current is supplied to the stepper motor. This can cause skipping or a shutdown. Some drivers have an automatic safety feature that shuts the driver down when the controller IC gets too hot. When it cools, the driver resumes. To adjust the amount of current supplied, a potentiometer (also called a trimpot) is built into the driver. This is a small round device that looks like a screw head. An example can be seen in the following image:

10. Sometimes it can be a small screw on a box, as seen in the following image:

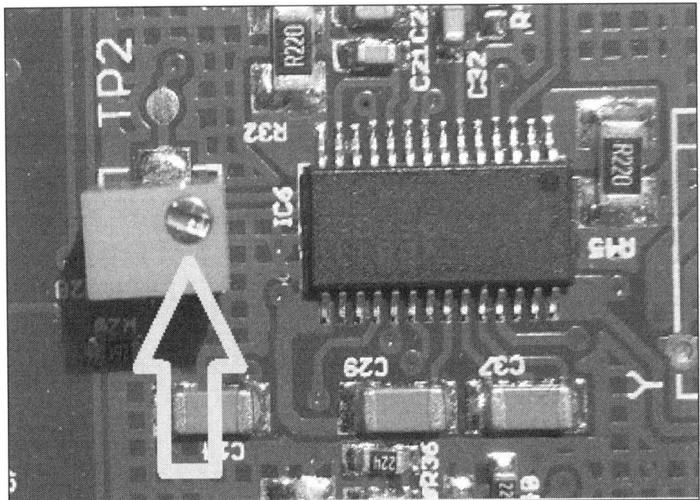

11. By turning it counterclockwise all the way, it will shut the current OFF. A rule of thumb is to increase the current by turning the potentiometer one-fourth of a revolution clockwise.

12. A stepper motor that isn't providing enough torque can cause skipping as well. Increase the current by turning the potentiometer clockwise in small increments until the proper torque is obtained by the motor. If the motor runs too hot, then you are supplying too much current. The motor can get very warm but never too hot to touch.

More precise adjustments can be made with a multimeter. Refer to `http://reprap.org/wiki/Pololu_stepper_driver_board` and `http://reprap.org/wiki/RepRapPro_Setting_Motor_Currents`. Keep in mind that the specific VREF voltages may vary for your driver. Check your specifications first!

13. If your stepper driver uses a heat sink, make sure it's still attached. Heat sinks are usually small fin-like objects that are taped to the top surface of the stepper driver's IC controller. This can be seen in the following image:

14. This object allows greater dissipation of the generated heat in the IC controller. Pololu stepper drivers have a tendency to run hot. For this reason, you should make sure that you have heat sinks when using this particular driver.

How it works...

The current that is sent to the stepper motor must be set correctly. This one adjustment can make an incredible difference in the precision and health of your printer. If the voltage is too low, enough current will not be sent to your stepper motor. This will decrease its torque and cause the stepper to skip steps.

If the voltage is too high, the stepper motor and driver may suffer damage due to the heat. The motor mounts can soften and distort. A printed pulley mounted on the stepper motor shaft can become permanently loose. These scenarios can cause problems for the belt system.

Some newer controller designs such as the RAMBo 1.2 have digital trimpots for the stepper drivers, which are controlled by the firmware.

If you can't get the stepper motor to work and you suspect that it's burned out, you're probably wrong. Stepper motors on a RepRap 3D printer very rarely burn out. If you need peace of mind, simply connect the suspect stepper motor's leads to another axis that is working and test move it. This will indicate its condition. Be careful! Never remove the leads from the driver while it is powered ON. Make sure that the printer is powered OFF before making any electrical adjustments, or you may damage your stepper drivers or other components permanently.

Please be careful with all of your printing activities!

Understanding and Editing Firmware

Firmware is a program code that is stored in the CPU of a 3D printer's controller. It provides a set of instructions on how the printer works mechanically. Most of the time, the contents of a firmware package uploaded to the controller only need minor adjustments to work properly. These adjustments make minor changes to the values in the source code. These values will specify the hardware and calibrate your particular machine.

Most companies selling 3D printers fully assembled and in kit form provide edited versions of popular firmware for their machines. In most cases, if changes are needed to be made, it is probably better to follow the instructions on their website. Sometimes, these companies don't keep up with the recent firmware upgrades. If this is the case, you may decide to upgrade to a more recent firmware.

Firmware is continually updated and improved upon. There are eleven active firmware listed on the RepRap site at `http://reprap.org/wiki/List_of_Firmware`.

Here are the two most popular firmware that work with Prusa Mendel designs:

- Sprinter (`https://github.com/kliment/Sprinter`)
    - Supports printing from an SD card
    - Supports PID temperature control
    - Supports acceleration

- Marlin (`https://github.com/ErikZalm/Marlin`)

    - Supports all of the preceding Sprinter-supported features

    - Supports look ahead for smoother corners

    - Supports the Arc feature

    - Saves to EEPROM

    - Automatic build platform leveling

An Arduino IDE program

Firmware is updated on most RepRap controller boards by using the Arduino **Integrated Development Environment** (**IDE**). It's an open source software application that allows programs and data (such as the RepRap firmware) to be loaded and stored permanently in the microcontroller chip.

In order to access the firmware and make changes, you'll need to download the recent version at `http://arduino.cc/`. It's available for Windows, Mac, and Linux OS systems. Some recent versions of Marlin and older firmware will require the use of legacy versions such as v0.23. They can be found on the previous release page of the download site. If you're having problems uploading basic data changes, it's a good idea to check a previous version of the Arduino IDE that you are using. Sometimes, the firmware updates don't keep up with the recent Arduino versions.

For Windows users, you can place the unzipped `Arduino` folder in your `Program Files` folder. Create a desktop icon from the `arduino.exe` file and use it to start the program.

Getting Windows to recognize the controller

This appendix will cover two basic controller designs that are common for RepRap-based printers:

- Arduino Mega 2560 is based on the ATmega2560 microchip (the older ATmega 1280 may also be used on older machines)

- Sanguinololu is based on the ATMEGA644P microchip

If this is the first time you have tried to upload some firmware, you'll discover that there is a need to install the drivers that are specific to the controller.

For the Arduino Mega, you'll need to follow these steps:

1. Plug the board in using the USB connection. Windows will attempt to find a device driver for the board and will most likely fail.

2. Open **Device Manager** in your system. Locate the yellow exclamation mark labeled **Arduino Mega 2560** under **Ports** or **Other Devices**.

3. Choose the **"Browse my computer for driver software"** option. Locate the `drivers` folder in the `Arduino` folder. Select the `drivers` folder and then click on **Next** to install. The Arduino Mega should now be recognized and assigned with a port number. Take note of this number.

If you plug in a controller and it's not recognized at all, you'll need to install a Virtual COM Port driver. You can download this from `http://www.ftdichip.com/Drivers/VCP.htm`. Extract all the folders and install the driver.

Getting the Arduino IDE to recognize the Sanguinololu

The Arduino IDE is written for authentic Arduino controllers and thus only comes loaded with these controller-board options. Its open source environment has allowed developers to create the addition of ATmega boards such as the Sanguinololu. In order for this to work, additional files are needed.

For Arduino Version 1.0.1, download the zipped file `sanguino-0101r1.zip` via `https://code.google.com/p/sanguino/downloads/detail?name=Sanguino-0101r1.zip&can=2&q`.

For Arduino Version 0023, download the zipped file `sanguino1284p-master` via `https://github.com/jmgiacalone/sanguino1284p`.

Place the folder's contents into the `hardware` folder nested in the `Arduino program` folder. If Windows asks you to merge or overwrite files, indicate yes. The Sanguinololu boards now become available.

Setting up the Arduino IDE for your controller

Once you have plugged in your controller to the USB port and started up the Arduino IDE, two selections must be made. Refer to the following steps:

1. Go to **Tools** in the menu and then go to **Boards**. From the cascaded menu, choose the controller board that you are using.

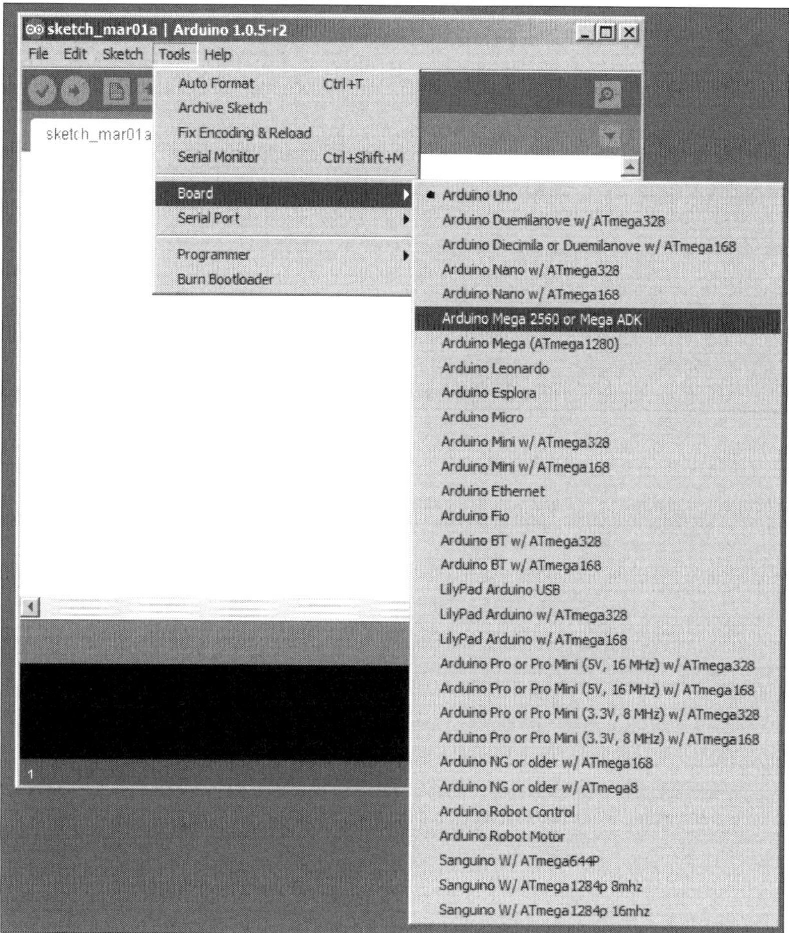

2. Go back to **Tools** and choose **Serial Port**. From the cascaded menu, choose the COM port that your controller is using.

Setting up the firmware in the Arduino IDE

When the Arduino IDE is initially started, an `Arduino` folder is created in your Windows `Documents` folder. This is where the sketches (programs such as our firmware) are stored. Make sure your downloaded firmware is unzipped in a folder and stored here.

From the Arduino IDE menu, select **Files** and then **Sketches**. The list of firmware that you have stored in the `Arduino` folder becomes accessible. If the firmware doesn't appear, try restarting the Arduino IDE.

Comparing firmware versions with WinMerge

The first thing to keep in mind is that a backup of the firmware that is loaded and working on your controller board is necessary if you plan to revert to it. This requires the actual folder contents that are loaded in the board. There is no easy method of retrieving or reading the firmware stored on your controller. Any new uploads to the controller will permanently erase the old firmware.

There are many different settings that may be specific to your printer that may need to be transferred to a new firmware update. These differences can easily be seen by using a program called **WinMerge**. It's a free open source program available at `http://winmerge.org/`.

Using this program allows a complete comparison between each file in the firmware folders. Follow these steps:

1. Start by selecting **File** in the WinMerge menu and then click on **Open**. A pop-up window stating **Select Files or Folders** will appear.

2. Browse for the old firmware folder on the left. Click on **Open the folder** and then click on **Open** when the filename reads **Folder Selection**.

3. Do the same with the new firmware folder on the right and select **OK**.

A list will appear with the contents of both firmware folders. There will be a column that indicates the comparison of files, as shown in the following screenshot:

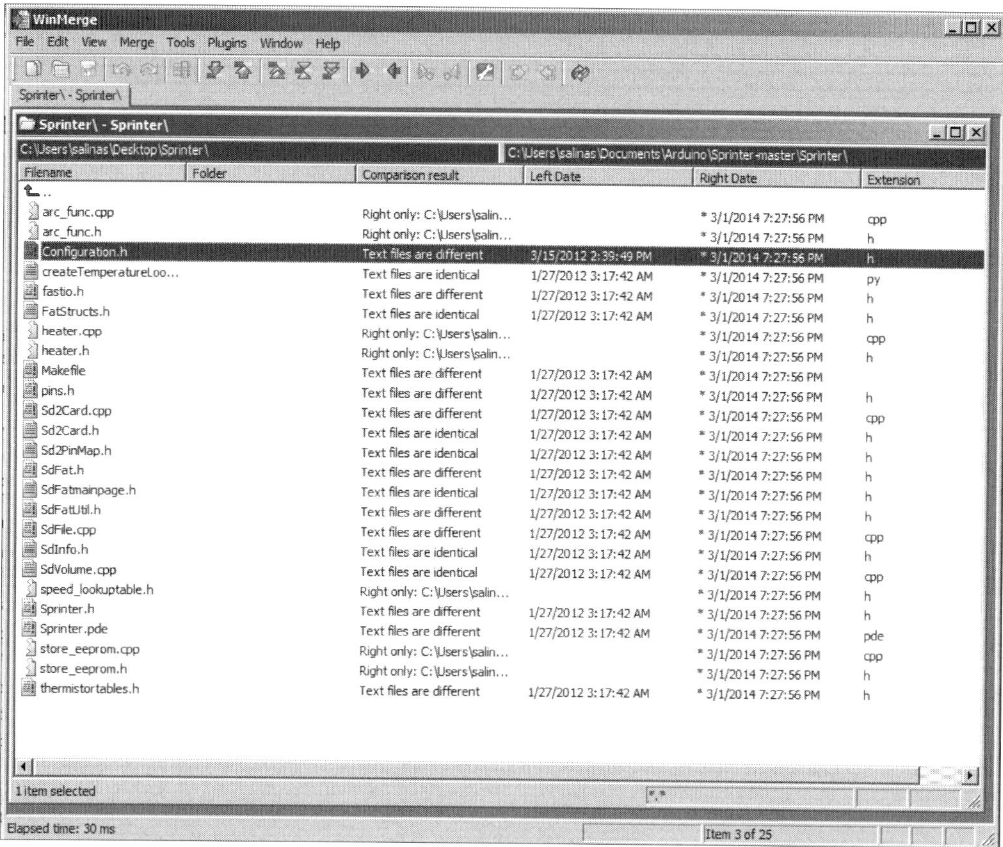

The following are the observations from the preceding screenshot:

- Text files are identical
- Text files are different
- Left or right indication of an additional file

Scroll down the file list and open the `configuration.h` file by double-clicking on it.

A new window will appear showing a side-by-side comparison of the two files. The yellow highlights will indicate a change in information, and the gray areas will indicate added information, as shown in the following screenshot:

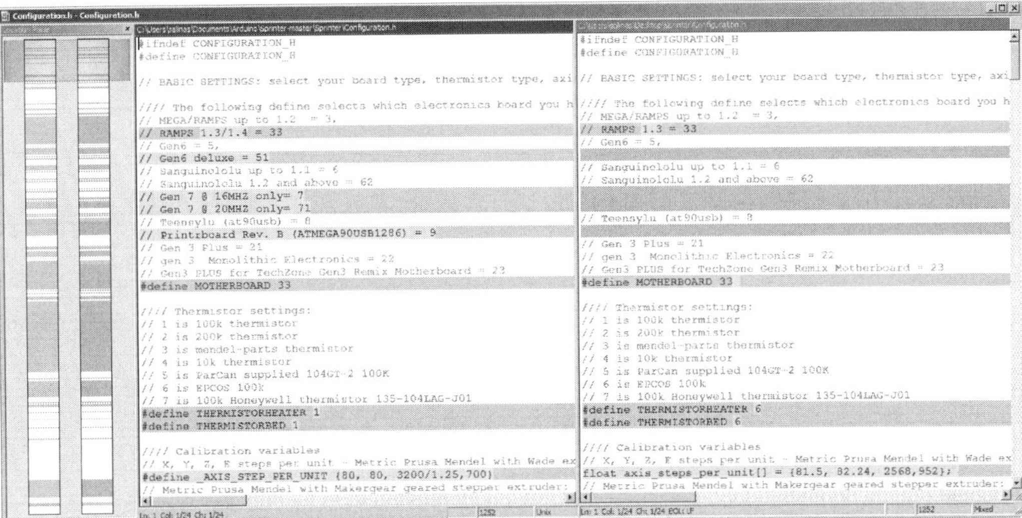

Permanent changes can be made to the firmware with WinMerge, but it's better to use the Arduino IDE for these changes. The IDE has a **Verify/Compile** function that will alert you of any errors.

Editing the firmware with the Arduino IDE

The `configuration.h` folder is usually the only file that most RepRap printers will need to adjust. This file contains the data that describes your particular electronics and stores the numerical data that calibrates your printer.

The line that is most commonly changed with a working unmodified 3D printer contains the **X**, **Y**, **Z**, and **E** steps per unit values. These values calibrate the movement of the printer and the amount of filament extruded.

In Sprinter, this can be easily found at the beginning of the `configuration.h` file. In Marlin, this is closer to the bottom-third of the file. Marlin can be seen open in the Arduino IDE in the following screenshot:

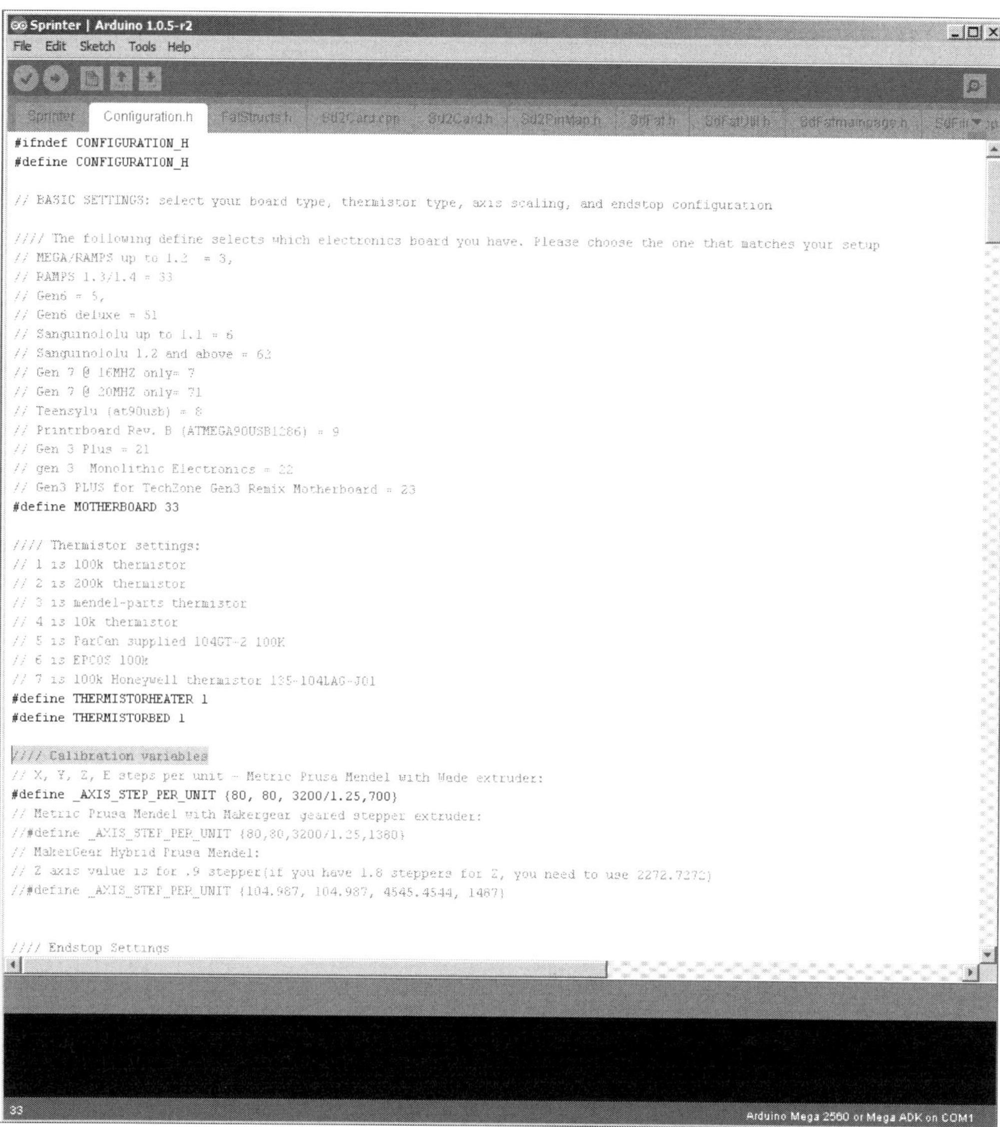

Any data recorded with two forward slashes `//` is the data that is commented out and disabled. It can also precede comments for information purposes or records. When changing values in the firmware, it's a good idea to comment out your old values with the `//` for record-keeping in case you would like to revert to the old values.

There are many other variables that can be adjusted. These are usually made during the initial setup of a newly built printer. Most kits and fully-assembled printers will have the necessary changes made in its firmware and uploaded to your controller. For more information, one of the best overviews of the options available in the `configuration.h` file can be found at `http://airtripper.com/1145/marlin-firmware-v1-basic-configuration-set-up-guide/`.

Uploading the firmware to the controller

Once the firmware is edited, the firmware needs to be compiled and uploaded to the controller. If you are concerned about the possibility of a mistake in the syntax of your firmware, you can choose **Sketch** in the menu and then select **Verify/Compile**. If there are any errors, they will be noted in the window at the bottom.

Most syntax errors in a line will be highlighted in yellow. This will make it easier to locate. Most of the values, if wrong, may be more difficult to discover. They will not generate compiling errors, but they could create faulty or erratic machine operation.

If all is well, the firmware can now be uploaded to the controller. Select the right-pointing arrow for the **Upload** option in the row of icons under the menu. Within a minute, the firmware is loaded.

Some host software can make changes to firmware settings by sending the G-code instructions. This will be examined in *Appendix B, Taking a Closer Look at G-code.*

B

Taking a Closer Look at G-code

G-code is a numerical control programming language. It's a set of instructions used as a means of controlling automated machines. In this case, it will instruct your 3D printer how to move and how much filament to extrude. It's unlikely that you'll need to examine the G-code that is generated by your slicer. However, knowing a handful of G-code commands can be useful at the command window of your host.

Generating G-code

G-code is generated by your slicer. The slicer is a program that takes the file of your 3D model and slices it up into many layers. A model created for 3D printing is constructed by a contiguous surface of triangles. This forms the entire skin of your model, without any gaps or overlapping.

The following image is a model created with TopMod.

When the slicer program slices the model, it generates a perimeter of each Z layer. A sliced layer is illustrated in the following image:

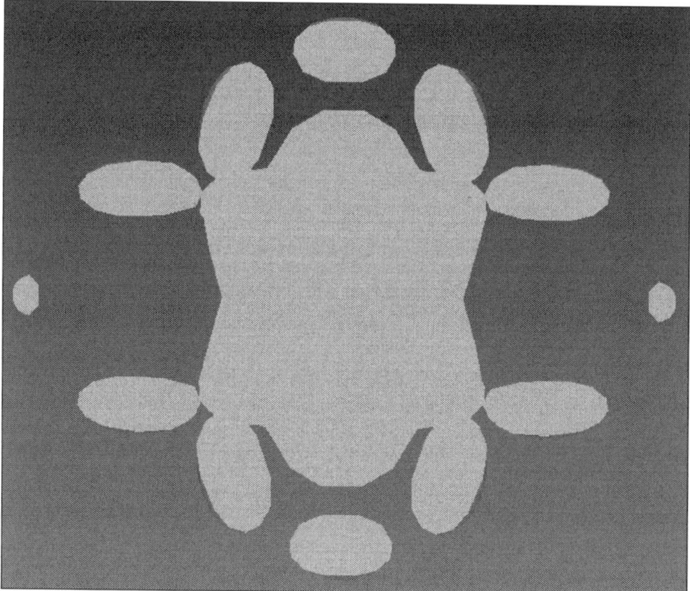

In order to create a perimeter for the slicer, some or all of the triangles that intersect the XY plane for the Z height may be used. In the following image, we can see the places where some triangles may be eliminated due to size or redundancy:

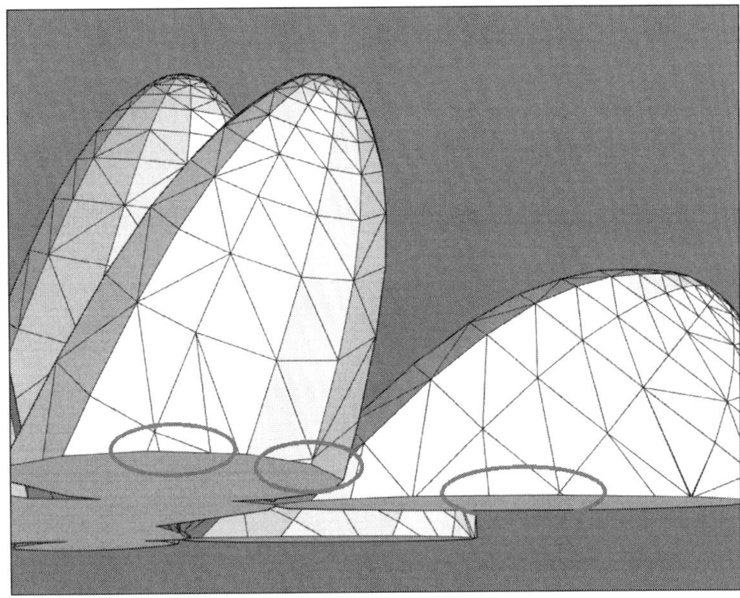

This is one reason why different slicers may produce different results. As shown in the following image, we can see a difference in the 39th Z height layer of this model:

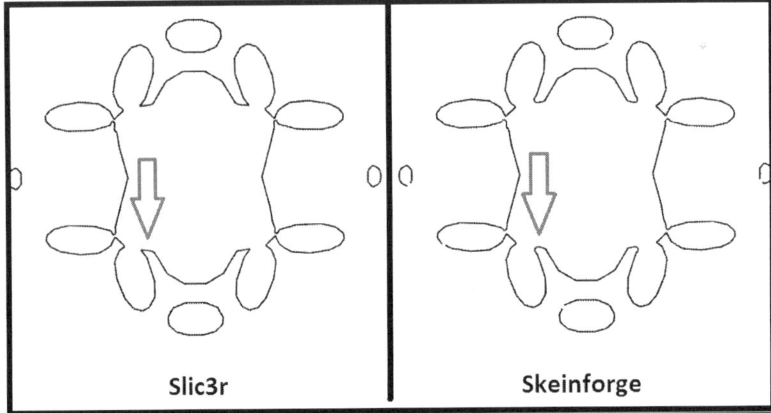

The narrow undercut of the perimeter is sharper in the Slic3r profile as opposed to the more rounded Skeinforge interpolation. This is a subtle difference, but it illustrates how there can be a difference between different slicer interpolations.

Another difference between slicer profiles will be how the extruder's actual path is generated. In the following figure, we can see the difference between Slic3r and Skeinforge:

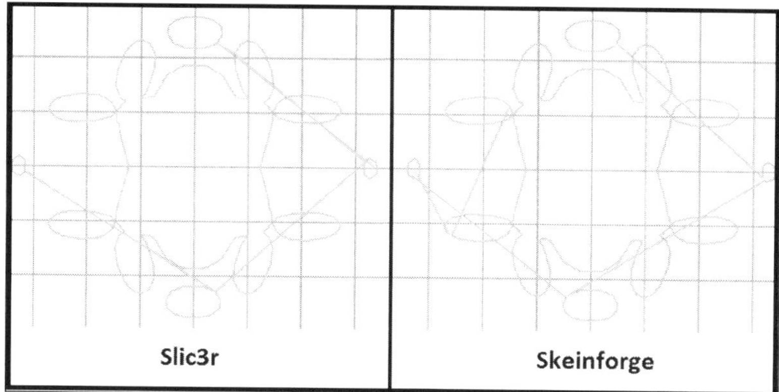

It's very unlikely that a difference in the actual movement path of the extruder will make a difference, unless the end and start of a Z height layer occurs in the same XY coordinate, and this creates a ridge in a detailed sensitive area of the model. Of course, this can be alleviated by selecting a random start point for each Z height in the slicer profile.

Repetier-Host, Pronterface, and other host software have good G-code viewers, but there is also a web browser G-code viewer that is useful. It is called G-code Visualizer. It's an open source web app that was created by Alex Utsyantsev, and it's available freely at `http://gcode.ws/`.

Viewing G-code

There are many options available to see the written G-code generated by your slicer. Both Repetier-Host and Printrun have the ability to show and edit the text of G-code.

An ordinary text application such as Windows Notepad can also be used. The following example is a G-code of a 20 mm test cube generated by Skeinforge and Slic3r:

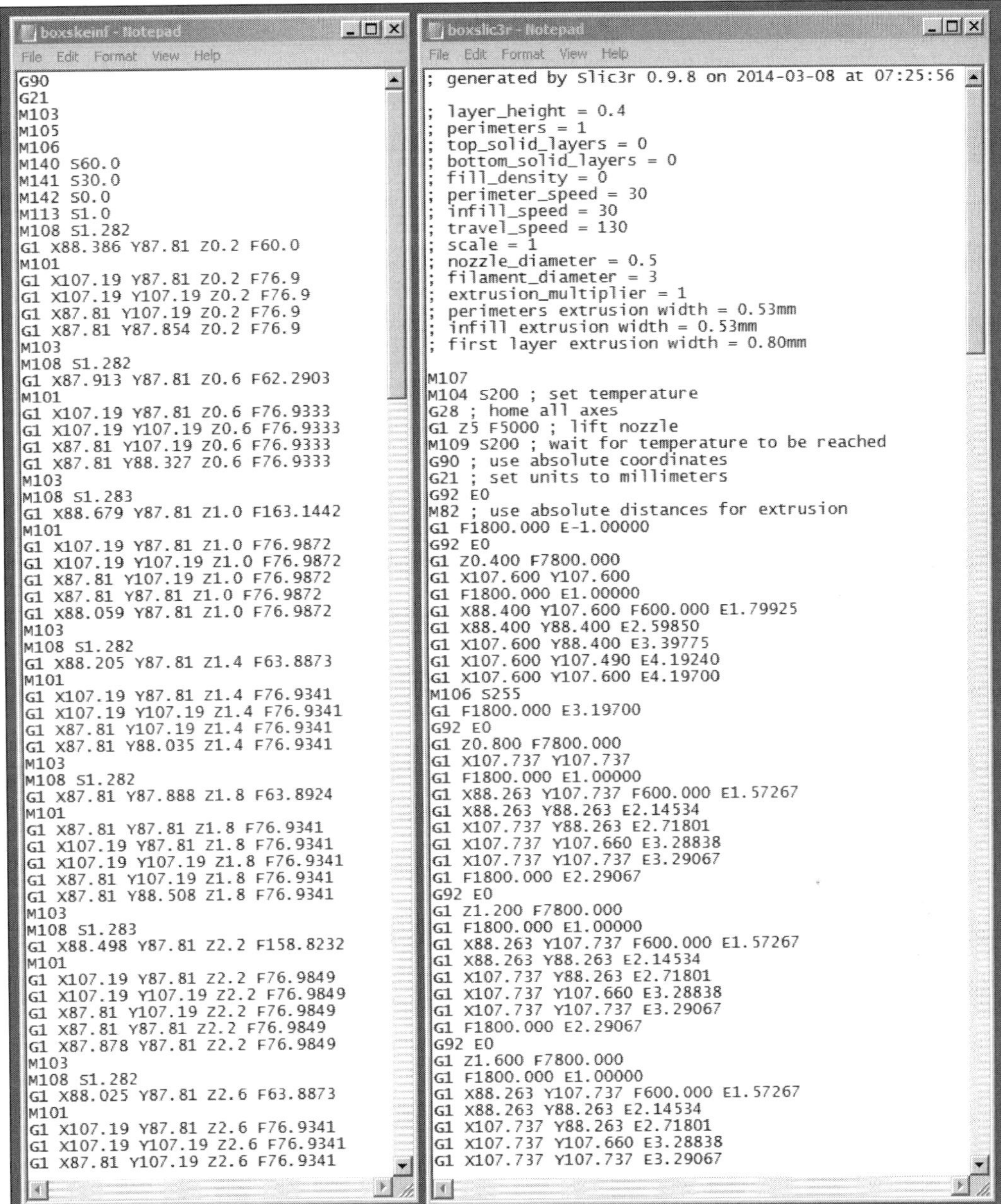

boxskeinf - Notepad
File Edit Format View Help
G90
G21
M103
M105
M106
M140 S60.0
M141 S30.0
M142 S0.0
M113 S1.0
M108 S1.282
G1 X88.386 Y87.81 Z0.2 F60.0
M101
G1 X107.19 Y87.81 Z0.2 F76.9
G1 X107.19 Y107.19 Z0.2 F76.9
G1 X87.81 Y107.19 Z0.2 F76.9
G1 X87.81 Y87.854 Z0.2 F76.9
M103
M108 S1.282
G1 X87.913 Y87.81 Z0.6 F62.2903
M101
G1 X107.19 Y87.81 Z0.6 F76.9333
G1 X107.19 Y107.19 Z0.6 F76.9333
G1 X87.81 Y107.19 Z0.6 F76.9333
G1 X87.81 Y88.327 Z0.6 F76.9333
M103
M108 S1.283
G1 X88.679 Y87.81 Z1.0 F163.1442
M101
G1 X107.19 Y87.81 Z1.0 F76.9872
G1 X107.19 Y107.19 Z1.0 F76.9872
G1 X87.81 Y107.19 Z1.0 F76.9872
G1 X87.81 Y87.81 Z1.0 F76.9872
G1 X88.059 Y87.81 Z1.0 F76.9872
M103
M108 S1.282
G1 X88.205 Y87.81 Z1.4 F63.8873
M101
G1 X107.19 Y87.81 Z1.4 F76.9341
G1 X107.19 Y107.19 Z1.4 F76.9341
G1 X87.81 Y107.19 Z1.4 F76.9341
G1 X87.81 Y88.035 Z1.4 F76.9341
M103
M108 S1.282
G1 X87.81 Y87.888 Z1.8 F63.8924
M101
G1 X87.81 Y87.81 Z1.8 F76.9341
G1 X107.19 Y87.81 Z1.8 F76.9341
G1 X107.19 Y107.19 Z1.8 F76.9341
G1 X87.81 Y107.19 Z1.8 F76.9341
G1 X87.81 Y88.508 Z1.8 F76.9341
M103
M108 S1.283
G1 X88.498 Y87.81 Z2.2 F158.8232
M101
G1 X107.19 Y87.81 Z2.2 F76.9849
G1 X107.19 Y107.19 Z2.2 F76.9849
G1 X87.81 Y107.19 Z2.2 F76.9849
G1 X87.81 Y87.81 Z2.2 F76.9849
G1 X87.878 Y87.81 Z2.2 F76.9849
M103
M108 S1.282
G1 X88.025 Y87.81 Z2.6 F63.8873
M101
G1 X107.19 Y87.81 Z2.6 F76.9341
G1 X107.19 Y107.19 Z2.6 F76.9341
G1 X87.81 Y107.19 Z2.6 F76.9341

boxslic3r - Notepad
File Edit Format View Help
; generated by Slic3r 0.9.8 on 2014-03-08 at 07:25:56

; layer_height = 0.4
; perimeters = 1
; top_solid_layers = 0
; bottom_solid_layers = 0
; fill_density = 0
; perimeter_speed = 30
; infill_speed = 30
; travel_speed = 130
; scale = 1
; nozzle_diameter = 0.5
; filament_diameter = 3
; extrusion_multiplier = 1
; perimeters extrusion width = 0.53mm
; infill extrusion width = 0.53mm
; first layer extrusion width = 0.80mm

M107
M104 S200 ; set temperature
G28 ; home all axes
G1 Z5 F5000 ; lift nozzle
M109 S200 ; wait for temperature to be reached
G90 ; use absolute coordinates
G21 ; set units to millimeters
G92 E0
M82 ; use absolute distances for extrusion
G1 F1800.000 E-1.00000
G92 E0
G1 Z0.400 F7800.000
G1 X107.600 Y107.600
G1 F1800.000 E1.00000
G1 X88.400 Y107.600 F600.000 E1.79925
G1 X88.400 Y88.400 E2.59850
G1 X107.600 Y88.400 E3.39775
G1 X107.600 Y107.490 E4.19240
G1 X107.600 Y107.600 E4.19700
M106 S255
G1 F1800.000 E3.19700
G92 E0
G1 Z0.800 F7800.000
G1 X107.737 Y107.737
G1 F1800.000 E1.00000
G1 X88.263 Y107.737 F600.000 E1.57267
G1 X88.263 Y88.263 E2.14534
G1 X107.737 Y88.263 E2.71801
G1 X107.737 Y107.660 E3.28838
G1 X107.737 Y107.737 E3.29067
G1 F1800.000 E2.29067
G92 E0
G1 Z1.200 F7800.000
G1 F1800.000 E1.00000
G1 X88.263 Y107.737 F600.000 E1.57267
G1 X88.263 Y88.263 E2.14534
G1 X107.737 Y88.263 E2.71801
G1 X107.737 Y107.660 E3.28838
G1 X107.737 Y107.737 E3.29067
G1 F1800.000 E2.29067
G92 E0
G1 Z1.600 F7800.000
G1 F1800.000 E1.00000
G1 X88.263 Y107.737 F600.000 E1.57267
G1 X88.263 Y88.263 E2.14534
G1 X107.737 Y88.263 E2.71801
G1 X107.737 Y107.660 E3.28838
G1 X107.737 Y107.737 E3.29067

The obvious difference between the two slicer versions is the inclusion of comments in the header of the Slic3r G-code.

Slic3r creates a list at the beginning. This list overviews the parameters that have been chosen in the profile. Each line is commented out using a semicolon (;) before each comment line. Skeinforge doesn't create any comments.

Adding comments can be a useful feature when experimenting with different slicer profiles. By adding a description of short settings to the G-code, the attached documentation won't be lost. A comment can be added by simply typing in the information after a semicolon and saving the change. Just be careful that the text editor saves the file with the `.gcode` extension.

Basic G-code commands

Most people do not need to learn G-code. This is why we have a slicer to do all of the work. However, there are a handful of G-code commands that are useful to know. All of these commands are useful while printing and can be entered by way of the host command line. Refer to the following commands:

- `G1`: This command designates a controlled move. Here's an example of the `G1` command-line syntax: `G1 X200 Y200 Z100 F500`. The X and Y motors should move the extruder 200 mm from the home position and at 500 mm/min (F500). We'll see shortly how this command is a useful one.

- `M302`: This command disables the cold extrusion prevention. This is very useful when testing the extruder movement without heating the filament. This allows the extruder motor to run when the hot end is colder than a firmware-specified temperature.

- `M106`: This command turns the cooling fan on. When used with an `S` parameter between 0-255, the speed can be adjusted. Here's an example of the `M106` command-line syntax: `M106 S127`.

- `M107`: This command turns the cooling fan off.

- `M503`: This command echoes the current settings from memory (not from EEPROM). This is very useful when you need to see the current calibration settings stored in the firmware.

- `M501`: This command echoes the current settings from EEPROM (if you need to reset them after you changed them temporarily).

- `M92`: This command sets `axis_steps_per_unit` to the same parameters as entered in the firmware. This is a good way to tweak the axes and E-motor calibration on the fly. Here's an example of the `M92` command-line syntax: `M92 X80 Y80 Z3200 E945`.

- `M303`: This command is the PID autotune. This generates the Proportional, Integral, and Derivative (PID) values for the hot end. Run this test every time you make a temperature change. The variables C = number of cycles to run test and S = target temperature. Here's an example of the `M303` command-line syntax: `M303 C8 S220`. Testing should be started with a cold hot end.

- `M500`: This command stores parameters in EEPROM.

More commands can be found at `http://reprap.org/wiki/G-code` and `http://www.thingiverse.com/thing:21546/`.

Using the command line

The host can also make changes to the G-code on the fly. This is handy if you want to make changes quickly, such as turn a fan on or off or adjust its speed. To do this, you simply enter the G-code command in a command-line window and click on **Send**.

The following screenshot shows the host program Repetier-Host:

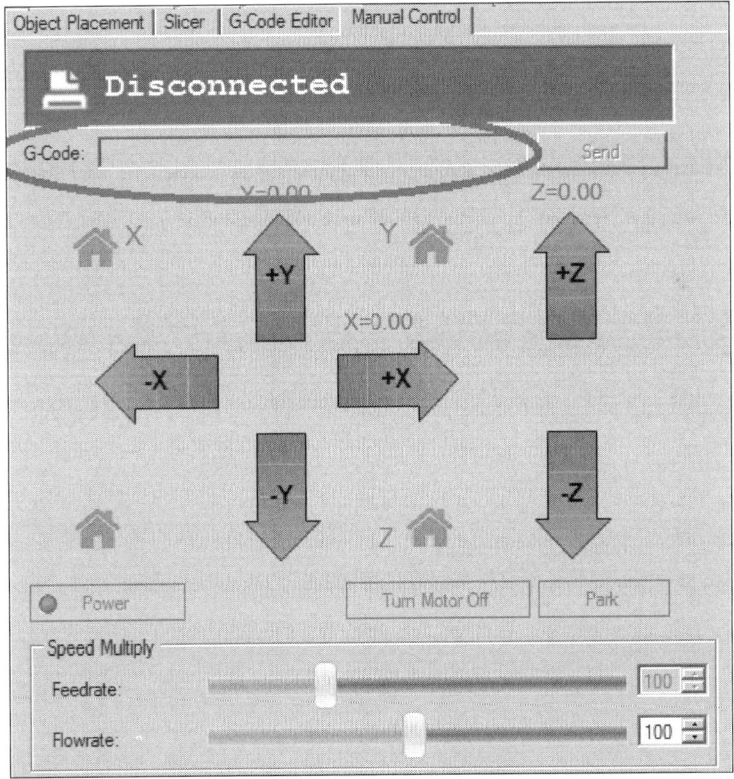

Its command line is located under the **Manual Control** tab. The following screenshot shows the host Pronterface:

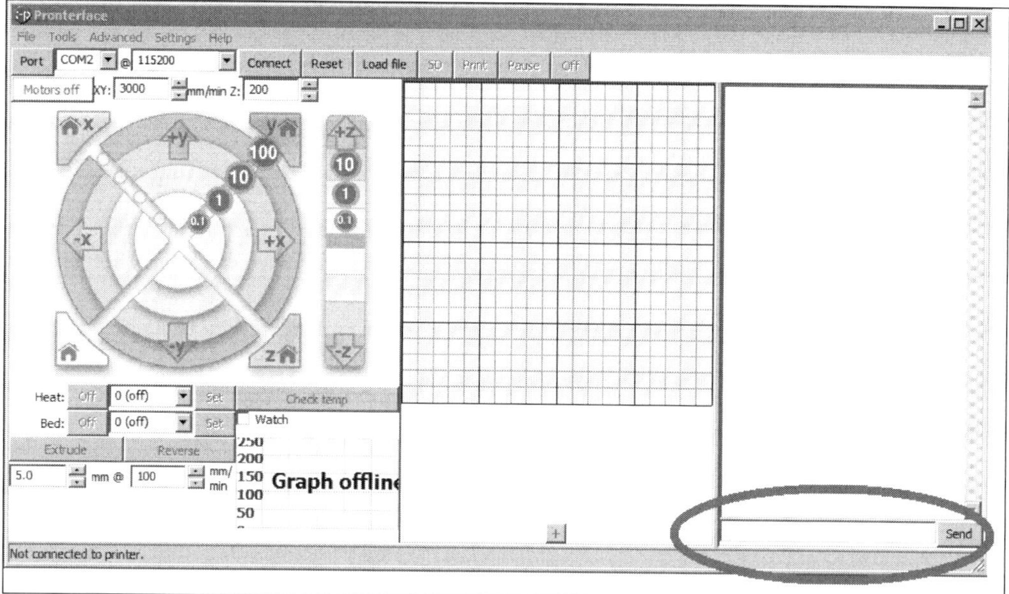

Its command line is located on the bottom-right corner of the program. A nice feature of Pronterface is its capability to create custom buttons that will send frequently used G-code commands. For instance, it's very convenient to have a set of buttons that will move the extruder to all four corners of the build platform when bed leveling.

We'll make the first button for a 200 mm x 200 mm bed by starting with the front-left position. To do this, left-click on the small **+** button at the bottom center of the program. A pop up will appear with the following three text fields:

- **Button title**: In this field, enter XY front left

- **Command**: In this field, enter `G1 X0 Y0 F10000`

- **Color**: In this field, enter a hex color code (check the following list):

    - For yellow, it is `#FFFF00`; for red, `#FF0000`; for blue, `#0000FF`; for green, `#00FF00`; for magenta, `#FF00FF`; and for cyan, `#00FFFF`

Also, continue to make buttons for the other three corners with the following data:

- XY front right: `G1  X260  Y0  F10000`
- XY rear right: `G1  X260  Y230  F10000`
- XY rear left: `G1  X0  Y230  F10000`

Making other buttons for G-code commands can be very convenient, for instance, a button for fan control. The Pronterface host doesn't have a manual control feature for the fan. By allowing the use of custom buttons, many useful G-code commands can be accessed.

Filament Options for RepRap Printers

Many different materials have become available for 3D printing, and more efficient and exotic filaments are bound to become available in the near future. This list is by no means an exhaustive review of the 3D filaments available, but it does provide a variety of materials that can offer enormous possibilities for home or small business manufacturing.

All of the listed filaments are available in 3-mm and 1.75-mm diameters. Considering the worldwide possibilities of acquiring filaments, the best source may be derived, depending on your geographical location, from the list at `http://reprap.org/wiki/Printing_Material_Suppliers`.

Health considerations

Before we begin the survey, let's look at some health issues when extruding with these filaments.

For your health, it's better to be aware of these dangers, and it's also better for the health of your printer. A cooler operating hot end will last longer. Make sure you are not extruding at a very high temperature. If you don't have the proper tools (such as a multimeter with a thermocouple) to take accurate readings, then be safe and don't exceed the maximum temperature specified for a material. When an ABS filament is burned, it will release carbon monoxide and hydrogen cyanide, which are hazardous to your health. When a PLA filament is burned, it will release carbon monoxide.

3D printers will release **ultrafine particles (UFPs)** into the air when they extrude plastic. There is no conclusive evidence that the volume of exposure is detrimental to your health, but proper ventilation is a good precaution.

An ABS filament

Acrylonitrile butadiene styrene (**ABS**) is a common plastic that is used in manufacturing most of our consumer products. It is not biodegradable and has a greater environmental impact than some of the other filaments. An ABS filament is a strong and flexible material suitable for mechanical parts. It has impact resistance, dimensional stability, and excellent heat and low-temperature resistance. It's easily sanded, glued, and receptive of most paint products. It is also available in many colors.

The average temperature for 3D extrusion should be around 225 degrees Celsius. Different colors may need to be adjusted with slightly different extrusion temperatures.

ABS has a tendency to warp, but this can be minimized using a heat bed at a maximum temperature of 120 degrees Celsius.

ABS should be used in a well-ventilated area. ABS products are capable of releasing small amounts of fumes at melting temperatures. While these fumes are generally considered tolerable, care should be taken to minimize exposure.

There are three special varieties that exhibit different characteristics. They are as follows:

- Glowing in the dark is available in a limited range of colors. It requires a slightly lower extruding temperature from 210 to 220 degrees Celsius.

- smartABS has a 30 percent lower warp tendency. It extrudes at normal temperatures, but if foam comes out of the nozzle, the material has to be dried at about 75 degrees Celsius for 2 hours.

- A conductive filament can be used for the conduction of electric current, antistatic dissipation, and electromagnetic interference shielding. It requires an extruding temperature from 200 to 230 degrees Celsius.

- A polycarbonate ABS alloy is an incredibly tough material designed for strong, resilient parts. It should be used in a well-ventilated area. It requires a much higher extruding temperature from 260 to 280 degrees Celsius.

A PLA filament

Poly-Lactic Acid (**PLA**) is a thermoplastic which is derived from plant-based starches and is biodegradable under the right conditions. It is a strong and stiff material suitable for many uses. It has a lower heat tolerance and less impact resistance than an ABS filament, but it adheres well to itself and all surfaces. It can be sanded, glued, and is receptive of most paint products. It's available in many colors and recognized for its shiny surface.

The average temperature for 3D extrusion should be around 180-200 degrees Celsius. Different colors may need to be adjusted with slightly different extrusion temperatures.

It has a low warp tendency and doesn't require a heat bed. If a heated bed is utilized, a temperature of 60 degrees Celsius is recommended. Printing on a blue painters tape will help in keeping the print adhered.

PLA should be used in a well-ventilated area. It releases a sweet smelling odor when it is at melting point.

There are two special varieties that exhibit different characteristics. They are as follows:

- Glowing in the dark is available in a limited range of colors. It requires a slightly higher extruding temperature from 210 to 220 degrees Celsius.

- Carbon fiber reinforced is a PLA filament composite with short chopped carbon fibers. It's a very stiff material with an incredibly solid feel. It has a dark metallic color. It requires a slightly higher extruding temperature from 190 to 210 degrees Celsius.

A PET filament

Polyethylene terephthalate (**PET**) is a very strong, fairly stiff, and impact-resistant material. It has excellent water and moisture barrier properties, making it a widely used material for plastic bottles manufactured for the beverage industry. For 3D printing, it is a great colorless, crystal-clear printing material, but it's also available in limited clear colors. The popular brand is **Taulman's T-Glase**.

The average temperature for 3D extrusion should be around 212-230 degrees Celsius. It has very low shrinkage and prints well on acrylic, glass, and Kapton tape. A heated bed temperature of 60 degrees Celsius is helpful.

There isn't any odor or release of fumes when printing, but it should be used in a well-ventilated area.

A nylon filament

Nylon is a synthetic polymer that is flexible and soft with a natural translucent surface color. It has high strength and is tear resistant. It also has an excellent resistance to chemicals, but it can be colored with acid-based clothing dyes.

Printing with a bed temperature from 60 to 70 degrees Celsius is helpful. Shrinkage is similar to an ABS filament.

There are three different varieties sold. They are as follows:

- **Taulman 618**: The average temperature for 3D extrusion should be around 245 degrees Celsius. It does not stick to glass or aluminium print beds. Use a Garolite sheet or an unfinished hardwood (such as poplar) to print on.

- **Taulman 645**: The average temperature for 3D extrusion should be around 230 to 265 degrees Celsius. It has high strength, durability, and is more transparent than Taulman 618. It requires a Garolite bed or substitute with wood.

- **Taulman Bridge**: The average temperature for 3D extrusion should be around 235 to 260 degrees Celsius. It easily adheres to any type of bed when printed on a coat of PVA glue.

A HIPS filament

High-impact polystyrene (**HIPS**) is a great lightweight plastic that has excellent dimensional stability. It's a common plastic that's used in the manufacturing of toys and product casings. It's very much like ABS and has a similar range of available colors.

The average temperature for 3D extrusion should be around 220 to 230 degrees Celsius. It has low warp characteristics and prints well on acrylic, glass, and Kapton tape. A heated bed temperature of up to 110 degrees Celsius is helpful.

Its special characteristic is that it's dissolvable in limonene (citrus cleaner). This makes it a good material for printing dissolvable support material with a dual extruder.

HIPS should be used in a well-ventilated area. HIPS products are capable of releasing small amounts of fumes at high temperatures. While these fumes are generally considered tolerable, care should be taken to minimize exposure.

A TPE filament

The primary characteristics of a **Thermoplastic elastomer** (**TPE**) filament are elasticity and resistance to oil, grease, and abrasion. It's an excellent material to print wheels, belts, and gaskets.

The popular brand is **NinjaFlex**.

The average temperature for 3D extrusion should be around 210 to 225 degrees Celsius. It prints well on aluminum, acrylic, glass, and tape. A heated bed temperature from 20 to 50 degrees Celsius is helpful.

In general, TPE performs best in printers with direct-drive extruders, using settings similar to a standard rigid ABS filament. It's not recommended to be printed with a Bowden Cable system.

TPE will degrade and lose its elastic properties when submerged in water for extended periods of time.

TPE should be used in a well-ventilated area. TPE products are capable of releasing small amounts of fumes at high temperatures. While these fumes are generally considered tolerable and less odorous than ABS, care should be taken to minimize exposure.

A wood filament

LaywooD3 is a filament composite of recycled wood particles and polymer binders. It prints wood-like objects with annual rings by making changes in the extrusion temperature. A rough or smooth surface is possible during one printing, and it can be tooled after printing with a saw and sander. The surface can be stained and painted.

The printing temperature can range from around 180 degrees Celsius for a bright color to 245 degrees Celsius for a dark wooden color. When the temperature increases, it also increases the "grain" of the wood tone. It prints well on aluminum, acrylic, glass, and tape, and it doesn't require a heat bed.

The material has no warping tendencies.

This filament is extremely sensitive to lower temperatures (60 degrees Fahrenheit and below). It will become extremely brittle in the cold.

LaywooD3 smells like wood, but it should be used in a well-ventilated area. It contains a polymer, so it's capable of releasing small amounts of fumes at high temperatures.

A stone filament

Laybrick is a mixture of milled chalk and harmless copolyesters. It has the visual characteristics of sandstone. It can be worked on further with a saw and sander, and the surface can be painted.

The printing temperature can range from around 165 degrees Celsius for a smooth surface to 245 degrees Celsius for a rough surface. It prints well on aluminum, acrylic, glass, and tape, and it doesn't require a heat bed. Caution is advised with regard to the surface bond of the material. It may be difficult to remove the print from the printbed surface without damage.

The material has negligible warping tendencies.

Printing with a cooling fan is recommended. It requires hardening time after printing. The object should be removed from the build platform 2-4 hours after printing.

Laybrick should be used in a well-ventilated area. It contains copolyesters, so it's capable of releasing small amounts of fumes at high temperatures.

A ceramic filament

LAYCeramic is an experimental filament that is a blend of ceramic powder and polymers. After printing, the object can be fired to a hard ceramic by heating it up to 1200 degrees Celsius in a kiln. The resulting product can then be fired with decorative glazes.

The printing temperature can range from around 250-280 degrees Celsius.

Special modifications should be made. A full metal hot end is required, and a hardened, steel-hobbed bolt is needed for the extruder drive. It's recommended that you preheat the filament from 35 to 40 degrees Celsius in a flexible tube before it reaches the extruder.

Printing with a cooling fan is recommended.

LAYCeramic should be used in a well-ventilated area. It contains polymer binders, so it's capable of releasing small amounts of fumes at high temperatures.

A water-soluble PVA filament

Polyvinyl alcohol (**PVA**) is a water-soluble synthetic polymer hydrolyzed from polyvinyl acetate. It's recyclable and nontoxic and is a quick dissolver. It is primarily used as a dissolvable support-structure material when used with a dual extruder. It can also be used to make dissolvable molds for casting.

The printing temperature can range from around 170-190 degrees Celsius.

As PVA is a water-soluble material, it must be kept dry!

Storage of 3D printing filaments

Storage is an important factor with all of these materials. All filaments will absorb moisture, which makes storing in a low-humidity environment preferable. An airtight, plastic storage container or heavy-duty Ziploc storage bag with desiccant is helpful.

If a filament has absorbed moisture, the usual symptom is the sputtering of filament material when it extrudes. This is caused when the moisture stored in the filament surpasses the boiling point of water in the heat chamber and exits the nozzle in bursts of steam.

It is possible to dry out small portions of filament in a normal kitchen oven. Lay the filament on a nonstick surface such as a tin foil and heat it at around 55 to 75 degrees Celsius for an hour. PLA shouldn't be heated over 50 degrees Celsius. Care must be exercised while drying all materials or the filament will deform if heated too much. Move the filament around during the heating and cooling processes to prevent sticking.

Index

Thank you for buying
3D Printing with RepRap Cookbook

About Packt Publishing

Packt, pronounced 'packed', published its first book "*Mastering phpMyAdmin for Effective MySQL Management*" in April 2004 and subsequently continued to specialize in publishing highly focused books on specific technologies and solutions.

Our books and publications share the experiences of your fellow IT professionals in adapting and customizing today's systems, applications, and frameworks. Our solution based books give you the knowledge and power to customize the software and technologies you're using to get the job done. Packt books are more specific and less general than the IT books you have seen in the past. Our unique business model allows us to bring you more focused information, giving you more of what you need to know, and less of what you don't.

Packt is a modern, yet unique publishing company, which focuses on producing quality, cutting-edge books for communities of developers, administrators, and newbies alike. For more information, please visit our website: www.packtpub.com.

About Packt Open Source

In 2010, Packt launched two new brands, Packt Open Source and Packt Enterprise, in order to continue its focus on specialization. This book is part of the Packt Open Source brand, home to books published on software built around Open Source licenses, and offering information to anybody from advanced developers to budding web designers. The Open Source brand also runs Packt's Open Source Royalty Scheme, by which Packt gives a royalty to each Open Source project about whose software a book is sold.

Writing for Packt

We welcome all inquiries from people who are interested in authoring. Book proposals should be sent to author@packtpub.com. If your book idea is still at an early stage and you would like to discuss it first before writing a formal book proposal, contact us; one of our commissioning editors will get in touch with you.

We're not just looking for published authors; if you have strong technical skills but no writing experience, our experienced editors can help you develop a writing career, or simply get some additional reward for your expertise.

Blender 3D Printing Essentials

ISBN: 978-1-78328-459-7   Paperback: 114 pages

Bring your ideas to life in Blender and learn how to design beautiful, light, and strong 3D printed objects

1. Design beautiful, colorful, and practical objects in Blender to print or export.

2. Master Blender's special 3D printing tools to maximize print quality and minimize cost.

3. Consider requirements unique to 3D printing such as structural integrity and stability.

3D Printing for Architects with MakerBot

ISBN: 978-1-78355-075-3   Paperback: 108 pages

Build state-of-the-art architecture design projects with MakerBot Replicator 1, 2, or 2X

1. Intelligently design a model to be printed on the MakerBot from the scratch.

2. Make the MakerBot replicator work for you, automating tasks and doing post processing on MakerBot output.

3. Full of practical tips, tricks, and step-by-step instructions to successfully design your model with MakerBot.

Please check **www.PacktPub.com** for information on our titles

Instant Slic3r

ISBN: 978-1-78328-497-9   Paperback: 68 pages

Unravel the mysteries behind taking a virtual model and turning it into a physical object

1. Learn something new in an Instant! A short, fast, focused guide delivering immediate results.

2. Use Slic3r to make your printed objects the best quality possible.

3. Make Slic3r work for you, automating tasks and doing post processing on Slic3r output.

4. The book is put together in a friendly and accessible manner to help walk you through the learning and how to use the software.

3D Printing Blueprints

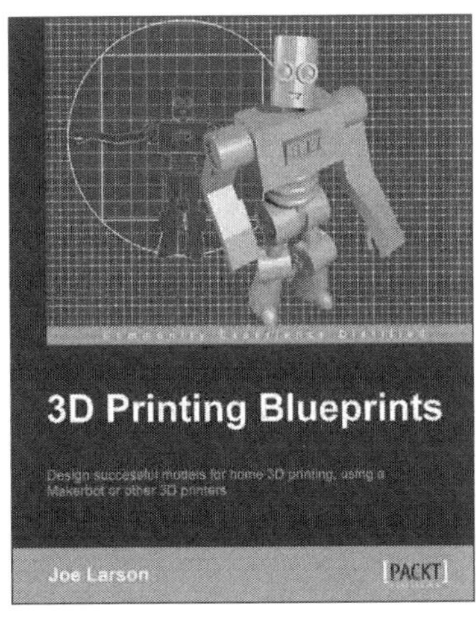

ISBN: 978-1-84969-708-8   Paperback: 310 pages

Design successful models for home 3D printing, using a Makerbot or other 3D printers

1. Design 3D models that will print successfully using Blender, a free 3D modeling program.

2. Customize, edit, repair, and then share your creations on Makerbot's Thingiverse website.

3. Easy-to-follow guide on 3D printing; learn to create a new model at the end of each chapter.

Please check **www.PacktPub.com** for information on our titles

16344580R00195

Made in the USA
San Bernardino, CA
29 October 2014